Praise for *Third Culture Kids: Growing Up Among Worlds, Third Edition*

"As an adult TCK, I have long wrestled with how I fit into this world. This book is the 'bible' for anyone who wants to understand the blessings and the curses of growing up multiculturally."

—Wm. Paul Young, New York Times Bestselling author of *The Shack*

"Growing up as a Third-Culture Kid is a gift that I will always treasure. As a senior military officer and US diplomat, I frequently interacted with world leaders and often drew upon my knowledge of different cultures to complete my work. My TCK experiences were invaluable in my efforts to negotiate international agreements. As a TCK, it was easy for me to understand various perspectives and to navigate through cultural nuances to achieve a positive outcome for both sides. I am delighted to see the lessons learned from the traditional TCK experience live on in this new edition of *Third Culture Kids*."

—Scott Gration, Maj. Gen., USAF (Ret), Executive Chairman, Champion Afrik and author, *Flight Path: Son of Africa to Warrior-Diplomat*

"Visionary, bold, and embracing. This may be the first book ever that hasn't left a single person out."

—Dr. Douglas W. Ota, author of *Safe Passage: How Mobility Affects People & What International Schools Should Do About It*

"I called the earlier editions of *Third Culture Kids* 'absolutely brilliant.' This third edition continues to earn that acclaim. It's a powerhouse of a book through which readers growing up 'among worlds'—and their parents and the professionals responsible for their care and teaching— become able to take leadership of the challenges and opportunities presented by such a rich and complex childhood."

—Barbara F. Schaetti, Ph.D., co-founder of Personal Leadership Seminars, LLC

"The additions on parenting of TCKs to this seminal book are life-changing. Though I own the first and second editions I need this one too. I wish I had read it before our TCKs became teenagers."

—Jo Parfitt, publisher, Summertime Publishing, author of *Career in Your Suitcase* and founder of the Families in Global Transition Writing Residency Program

"Ruth's writings consistently set a high bar in any discussion or writing on Third Culture Kids. The added value of this new edition is the inclusion of the thoughts of David's son, Michael. This makes it even more valuable, as the reader is able to catch a glimpse of the thoughts and reflections of the next generation."

—Lois J. Bushong, Author of *Belonging Everywhere & Nowhere: Insights into Counseling the Globally Mobile*

"This has been the single-most influential book in the field of personal intercultural transitions, drawing its audience both from individual TCKs who read it for self-discovery and the professionals who study and support them. With this important third edition, the authors continue their perceptive analysis. Written in an engaging style that crosses disciplinary bridges, there's critical information here for TCKs (at any point in their self-awareness) and the parents, researchers, educators, counselors and administrators who are cheering them on."

—Anne P. Copeland, PhD Executive Director, The Interchange Institute

"Michael Pollock and Ruth Van Reken do not disappoint with the third edition! Michael has deftly stepped in to fill his father's shoes and together with Van Reken they continue to explore the evolving implications of having lived a cross-cultural childhood. Expanded thinking on how expatriates can deal with re-entry and new transition models make this resource a must-read for anyone living the mobile life."

—Tina L. Quick, Author *of The Global Nomad's Guide to University Transition* and *Survive and Thrive: The International Student's Guide to Succeeding in the U.S.*

"As an early childhood educator, I am so excited that this book now includes more practical information on why the cross-cultural mobility in childhood matters. This goes hand in hand with the expanded chapter on practical tips for parents. The PolVan Cultural Identity diagram is a wonderful way to help the international schools have more knowledge about their students."

—Julia Simens, author, *Emotional Resilience and the Expat Child*

"When I read this book I understood why it was so special. I realized that I finally belonged somewhere... Knowing that I was a Third Culture Child, that other people experienced the same thing, was a sort of liberation."

—Amel Derragui, founder of TandemNomads.com

"This book is a MUST read for anyone raising children abroad or people having grown up overseas. The best parts are the practical and real life tips, experiences, and guidelines that Michael and Ruth bring to the discussion from perspectives of both parents of TCKs and TCKs themselves."

—Dr. Amos A. Lyso, Adult TCK, Vice Principal at Yew Chung International School - Secondary, Hong Kong

"Filled with profound insight and counsel, this essential book provides a glimpse into the world of globally mobile children (regardless of why they moved) and how to be supportive of all the transitions they may encounter."

—Amanda Bates, adult third culture kid raised bi-culturally between Cameroon and the US, and is founder/editor-in-chief of The Black Expat

"Michael Pollock and Ruth Van Reken have built on the foundational principles and ideas produced by Michael's father, David. This book is a wonderful tribute to Dave's life and ministry as the original co-author. It is full of new insight regarding transition and the TCK experience, and I would encourage you to open your heart and allow for God's still, small voice to speak into you – whether you are a TCK or work with TCK's.

—Dan Egeler, President, Association of Christian Schools International

"A deeply validating book for anyone who has lived and/or is living an intercultural life."

—Elizabeth Liang, Actor/Writer/Producer, including
ALIEN CITIZEN: An Earth Odyssey

"A must-read for those who identify as TCKs or who have lived cross-culturally, those who are raising families in cross-cultural settings, schools who are educating students from a variety of cultural backgrounds, and universities interested in helping cross-cultural students transition effectively."

—Dr. Dan Long, Upper School Dean of Students,
Taipei American School, Taiwan

"I will never forget the day I began reading *Third Culture Kids: Growing Up Among Worlds*. On each page I found more truth and tools that helped me understand, accept, and navigate the TCK experience. Building on the previous volume, this new edition provides more research, practical tips, increased attention to the complexity of terms, and the added bonus of questions for reflection. This book is a treasure, not only for TCKs, but for all those whose experience includes living between."

—Marilyn R. Gardner, Author of *Passages Through Pakistan: An American Girl's Journey of Faith* and *Between Worlds: Essays on Culture and Belonging.*

Third Culture Kids

third edition

Growing Up
Among Worlds

**David C. Pollock,
Ruth E. Van Reken,
and Michael V. Pollock**

NICHOLAS BREALEY
PUBLISHING

BOSTON · LONDON

First trade edition published in 2001 by Nicholas Brealey Publishing
This edition published in 2017 by Nicholas Brealey Publishing
An imprint of John Murray Press
An Hachette company

23 22 21 20   6 7 8 9 10

A CIP catalogue record for this title is available from the British Library

Library of Congress Control Number: 2017942481

ISBN 978-1-47365-766-3
US eBook ISBN 978-1-85788-408-1
UK eBook ISBN 978-1-47364-514-1

Printed in the United States of America

Nicholas Brealey Publishing policy is to use papers that are natural, renewable and recyclable products and made from wood grown in sustainable forests. The logging and manufacturing processes are expected to conform to the environmental regulations of the country of origin.

Nicholas Brealey Publishing
Carmelite House
50 Victoria Embankment
London EC4Y 0DZ
Tel: 020 3122 6000

Nicholas Brealey Publishing
Hachette Book Group
53 State Street
Boston, MA 02109, USA
Tel: 617-263-1834

www.nicholasbrealey.com

For Betty Lou, David, and Kristen, our lifelong partners and unfailing supporters throughout our journeys. And to our children, who have taught us so much—TCKs "for true."

Contents

Part III   The TCK Journey

Part IV   Maximizing the Benefits; Overcoming the Challenges

Appendices

Acknowledgments

Without Lois Stück's original encouragement, transcriptions of seminar tapes, suggestions, and expert help throughout the initial creative process of this book, it would have remained only a dream. Without Professor Barbara Cambridge's original guidance in the writing process or Professor Jon Eller's most helpful ideas about organization, the manuscript would never have gotten back to Lois or our publishers. Thinking partner and artist Barb Knuckles has shaped all three editions with her ideas as well as her art. Anthropologist Ken Barger; friends Margie Becker, Lori Beuerman, Christine Dowdeswell, Janet Fischer, Stephanie Hock, Brenda Keck, Ann Kroeker, Erica Lipasti, Paul Pedersen, Paul Seaman, Alan Shea, Francisco West, and Elisabeth Wood; wife Betty Lou Pollock; and daughter Stephanie Van Reken Eriksen have all given most helpful suggestions while reading various drafts of the manuscript. Helen Fail's insights into international schooling have been invaluable. The list could go on and on.

Above all, without each TCK and ATCK who has shared his or her story with us through the years, without the honest dialogue we have witnessed among so many, there would have been no story to tell. In particular, we thank the Global Nomad chapter at Valparaiso University for the time they gave to engage in dialogue specifically designed to address issues we are raising in this book. And a huge thanks to "Erika," not only for letting us use her story but also for helping in the early stages of writing it.

And many thanks to our original editor, David Hoopes, for having the vision that this is a topic whose time has come—to say nothing of his masterfully helping two people join their different thoughts and writing styles into one text. He did not have an easy job. Thanks also to Toby Frank for her further suggestions and Judy Carl-Hendrick for substantial help in the final editorial process of the first edition. Without each of them this book couldn't have been written in the readable form we trust it now is. And thanks to the original Nicholas Brealey Publishing team for having the vision to make this book more available to the public, to Trish O'Hare for her encouragement to update and expand this book, to Mr. Nicholas Brealey and Chuck Dresner for agreeing, and to Erika Heilman and Rebecca Greenberg for their great help in the final editing process.

And now, thanks to the new team at Nicholas Brealey Publishing: Alison Hankey and Michelle Morgan, for working with us to publish this third edition. We appreciate that they have invited Michael Pollock to add his wisdom to the great heritage his father left. Thanks to those who have added their thoughts and expertise for this update, including Danau Tanu, Myra Dumapias, Ute Limacher-Riebold, Rita Rosenback, Donnyale Ambrosine, Doug Ota, John Berry, Heidi Tunberg, Libby Stephens, and all who shared their stories in the coming pages. Michael thanks Kristen Pollock and Anna Pollock for sharing the burden of new authorship and Abigail Pollock and Steffen Pollock for adding their unique perspectives and challenging assumptions. And thank you to David Van Reken for all the thirty-five years of support he has given to this evolving topic and each revision of this book. Special thanks to Sally Rushmore, who helped us blend our work into one whole piece. Thanks for your patience and expert guidance, Sally!

We've decided it not only takes a village to raise a child, but it also takes one to birth a book. Last, but certainly not least, we thank God, not only for life but for the richness of our lives. We have experienced much joy in our journeys as we have studied this topic—and lived it as well.

Introduction

By Ruth E. Van Reken

Some may ask, "Why a third edition of *Third Culture Kids: Growing Up Among Worlds*? What more is there to say than has already been said?" A lot. In 1999, David Pollock began the first edition of this book with the following words. "Third culture kids (TCKs) are not new, and they are not few. They have been a part of the earth's population from the earliest migrations. They are normal people with the usual struggles and pleasures of life. But because they have grown up with different experiences from those who have lived primarily in one culture . . . we have seen a set of patterns of behavior or reactions to life emerge that stem from the cross-cultural and high-mobility aspects of their upbringing. As I have shared these observations with TCKs, their parents, teachers, and caregivers throughout the world . . . a multitude of TCKs have validated that this is, indeed, their story."

That remains true, but David went on to caution, "Since we are dealing with people, we are writing about process and progress, not a fixed entity. In the past two decades alone, dramatic changes related to the care of children and adults have occurred in the global nomad community, and undoubtedly new theories and practices will continue to evolve."

And they have. In the first edition, our focus was primarily on those who had grown up outside the parents' passport country due to a parent's occupation. Most of the early TCKs we studied had parents who shared the same nationality, and the TCKs often grew up in primarily one, two, or maybe three host countries. Skype and Facebook were nowhere around and international phone calls were expensive.

Even as the first edition of our book saw the light of day, change continued to sweep across the globe, altering the landscape for the traditional TCK experience itself. For one thing, TCK demographics were becoming more culturally complex. Questions arose, such as: What is the same or different for TCKs who also happen to be part of a minority group in their passport culture? What about bicultural or mixed-racial heritage TCKs? How do non-Western TCKs relate to their parents and passport culture after attending school in primarily Western-based international educational systems? Was this increasing cultural complexity changing in some way the fundamental story of the TCK experience about which we had written or simply adding more layers to it?

This growing cultural complexity only underscored the skepticism that some who thought of culture and belonging in traditional ways already had about the TCK topic. In fact, a university professor of sociology once asked me, "Are you saying that no matter where TCKs come from or where they grow up, there is something that they share?"

I stopped for a moment to think. "Well, I guess I am. No matter where I go and talk about these things, despite all the differences in demographic details, there is something that connects them."

"Well," responded the professor, "if you can prove that, you will change the face of sociology."

I was rather stunned! But I understood how he, like others, initially couldn't imagine how such a wide-ranging group of people from different nations, races, ethnicities, and experiences could be collected into one discussion. Certainly when judged by traditional patterns of assigning cultural or ethnic identity, where often we are defined first by our differences, it seems impossible that this cohort would have much in common. But over and over, we were seeing that TCKs from many places and varied backgrounds in terms of passport and host cultures still shared and related to the many common characteristics Dave Pollock developed as the *TCK Profile*. And so the sense that there was something important to explore that transcended the individuals involved but reflected some definite sociological and anthropological changes for our times deepened.

After our first edition, some folks agreed that in the past, TCKs might have had trouble staying connected to their passport culture or friends from other places, but they believed all of that had changed for today's TCKs. After all, Skype, Facebook, online local newspapers, and local sports could now keep them virtually connected if not connected in person. But as we watched the burgeoning TCK groups forming on social media, it seemed that, if anything, questions of belonging and identity were only increasing for the current generation of TCKs. Why? It seemed counterintuitive. We wanted to begin thinking more about this.

Another interesting development emerged between our first and second editions. No matter where we presented on the topic of TCKs, people came up after seminars or wrote emails to say, "I am not a TCK as you define it, but I related to nearly everything you mentioned as part of the TCK Profile. Why?" Some had grown up as immigrant children, or refugees, or in different cultural worlds in one country. Others were international adoptees or children of minorities. In our first edition, we mentioned why these types of experiences were different from the traditional TCK life we were writing about. But eventually we could not ignore the reality that for all the overt differences in these various experiences, *something* connects all of these journeys of people who grew up in a multiplicity of cultural worlds, no matter how it happened. What is it?

To find a way to look at all the experiences (traditional TCKs, the more culturally complex TCKs, and non-TCKs who related to what we were describing) without confusing the research, in our second edition we added our new term *cross-cultural kid (CCK)* to the lexicon as a way to include all of those who have interacted or are interacting significantly with two or more cultural worlds during childhood.

As we did this, we also began to wonder if the traditional TCK experience might be like a microcosm of what is now happening on a global scale. In other words, about fifty years before it was common for so many to move and grow up cross-culturally, the effects of cross-cultural mobility were already being observed and researched in this particular cohort of people from many countries and races called TCKs. Could our research and observations be like scientists who first isolate a simple organism in order to define and understand its structure and functions and move on to apply those understandings to more-complex organisms?

If so, then what were we studying? We decided it was here we could begin to see the first results of a great, but not yet fully explored, cultural shift of our changing world—the difference between being raised in a monocultural environment or in a many-layered cultural setting. We believe the TCK experience is an area where certain factors related to growing up in a culturally mixed lifestyle that are not limited by race, nationality, passport culture, or even economic status per se have already been identified. The more we understand the common responses from such an experience for what they are, the better we can then apply this knowledge to other types of cross-cultural childhoods and their long-term effects. Introducing this concept was the major expansion of thinking in our second edition of *Third Culture Kids*. But we could offer only preliminary thoughts about some commonalities we saw among the larger cohort of CCKs and invite others connected to CCKs of all backgrounds to join us in our wonderings.

Since then, as we have continued to hear more stories from those who have grown up as CCKs of all sorts, our understanding of the importance of this topic has grown. Based on the responses we have received and watching the themes emerging in books, movies, YouTube videos, TED talks, and so on, we are satisfied that *a childhood lived in, among, and between various cultural worlds is indeed becoming the norm rather than the exception.* And as we have seen CCKs of all backgrounds and all levels of cultural complexity take lessons learned from the TCK Profile and intuitively apply it to their own life story, we feel affirmed in what we were seeing about the relevance of the TCK story. Because of that, we now want to explore more fully the changes happening in the TCK experience with the belief that what we continue to learn from this particular subset of CCKs will give us new insights for many other types of CCKs as well.

To help do that, I am beyond delighted that David Pollock's son, Michael V. Pollock, is joining me to continue building on the brilliant work his father did for us all. Michael is eminently qualified for this assignment. As a child, he not only grew up as a TCK but, unlike most of us older ATCKs who never heard the TCK term until adulthood, Michael had language for his experience from an early age as he traveled with his dad to various TCK seminars. As an adult, Michael has lived and worked as an expat in the field of international education, raising his own now millennial TCKs in the process. He is founder of Daraja, an organization whose goal is to care for, encourage, and equip TCKs through a variety of means so they can address challenges and take hold of the gifts bestowed on them through their global childhoods, applying them in the places of great global opportunity and need.

One reason Michael feels so passionately about Daraja is because he also believes the same global mobility that offers rich diversity for those willing to engage with it positively can lead to increased cultural clashing and disruption between those who haven't yet learned to do so. The need is great for individuals who can bridge those differences with empathy, intelligence, patience, and flexibility. Surely TCKs and other types of CCKs are poised for such roles in business, education, arts, community development, politics, etc., if they can learn how to develop the skills and tools their life experiences have given them.

To help reach these goals of assisting young people to develop their full potential, Michael will be sharing his expertise through a completely revamped and expanded section on transition. Not only will we talk as before about personal transition (chapters 13 and 14), but Michael will specifically focus on how parents (chapter 17) and organizations can develop a "flow of care" (chapter 18) that will support families from the first day of their cross-cultural assignment through reentry and resettlement. Michael has developed a unique way of thinking through the needs of individuals and families by overlaying transition with Maslow's hierarchy of needs. He has presented this model in several national and international conferences, including Families in Global Transition.

In addition, Michael comes with the freshness of being a younger (than Ruth!) ATCK who, as we said above, has raised his children as millennial TCKs, taught TCKs in international school, and worked with them through transition to college and beyond. From what he has learned by his interactions with them as well as his own life, he brings a fresh perspective and updated stories to this topic throughout the book. Working together and joining past and present realities, Michael and I hope to accomplish several things in this new edition.

We want to look more closely at today's TCKs and build on what we have learned in the past to try to help all TCKs, as well as those who love and work with them, understand their stories better within the context of the current global changes. We will continue to probe more deeply such questions as: Does the presence of the Internet, constant social media innovation, new patterns of overseas assignments for their parents, multiple cultures in their international schools, or higher levels of security risk change the basic TCK Profile as previously described? If so, what are the changes? If not, why do the historical TCK characteristics remain essentially the same despite these external changes in our environment? What are some new strategies that might be needed to help today's TCKs better maximize the strengths of their upbringing?

We consider these questions in the hope of continuing to achieve our original goal: to help TCKs, adult TCKs (ATCKs), their families, and all who work with them understand how they can build well on the many gifts of this upbringing while dealing effectively with the challenges. That is the heart of our ongoing theme for all generations of TCKs, ATCKs, and their families.

But as we continue to study this particular TCK phenomenon in greater depth, we want to add a new section in most chapters—"Expanding Our Vision"—a few thoughts on how lessons learned in that chapter about the TCK experience might give more language and understanding to all who grow up among many cultural worlds for whatever reason. We will follow that with some questions that can be used for personal reflections or group discussions.

And with all of this, our greatest hope is that no matter the specifics of each person's story, all who have grown up cross-culturally for any reason will discover more fully and use with joy the hidden treasures they have acquired in their life journey so they may use them well for "such a time as this."[1]

Guide for Using This Book

If this is the first time you have read anything about Third Culture Kids (TCKs) or Cross-Cultural Kids (CCKs), read from the beginning and straight through; each section builds on the one before. Even if you already feel you know the "basics," you may be surprised to find what has changed and what has been affirmed in the eight years since the release of the first revision.

Earlier editions had three sections:

- Part I primarily explained *who* we were talking about and *why* a life of growing up cross-culturally, and often with high mobility, leads to common themes related to identity and dealing with loss that TCKs often face.
- Part II gave the *what* of the story. What are the common benefits and challenges of this experience? What are characteristics often found in current and adult TCKs?
- Part III concentrated on *how* parents, teachers, organizations, and even TCKs/adult TCKs can help to maximize the many gifts of a TCK childhood and deal well with the challenges.

Our third edition keeps the same basic format with new information in each section that has arisen from our changing world.

- Part I includes more accounts of TCKs who may have nontraditional stories. Under CCKs, we add new awareness for other ways children can grow up cross-culturally. The growing cultural complexity of all is highlighted, along with how this leads to a hidden diversity.

- Part II continues to examine the historical TCK Profile but also explores what may or may not continue to be relevant for today's TCKs. Because these characteristics are from past and present research on TCKs and ATCKs, each chapter concludes with considering which of the lessons learned might also be applied to other cohorts of CCKs.

- Part III is different from our former Part IIIs. Because transition between places and cultures is such a pivotal part of the TCK experience, Part III focuses on transition and reentry, gathering the pieces to bring greater clarity and tips for enjoying the journey. The chapter for Adult TCKs offers suggestions for those who are grown up and continue to seek understanding, healing, and growth.

• Part IV offers a rationale for care and specific strategies for how parents and organizations can help TCKs and their families thrive through *a flow of care*. The book finishes with a chapter of Ruth's and Michael's thoughts on the future of the topic.

The resources are by no means exhaustive but give a rich sampling of all that is available as we write this edition to help TCKs, their families, and the organizations that create TCKs by moving families cross-culturally. The appendices are meant to supplement areas in chapters and offer historical context so the chapters do not get buried in details. And don't miss Danau Tanu's thought-provoking insights in Appendix C adding to and challenging some of our preconceptions about TCKs.

Part I

Understanding the World of TCKs

This first section of the book looks in detail at who a third culture kid (TCK) is and why the two major realities of this experience—growing up among many cultural worlds and high mobility—have such a significant effect on TCKs. We will also consider how (and why) lessons learned from the TCK journey can be applied to other types of cross-cultural childhoods, even when the details of these other experiences may be quite different from the traditional TCK lifestyle.

CHAPTER 1

Where Is Home?

Erika's Story

> As the Boeing 747 sped down the runway, Erika sat with
> her seat belt secure, her chin propped against a clenched
> fist, staring out the window until the final sights of her be-
> loved Singapore disappeared from view.
>
> *How can it hurt this much to leave a country that isn't
> even mine?* Erika closed her eyes and settled back in the
> seat, too numb to cry the tears that begged to be shed. *Will I
> ever come back?*
>
> For nearly half of her twenty-three years, she had
> thought of Singapore as home. Now she knew it wasn't—and
> the United States hadn't felt like home since she was eight
> years old.
>
> *Isn't there anywhere in the world I belong?* she
> wondered.

Countless people of virtually every nationality and from a great variety of backgrounds identify with Erika's feeling of not fully belonging anywhere in the world. Like her, they may be North Americans who grew up in Singapore. But they may also be Japanese children who grew up in Australia, British kids raised in China, Turkish youth reared in Germany, African children currently living in Canada, or the child of a Norwegian father and a Thai mother growing up in Argentina. All of them have one thing in common: like Erika, they are spending, or have spent, at least part of their childhood in at least one country and culture other than their own. They are *third culture kids (TCKs)* or, by now, *adult TCKs (ATCKs)*—those who have grown up as TCKs.

Children are TCKs for many reasons. Some have parents with careers in international business, the diplomatic corps, the military, or religious missions. Others have parents who studied abroad. While these were the groups or *sectors* researchers initially named and studied as TCKs, an increasing number of children now grow up (or grew up) outside their parents' passport country and culture for many different reasons. Understanding their story is important for three reasons:

1. To help these individuals recognize and use well the gifts such a childhood provides;
2. To help them recognize and deal successfully with the challenges that are also inherent in this experience; and
3. To help normalize the third culture experience for this growing population.

TCKs are raised in a "neither/nor" world. It is *neither* fully the world of their parents' culture (or cultures) *nor* fully the world of the other culture (or cultures) in which they were raised. Contrary to popular misconceptions, however, this neither/nor world is *not* merely a personal amalgamation of the various cultures they have known. Instead, it is a way of life shared by others who also grow up living first in one culture and then moving to another one—maybe even two or three more—and often back and forth between various cultures. For reasons we will explore, through this particular lifestyle TCKs often develop common characteristics that differ in various ways or degrees from characteristics of those who are basically born in and live their entire childhoods in one place. Most TCKs learn to live comfortably in this in-between space they share with other TCKs, whether they stop to define it or not.

Why TCKs Are More Visible

TCKs are not a new phenomenon. Children have traveled into other countries with their parents throughout history, or at least for several centuries, in various patterns of migration including accompanying their parents with international careers (e.g., colonial officers, diplomats, missionaries, military personnel). Until the end of the twentieth century, however, they were largely invisible as a recognized entity. How and why is that changing?

THE NUMBER OF TCKS IN THE WORLD IS INCREASING

Carolyn Smith gave some historical perspective on the changes taking place in one of the earliest books written on this topic, *The Absentee American*.

> Since 1946, therefore, when it was unusual for Americans to live overseas unless they were missionaries or diplomats, it

has become commonplace for American military and civilian employees and businesspeople to be stationed abroad, if only for a year. The 1990 Census counted 922,000 federal workers and their families living overseas, and the total number of Americans living abroad either permanently or temporarily is estimated at 3 million.[1]

By 2015, this estimated number had grown to 8 million, with no end in sight of how high this tally might rise.[2] That's a lot of people—equivalent to the combined populations of Chicago, Los Angeles, and Philadelphia!

But these figures only account for U.S. citizens. Australia has more than 1 million citizens living outside its borders on either a long- or short-term basis.[3] In 2013, Japan disclosed that 1,258,263 of its citizens were living for longer than three months as expatriates all over the world.[4] Add to these figures the burgeoning number of citizens from every other country working and living outside their home cultures and we can only imagine the total number of expatriates worldwide.

Of course, as more adults have international careers or live abroad for whatever reason, there are more children accompanying parents into new lands. In the days of early explorers, traders, colonial governors, or pioneer missionaries, children often remained in the home country to avoid the rigors of travel and disease or for educational purposes. It is now normal for children to accompany their parents overseas rather than to stay in the homeland or go to boarding schools in another part of the host country (or a different country), as was common in those earlier days. Traveling between home and a host country now rarely takes more than one day—an easy trip compared to the three months it used to take on an ocean liner. International schools exist everywhere. Advanced medical care is an airlift away (and even more immediate with telemedicine). In fact, the International School Consultancy reports that in 2016 there were more than 8,257 international schools teaching 4.53 million K–12 students (in English) worldwide. The estimate is that by 2026 this number will have more than doubled to 10 million students in international schools using English as the language of instruction.[5] Consider how many more there are if you add all the students in non-English-speaking international schools and TCKs being homeschooled by parents while living outside their passport culture. The growth of this population is astounding.

THE PUBLIC VOICE OF TCKS HAS GROWN LOUDER

As these increasing numbers of TCKs become adults, they are becoming more vocal. Through alumni associations or online communities (such as *www.tckidnow.com*), TCKs and ATCKs have formed visible, identifiable groups. The proliferation of blogs; countless memoirs published by ATCKs; popular and scholarly articles in various online and print magazines; and anthologies such as *Unrooted Childhoods, Writing Out of Limbo,* or *The Worlds Within* have also created higher visibility of this cohort. Visual media such as Rahul Gandotra's Oscar-nominated short film *The Road Home,* Mira Nair's movie *The Namesake,* and Pico Iyer's TED talk *Where Is Home?* bring the reality of the TCK story to life on our screens. Many ATCKs have become well-known politicians, newscasters, actors, actresses, sports figures, and authors. The election of President Barack Obama in 2008 made the entire world aware that this type of childhood exists, whether or not they knew there was a name for how he grew up. As these TCKs and adult TCKs share their stories, they encourage others to do the same, and their voices are being heard.

BEING A TCK OR ATCK HAS BECOME SIGNIFICANT

The TCK experience is a microcosm of what is quickly becoming normal throughout the world. In 1984, sociologist Ted Ward said that TCKs were the prototype citizen of the future,[6] and it seems that day is nearly, if not already, here. Few communities anywhere will remain culturally homogeneous in this age of easy international travel and instant global communication. Growing up among cultural differences is already, or soon will be, the rule rather than the exception—even for those who never physically leave their home country. Experts are trying to predict the outcome of this cultural juggling. Looking at the TCK world can help us prepare for the long-term consequences of this new pattern of global cultural mixing. We look at these new trends in depth when we focus on the broader group of *cross-cultural kids (CCKs)* in chapter 3.

The benefits of the TCK lifestyle are enormous. Many TCKs and ATCKs are maximizing the potential of these benefits in their lives, both personally and professionally. In part II we look in detail at what these benefits are. Unfortunately, for some TCKs and ATCKs, the challenges of their experience have seemingly canceled out the many benefits—a sad waste for both the TCKs and the world around them. It is our hope that a better understanding of some of these benefits and challenges will help TCKs and ATCKs everywhere use the gifts of their heritage well. That's why, throughout this book, we examine the paradoxical world of the TCK and other cross-cultural experiences during childhood from a variety of perspectives.

We return to Erika for a better look at one young woman's true story. Only the names and places have been changed.

Back to Erika's Story

Erika didn't notice that the captain had turned off the "fasten seat belt" sign until a flight attendant interrupted her reverie.

"Would you like something to drink?" he asked.

How many Cokes and miniature pretzels have I eaten on airplanes? she wondered. Far too many to count. But today her grief outweighed any thought of food or drink. She shook her head, and the attendant moved on.

Erika closed her eyes again. Unbidden memories flashed through her mind. She remembered being eight years old, when her family still lived in upstate New York, Erika's birthplace. One day her father entered the playroom as she and her younger sister, Sally, performed a puppet show for their assembled audience of stuffed animals.

"Wanna' watch, Dad?" Erika asked hopefully.

"In a few minutes, sweetie. First, I have something special to tell you."

Puppets forgotten, Sally and Erika ran to their dad, trying to guess what it could be.

"Are we gonna have a new baby?" Sally began jumping up and down in excited anticipation.

"Did you buy me a new bike?" Erika inquired.

Erika's dad shook his head and sat in the nearby rocking chair, gathering one daughter on each knee. "How would you like to take a long airplane ride?" he asked.

"Wow!"

"Sure."

"I love airplanes."

"Where, Daddy?"

He explained that his company had asked him to move from the United States to Ecuador to start a new branch office. The family would be moving as soon as school ended that June.

A flurry of activity began—shopping, packing, and saying good-bye to relatives and friends. It all seemed so exciting until the day Erika asked, "Mom, how is Spotty going to get there?"

"Honey, it's not easy to take a dog. Grandma's going to take care of him 'til we get home again."

"Mom, we can't leave Spotty! He's part of our family!"

No amount of pleading helped. Spotty was sent to his new home and finally, with a mixture of eagerness for the adventures ahead and sadness for the people and things they were leaving, Erika and her family flew off to their new world.

Wanting to stop this flood of memories, Erika opened her eyes, trying to focus on her fellow passengers. The diversion didn't work. As soon as she had adjusted her cramped legs and resettled into a more comfortable position, the flashbacks continued. It was almost as if every few seconds a virtual click inside her brain advanced her mental Power-Point show. Pictures of Ecuador replaced those of New York. She had been so scared the first time her family flew into Quito. How would the airplane wiggle its way between the mountain ranges and find a flat place to land? Yet Erika remembered how, in time, those same Andes mountains gave her a deep sense of security each morning when she woke to see their towering peaks looming over the city, keeping watch as they had for centuries. But what did these memories matter now? She put on her headset, hoping that music would divert her thoughts. Unfortunately, the second channel she switched to played the haunting music of the hollow-reed flute pipes that always evoked a twinge of melancholy whenever she heard it. The sound brought instant memories of going to fiestas with her Ecuadorian friends and dancing with them while the pipers played. Certainly, listening to this music wouldn't help her now. She took the earphones off, letting them dangle around her neck.

By now the images of an in-flight movie were on the monitor in front of her, but Erika never saw them. Her own internal picture show continued with its competing images—the scene changing from towering mountains to the towering skyscrapers of Singapore. After two years in Ecuador, her father had been transferred once more, and for the thirteen years since then—including the four years she attended university in Wisconsin—Erika had considered Singapore her home. Now she knew Singapore would never truly be home. But the question continued to haunt her: where was home? Still refusing to dwell on that topic, her mind searched for a new show to look at. Pictures of countless scenes from other places she had visited with her family through the years appeared—the Kathmandu Valley in Nepal at the beginning of the rainy season, the monkey cup plants in the Malaysian rain forest, the Karen tribal people in the hills of northern Thailand, winter on the South Island of New Zealand, the water-derrick wells of the Hortobagy in Hungary. One after another the images flashed in her mind's eye. Even to herself, it seemed incredible how much she had done, seen, and experienced in her first twenty-three years of life. The richness and depth of the world she knew was beyond measure—but what good did that do her today?

Finally, the other pictures ran out and Erika was left with the visions of life in Singapore that kept returning, insisting on a paramount spot in the show. Now instead of places, however, she saw people—her amazing collection of friends from her international school in Singapore: Ravi, Fatu, Sam, Kim Su, Trevor, Hilary, Mustapha, Dolores, Joe. One after another they came to her memory. How many races, nationalities, styles of dress, cultures, and religions did these friends represent? With diversity as their hallmark, who could say what was "normal"? Erika never stopped to realize that others might be surprised to know that this diversity among her friends reflected the norm rather than the exception of her life. Instead, she reminisced about how she hated parting from them each summer when her family returned to the States for vacation. (It was never America or the United States—simply "the States.") Somehow she always felt much more like a fish out of water with her Stateside peers than she did in Singapore.

For the first time since the airplane had lifted off, a wry smile came to Erika's face. She remembered how strange she had felt the first time her American cousins had asked her to "go cruising." She presumed they meant some type of boat ride—like when she and her friends in Singapore rented a junk and sailed to a small island for a day of sunbathing, swimming, and picnicking. She was eager to go.

To her amazement, cruising for her cousins had nothing to do with boats and water. Instead, it meant endless driving about town with no apparent purpose. Eventually, they parked at a shopping mall and simply stood around. As far as Erika could see, it seemed their purpose was to block aisles rather than purchase any goods. What was the point? For Erika, "going home" meant something entirely different than it did for her parents. When her parents spoke of "going home," they meant returning to the States each summer. For her, "going home" meant returning to Singapore at the end of summer. But where was home now? The nagging question returned.

Temperatures dropped inside the airplane as the short night descended. Erika stood up to get a blanket and pillow from the overhead compartment, hoping for the comfort of sleep. But would sleep ever come on this journey? Not yet. Another set of pictures pushed their way into the muddle of her mind—now with scenes of the time she left Singapore to attend university in the States.

"Don't worry, darling. You'll be fine. I'm sure you'll get a wonderful roommate. You've always made friends so easily. I know you'll have no trouble at all," her parents had reassured her as she faced that transition.

But somehow it hadn't been that easy. Fellow students would ask, "Where are you from?" At first, Erika automatically answered, "Singapore." The universal reply was, "Really? You don't look like it," with the expectation of some explanation of how she was from Singapore.

Soon, Erika decided she would be from New York—where her grandparents lived. She hoped that would simplify these complicated introductions.

Eventually, as she adapted outwardly, picking up the current lingo and attire, others accepted her as one of them. By the end of her first year, however, she felt angry, confused, and depressed. *How could anyone care so much about who won last week's football game and so little about the political unrest and violence in Syria or Sudan? Didn't they know people actually died in wars?* Perhaps they never read the global news that crawled across their TV screens while supposedly erudite "news" commentators went on endlessly about the latest celebrity or local political scandal. They couldn't comprehend her world; she couldn't understand theirs.

As time went on, Erika found a way to cope. Once she realized most of her peers simply couldn't relate to what her life had been, she no longer discussed it. Her relatives were happy to tell everyone she was "doing fine." Just before graduating from university, however, she lost the last internal vestige of home. Her father was transferred back to the States and her family settled in Dayton, Ohio. For school vacations, she no longer returned to Singapore. Erika closed that chapter of her life. The pain of longing for the past was just too much.

As she stared at the rhythmic, almost hypnotic, flashing red lights on the jet's wings, Erika continued her reflections. That chapter on Singapore didn't stay closed for very long. *When did I reopen it? Why did I reopen it?*

After graduation, she had decided to get a master's degree in history. Thinking about that now while flying somewhere over the Pacific Ocean, she wondered why she had chosen that particular field. *Was I subconsciously trying to escape to a world that paralleled my own—a world that was once exciting but is now gone forever?*

Who could know? All Erika knew was that her restlessness increased in graduate school, and she finally dropped out. At that point, Erika decided only a return to Singapore would stop this chronic unsettledness, this sense of always looking for something that might be just around the corner but never was. But also, she couldn't define what she wanted. Was it to belong somewhere? Anywhere?

Although her family no longer lived in Singapore, she still had many Singaporean friends who had often invited her to stay with them. Why not live her own life overseas? Surely it would be far better to live in a place where she belonged than to wander forever in this inner limbo.

Erika went online and booked a flight to Singapore. The next step was to call one of her former classmates still living in Singapore. "Dolores, I want to come home. Can you help me find a job? I'm coming as soon as I get my visa, and I'll need a way to support myself once I'm back."

"That's wonderful! I'm sure we can find some kind of job for you," came the reply. "You can stay with me and my family until you get everything lined up."

Erika was ecstatic! It felt so familiar, so normal to be planning a trip overseas again. She couldn't wait to return to the world in which she so obviously belonged.

When she arrived in Singapore, her dream seemed to have come true. What airport in the world could compare to the beauty of Changi? Graceful banners hung on the walls, welcoming weary travelers in their own languages. Brilliantly colored flowers cascaded down the sides of the built-in garden beds throughout the terminals. Trees grew beside waterfalls that tumbled over rocks to a pond below. The piped-in sounds of chirping birds completed her sense of entering a garden in paradise. How could anyone not love this place?

As she walked out of the terminal, she took a deep breath. How wonderfully familiar were the smells: tropical flowers and leaded petrol fumes—what a paradox! Living, life-giving plants and dead, polluting fuel—intermingled. *Was it possible her whole life was a paradox? A life full of rich experiences in totally diverse cultures and places, each experience filled with a special vibrancy that made her want to dance and celebrate the joy of life. And yet, a life in which she always felt a bit like an observer, playing the part for the current scene but forever watching to see how she was doing.*

Erika quickly brushed these thoughts aside. Those times of being an outsider were gone now because she knew where she belonged—in Singapore. How wonderful finally to be home!

As the days progressed, however, life seemed less familiar. She discovered that many things she had taken for granted as a child in the expatriate business community of Singapore were no longer hers to enjoy as a young, single, foreign woman living with a Singaporean family—no maid, no expensive restaurants, no car, fewer friends. Instead, she had to wash her clothes by hand, grab cheap rice dishes from street vendors, and get around the city by walking blocks in the hot sun to take a crowded bus.

While growing up, her family might not have been classified as wealthy, but there had always been enough money for them to be comfortable and not worry about paying the bills, to take little side trips or splurge on a particularly nice outfit. Now she had to consider seriously such mundane questions as how much lunch cost and how she could pay for her barest living expenses.

Finding a job was harder than she had imagined it would be. Jobs that paid enough for her to rent a reasonably modest apartment and buy food and clothes had to be contracted with international companies before entering the country. Now she realized that was what her father had done. To make matters worse, she learned that available jobs were next to impossible for a noncitizen to get. Because the government wanted to save jobs for Singaporeans, it rarely issued a work permit for local jobs to a foreigner. Besides, the jobs for local hires that she could find would not pay enough for her to live safely, let alone well. Because a young white woman was so obvious in a cheaper rent district with higher crime rates, Erika feared she would present a far too easy target for someone bent on robbery or assault.

Here, in the world she had always thought of as home, Erika realized she was seen as a foreigner—an outsider. There was no such thing as an international passport.

The sad day came when she finally had to admit that she didn't fit in this country either. Sitting in her friend's tiny apartment in a world she had thought was home, despair swept over her. She was lost. The promises of big dreams seemed foolish and childish. She belonged nowhere. With a muffled sob she picked up her cell phone and called her parents.

"Mom, I can't make it here, but I don't know what to do. I don't fit in Dayton, but I don't fit here either. Somehow I seem to have grown up between two totally different worlds, and now I've found out I don't belong to either one."

With infinite sorrow this time, she made one last airline reservation, and now she was here, 40,000 feet in the air, going—home?

Erika's story is only one of thousands we have heard from TCKs all over the world. The particulars of each tale are different, yet in a sense so many are alike. They are the stories of lives filled with rich diversity and amazing experiences but often conflicted by the underlying question of where they really fit in. What are some of the reasons for this common thread among TCKs? Who, indeed, are these TCKs and what are some of the benefits and challenges inherent in the experience they have had? How does this relate to those who have grown up among various cultures for many reasons besides moving physically or internationally? These are the questions we address in the chapters that follow.

Questions for Chapter 1

1. Which part(s) of Erika's story seem universal, perhaps to TCKs and non-TCKs alike?
2. Was there any particular place you felt connected to Erika's story? Or her feelings about the moves in her life? Please explain.
3. How would you define home?
4. Is it possible to feel at home in more than one place? Please explain your answer.

CHAPTER 2

Who Are "Third Culture Kids"?

I am fourteen years old and I speak around four or five languages. When I was younger, my father spoke German to me at home, my mother used Swiss-German, most of my international friends communicated in English, and my local friends talked to me in Albanian. Now I study French at school so I have added one more language to my life. At our dinner table in the evening, our family speaks a mixture of all of these languages. So far I have been to twenty-one countries, which are mostly in Europe but include the United States and part of Africa too.

I think technology has definitely helped me to stay in touch with my friends around the world, but for me it also can be hard when I see pictures online of some of my best TCK friends hanging out together in some place where we used to all live and know that I cannot be a part of it.

—Hannah Steets, German Swiss TCK

Hannah's story reflects more of the amazing paradox of the TCK story. Consider all she has experienced and learned in her short fourteen years! Look at the gift technology offers her to stay in touch with her multiple worlds. And yet, despite all of that, there is a wistfulness that she can't quite keep her worlds together as they once were.

Let's look more deeply into who TCKs are and what this acronym means. In 1989 David Pollock defined and then described them:

A Third Culture Kid (TCK) is a person who has spent a significant part of his or her developmental years outside the parents' culture. The TCK frequently builds relationships to *all of the cultures, while not having full ownership in any. Although elements from each culture may be assimilated into the TCK's life experience, the sense of belonging is [often] in relationship to others of similar background.*[1]

We'll look in detail at Dave's basic definition first: "A Third Culture Kid (TCK) is a person who has spent a significant part of his or her developmental years outside the parents' culture."

"A Third Culture Kid (TCK) . . ."

Some of the most vigorous discussions about *third culture kids* (TCKs) start with a debate over the "third culture" term itself. What does that mean? Many wrongly assume it is related to the term "third world," an unfortunate misnomer itself with its roots in the Cold War.

Appendix A includes an extensive history of the progression of this term from the beginning until now and acknowledges other significant pioneers in the field. For now, a brief synopsis will do.

Ruth Hill Useem, a sociologist from Michigan State University, is considered to be the "mother of TCKs." She coined this term in the late 1950s when she and her husband, John, went to India to study how U.S. Americans who lived and worked there as foreign service officers, missionaries, technical aid workers, businesspeople, educators, and media representatives interacted professionally with the local Indians (and vice versa) in those early postcolonial days.[2] At the time, the Useems called the interaction between these two communities the "third culture." Ruth Useem took particular interest in the children of the expatriates they were studying and called them "third culture kids" or "TCKs." She defined them simply as "children who accompany their parents into another culture."[3]

These are examples of the main groups Dr. Useem studied at this point:

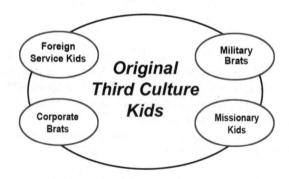

Figure 2–1: Original Third Culture Kids
©1996 Ruth E. VanReken, updated 2017

As the concept of what the Useems called an "interstitial culture" has evolved over the years, the term *first culture* refers to the *home* or *passport* culture of the parents, and the term *second culture* references the *host culture* to which the family has moved or in which they have lived. The term *third culture* then refers to *a way of life* that is neither like the lives of those living back in the home culture nor like the lives of those in the local community, but is *a lifestyle with many common experiences shared by others living in a similar way.*

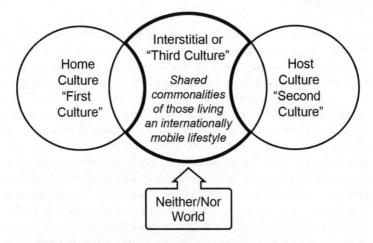

Figure 2–2: The Third Culture Model
©1996 Ruth E. Van Reken, updated 2017

When Ruth Van Reken and Dave Pollock asked Ruth Hill Useem what she thought about their slightly different way of describing the different cultures from her original studies, she replied, "Because I am a sociologist/anthropologist I think no concept is ever locked up permanently. . . . Concepts change as we get to know more; other times concepts change because what happens in the world is changing."[4]

That, in itself, is an important lesson to remember as the world continues to change. In today's world, not only is the cohort of people who accompany their parents into other cultures expanding, but also there are various permutations of this reality. How does all of this fit in?

One question people often ask is, "How can you possibly say those with such incredibly diverse cultural backgrounds and experiences can make up a 'culture,' when the word *culture*, by definition, means a group of people who have something in common?" Good question! However, those who ask it don't realize that TCKs are actually an example of some of the changes going on in our world. In 2000, anthropology student Ximena Vidal wrote, "Third Culture Kids [are] an example of a people whose experience and cultural identity cannot be understood within the limiting [traditional] frameworks of culture."[5] She further explained that TCKs are an example of a new way to define culture that is emerging in our postmodern world. Vidal claims that culture can be *what we share experientially* as well as the more traditional ways we have defined it.

The question then becomes, of course, what are the shared universals of a traditional TCK experience that shape their lives in ways that transcend their family, ethnic, national, or sector background *alone*? These are the things we believe are part of this shared experience. First, we see two realities that arch over the TCK experience:

1. **Being raised in a genuinely cross-cultural world.** Instead of simply watching, studying, or analyzing other cultures, TCKs actually live in different cultural worlds as they travel back and forth between their passport and host cultures. It can include not only geographic moves by airplane, but also the changing interaction when they play with their host culture friends in the village and come home at night to a different culture/language at home. Some TCKs who have gone through multiple moves or whose parents are also in an intercultural marriage have lived in or interacted closely with four, five, six, or more cultures either sequentially or even on any given day.

2. **Being raised in a highly mobile world.** Mobility is normal in the third culture experience. Either the TCKs themselves, or those around them, are constantly coming or going. The people in their lives frequently change and the backdrop of physical surroundings may often fluctuate as well. Even TCKs in more stable communities can assume a change is coming for them because of what is often the fluid nature of how those around them come in and out like the ebb and flow of the tide. Interrupted relationships are the norm for many, even though they often develop an amazing ability to pick up where they left off when they meet years later.

In our first editions, we named four other common factors of the TCK experience as we observed them at that point. In reality, all four were by-products of the first two. *Expected repatriation* happened because the TCKs' parents had moved temporarily for a career or further education, not as immigrants. That meant that in the end they expected to return to their home culture. *Distinct differences* referred to the fact that moving to a new culture often meant living where the TCK was a clear foreigner—by looks, language, or both. *Privileged lifestyle* referenced the perks offered by companies and organizations to those living outside the company's home culture (a driver or household help or living in a compound), which often did not come with jobs in the home country. In addition, these expats often lived at a higher economic position than those in the host cultures. *System identity* was a result of studying or working overseas through the sponsorship of specific companies, foreign-service departments, religious missions, or branches of military, and the children strongly identified with those same organizations.

While we believe the first two observations of a cross-cultural lifestyle and high mobility remain virtually universal for today's TCKs, these other four characteristics we saw of the typical TCK's "third culture" or shared lifestyle bear a closer look to see whether they still hold true as well, or even how they might have changed. If we do that, perhaps we can further hone the essence of what it is that produces the classic characteristics of the TCK Profile and then see later which of these may or may not be shared by others raised cross-culturally in today's changing world.

- **Expected repatriation.** Unlike immigrants who usually move with the expectation of settling permanently in the new place, traditionally when third culture families go to another country because of a career, they generally expect they will be able to go "home" when that job is done. Likely this assumption remains true for many who begin their first overseas assignments and continues to shape countless decisions along the way that affect their children, such as educational choices or making efforts to learn or not learn the local language.

  But it is also true that more and more families do not totally repatriate as in earlier days, for various reasons. The global economy means that some families remain as mobile expats, moving from one job and/or country to another. In the end, some find they have become "unintended immigrants" to one of those places. Changing political situations at "home" sometimes make it unfeasible for the family to return.

  > During a seminar in one international school in the Middle East, Ruth began talking about the challenges of reentry and one student put up his hand. "What if you don't have a place to go back to? And other countries may not let you in?" His entire village had been burned to the ground and all those he once knew from there were either dead or scattered. He literally had no idea where he would go when he graduated from high school at the end of that semester.

  There is another interesting twist in regard to repatriation that we didn't stop to notice in our earlier editions. In the "old days," without historical precedent to consider, parents assumed their children would repatriate with them one day. The unexpected, and growing, reality is that ATCKs often discover that once they have seen and experienced the world "out there," they feel far more at home in that bigger world than the place and culture their parents call home. That means the historical expectation of repatriation has morphed for some into the more fluid mobility of today's TCKs with parents, their adult children, and ultimately grandchildren often living on different continents. For example, Erika of chapter 1 finally found her sense of home and belonging when she met and married a man from a European country. They now live and raise their family in France—while her parents remain in Dayton, Ohio! In our next chapter we take a look at these experiences as well and the implications for what's going on in our world for so many families beyond traditional labels.

Bottom line, our conclusion about whether or not "expected repatriation" is still a characteristic of the TCK experience is that although this may be the parents' original default expectation, repatriation can no longer be presumed to be as automatic as once thought for all members of the family. This is an important awareness families should have as they make that first decision to embark on their global careers.

- **Distinct differences.** In the days when Ruth Useem first identified TCKs, globalization was in its infancy. The expatriate families she studied during those colonial and neocolonial days (e.g., U.S. Americans living in India) were usually clear foreigners in their host cultures based on either appearance or language alone. While this may remain true for many TCKs (e.g., a Ghanaian family living in Russia), for others this is no longer so. With people moving back and forth among nearly every country, more TCKs are raised where they physically resemble members of the dominant local culture and blend in at first sight (e.g., a Chinese Australian family working in Shanghai). Some may grow up in places where the mixture of racial heritage and multiethnic makeup of their new city or country is so great that these TCKs can melt into the surrounding environment more easily than before because there is no particular standard look.

When we first wrote about distinct difference as a common characteristic, we said that "whether or not they blend in by appearance, TCKs often have a substantially different perspective on the world than their local peers simply because their life experiences have been different." In today's world, with the Internet, Facebook, Instagram, Skype, and all other forms of social media, many argue that there will be less difference in how people think and see the world, and we can agree. But we have also seen a twist here as well. Because many TCKs assume they share a common culture with their peers no matter which country they live in, some remain unprepared for the day when they actually go live in another place and bump into quite different social patterns or traditions than they had realized via social media.

Also, with the plethora of books and movies coming out featuring TCK-related themes and issues, this lifestyle of growing up among and between different cultural worlds is becoming more common, so people can no longer say to a TCK, "My goodness, your experience is so unique"—not if millions of others share the same thing! So we would say this characteristic is again not as strong a reality for many as it once was, but is probably more dependent on the particular situation each TCK is in. Certainly we continue to hear that upon reentry to the passport culture, often the feeling of "being different" is strong.

- **Privileged lifestyle.** This is another characteristic that bears more scrutiny as times and international assignments have changed. We noted in our earlier editions that historically, employees of international businesses and members of religious missions, the military, and the diplomatic corps have been part of an elitist community—one with special privileges bestowed on its members by the sponsoring organization, the host culture, or both. We also included stories of others such as Turkish children whose parents had worked in various trades or more "blue collar" types of jobs in Germany. Because, however, Dr. Useem's initial studies were done in this cohort of those sent overseas by a sponsoring organization or corporation, the impression may still remain for some that these groups are the *only* ones included when we talk of TCKs. But the world has changed and so has those we look at as TCKs. Does this characteristic of a privileged lifestyle still apply as part of the shared realities of current TCKs?

There were, and often still are for TCKs who continue to be part of the original communities Dr. Useem studied, systems of logistical support or "perks": those in the military can use the commissary or PX; embassy or missionary families may employ domestic help; and diplomatic families may have chauffeurs to drive the children to school or around town. Even without the perks, there are entitlements such as worldwide travel to and from their post—all at the expense of the sponsoring agency, or "supporters" in the case of missions. In addition, while some third culture careers such as religious missions or educators might not be financially privileged compared to others from their passport culture, those who moved into these types of careers generally had another type of privilege or elitism—their educational background. To move into an international career usually requires advanced training of some kind and that, in itself, is a privilege many in this world do not have.

The question, however, remains as to whether or not this view that the TCK experience is one of high privilege still holds true in today's world. Initially, the TCK experience was also seen primarily through the looking glass of the Western-based TCKs from fairly affluent countries. What about those whose families come from less affluent countries? For example, many governments from poorer countries cannot offer their diplomatic families the financial perks usually associated with state department employees, such as sending the children to international schools or taking frequent trips back to the passport country. Their salaries are not at the level others might presume. Some TCKs raised in these situations say it is hard when people assume by virtue of their parents' job title they are rich or have these extra perks. Myra Dumapias, an ATCK whose father was a Filipino diplomat, wrote:

> As a diplomat's daughter, I noticed differences in who lived in which neighborhoods, who was able to afford all the IB [International Baccalaureate] programs, what kind of cars people drove, who had memberships at the expat clubs. I

didn't grow up with my tuition paid by the government after elementary years, and my family was not always able to afford to keep me in international schools. This defined my educational experience. Not every TCK can stay in international schools throughout the whole time they are abroad. Although I grew up with certain privileges typically associated with middle class, [as one of the] children whose passport country was developing or poorer, [I] didn't grow up with the same privileges and luxuries as [children of] families from richer passport countries. Yet, when people hear I was a diplomat's daughter, the default thought about my class experience is a sheltered upper-class life of luxury.[6]

But even TCKs like Myra who were not as financially well off as some of their peers still had the privilege of seeing the world and meeting folks from so many countries in ways their peers at home might not have had. So, while we realize the great discrepancies of some types of privilege in different TCK experiences, we believe that overall, in many different ways, there are still great privileges to this lifestyle. But what those privileges are or are not might be more dependent on each TCK's story by now. In time the work of Danau Tanu, a Japanese Indonesian ATCK who has done her Ph.D. work in studying the varied experiences of children who grow up what she calls "transnationally," and others will continue to inform our understanding of how issues of class, power, and privilege impact the TCK story as well. (See Appendix C for more on this topic.)

- **System identity.** While Ruth Useem believed that many of the characteristics she observed among TCKs stemmed very directly from the strong identity TCKs had with their parents' sponsoring organizations, it seems this factor is also likely becoming more a case-by-case matter for TCKs. On the whole, having a "representational role" appears less of an issue in general than in former generations for several reasons. First, many TCKs blend into the local culture more easily, and the pressure to behave in a certain way is less when others aren't as aware of who their parents are or what group they represent. Second, it is our impression that in most cases parents are no longer as directly credited with or blamed for their children's behavior as they were in earlier generations. If so, perhaps they do not remind children as frequently of their "duty" to uphold the reputation and traditions of the organization or system that sent them overseas as former generations may have done. Third, because parents often don't stay with one company or organization for a lifetime as they did in the past, TCKs' sense of loyalty to, or connection with, the sponsoring organization may be less.

Having said that, however, there are certainly some—e.g., military or missionary kids—who seem to maintain that strong system identity as one of their primary identities. For more insight into the power of the system for those who are still part of a strong organizational system, read "The Powerful Impact of Systems on the Globally Mobile" by Lois Bushong and Ruth Van Reken at *http://quietstreamscounseling.com/wp-content/uploads/2016/05/ The-Powerful-Impact-of-Systems.pdf* or in the appendix of Lois's book for therapists, *Belonging Everywhere and Nowhere: Insights into Counseling the Globally Mobile*. Bottom line, this characteristic for TCKs may be another one that is more variable according to each situation than in the past.

Now that we hopefully understand the first four words of our TCK definition, let's look at the rest of it. "A Third Culture Kid (TCK) *is a person who has spent a significant part of his or her developmental years outside the parents' culture.*"

" . . . is a person . . ."

Why are these words critical to all further discussion on third culture kids? Because we must never forget that, above all else, a TCK is a person. Sometimes TCKs spend so much time feeling different from people in the dominant culture around them that they (or those who notice these differences) begin to feel TCKs are, in fact, intrinsically different—some sort of special breed of being. While their experiences may be different from other people's, TCKs were created with the same need that non-TCKs have for building relationships in which they love and are loved, ones in which they know others and are known by them. They need a sense of purpose and meaning in their lives and have the same capacities to think, learn, create, and make choices as others do. The characteristics, benefits, and challenges that we describe later arise from the interactions of the various aspects of mobility and the cross-cultural nature of this upbringing and how they do or don't help meet these most fundamental needs, not from some difference in them as persons. We will look at that in more depth in chapter 6.

" . . . who has spent a significant part . . ."

Time by itself doesn't determine how deep an impact the third culture experience has on the development of a particular child. Other variables such as the child's age, personality, and participation in the local culture have an important effect. For example, living overseas between the ages of one and four will affect a child differently than if that same experience occurs between the ages of eleven and fourteen even though both are TCKs by definition.

While we can't say precisely how long a child must live outside the home culture to develop the classic TCK characteristics, we can say it is more than a two-week or even a two-month vacation to see the sights. Some people are identifiable

TCKs or ATCKs after spending as little as one year outside their parents' culture. Of course, other factors such as the parents' attitudes and behavior or the policies of the sponsoring agency or how the surrounding culture received or didn't accept or interact with the family add to how significant the period spent as a TCK is—or was—in shaping a child's life.

There is another caveat to add here. When Dave Pollock wrote this definition in 1989, he intended to include those children currently in the third culture, children who might already be repatriated after some time in other countries and adults who had grown up as TCKs. Perhaps in today's world, he might have written, "A TCK is a person who is spending, or has spent, a significant number of developmental years outside the parents' culture(s)," and, "an Adult TCK (ATCK) is one who grew up as a TCK." Times have changed but the underlying factors of TCK life have not, and it is important to recognize all TCKs, wherever they may be in their development.

Why might this be important? Over the years, we have seen how certain factors in a global childhood result in some common characteristics long term but they may not be as obvious while the child is growing up and still living in this third culture experience. When we share some of these common characteristics with ATCKs, many have what has become known as the "Aha!" moment—the instant they realize there is a reason for many things they have felt and experienced through the years but for which they had no language or understanding until that point. On reflecting back, they can see how the benefits and challenges in Dave's classic Third Culture Kid Profile describe them and recognize how both grew out of this third culture lifestyle that they didn't recognize at the time.

We have noticed, however, that often parents of younger or current TCKs aren't so sure that the TCK Profile is accurate. They may be happily willing to believe the gifts are forming as they see the wonderful opportunities their children are having to explore the world in so many positives ways. That is terrific and they are right. But at times, when we talk of the challenges that can also be here, some will tell us that these might have been true in the past, but everything is different now—their children are doing "just fine." Educators in international schools have expressed similar feelings as they observe their students apparently thriving day-to-day. Even human resource managers of large international companies assure us their families do not experience what we talk about. Some presume the expat bubble they provide their employees overseas shields them from some of the historic challenges we describe.

Sadly, when adults maintain this view, they aren't as prepared to help their children or students deal well with the challenges that may remain more hidden as they are happening. What parents may not realize is that children do not have sophisticated language to express the paradoxical feelings of their experience. It's confusing for young TCKs to feel excited for the upcoming flight to see grandparents and cousins while simultaneously feeling great sadness to leave a place and friends they love. Educators may forget that the international school is part of the life TCKs know. It *is* the world where they belong—one filled with many friends who share their experience of living globally mobile lifestyles. These students are not yet facing the issues related to reentry or finding a place of belonging when they seek to return to their passport cultures. When the children are outside their parents' passport culture, life is often so "normal" for them and their parents that the common characteristics ATCKs recognize later may not be obvious—although those with eyes to see can notice them forming!

" . . . of his or her developmental years . . ."

While the *length* of time needed for someone to become a true TCK can't be precisely defined, the time *when* it happens has also come under scrutiny. When Dave made his original definitions, experts presumed adolescence ended around eighteen or nineteen, so this age group was in Dave's mind for what "developmental years" meant. We understand with new discoveries in brain science that some concepts of development are changing, but for our initial purposes, we are generally talking about those who had this experience in their first eighteen years of life.

We recognize people do continue developing throughout life and that a cross-cultural experience affects adults as well as children. In 2000, during the Families in Global Transition conference in Indianapolis, Paulette Bethel, Joanna Parfitt, and Christine Dowdeswell convened a group of interested attendees to look at what they called *third culture adults* (*TCAs*): those who go overseas for the first time after growing up in a more traditional "monocultural" environment of their passport culture. The difference for a TCK, however, is that this cross-cultural experience occurs during the years when that child's sense of identity, relationships with others, and view of the world are being formed in the most basic ways. While parents may change careers and become former international businesspeople, former missionaries, former military personnel, or former foreign service officers, no one is ever a *former* third culture kid. TCKs simply move on to being *adult* third culture kids because their lives grow out of the roots planted in and watered by the third culture experience. This matters because the term TCK does not mean the person is still a child (whether or not they use the term ATCK). It is a description of the experience at a formative age.

" . . . outside the parents' culture."

All of those originally studied by Dr. Useem had grown up outside at least one of their parents' passport country(s) as well as culture. For that reason, we use the terms *passport country* or *passport culture* to mean the country(s) or culture(s) from which at least one of the parents come. These terms are becoming a bit less clear, however, because increasingly many TCKs have parents with multiple passports. In addition, some TCKs not only carry the same national passport(s) as their parents, but one from the country where they were born that is not the same as any passport their parents carry.

Updating the Definition

We take a momentary diversion from Dave's definition to add a few thoughts. It is interesting that although Ruth Useem and Dave Pollock worked primarily with those who had accompanied parents into another culture because of a parent's career choice, neither included in their definition a geopolitical description to clearly state that this culture was also in a different country or the reason the parents made the move. Some would argue then that children whose parents move to another culture within a country's borders—for example, a Nigerian family from Lagos who move to a small remote Nigerian village so the parents can set up a medical clinic for the underserved population—should be called TCKs even if they have not crossed country borders. Others would say some refugees have also experienced moving into another culture with their parents. This is true. Certainly, before his death in 2004, Dave Pollock had begun to work with refugee organizations as well as traditional TCKs because he found many places the two groups shared emotional and psychological responses. Are all of these children then also TCKs? If so, how can the incredible differences in all of these and other similar experiences be included under one umbrella? If not, why not?

The questions are, indeed, becoming complicated! We promise to look at them in detail in chapter 3. In order to compare and contrast the TCK experience with these other ones, however, we need to first make a less ambiguous definition for TCKs but based on what we believe were the original assumptions and intent of Dr. Useem and Dave Pollock when they made their definitions several decades

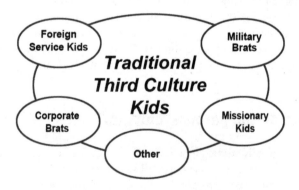

Figure 2–3: Traditional Third Culture Kids

© 1996 Ruth E. VanReken, updated 2017

ago. Hopefully, by clarifying the TCK definition, we can have a more productive discussion comparing and contrasting this experience with others for the good of all. Here is our updated definition for traditional TCKs.

> *A traditional third culture kid (TCK) is a person who spends a significant part of his or her first eighteen years of life accompanying parent(s) into a country or countries that are different from at least one parent's passport country(ies) due to a parent's choice of work or advanced training.*

We use the term "work" rather than "career" to make clear it is not only those with sponsored careers we are discussing. We understand there are TCKs who come from many social classes or economic situations, who also go to another country with parents who have many different types of jobs but who are not going as permanent immigrants. Before Dave Pollock's death in 2004, he always included any child who went with parents into another culture for a "significant part of his or her developmental years" in his presentations, no matter what the parents' work was or what nationality or culture they came from. The problem has become that without a clearer definition from Dr. Useem or Dave of where this other culture was or why the parents took their children there, the conversations about who does or doesn't *qualify* as a TCK have gotten in the way of looking at the bigger picture of what is happening for so many in our world. Our hope is that if we can provide a clearer definition for TCKs per se, we can move on to seeing how the principles we have learned from this group can help inform a much broader and global conversation in the end. We will explain our vision more in chapter 3.

And now back to Dave Pollock's description of what TCKs often experience:

"The TCK frequently builds relationships to all of the cultures, while not having full ownership in any."

This brings us back to Erika.

> As she flew back to the United States, Erika wondered how it could be that life felt like such a rich dance in and through so many cultures, while at the same time that very richness made it seem impossible to stop the dance. To land in Singapore would mean she could celebrate the hustle and bustle of that wonderful city she loved so much, but then she would miss the mountains of Ecuador and the joy of touching and seeing the beautiful weavings in the Otavalo Indian markets. To end the dance in Ecuador meant she would never again see the magnificent colors of fall in upstate New York

or taste her grandmother's special Sunday pot roast, but to stop in New York or Dayton, where her parents now lived, meant she would miss not only Singapore and Ecuador, but all the other places she had been and seen. Erika wished for just one moment she could bring together the many worlds she had known and embrace them all at the same time, but she knew it could never happen.

This is at the heart of the issues of rootlessness and restlessness we will discuss later. This lack of full ownership is also what gives that sense of simultaneously belonging "everywhere and nowhere" that so many TCKs identify with well into their adult years.

"Although elements from each culture may be assimilated into the TCK's life experience . . ."

Obviously, there are specific ways each home and host culture shapes each TCK. British TCKs celebrate Guy Fawkes Day while living in Kenya. Liberians in Russia meet every July 26 for Independence Day festivities. Finnish TCKs who grew up in Malaysia search the international food markets for durian candy or jelly even if they cannot find the fruit itself. U.S. Americans raised in Australia search high and low for a jar of Vegemite in Indianapolis, not wanting to settle for the growing number of Marmite jars beginning to appear there in stores as more international companies sprout up in that city. But it's not only food and language that shape them. Cultural rules do as well. Here are just two examples:

After living in London where his dad served as ambassador for six years, Musa had trouble with how people dealt with time when he returned to Guinea. Instead of relaxing as others from his passport culture could when meetings did not begin and end as scheduled, he felt the same frustration many expatriates experienced. Unknowingly, Musa had exchanged his passport culture's more relational worldview for a time-oriented worldview during his time abroad.

At his summer job in Canada, Gordon's boss thought he was dishonest and lazy because Gordon never looked anyone in the eye. But where Gordon had grown up in Africa, children always kept their eyes to the ground when talking with adults as a sign of respect.

Certainly cultural practices are incorporated from the unique aspects of both host and home cultures, but the third culture is more than the sum total of the parts of home and host culture. If it were only that, each TCK would remain alone in his or her experience, for no one else would share the precise details of his or her life story.

" . . . the sense of belonging is in relationship to others of similar background."

This is one of the strange paradoxes about TCKs. Looking at the differences among them—of race, nationality, sponsoring organizations, and places where they are growing (or have grown) up—you would think TCKs could have little in common. But if you have attended a conference sponsored by Global Nomads International,[7] Families in Global Transition,[8] or the World Reunion weekends that Dave used to host for Adult TCKs (ATCKs) and have watched the animated, nonstop conversation of the participants throughout the weekend, you wouldn't question the powerful connection between them. Norma McCaig, founder of Global Nomads, called it a "reunion of strangers." What is this almost magical bond? What is it they share from this "third culture" experience that transcends how we usually define and categorize people?

> Erika returned to Dayton, Ohio, after her long, final flight back from Singapore. She began teaching high school French and Spanish during the day and tutoring international businesspeople in English in the evenings. Once more she tried to accept the reality that her past was gone. Life must go on, and she couldn't expect anyone else to understand her when she didn't understand herself.
>
> Then a remarkable thing occurred. Erika met Judy.
>
> One evening Erika went to see a play and got there a few minutes early. After settling in her seat, she opened her program to see what to expect.
>
> Before she could finish scanning the first page, a middle-aged woman with curly, graying hair squeezed past her, settling on the next seat.
>
> *Why couldn't she have a ticket for the row in front? That's wide open.* Erika rolled her eyes to the ceiling. *All I wanted was a little space tonight.*
>
> Then it got worse. This woman was one of those friendly types.
>
> "Hi, there. I'm Judy. What's your name?"
>
> *Oh, brother, lady. I'm not into this kind of chitchat.* "I'm Erika. It's nice to meet you."

There, she thought, *that's over with.* And she turned her eyes back to study the program again.

"Well, I'm glad to meet you too."

Why won't she leave me alone? Erika wondered.

The lady went on. "I come for the plays every month but I haven't seen you before. Are you new here? Where are you from?"

C'mon, lady. Erika was becoming more agitated by the moment. *This is the theater, not a witness stand. Besides, you don't really want to know anyway.* "I live here in Dayton," Erika replied, with cool politeness. *That ought to end it.*

But Judy continued. "Have you always lived here?"

Why does she care? Erika was definitely losing composure at this point. "No, I've only lived here for two years." *Now shut up, lady.*

"Oh, really? Where did you come from before that?"

With a sigh, Erika half turned to look at this pesky woman and said, "I've lived in lots of different places." *So there.*

"Hey, that's great. So have I! Where have you lived?"

For the first time, Erika looked Judy in the eye. She couldn't believe it. This lady genuinely wanted to know. Erika hesitated. "I lived in Ecuador and Singapore."

"How long?"

"Oh, about ten years between the two places, if you're talking about actually living and going to school there full time."

"You're kidding! I grew up in Venezuela. I'd love to talk to you about it. It's not always easy to find someone here in Dayton who understands what it's like to grow up in another country."

Just then the curtain went up for the play so they stopped talking. Afterward they went for coffee and Erika found herself amazed. Here they were, two women from two totally different backgrounds and generations—Judy's parents had been in the foreign service while Erika's were in business; Judy had lived in Venezuela and Erika had lived in Ecuador and Singapore; Judy was forty-seven, married, and the mother of four grown children, while Erika was twenty-six, single, with no children. Yet they were soon talking and laughing together like long-lost friends.

"I remember when the CEO's wife first came to our house for dinner," Erika said with a chuckle. "She had just arrived in Singapore and kept talking about how awful everything was. My sister and I made up all sorts of stories about how big the roaches were and how poisonous the spiders were just to scare her."

Judy laughed. "I know how you felt. I hated it when new people came out and complained about everything. I always felt so protective for what seemed like my personal Venezuela."

"Well, I guess it was kind of mean," Erika said, "but we didn't like her barging into our world without trying to understand the parts we loved so much. We thought she was arrogant and narrow-minded and didn't deserve to be there—and she probably thought we were the same!"

They laughed together and continued talking for three hours. Erika couldn't believe it. For the first time in years she could speak the language of her soul without needing a translator. A space inside that had almost dried up suddenly began filling and then overflowing with the joy of being understood in a way that needed no explanation.

This is perhaps one of the most amazing things about the TCK experience—that someone from Australia who grew up in Brazil can understand the inner experience of someone from Switzerland who grew up in Hong Kong (or any other combination of passport and host countries). Some say that this might have been true in the past when more TCKs came from Western countries so their roots were more similar, but now it is not so likely with more stark differences in their passport cultures. Based on our interactions with TCKs and ATCKs of many different countries and backgrounds, plus all the chatter on TCK/ATCK blogs, we believe this sense of connection is as strong as ever. In fact, one researcher who has past and present data on this is Alice Wu, an intercultural communication consultant and adjunct lecturer at Cornell University. In 1994, Alice produced what, as far as we know, was the first video of a TCK (aka Global Nomads) panel. In *Global Nomads: Bridges for the Future* the students she interviewed clearly demonstrated this bond across a wide variety of backgrounds. Among the TCK panelists were:

- Kelvin, who was born in Hong Kong, raised in Nigeria, England, and the United States;
- Marianne, a Danish citizen who grew up in Egypt, the United States, and Denmark;
- Kamal, an Indian who lived in Japan as a child;
- Ali, a young Turkish man who spent his childhood in Germany, England, and the United States;
- one North American who grew up in the Philippines; and
- another North American reared in France.

Although each person in the video has differing points of identification with his or her host culture (e.g., the Turkish man feels he is extremely punctual as a result of living in Germany for many years), throughout the discussion it is obvious that their commonalities of feelings and experiences far outweigh their differences. It is equally obvious how delighted they are finally to find a forum where simply naming how they have felt in various circumstances brings instant understanding. No further explanation is needed to elicit a sympathetic laugh or tear from their peers.

Alice traced the Global Nomad/TCK experience in a follow-up video in 2001 called *Global Nomads: Cultural Bridges for the New Millennium* and another in 2014, *Global Nomads: Cultural Bridges in the Age of Technology.* We will talk about her findings of how technology affects this experience later in this book, but in her ongoing research, Alice also reinterviewed fourteen of her 1994 and 2001 panelists through an online survey in 2006 and again in 2010. Here is what she says about those results:

> The results of the survey were striking in terms of the similarity of the student panelists' answers. Almost all of them felt that their Global Nomad [aka TCKs] backgrounds had significantly influenced all of their major life choices (relating to career/education, spouse, and child rearing). These similarities in their viewpoints occurred regardless of whether they completed the survey in 2006 or 2010, whether they participated in the 1994 or 2001 videos, and across various schools and backgrounds.[9]

But the question lingers: What is it about growing up in multiple cultures and with high mobility that creates such instant recognition of each other's experiences and feelings? We'll continue to explore this and other questions about TCKs, but first we'll look at some of the growing cultural complexity in our world today for both TCKs and others who grow up cross-culturally for other reasons and see why all of this matters for not only families but our world itself.

Questions for Chapter 2

1. Before reading chapter 2, what had been your general idea of what "third culture" means?
2. Has that answer changed after reading this chapter? Please explain.
3. The very term Third Culture Kid (TCK) seems to have been a problem to explain easily from the beginning. Properly understood, it makes sense, but when misunderstood, it creates even more confusion. Have you experienced that for yourself or in trying to explain this to others? Please explain.

4. Does the updated definition for TCK or ATCK describe you or someone you know? Look at figure 2-3. Into which of these circles would you put yourself or the person(s) you know in?
5. When you read the classic TCK definition, can you separate what is a definition and what is a description of the TCK? Is that important? How do you relate to these statements?
6. Is there anything else you would like to comment on from this chapter?

CHAPTER 3

Who Are "Cross-Cultural Kids"?

My name is Brice Royer and I'm from Ottawa, Canada. Actually, that's a lie, but that's the answer I give to acquaintances.

So where am I really from? You be the judge. My father is a half-French and half-Vietnamese peacekeeper, and my mother is Ethiopian. It was an unlikely love story that transcends race, culture, and values, but they found love across barriers. I'm grateful for the diversity of my heritage.

And where do I belong? I'm not French, Vietnamese, Ethiopian, or Canadian, and I certainly don't belong everywhere and nowhere. I belong to a group of multicultural people—cross-cultural kids. I've always been the 'Foreigner.' I look different and feel different. I even sound different—including among family members. I eat French food for breakfast, Ethiopian food for lunch, and my own special multicultural recipe for dinner. The truth is, I order Chinese takeout more often than I would like to admit, because let's face it, it's convenient and I can be lazy.[1]

—Brice Royer, developer of TCKID.com

So who is Brice? Certainly he is a TCK, because his father had an international career and Brice traveled the globe with him. But what do we do with the rest of his story? It seems far more complicated than those we have looked at so far.

All over the world, we meet people like Brice whose stories defy simple categorization based on traditional definitions—even for TCKs! Consider the angst of the news broadcasters as they tried to define the forty-fourth U.S. president,

Barack Obama, during the 2008 campaign. Here was a man running for president who had a white U.S. American mother and a black Kenyan father. After his parents divorced, Obama's mother married a man from Indonesia and they moved to Jakarta. Because they had little money, Obama attended the local Indonesian school, where Indonesian was the language of instruction during the day. In order to help him stay fluent in an English-based curriculum, his mother also taught him for some hours every day at home. In time, Obama had a half-sister who was also biracial but not the same two races as himself. After his mother divorced her second husband, she moved to Hawaii with Obama and her white parents, originally from Kansas, and raised him there. So how were the news reporters to describe Obama? Should they call him an African American? Half-white? Half-black? Mixed? While the pundits worked hard to define Obama by his mixed racial heritage[2] and ethnicity, few seemed to understand one of the most basic facts about his life story: Former President Obama not only has a mixed racial heritage, but, as Brice describes himself, he is *culturally mixed* as well.[3]

Increasing Cultural Complexity for TCKs

In chapter 2, we explained the basic history and progression of the TCK concept. But, as Ruth Useem said, concepts grow and change as time goes on, and so it has been even for the cohort she first studied—those who travel to other countries because of their parents' careers.

When Dr. Useem first looked at TCKs, she studied U.S. American kids living in India with parents who most likely were both U.S. citizens working in this one place. Part of the progression of the TCK story began when Dave and Betty Lou Pollock went to Kenya in 1976 and began working with students at an international school. Although the TCKs in this school carried different passports, most were still from Western nations and the majority had parents who shared the same national passport. The students had lived in different host countries but primarily these were nations in Africa.

But the times, they are a-changin'. Now when many TCKs share their stories with us, the layers of cultural complexity in them seem endless. They are not just dealing with a passport culture, host culture, and general shared realities of the internationally mobile experience we call the third culture, but many subsets in each. Those whose family roots are not rooted in a Western-based culture often find the ways of the expat third culture or international schools they attend to be steeped in values quite different from what they experience in their homes each night.

> One African ATCK challenged our belief that TCKs are generally more sensitive to others because of their exposure to many cultures. "I am not so sure that simply growing up as

a TCK makes someone an automatic skilled interculturalist. When I attended my international schools, I had to be Western to fit in there. Everyone thought they knew me, but no one had any idea of who I was when I went home each night to my African cultural world. I don't think it ever occurred to them to ask what might be different between my school and home worlds."[4]

Frankly, before hearing his story, it hadn't occurred to us to ask that question either. Since then, when interviewing TCKs individually or on a panel during a presentation at their schools, we include the question, "Is there anything different for you at home from how things are for you here at school each day?" Speaking in a different language is frequently mentioned, but so are such things as bowing to elders and the way you verbally address adults. Contrary to what many TCKs may be taught in school about the positive value of questioning and exploring every option related to a topic, some TCKs return to a home culture each evening where what the parent says must be respected no matter the child's personal opinion. We have heard some interesting stories about the consequences of mixing these two worldviews!

Increasingly, TCKs have parents from at least two cultures or nationalities. Which country do they visit while on leave? Which language is spoken at home? In the local culture? At school?

Max and Maria are parents of one such family. Max is from France but did a medical residency in the United States. Maria is from Nicaragua, and they met while both worked for a relief agency in Africa. They returned to work in the same region where they met after they married, and their three children all speak French, Spanish, Arabic, and a smattering of English. The children are home-schooled because it is the best viable option in their situation. When Dad teaches them, he uses French. When Mom teaches, the classes are in Spanish. Mom or Dad give a daily lesson in English and a local tutor helps with the Arabic.

For the children, their way of life seems "normal" despite the political tensions around them. It's what they know. But life feels infinitely more stressful when it's time for the parents' annual leave. Both of their extended families want them to come "home" each time, but France and Nicaragua aren't exactly next-door countries. Donors to their agency who live in the U.S. would like a report of how things are going. If Max and Maria try to see everyone during each leave, both sets of grandparents get upset that they didn't have enough time with their grandchildren. Of course, the children get tired of so much travel, and Max and Maria

wind up exhausted. If they try to alternate years for returning to each passport country, the grandparents not on the
schedule for that year feel cheated.

This new reality of multinational parentage is something many third culture families now face that the colonialists of old never considered when both
parents were usually from the same country. In those days, all the grandparents
most often lived in the same country as well, so visiting them wasn't such a
problem.

For Western TCKs in former generations, reentry to the passport culture
was a challenge, but most had gone to school overseas in their first language as
they attended British, American, German, or French schools. Their command of
language and accents mirrored others in their passport countries and their TCK-
ness could remain hidden at least initially when they repatriated.

Now, in many international schools it is not uncommon to have forty or fifty
nationalities (the most we encountered was over 120 in one particular school!).
That means many students are not studying in their primary language. When
the educational language is English, students from non-English-speaking countries generally pick up the particular accent of the majority culture of that school
rather than the accent others from their passport countries might typically have
when speaking English. When they repatriate, such students are often mocked
for the American or British accents they acquired at school or because they cannot speak their own "mother tongue" correctly.

Here is part of Joyce Mann's story, an ATCK from Hong Kong:

> I will no longer apologise for my flawed Cantonese and for-
> eign ways. I am that Westernised child who emigrated in the
> 1990s, returned later, and attended expensive international
> schools and a foreign university. I speak English fluently
> and Cantonese with an accent.
>
> I am also, if you like, the product of the struggles,
> hopes, and fears of upper-middle-class Hongkongers in
> the handover era. Out of fear, our parents uprooted us to
> Canada, Australia, the U.S., and Britain before 1997. Out of
> frustration from not finding jobs, they later moved us back,
> but invested heavily in international education.
>
> For us, the children, that meant growing up speaking
> English. Between studying Western curriculums and doing
> after-school activities, all in English, there was not much
> time left to absorb Hong Kong culture.
>
> Moreover, at my school, Cantonese was forbidden. . . .
> Relatives, friends, colleagues, acquaintances, and even
> strangers have laughed at me for the way I speak Canton-
> ese. I have been accused of forgetting my roots or, worse,
> of not being a Hongkonger. Last year, a restaurant owner

> yelled at me in front of her entire clientele. "Do you even
> speak Chinese?" . . . All the skills I have gleaned from my
> cross-cultural background apparently count for nothing
> when I say or do something differently from a "local" Hon-
> gkonger, because supposedly I have turned my back on my
> roots.[5]

And, depending on which country or countries the parents are from and the geopolitical realities of each, things can be very complicated when an adult TCK tries to return to the family after college and finds out that governments are not geared to considering all the cultural nuances of his or her story or the increasing global fluidity of ATCKs!

> Eun-chae (Doris) was born to a Singaporean mother and a
> Korean father and grew up in western China. While at-
> tending college in the U.S., she turned twenty-one at the
> same time that her parents moved back to Singapore, which
> meant that she could not be registered as a dependent. Un-
> able to join her family, she spent a year working in India
> and then decided to try again. Doris obtained a tourist visa
> because Singapore does not allow dual citizenship. Upon
> arrival, she applied for a work visa so she could remain in
> Singapore with her family. After months of effort and wait-
> ing, her work visa was denied and she was forced to leave
> her family to find work elsewhere. Since she had never lived
> for an extended period in her passport country, Korea, Doris
> had neither the relationships nor necessary cultural and
> linguistic capital to find work and live at ease there. In the
> end, she joined an NGO in Bangladesh.

While the above stories are about the increasing cultural complexity of to-day's TCKs, this experience of growing up in a culturally mixed environment is becoming increasingly common, not only for TCKs but for many others as well. These people may have grown up as children of immigrants or refugees or as international adoptees or minorities. Some simply grew up in an environment where they commonly interacted deeply between and among various cultural worlds around them, rather than moving to other cultures with parents who were engaged in international careers. Although their experiences differ mark-edly from those of the traditional TCKs first described by Ruth Hill Useem, peo-ple from this wide variety of cross-cultural experiences as children tell us how much they relate to the common characteristics for TCKs. They want to know: *Am I a TCK or not?* Pravin was one who asked this question.

> Pravin began life in normal fashion—being born in his
> parents' homeland, India. From the moment of his birth,
> Pravin's parents wanted one thing: to give him every

opportunity they could to be successful in a changing, internationalizing world. Part of their dream included helping him develop proficiency in English. With this goal in mind, they sent him to a British boarding school high on a mountainside in the north of India, which required students to speak and write only in English.

Because his parents lived quite far away, they were not able to see Pravin during the school holidays. Finally the end of term came, and the day six-year-old Pravin had waited for all year: his parents were coming to pick him up for summer vacation. He could hardly contain his excitement! Yet he did have a slight fear—what if he didn't recognize his parents? How would he find them?

Finally, he saw them. He did know them after all! He ran to his parents, they picked him up, and then the unthinkable happened. Pravin couldn't understand what they were saying. Their words sounded vaguely familiar, but he could not respond even to the few words he understood. During that year away from home, he had forgotten his mother tongue, and his parents didn't know English. When they took him back to their village for summer vacation that year and each year thereafter, he could no longer communicate with his former playmates. From that day to this, he has lived in and among many cultural worlds without feeling totally at home in any—but all within one country.

Stories abound of those who have grown up in a multiplicity of cultural worlds for many different reasons besides the more traditional TCK experience about which we usually think. Foreign exchange students are one example as they change cultural worlds often for a year without their parents around at all. *NBC Nightly News* carried the story of "satellite babies"—children born to immigrants in the U.S. whose parents find child care expensive and also want to keep their child connected to the home culture. These children stay with relatives back in the "homeland" until school age. At age five or six they are reconnected to parents and a land in which they are citizens by birth but not by culture. Another trend we have seen is that some parents in non-English-speaking countries send children to a local international school or a more distant boarding school whose instructional language is English. They want their children to learn fluent English so they can be successful international businesspeople later. Technically these children are not TCKs since they have not gone to a new culture with their parents, but the students attending local international schools change cultural worlds on a daily basis. Those who go off to boarding school not only change cultural worlds but face other issues, such as attachment and loss, familiar to TCKs who went to boarding school at young ages.

All of these examples raise the legitimate question: Can all who grow or grew up among many cultures for whatever reasons be considered TCKs or ATCKs, per se?

Some who work with or know about TCKs say no. They believe there are so many differences between these types of experiences that none can be properly researched if all are included under one umbrella. The problem then is that there seems to be little effort to understand why there exists such a commonality of response to the TCK Profile from those with greatly assorted, cross-cultural backgrounds. Instead, each group is left on its own to understand from scratch its collective story.

Conversely, those who see themselves or others relating to the TCK Profile, even if they never lived as traditional TCKs, say, "Yes, include everyone." They believe any child who has grown up among various cultural worlds is a bona fide TCK. Then the first group asks, "How can the child in the refugee camp have anything in common with the ambassador's kids living in a mansion and taking private riding lessons?" Good question. Yet, amazingly, there are indeed points of connection in their stories.

> During the height of the Liberian civil war, Ruth (Van Reken) and her husband traveled to Ghana and learned that many friends from their nine years spent in Liberia lived in a nearby refugee camp.
>
> Ruth wanted to see her friends, but what would she say? Their experiences since their last meeting were beyond belief. How did anything in her life relate to the horrors of war and displacement they had known?
>
> In the first moments of meeting, it seemed like old times. The familiar sounds of Liberian English rang like music in her ears. They all chatted to catch up on news of family and friends. But soon the conversation began to include the sadder stories of the many friends who had died in the war and the atrocities so many had been through. Ruth could only grieve for them. How could anything in her life relate to theirs?
>
> One friend finally asked what she had been doing since their last meeting. To Ruth, all she had done seemed rather irrelevant in this situation. Her fairly routine activities paled in comparison to their dramatic and sad stories. Yet in sharing her life story and also her work regarding TCKs, her Liberian friends began telling her their stories—what it felt like for them to realize their children had no idea about the Liberia they as parents had known and how their children were now caught in a world between worlds, neither fully Liberian nor fully Ghanaian.

There they were: a white ATCK woman with enough means to travel to Ghana for a family visit, and her friends—black men, women, and children, victims of a terrible civil war, living on the rations given by the U.N. Still, in that moment of talking about the impact of living and growing up outside the environment defined as "home," they connected in a shared experience that transcended, for those moments, all the differences in their outer circumstances.

Are these children of refugees TCKs or not? If so, what do we do with what it means to live as a refugee rather than a TCK who may happen to be a privileged "expat" child? If not, why do they relate? What are their points of connection?

As the cultural mixing of today's world increases, these questions regarding who can or cannot be included as an "official" TCK are important ones to address. The point is not to include or exclude others as from some special "club" but to continue growing collectively in our understanding of how the many events going on in our globalizing world specifically impact children and families. The reality is that if we throw a huge net over all of those who have a point of connection to the TCK profile and say all are TCKs, not only may it make research into each type of experience more difficult, but we can minimalize parts of someone's story. As one example, the children growing up in the Liberian refugee camp Ruth visited have significant overlap with TCKs who feel culturally displaced and may have lived with much mobility, but the trauma and statelessness of what they have experienced would be sadly lost by labeling their story "the same" as children who move because of a parent's choice or the decision of the sponsoring agency. At the same time, as a community of TCKs, we want to throw our arms around them and, because of our points of connection, say, "Come, be part of us too." How do we find a way to share strategies that we have learned from the TCK experience related to the effects of growing up among different cultural worlds, while honoring that the sad trauma of war and forced mobility is an added reality most traditional TCKs have not known?

Another example of how our changing world has made the discussion of who is or isn't a TCK a bit more complicated is how the immigrant (or simply "migrant" experience as it is named in some parts of the world) has changed. Historically, we assumed the difference between the TCK experience and that of immigrant children was simple: immigrants moved to a land to stay and many never took even one trip back to the homeland after arriving in the new country. TCKs moved with the expectation of one day returning to their original country. We assumed that difference in expectation regarding potential repatriation changed how each group related to the host or new country. But in today's highly mobile world, immigrant children go back and forth, often with great regularity, between their country of origin and their adopted land just as TCKs do. Yet, the expectation of "settling" is different for TCKs and immigrant children despite these growing commonalities. How do we factor all of these changes into our understanding to more accurately describe the new normals of our world of both the commonalities many of these children share while also recognizing the particular strengths or challenges of each experience?

And we circle back to the questions with which we began this chapter—the cultural complexity of so many of today's TCKs as well as some who are already ATCKs. How do we acknowledge the additional layers of cross-cultural experiences that TCKs like Brice Royer or Barack Obama have experienced that potentially add extra nuances to their lives beyond what the traditional TCK has known? Can we offer a way to help them look at the many factors that have shaped them rather than trying to jam everything about their lives into one simple "TCK box"? And, again, what about those who have not lived a traditional TCK experience yet say they relate to so much of the traditional TCK's common characteristics. Is there a better way to keep open the possibility for more research into all of these fascinating and evolving realities rather than being forever stuck on terminology?

We believe there is.

We need new language.

Identifying Cross-Cultural Kids

In 2002, Ruth Van Reken coined the term *cross-cultural kids (CCKs)* as a way (hopefully!) to move past the arguments on language for who could or couldn't be named a TCK so the larger story of what is going on in our world could be better studied. She defined them as follows.

- A *cross-cultural kid (CCK)* is a person who is living/has lived in—or meaningfully interacted with—two or more cultural environments for a significant period of time during the first eighteen years of life.
- An *adult CCK (ACCK)* is a person who has grown up as a CCK.

Ruth believed that just as we had included children from the various communities of those who work or do advanced training internationally (e.g., corporate, military, missionary, foreign service, NGOs, graduate students) under the broader language of *third culture kids*, so we could enlarge our language and make room under one umbrella of *cross-cultural kids (CCKs)* for all types of cross-cultural childhoods, *including* traditional TCKs. In this model (see figure 3-1), the wide variety of ways children can grow up cross-culturally are recognized under a unified whole while not losing the distinctions of a particular experience. In addition, we can see more clearly the reality and cultural complexity of each person's story within a larger context. For example, when we look carefully at Obama's story, we can see that he is in at least six CCK circles—traditional TCK, bicultural, biracial heritage, domestic TCK, minority, educational CCK. In the CCK model researchers can still choose a specific group to study in depth. Hopefully, in time, these researchers can join in comparing and contrasting the longer-term outcomes of children who grow up in these different environments to see what are the universals and what are distinctions for each group.

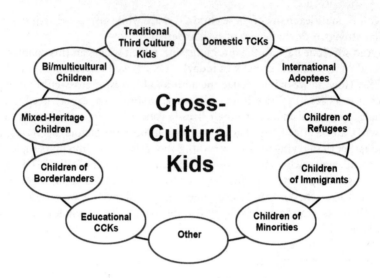

Figure 3–1: The Cross-Cultural Kid (CCK) Model
©2002 Ruth E. VanReken, updated 2017

This model is a representation of *some* of the types of CCKs we can consider:

- *Traditional TCKs:* Children who accompany parents into a country or countries that are different from at least one parent's passport country(ies) due to a parent's choice of work or advanced training.
- *Children from bi/multicultural/multiethnic parents:* Children born to parents from at least two cultures—may or may not be of the same racial heritage.
- *Children with mixed-racial heritage:* Children born to parents from at least two racial heritages—may or may not be of the same culture.
- *Children of borderlanders:* Children who cross borders frequently, even daily, as they go to school, or whose parents work across national borders.
- *Educational CCKs:* Children who attend a school with a different cultural base from the one they return to at home each night.
- *Other:* Any other way children grow up cross-culturally. You fill in the blank.
- *Children of minorities:* Children whose parents are from a racial or ethnic group that is not part of the majority race or ethnicity of the country in which they live.
- *Children of immigrants:* Children whose parents have made a permanent move to a new country where they were not originally citizens.
- *Children of refugees:* Children whose parents are living outside their original country or place due to circumstances they did not choose, such as war, violence, famine, or natural disasters.
- *International adoptees:* Children adopted by parents from another country other than the one of that child's birth.
- *Domestic TCKs:* Children whose parents have moved in or among various cultures or subcultures within that child's home country.

These designated groups represent just a few of the many ways children can grow up as CCKs in our modern world. As you can see, one of the great things about this CCK model is that there are, and will continue to be, more categories than those named here, and we can simply add another subgroup each time that happens. The different types of experiences that could go in "other" are almost endless. Oya Ataman has written a wonderful blog on how this model of cross-cultural upbringing applies to children of deaf parents. These CCKs serve as bridges between the Deaf culture with its own distinct language and the hearing world around it.[6] Many other types of disabilities could be included here as well. Children of divorced parents who spend half their time in one parent's home and half in the other's house often tell us they switch cultures each time they move from one home to the other because the rules for what is allowed or not allowed by each parent can be quite different. In some countries children move cross-culturally from village life with its subsistence farming and strong communal living to the chaos of the capital city where congested traffic patterns, anonymity, and cash economy are the way of life. But for now, we begin with these few examples of CCKs.

Cross-Cultural Kids Subgroups and Subsets

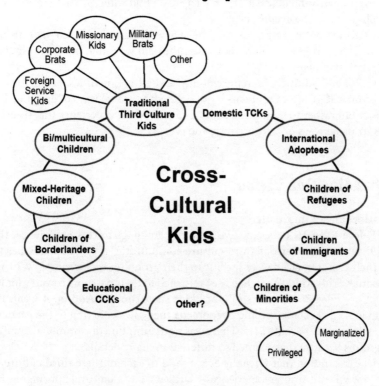

Figure 3–2: The Cross Cultural Kid (CCK) Model Expanded

©2002 Ruth E. Van Reken, updated 2017

Please note several things about the CCK definition and our model:

• The traditional TCKs discussed in this book are also CCKs. Just as corporate "brats" or missionary kids are TCKs, traditional TCKs are also a subgroup of CCKs, as our paradigm shows. Each category listed under CCKs could have additional subsets, just as TCKs do. See figure 3-2. In other words, just like corporate, foreign service, military or missionary children are subsets of the TCK subgroup, so under immigrants, various ethnicities, generations, or types of immigration (e.g. political asylum) might be listed. For refugees, studying those living in camps versus those who are granted asylum in another country is possible. This means each individual subset can be studied independently at whatever level the researcher decides but, if desired, those findings can then be compared to what others discover while looking at their particular area of interest. We believe this is a way to create a more cohesive discussion for all rather than having many isolated conversations.

• Unlike the definition for TCKs, the CCK definition is *not* dependent on the question of *where* CCKs grow up, such as outside the passport culture or overseas. This definition focuses on the multiple and varied layering of cultural environments that are impacting a child's life rather than the actual place where the events occur.

• CCKs are not merely living side-by-side with those from other cultures, but are interacting with more than one culture in ways that have meaningful or relational involvement.

• CCKs and adult CCKs represent any and all nationalities, ethnicities, and economic groups. Our focus is not on the traditional ways of defining diversity but rather to look at the commonalities of the experience that transcend our usual ways of categorizing people.

Expanding Our Vision

Why does any of this matter?

Before Ruth Hill Useem gave unifying language to this experience, those who lived in these various third culture communities assumed the issues they and their children faced were specific to their group (or sector) alone. Why were missionary kids so strange when they returned to their passport country for high school or college? Why were military kids such "brats"? And on it went. Each group looked at sector-specific phenomena they saw occurring in the particular system where the parents were. There was no assumption of commonality among the groups because they seemed so different in many details.

Understanding that virtually every child in each of these third culture sectors grew up with similar experiences—such as a cross-cultural upbringing, high mobility, expected repatriation, and often a system identity as we mentioned in chapter 2—expedited the discussion for everyone. Each group no longer had to

think through from scratch why they were seeing certain behaviors or characteristics or presume these things came from the specific nature of their sector.
As the broader themes emerged, understanding and resources could be shared
among all the sectors.

By looking at the shared whole, however, issues that applied specifically to
each sector became more visible as well. For example, how did the long and often
multiple separations from at least one parent, coupled with the fear (for those in
a war zone) that this parent might never return, play out specifically for military
kids? How did the sense that they and their families represented an entire nation affect children growing up in the foreign service? How did the *God piece* of
growing up in a religious system impact the missionary kid? How did watching
decisions made by a parent's corporation based on the *bottom line* that might
adversely affect the family or influence the local economy shape a business kid?
Figure 3-3 illustrates both what is shared and what is more specific among traditional TCK sectors.

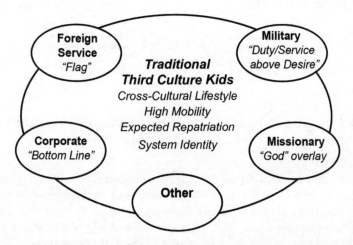

Figure 3–3: Third Culture Kids: Potential Commonalities and Differences
©1996 Ruth E. VanReken, updated 2017

In other words, it's not entirely God's fault that a missionary kid might carry
unresolved grief; that is a common characteristic for TCKs of all sectors. On the
other hand, dealing with separating a view of God from the religious subculture
may be a common challenge unique to TCKs in the mission sector. Neither is the
military to blame for a person who has "itchy feet" and is always looking to move
after two years, but the fear of a black limousine pulling up to the front door to
announce a parent's death may be a common characteristic for a child raised in
this subset of the TCK experience. Once universals are defined, other specific
issues can be discussed.

These same lessons apply to understanding CCKs. Figure 3-3 gives us examples of what CCKs of all backgrounds share and what issues may be specific for each particular type of experience.

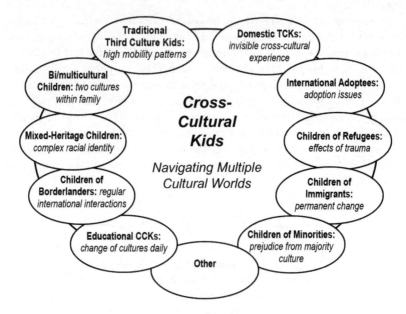

Figure 3–4: Cross-Cultural Kids: Potential Commonalities and Differences
©2004 Ruth E. Van Reken, updated 2017

While the idea of CCKs is a growing concept, there is one thing we know for sure that virtually all CCKs share. By definition, each of them grows up in some sort of cross-cultural lifestyle or environment, no matter the particular circumstance. An exception might be children of mixed-racial heritage whose parents are from the same culture and they are not in any of the other subsets, but even there, how the culture around them mirrors back how they are seen would likely still be a cultural factor. That means that discussions of the impact of frequent switching between cultural worlds during childhood could be a relevant issue to talk about for every group.

> One friend who has worked with the refugees of Darfur looked at the CCK model and said, "This is the first time I see my friends at Darfur being invited back to the human race. We are so used to thinking of all their issues as a result of the violence, which is, indeed, terrible. But we have been forgetting that in addition to that, they have lost their cultural world as well and feel that loss as all others do when it happens to them for whatever reason."

Some of the most invisible CCKs, however, may be domestic TCKs—those who have moved in and among various cultures right within their homeland. Jennifer is one.

> Both of Jennifer's parents grew up in the upper-middle-class suburbs of Toronto. When Jennifer was nine, they became teachers for five years on a First Nation (Native American) reservation near Vancouver. Jennifer went to school, played, ate, and visited with her First Nation playmates almost exclusively during those years—yet her lifestyle was not the same as their lifestyle. For example, there were celebratory rituals in the First Nation culture that Jennifer's family never practiced. Her parents had rules for curfew and study hours that many of her friends didn't have, but Jennifer accepted these differences between herself and her friends.
>
> When she was fourteen, Jennifer's parents returned to Toronto. They wanted her to have a more "normal" high school experience. Unfortunately, it wasn't as normal as they had hoped. For one thing, Jennifer's new classmates seemed to judge one another far more critically by clothing styles than she had ever before experienced. Far worse, however, was that Jennifer saw this emphasis on apparent superficiality as stemming from a lack of concern for what she considered the real issues of life.
>
> When newspapers reported the ongoing conflict of land issues between the First Nation people and the Canadian government, she read the accounts with keen interest. She personally knew friends whose futures were directly affected by these political decisions. But when she tried to discuss such things with fellow classmates or their parents, their response was almost dismissive: "I don't know what those people are complaining about. Look at all we've already done for them." The more she tried to explain why this topic needed attention, the more they labeled her as radical, and the more she labeled them as uncaring. Jennifer sobbed herself to sleep many nights, wishing for the comfortable familiarity of the world and friends she'd known before.

Although she had never left Canada, Jennifer had become a domestic TCK—someone raised in that world between worlds—within her own country.

The military is another place where domestic TCKs often develop, even though the parents may never have gone overseas. Because the military subculture is quite different from that of the civilian population around it, a particular life-style develops (see Mary Edwards Wertsch's book *Military Brats*). When military parents return to civilian life, their children often experience many of the same feelings that internationally mobile TCKs describe when they return to their passport countries, despite the fact that they may have lived their entire lives on homeland soil.

> Raised on U.S. Navy bases in California and Washington, D.C., Bernadette was fourteen when her father retired from the navy and her family settled in the midwestern town of Terre Haute, Indiana. Bernadette later described the experience as one of total alienation from her peers, whose life experience was completely foreign to her. "They had no idea what the PX was, how much life on a base is governed by the security issues surrounding it, or how normal it was to mix with those of different races on a daily basis because our parents were all working as peers in their various assignments. And I had no idea what it felt like to grow up in one town in the Midwest with little interaction with others who were not from your presumed social group or race."

This is where the idea of TCKs as prototypes for others becomes reality. As we consider why a cross-cultural childhood matters in a TCK's life, we can begin to see what lessons learned from that experience can be applied to other CCKs as well. For example, although the way cultural interactions occurred and the degree of mobility were different in other types of CCK experiences from the traditional TCK's world, many other CCKs shared the common emotional experience that when they tried to relate to those who "should" be their own, they didn't feel as if they fit or belonged to that group any longer. This is the part about "relating to others of like experience" described in the TCK definition—one of the new places of connection in our changing world. As we continue to find the common points that CCKs of all backgrounds share, we can see more clearly what, in fact, are unique issues to consider for those various subgroups as well.

But then, the beauty in the CCK model is also that TCKs like Royer and Obama can look and instantly recognize the multiple layers of their story as well as looking at the TCK factor. For Obama, that might mean in addition to understanding his basic TCK experience as described in this book, he also considers what it was like to grow up with no mirror for himself even in his own family, as others from a mixed-racial heritage frequently write about. How did he navigate the two cultural worlds of his biological and then stepfather's different cultural worlds?

The Ngujos are a family who knew what it was to be in more than one grouping of CCKs.

The Ngujos laughed when they saw the CCK model. "We never stopped to think of how many of these groups our kids are in." When asked to explain, Mrs. Ngujo said, "Well, I came from one region in Kenya; my husband came from another. We both spoke Swahili and English, but neither of us spoke each other's mother tongue. I guess that makes my kids members of the bicultural group. My husband took a job with a large international bank, so our family immigrated to the States. There we became part of a minority population for the first time, but soon his bank began sending us on assignments all over the world. At that point, our kids became traditional TCKs. I'm glad to know there is a term to describe all four experiences at the same time!"

These are factors other TCKs don't all have to face, but non-TCKs in those other groups may have much to share with the Ngujo children if they have also been immigrants or minorities or bicultural. As the Ngujos' children (now adults) share some things they have learned from being TCKs, it will help other CCKs see some of the more invisible realities of their own life lived among many cultures. What are the gifts this childhood might offer them? What are the challenges they might also face simply because of the cultural interactions, per se? And as the Ngujos read more of the studies of first-generation immigrants, they may have new insights into the complexity of their story. Our hope is that much more mutuality and camaraderie could be fostered between all the groups that lead to growth for all.

The question, however, remains: While it may be good to find a common term to describe children who grow up among many cultures, how is this going to help us compare and contrast the different experiences if we don't really understand each one?

That is an important question. We know, for sure, that we don't know the details of how it is to live in many of the groups we listed earlier. But we do know how it is to live as, work with, and study about TCKs.

For this reason, we will continue to focus *primarily* on the specifics of the traditional TCK experience as we proceed through this book. We do so for two reasons.

1. This is the experience we know in detail. We want to continue giving TCKs and ATCKs language and understanding for the depth and unique aspects of their own cross-cultural journey. We have seen for many years how important that is.
2. We also invite everyone to consider common themes for the larger cohort of CCKs that may emerge. What are the principles and basic understandings that can apply to other experiences as well? This book will not finish

that discussion, but we trust it will start it with the hopes of expediting and expanding that ongoing discussion.

With that in mind, we move on to why a cross-cultural childhood matters for TCKs and, presumably, other groups of CCKs as well.

Questions for Chapter 3

1. Refer to Figure 3-1. How many of these circles are you in? How many circles do your friends fit? Please explain why you count yourself in each circle if you are in at least one.
2. What are the places of connection you see in your story with these different types of cross-cultural experiences? What others might you add?
3. What do you think about the idea of growing "cultural complexity" in our world? How does that impact our communities?
4. What other thoughts did you have about a wider conversation on these different types of cross-cultural childhoods?

CHAPTER 4

Why a Cross-Cultural Childhood Matters

I am
a confusion of cultures.
Uniquely me.
I think this is good
because I can
understand
the traveller, sojourner, foreigner,
the homesickness
that comes.
I think this is also bad
because I cannot
be understood
by the person who has sown and grown in one place.

They know not
the real meaning of homesickness
that hits me
now and then.
Sometimes I despair of
understanding them.
I am
an island
and
a United Nations.
Who can recognise either in me
but God?[1]

—"Uniquely Me" by Alex Graham James

Who Am I?

This poem by Alex, a business TCK from Australia who grew up in Sabah (Borneo), Malaysia and married an Australian TCK who grew up in India, captures the paradoxical nature of the TCK experience—a life where the soil that nurtures the growth of their richest gifts exists in the same garden where some of their deepest challenges also sprout. How is it possible for Alex, Erika, and countless other TCKs to feel so profoundly connected, yet simultaneously disconnected, to people and places around the world? How do they develop the beautiful potentials of their life story while not denying the harder places?

To answer these questions, we will take a closer look at the world in which TCKs grow up, a world filled with cross-cultural transitions and high mobility. These two related but distinct forces play a large role in shaping a TCK's life in this paradoxical way.

Of course, we realize that many people who make their first international moves as adults—third culture adults (TCAs) as we call them—also experience cross-cultural transitions and high mobility as they embark on international careers. Their lives are inevitably changed in the process. TCAs, however, must understand some distinct differences between making a cross-cultural move for the first time as an adult and *growing up* cross-culturally as TCKs do.

People who initially go to live in another culture as adults (TCAs) undoubtedly experience culture shock and need a period of adjustment. They have lifelong shifts in their worldview after a major cross-cultural move, but their basic value system, sense of identity, and the establishment of core relationships with family and friends have usually already developed in the home culture. Most often, they clearly see themselves as Koreans, Germans, Australians, Kenyans, Indonesians, or (you fill in the blank), who happen to be living in another place or culture. Their basic sense of who they are and where they are from is intact—at least until they feel like strangers in their home country on repatriation! At that point they might need to do some reassessment of who they have become, but the fundamentals of identity for most TCAs remain even then.

Unlike third culture adults, TCKs move back and forth from one culture to another *before* they have completed the critical developmental tasks of forming a sense of their own personal, cultural, or national identity. A British child taking toddling steps on foreign soil or speaking his or her first words in Chinese with an *amah* (nanny) has no idea what it means to be a human being, let alone "British" yet. He or she simply responds to what is happening in the moment.

To have a meaningful discussion about TCKs, it is essential to remember that it is an *interplay* of these factors—living in both a culturally changing *and* highly mobile world during the *formative* years—rather than any single factor alone, that leads to the evolution of the benefits, challenges, and personal characteristics described later in the TCK Profile. To better understand how the interplay of these factors works, we need to look first at each one separately. We will begin by taking a look at the cross-cultural nature of the TCK's childhood. Then, in chapter 5, we will move on to high mobility, and then we will see how the intertwining of these two realities is life-shaping for TCKs in terms of their sense of identity, feelings of grief and loss, and knowledge of belonging and purpose.

The Significance of Culture

All children, including TCKs, face a myriad of developmental tasks as they grow from helpless infants into healthy adults. One of those is the need to develop a strong sense of personal identity that is rooted in an identity as part of a group, answering the questions *Who am I?* and *Where do I belong?* Traditionally, the family and community mirror back similar answers as the child sees his or her image reflected in them. Hans Christian Andersen's fable *The Ugly Duckling* shows how this process of finding personal and group identity works.

> A baby swan emerged from its shell in the midst of a nest of ducklings. The mother duck was shocked at the appearance of this baby. The ducklings laughed at the clumsy, overgrown, freakish supposed-specimen of a duck. The ducklings bullied and mercilessly teased the odd creature. Soon the young swan accepted the judgment of his community, believed he was ugly, and ran away.
>
> Eventually he saw a group of swans. As he swam out to try to join them, he looked into the lake and realized they reflected his own image in a beautiful way. At last this little ugly duckling understood both his personal identity in being a swan and that he did, in fact, belong to a community.[2]

Through the ages, this process of learning culture as part of our identity formation has occurred so naturally that it's been like breathing. We breathe all the time, but until someone chokes and can't catch a breath, no one notices what's going on. Because learning culture and identity are such an unconscious process, however, we need to dissect it so that we can find some important keys to unlock the mystery of *why* common TCK characteristics occur. Let's look first at what culture is, how it's learned, and why it's important. Second, we will compare how the process of cultural learning for those who grow up among many cultures is the same as or different from that of children born and bred in the more traditional monocultural experience.

WHAT IS CULTURE?

When we think of the word *culture*, obvious representations such as how to dress, eat, speak, and act like those around us come to mind. Culture is also a system of shared concepts, beliefs, and values.[3] It is the framework from which we interpret and make sense of life and the world around us. As cultural anthropologist

Paul Hiebert emphasized, culture is learned rather than instinctive—something caught from, as well as taught by, the surrounding environment and passed on from one generation to the next.[4]

The Role of the Visible and Invisible Layers of Culture

Anthropologist Gary Weaver suggested looking at culture as a kind of iceberg: one portion is clearly visible above the surface of the water, while the much larger chunk of ice is hidden below. The part above the water can be considered *surface culture*—what we can physically see or hear, including behavior, words, customs, language, and traditions. Underneath the water, invisible to all, is the *deep culture*.[5] This place includes our beliefs, values, assumptions, worldview, and thought processes, which, of course, also include language. Figure 4-1 depicts the cultural iceberg Weaver envisioned.

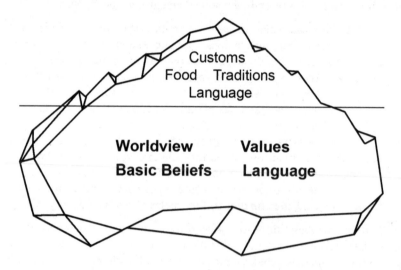

Figure 4–1: The Weaver Cultural Iceberg (adapted)
©1981 Dr. Gary Weaver. Used by permission.

The basic thesis behind this model is that traditionally the elements in the surface, or visible, layer of culture traditionally have been used to identify what is in the deeper, or invisible, layer. The visible is where the invisible is expressed. Thus, what we see becomes our shorthand method to make early assessments and identify expectations of others. Is this person an "us" or a "them"? Will we relate from "likeness" or "difference"? The following are examples of how this works.

- In some places, tribal markings on the face make it clear whether strangers will interact as fellow tribespersons or foreigners from the first moment of their meeting. Because of these symbols, they know (or assume!)

immediately whether they can use their tribal dialect or must speak in a more universal language before either has said one word.

- When we watch a sporting event, we cheer or boo the players based solely on the color of their uniform. We look around the grandstands and assume those who wear the blue jerseys or bandanas, like us, share our hopes for a home team victory. We are equally confident that those with red jerseys have come to root for the opposing team. In each case, without knowing one other thing about the people surrounding us, we have made decisions about who they are and what they want based on something we can see.

- Certain religions require their followers to wear specific types of clothing or hairstyles as part of living out a tenet of faith. Other religions have clear symbols representing core beliefs and their believers often wear these symbols as jewelry. Because of that, when others meet someone wearing that particular style of clothing, hair, or jewelry, they automatically assume they know what the person believes and interact with the person based on that premise, often without first checking if those assumptions are right or wrong.

Stereotypes and racism can form easily when we make assumptions about who another person is in these deeper layers of culture based on appearances alone. Without doubt, we must guard against that.

On the other hand, assumptions based on the visible expressions of culture also help us create order and structure in our lives and social relationships. Imagine the chaos teams would face if they had no uniforms. What would happen if every time a soccer player wanted to kick the ball to a teammate, that player had to stop and ask the intended receiver what team he wanted to win? How could we locate our desired item in a new store if we couldn't find someone wearing the right color shirt and logo that silently announces "This person works here; you can ask her your question"?

The Dangers of the Invisible Layers

But a special danger lurks from the iceberg. The *Titanic* didn't sink because it hit the visible portion of the iceberg. Disaster struck when the ship's captain assumed he knew where the iceberg lay because of what he saw. He had no idea of its mammoth size below the surface. The same can happen with cultural clashes. We can make many allowances for differences we recognize, but when our values, beliefs, or worldviews are at odds with others in ways we haven't stopped to consider and cannot see, our relationships can sink like the Titanic without our knowing what we hit.[6]

Though the iceberg model explains many historical clashes as well as present-day situations, Weaver gave a warning more than thirty years ago of new challenges coming for our globalizing world. He predicted that because we use the visible to make assumptions about the invisible and, thus, how we will relate to another person, as the visible layers of culture became more similar in dress, manners, and even language, people would then also assume commonality of thought, worldview, and beliefs at the deeper level. He realized that people change external cues of culture, such as dress and food, far more quickly than they alter their core values, manner of thinking, and belief system. Weaver stated that this developing discrepancy between who we *expect* others to be based on appearance and who they *are* in their invisible spaces will create more cultural clashes than previously seen unless we find new ways to recognize and address this issue.

In many ways the time that Weaver predicted is now. Cultural mixing and matching in every country are happening faster than we can understand. The normal feeling of many is to retrench and long for the good old days when things seemed more in our control. We feel more comfortable and safer when we understand what's going on based on how things have always been.

With the advent of the Internet and worldwide social media, a global pop culture where teens everywhere wear the same kind of athletic shoes or adore the same musical groups, to the worldwide syndication of TV and movies, the visible layer of culture for people and groups around the world is more similar than in previous eras. In fact, many have told us they don't believe the cultural issues or challenges we discuss for TCKs are relevant in today's world because of what they consider as some sort of "global culture." But when we read the TCK blogs or chat rooms, more than ever the questions of *Where do I belong?* and *Where do I fit?* fill cyberspace. The nastiness of so many comments on Facebook, Twitter, and Instagram, or responses to articles posted online belies any sense of "one big happy family" forming in this world despite more external similarities.

Once we see the importance of both the surface and deeper layers of culture, we can understand how they work together to give the important sense of cultural balance we all need, and then see what can add challenges in finding this sense of balance for TCKs and other CCKs.

HOW CULTURE IS LEARNED

Learning culture is more than learning external patterns of behavior. Understanding who we are and where we belong is a developmental task for everyone that takes place in the context of the surrounding community. Young parents don't buy books titled *How to Teach Your Child Culture*. From the moment of birth, children are learning the ways of their community. Parents speak a particular language to them. They are clothed and carried in ways defined by that community as "right": "Pink is for girls, blue is for boys." "Tie the baby on your back." "Put the baby in a safe car seat." Basically, culture is "caught" from those around us, not intentionally taught. This is how, while we are children, we unconsciously learn the basic rules and values by which our particular culture operates and the way these mores are appropriately expressed. We have role models for how life is one day supposed to be as we watch how older siblings, parents, and others in our community live.

As the children grow, extended family members reinforce the concepts of how life is approached and lived. "What do you say?" asks Grandma as she hands her grandchild a cookie. This is a basic lesson on the importance of saying "thank you" for gifts received in this culture. Later, teachers, peers, and others in the community reflect and teach how life is to be lived "properly" in this place through the same ongoing, everyday process of living life together. In past generations, teenagers typically began to test and challenge some of these assumptions and practices of their parents and others in the community in their quest to "individuate"—meaning to establish their sense of personal identity as different from others. Part of that normal testing might have included wearing some outlandish clothes or crazy (to Mom and Dad) hairstyle, or letting parents know they no longer held the same religious or political beliefs. It wasn't so hard to challenge these things when the teen knew how life was supposed to be and the assumptions were clear and were shared by the larger community. It was often called teenage rebellion!

In that traditional process, ultimately teens decided which practices or beliefs they wanted to keep for themselves. Whether or not they kept the same worldview or beliefs, they still knew how life worked there and how their internal values and practices fit, or didn't, within the context of their community. At that point, they were living in what is called *cultural balance*—that almost unconscious knowledge of how things are and work in a particular community and their place in relationship to it. Being at this place gave both a sense of belonging to young people and the capacity to move into adulthood with a basic sense of confidence. Why?

THE IMPORTANCE OF CULTURAL BALANCE

When we as humans are in cultural balance, we are like a concert pianist who, after practicing for years to master the basics, no longer thinks about how to touch the piano keys or do scales and trills. Those functions have become automatic responses to notations in the music score, and this freedom from *conscious* attention to details allows the pianist to use these very skills to create and express richer, fuller music for us all.

A sense of cultural balance allows that same freedom. Once we have internalized a culture's customs and underlying assumptions, or know who we are in relationship to this culture, an intuitive sense of what is right, humorous, appropriate, or offensive in any particular situation develops. Instead of spending excessive time worrying whether we are dressed appropriately for a business appointment, we concentrate on developing a new business plan. Being "in the know" gives us a sense of stability, confidence, deep security, and belonging, for we have been entrusted with the "secrets" of our tribe. We may not understand *why* cultural rules work as they do, but we know *how* our culture works. In the days when most people lived in a basically monocultural environment and community, members shared essentially the same values, assumptions, behavioral styles, and traditional practices with one another. Achieving cultural balance wasn't hard because everyone reinforced what lay in the deeper layer of culture as well as the seen layer. Patterns of the past were repeated for generations and change came slowly enough to be absorbed without rocking the cultural boat too wildly.

Perhaps one of the best illustrations of this type of traditional cultural community is seen in *Fiddler on the Roof,* the musical about a farmer named Tevye and his Russian Jewish village of Anatevka. For decades Tevye's culture had remained basically the same. Everyone knew where he or she fit, both in relating to one another and to God. There had been no major outside influences. The way things had always been was the way things still worked—with the milkman, matchmaker, farmer, and all others clearly aware of their assigned roles within the village. Roles assigned by whom? By *tradition*—another word for how cultural beliefs are worked out in practice. As Tevye says:

> Because of our traditions, we've kept our balance for many, many years. Here in Anatevka we have traditions for everything—how to eat, how to sleep, how to wear clothes. For instance, we always keep our heads covered and always wear a little prayer shawl. This shows our constant devotion to God. You may ask, how did this tradition start? I'll tell you—I don't know! But it's a tradition. Because of our traditions, everyone knows who he is and what God expects him to do. . . . Without our traditions, our lives would be as shaky as—as a fiddler on the roof![7]

Tevye then laments that tradition is breaking down. As the old ways he knew rapidly begin to change, he loses his former sense of balance. His grip on life slips and his comfortable world is shattered. Mentally and emotionally, Tevye can't keep up and he becomes disoriented and alienated, even from his own children.

This story serves as a great metaphor for what is happening in our world at an ever quickening pace. The ways generations have known and taken for granted as defining and "doing life" complete with neat little boxes of where racial heritage, nationality, or ethnicity fit are quickly breaking down. Clear role models are no longer seen ahead because the way life happened before is no longer how it is now. Each generation seems to be charting a new course. Cultural mixing and matching in every country is occurring faster than we can understand. The normal feeling of many is to retrench and, like Tevye, long for the "good old days" when things seemed more in our control. We, as humans, feel more comfortable and safe when we understand what's going on based on how things have always been. It's not hard to see on the global scene how this undefined, but real, sense of losing our cultural balance has led in many places to more attempts to define "us" and "them" by new rules regarding such things as immigration, dress, or specific behavior in hopes of regaining the sense of comfort that being in cultural balance can give us.

A World of Changing Cultures

Cultural balance is important for all the reasons mentioned, but many TCKs often feel out of cultural balance. Why? Because for them, the world of rapid cultural change has been their norm during a significant part of childhood as they bump into new icebergs that not only have different dress and food, but completely different sets of worldviews, expectations of behavior, and even languages—with an overnight airplane ride. As the role models in one place disappear, they search for who they should look to in the new place. Before they know how they are to behave or how people think here, they must figure out where they are.

Ironically—and one of the paradoxes of this TCK experience—it is also in this very place of trying to adjust to various cultural norms and languages that some of their strongest gifts of becoming cross-culturally adept develop. This can serve them well in their future lives and careers. We have heard human resources personnel tell the audience of international school educators that they will not look at any applicant's resume unless that person speaks at least two languages fluently. Companies are looking for those individuals who exhibit "cross-cultural competency"—or at least can pass the test designed to measure such a skill set.

The truth is when Ruth took such a test, she wasn't so sure she passed it because she got stuck on the first question. It read, "When did you make your first cross-cultural move?" *H-m-m-m. What were they asking? From where?* As a U.S. American born in Nigeria, was it at birth? Did they mean at the age of three when she first went to the United States? Were they factoring in the reality that every day of her childhood she moved between local culture and her home or the expat third culture? After a few more questions like that, Ruth gave up taking the test. Even though she has always felt learning to know people of totally diverse backgrounds and living in so many cultures is one of her greatest gifts—in addition to being just plain fun and interesting—it didn't seem easy to quantify even for those who supposedly know about such things!

But despite the long-term gain from these encounters with many cultures, there are also times such as returning to the passport culture or moving to an entirely new land when a sense of cultural imbalance also occurs. This is not easy for the child or teen or even ATCK. Without an understanding of why this sense of imbalance is happening, TCKs can begin to wonder *What is wrong with me? Why don't I ever quite 'get it'?* when what was normal in one place is seen as strange in the next. One ATCK told us about such a moment during his childhood (before most suitcases had rollers!).

My parents lived and worked in a remote village in Africa for ten years. They home-schooled us and wanted to make sure we four kids could slide back into our passport culture with little notice when it came time to go "home." They wrote friends at home to send us clothes that would be appropriate for our ages and the change in weather.

Before leaving, Mom and Dad gave each of us our designated outfit. The clothes felt a bit stifling to us compared to the usual attire of flip-flops, T-shirts, and shorts we wore in the village. Now we had on jeans, jackets, and boots, so we were not only more stylish but ready for colder temperatures in the airplane and when we disembarked.

We arrived in London and went to pick up our luggage. My parents gave each of us a suitcase to carry and then they led the way to the last customs checkpoint. Suddenly, they realized people were staring at us. How could this be when they had worked so hard for us to be "normal"?

Imagine their chagrin—soon turned to laughter—when they turned around and saw us in perfect single file, each with our designated suitcase perched in perfect balance on our heads. This is how we had always carried things in the village. Apparently, while it was normal for us, it seems this wasn't a common sight at Heathrow! I think my parents gave up trying to normalize us quite so hard after that and just let us use the skill sets we had acquired—including balancing loads on our heads.

Over and over, TCKs and ATCKs recount their tales of being out of cultural balance. Many of the stories are told at international school reunions and bring laughter from their by-then-adult peers. They describe how, no matter what situation they were in or how hard they tried to do or say everything right, they often found themselves making what others saw as a dumb mistake or remark. Like the TCKs carrying suitcases on their heads, what had been normal and part of their everyday life suddenly made them seem weird. Often, TCKs describe moving from a school culture where children stood when the teacher walked into the room to one where no one ever thought to do such a thing. This was how the deeper value of respect for those in authority expressed itself in the previous world. On the first day of school, the TCKs stood and heard fellow students laughing, and that horrible feeling of shame penetrated the deepest places inside. *Why are they laughing? What did I do wrong?* swirled in their heads as they slithered to a seated position after realizing no one else was standing. But the damage to reputation and heart had already begun if no one had stepped in to help the child (and the other children around when appropriate) understand that there is a big difference between ignorance and stupidity. It is one thing to not know how things are done in this new place or how values are expressed because they haven't been here before. They can learn. However, stupidity is quite something else!

When someone does notice these children's bewilderment and can help them put words to what they are feeling and understand why it happened, then some of the biggest life lessons can take place. From earliest days these children are learning that different cultures have different ways of doing things and it is important to pay attention to cultural cues. Sometimes parents are surprised to realize their children don't know something as simple as how luggage is carried or when to stand or not stand for a teacher. Like Tevye, the parents "caught" this as such a normal part of their cultural upbringing, they never thought of it as something that might need to be taught. These constructive moments are key for helping the challenges of a cross-cultural childhood ultimately become part of the benefit of being a TCK.

On the other hand, when the TCK or the community doesn't understand what is happening in terms of culture, those around the TCKs wonder at their strange behavior, and the TCKs and ATCKs are left feeling ashamed that once more they are so "out of sync" socially. Like the ugly duckling, they may accept the judgment of the community that something is wrong with them and they definitely don't belong. Because children often don't have words to express or understand what they feel or experience, it is vital for adults to help give them language and concepts to normalize what they are going through as they navigate their way into a new culture. The last thing we want is for this sense of being the ugly duckling to become deeply imprinted as some kind of long-term identity—which sadly, we have seen in some ATCKs who never understood their story.

HOW TCKs LEARN CULTURE

Perhaps ironically, the struggle many TCKs face in trying to find a sense of cultural balance and identity is not because they learn culture differently from the way others do. The real challenge—and accompanying gift—comes because they *learn culture the same way* everyone does—by "catching it" from their environment rather than by reading a book or getting a master's degree in cultural anthropology. The point isn't the process of *how* they learn cultural balance, but the *environment in which they are trying to learn it*—a world filled with many cultures—sometimes simultaneously, sometimes changing with an airplane ride, sometimes flowing back and forth every day as they move between their home environment and the world outside. The various individuals in their communities with whom they interact on a daily basis may hold markedly different worldviews and life views from each other. What was acceptable behavior and thinking in one setting (in a school, with a nanny, or in another country) is seen as crude or ridiculous in the next. Which culture are they supposed to catch? Do they belong to all of them, none of them, or some of each of them?

One of the shared experiences of TCKs is that their truest sense of being in cultural balance is often in this world where moving between different cultures is the norm rather than the exception. The main problem here is not that many TCKs do, indeed, find a deep sense of belonging and cultural balance in a culturally mixed setting where "different" is the norm. The problem comes when they and others may tend to invalidate that sense of belonging since it doesn't match a traditional expectation of how people find personal and group identity.

Let's look more closely at how the normal process of learning cultural balance may be both complex and rich as TCKs often interact daily, or regularly, with many potentially different cultural groups in their lives: parents, caregivers, peers, "home" culture, "host" culture, school, media (TV, Internet, social media), and sponsoring agency. Norma McCaig, founder of Global Nomads, designed the model in figure 4-2 to express this multiplicity of communities with which TCKs interact regularly and in which TCKs (aka global nomads) learn culture.[8]

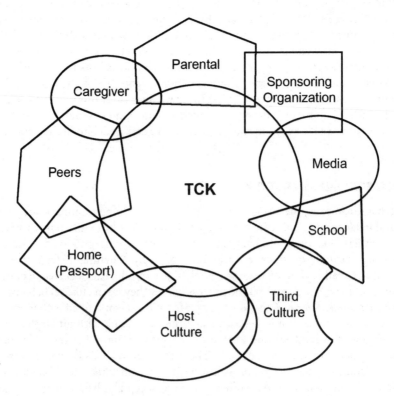

Figure 4–2: Possible Multiple Cultures in a TCK's World

© 1998 Norma McCraig adapted. Used by permission

When we show this model in our seminars and ask how many TCKs assumed that code-switching from one language, cultural practice, or style of greeting to another—depending on who they were interacting with—was totally normal, most laugh and almost sheepishly raise their hands. Let's look at each of these cultural segments to understand better the process of cultural learning for TCKs.

Parents

TCKs, as all children do, hear the first sounds of the language(s) they will one day speak as parents cuddle them immediately after birth. Parents continue to teach both the visible and invisible layers of their passport culture(s) by example as well as words. They dress differently for a business meeting than for a tennis match. When talking about others, they speak respectfully. As needed, they teach it by correction: "Don't chew with your mouth open." "Don't look Grandma in the eye when you say hello to her. That's not respectful. Try again, but this time keep your eyes down." "You forgot to shake everyone's hand when you came into the room. Go out and come back in so you can do it right this time." Or they do it by praise: "What a good girl you are to share your toys with your brother!"

Whether in the passport culture or host cultures, most TCKs' families' cultural practices and values are rooted in the parents' home culture(s) and may be markedly different from the practices of the surrounding dominant culture. This includes something as simple as the style of clothing. Girls from Muslim homes may continue wearing a hijab no matter where they live. Dutch children will likely wear Western dress in the forests of Brazil even if the local people wear quite different styles. Of course, it's more than what is visible. Telling the truth at all costs may be a prime value at home, while shading the truth to avoid shaming another person may be the paramount value in the surrounding culture (or vice versa). And when we add in the stories of TCKs whose parents are from two different cultures, such as one young man we met who was born in the Philippines to a German father and Cambodian mother who used French as their common family language, we can agree that for some TCKs even this most elemental step of learning cultural rules and practices from parents is becoming quite complex indeed!

Caregivers

Like children all over the world, some TCKs are left with a caregiver while their parents work or socialize. While caregivers in the home culture generally share the parents' basic language and cultural outlook, TCKs are often cared for by members of the host culture who may only speak their national language, a village language, or a dialect. Ruth learned fluent Hausa as a child from her Nigerian nanny, who spoke no English.

Methods of child care in various cultures can be radically different. Instead of being pushed in a pram, Russian children raised in Chad will be carried on their African nanny's back until they can walk. Shaming may be the main method of training a child in the host culture rather than a more praise-based type of reinforcement in the home culture or vice versa.

Caregivers, like all of us, inevitably reflect their culture's attitude toward children and life. The story goes that when Pearl Buck was a child in China, someone asked how she compared her mother to her Chinese *amah* (nanny). Buck replied, "If I want to have a story read, I go to my mother. But if I fall down and need to be comforted, I go to my amah." Her mother's culture valued teaching and learning, while her amah's placed a greater value on nurture. Even as a child, Buck instinctively knew the difference.

Peers

When children play together, they instinctively parrot the cultural rules they have been taught: "You're cheating!" "Don't be a sissy!" "You made a great play!" They reflect what is considered to be, or not to be, in style. "Why are you wearing that ugly shirt?" "Wow! I really like your coat." Children enforce the cultural norms of a community as they shame or praise one another in this way.

Most TCKs attend school and play with peers from many cultures—each culture valuing different norms. Some friends practically live and die for soccer and cricket; others love American football and baseball. Some children are raised to believe that academic success is the highest priority; others value peer relationships over high grades. Styles of relationship can be very different. Males holding hands in one culture is a common expression of friendship. In another, it may have connotations related to sexual preference. How does a child decide which, among all these choices, is "correct" either in value or interpretation? Or is this one more place where life itself teaches lessons early on that there are many differences between people in both visible and invisible layers of culture, but you can still be friends as humans despite those differences? This is yet another place of paradox for TCKs and one of the greatest gifts of this background.

Home (Passport) Culture

Traditionally, most non-TCK children grew up in a community like Tevye's where other adults reinforced what the parents taught at home because the rules for home and community were uniform. The same characteristics—such as honesty, hard work, and respect for adults—brought approval (or, in their absence, disapproval) from the community as well as from parents. No one stopped to question by whose standards these practices and values existed. They were just what they were. Being in cultural balance was not hard in this place called "home."

Ironically, for many TCKs this "home culture" may be one of the places they feel most *out* of cultural balance. Although they will likely learn the basic language, values, and traditions of this culture from their parents even when living in another land, TCKs often remain unaware of what is hidden in the unseen layer of what is presumably their own culture. They have not lived there long enough to understand the nuances of how life operates by both seen and unseen cultural norms, and social media alone does not fully communicate such things. Some of these norms may, in fact, be quite opposite to the ways of the host culture. Add to this the fact that many TCKs have parents from different passport cultures, and it's not hard to see how although the ways of the passport culture(s) shape TCKs, it may not be to the degree it would have if this was the only culture they knew.

Host Culture

Depending on the individual situation, the local host culture can have a major or more minor effect on TCKs. Some TCKs move so often they never quite settle long enough to absorb the specifics of the deeper levels of each culture, even while they may enjoy the more surface aspects such as food, art, geography, or whatever. They, and those who live in a more isolated military, embassy, mission, or company compound, may never interact deeply with those in the local community but they will still learn how life can be run by different customs, values, and worldview in another culture. Simply doing the everyday tasks of shopping, watching how garbage is sorted (or not) and collected, and getting from one place to another through heavy traffic with horns blaring (or horns not blaring depending on where the TCKs are "from" and where they now live), make it obvious that people live and see life in different ways.

On the other hand, those who grow up for much of their childhood living in more remote areas where they are the only foreigners will likely learn the language, enjoy the food, play the games of and with the local people, and get to know the deeper layers of culture even though it is not by definition their own. Even those immersed in local city life for a long time can feel more affinity to the host culture than their passport culture. We met one U.S American teenager who had attended local schools during his entire childhood in Japan. His mannerisms, English accent, and sense of home were totally based in his Japanese experience. When his mother repatriated to the U.S., he asked to attend the Saturday Japanese school because he felt so much more at home with Japanese friends than with any of his local peers in the U.S. Often these TCKs have a better sense of cultural balance in a host culture than their passport culture because they know how life works in a way they have not yet learned for their "home" culture.

Third Culture

One of the most important communities for TCKs, however, is the "third culture"—the expat subculture the Useems first noted. It is here where TCKs often feel the most "at home" because it is here that they share a lifestyle and cultural norms with others. Most who live within this community understand what it is to move from place to place. They know what it is to say good-bye over and over. Just think of the powerful song written by one military ATCK, John Denver. "I'm leaving on a jet plane. Don't know when I'll be back again. Oh, babe, I hate to go . . ."[9] How many TCKs and ATCKs claim this as their theme song? A lot we know do! Others in their third culture community know what it is to enjoy trying new and seemingly esoteric foods of many lands. Or to wonder, *Where is home?* Many TCKs have grown up in schools where the population comes from all over the world. Their best friends have many looks and share interesting foods at lunch with them. It is normal to move between these different cultural communities we are currently discussing.

The truth is most TCKs do have a community, an "interstitial culture" to which they belong but one defined by a shared experience rather than by place or nationality. It has such a significant long-term effect that we can write an entire book about it! And one reason for wanting to explain this story in detail is because we have seen that when TCKs/ATCKs come to understand they have this place of belonging, they can more easily find new ways to name how they belong to the other cultures and places of their lives as well. They can begin to view their cultural roots in a "both/and" way rather than having to choose "either/or."

School

When children go to school, they also move into another subculture—the way of life in this school and the presuppositions behind how the school operates. In each school, as in any organization, there are underlying philosophies of how life should best work in this place. What subjects should be taught and how? Math can feel like a completely different subject depending on if they teach division with remainders going above the problem or below. The choices for literature may depend on whether it is a local school or an international school. Teachers learn a particular style of teaching based on the philosophy of how their culture believes children should be taught. In an international school, the educators themselves may have come from different philosophical backgrounds about the best way to educate children.

In a traditional monocultural community, both school and home reinforce what the other is unconsciously teaching at the deeper level of culture so each child clearly learns the values and practices in this culture. For many TCKs, however, what and how things are taught at school may be vastly different from home or the previous school as they shift from school to school while moving from one place to another. Additionally, because in an international community the individual teachers themselves often come from a variety of cultures, this can add some interesting twists to the child's cultural development—let alone his academic achievement. ATCK Joe's story is an excellent example.

> My siblings and I were the only U.S. Americans in an Anglo-Argentine culture and we went to British schools. But the Argentines also thought their education was pretty good, so Peron mandated an Argentine curriculum for every private school and, with what time was left over, the school could do what it wanted. We went to school from 8:00 to 4:00 with four hours in Spanish in the Argentine curriculum in the morning and four hours in an English public school curriculum in the afternoon.

Meanwhile, our parents fought desperately to keep some semblance of Americanism at home. They lost the battle of the crossed 7s. They lost the spelling battle. Worse, when they were told that in a given year there would be a focus on North American history, geography, and literature, they discovered, to their dismay, North American meant Canadian.[10]

As Dr. Weaver foresaw with the iceberg model, often the visible layers of culture in an international school setting give the appearance of likeness because students from different countries or cultures may share the same race or have learned to speak with a similar accent—and study the same curriculum. At that point, educators may easily forget to consider the differences in those students' deeper layer of culture. Anthropologist Danau Tanu, who is an ATCK and did her Ph.D. work examining the Asian TCK experience, writes:

Growing up as a TCK does not automatically make us inter-culturally sensitive. People assume that international school cultures are neutral. But this is not true. For some it may seem "international," for others many of these schools seem "Western." How you interpret it depends on your cultural and linguistic background. For me, I felt like a second-generation Asian immigrant in a Western country: I was Asian by night, and Western by day. Even though I grew up in Asia, I learnt how to count the American nickels, dimes, and quarters in math class before I learnt to count the local currency. By the time I finished high school in the mid-1990s, I could write convincing essays about Western civilization and history, but I knew next to nothing about Asian history. I was embarrassed when I realized this and went on to major in Asian Studies at university. At least English was my first language, which made it easier for me at school. But for my friends who spoke it as a second language, many found the Westernized culture at the international school difficult to adapt to.

Part of the side effect of this sort of an environment is that I experienced a sense of internalized racism. Because "Asia" and other parts of the world outside "the West" were mostly absent from the curriculum (except in tokenistic forms) and most of our principals and teachers (i.e., people in authority) were white, I subconsciously learnt that the West was superior and the rest were inferior. I knew this was wrong and did my best to not act upon this internalized belief toward others or myself, but the feeling lingered inside. It took me many years to unlearn it as an adult.[11]

Another false assumption is that a child who comes from a country that shares the same language as the host country (e.g., Spanish, or French, or English) will not have any cultural issues. Eleanor Nicolás discovered this was not true.

> When I first moved to Virginia at eight years of age, my elementary school called Franklin Sherman was just across the road from our house. I do not remember children remarking on my accent, but the adults did: "Say something, I want to hear your accent." Or they would clarify my vocabulary. "A plaster? What's that? Oh, you mean a band-aid?"
>
> When a book report was due, I thought my teacher meant *do* and I rehearsed my presentation on Harriet Tubman nervously the night before, only to be told off because my homework was not done. . . .
>
> My parents were perplexed, however, when they learnt I was being taken out of class for remedial lessons. The special education teacher gave me words like *you're* and *your* or *piece* and *peace*. The exercises were boring and pointless to me, but I didn't tell her. She would grade my pronunciation and intonation and point out spelling mistakes. They weren't mistakes; I was simply spelling the British way. Looking back, perhaps it hadn't occurred to her that before her did not stand an American child. Or maybe it had? I'll never know.[12]

If school is a place for learning the values as well as the behavior of the local or other nation's culture (e.g., German International School of Silicon Valley, or the Japanese International School in Singapore) in which it is embedded, what happens when children attend a school with completely different customs, values, or religious orientation from that of their parents? What happens when the basic educational needs (e.g., "correct" spelling, penmanship, math processes, language) required for success in their passport cultures aren't taught in the school they attend? This often occurs for globally nomadic families when the choices for schools that teach the academic curriculum of their home country may be limited to schools based on a belief system or in a language that doesn't match their own. Even something like the style of teaching—such as rote versus inductive methods—can add to the stress of learning—and later relearning.

The timing of schooling also has an influence on students, as different school systems have different beginning and ending of the school year and holiday schedules. For instance, while Southern Hemisphere schools often have a summer break over December and January, Northern Hemisphere schools have summer break in June, July, and August. Some schools in countries on the Equator, like Kenya, go for three months and then a month off year-round. The result is that students come in and out of systems at different times with different curriculums, and that movement affects rapport-building and has an impact on the daily life of the school and the student's learning.

TCKs who go to boarding school experience another distinct subculture twenty-four hours a day rather than only during school hours. Without question, different rules are needed to organize scores of children in a dormitory environment rather than two or three in a home. Some TCKs talk of being raised by their peers more than by adults in such a setting. Some consider this the most positive thing about boarding school; others say it was the most difficult. Either way, it is a different experience from going to a day school and returning to parents each night.

Obviously, from the length of our discussion here on the impact of different educational systems on a TCK's story, there is much for parents, educators, and TCKs themselves to consider about the educational process for TCKs.

Media

The shaping influence of radio, magazines, and television may once have been more localized when radio was the way people caught up on world news. Now at the click of a mouse or the swipe of a finger TCKs have access to local and global newspapers, satellite radio, e-zines, news blogs, and Twitter updates in real time. The influence is pervasive and, at times, contradictory. The idea of a trusted source of news, at this point in time, is elusive, and we hear many TCKs discuss how they have a list of go-to sources they use to figure out what is actually going on when they hear about an event, analysis, or commentary. It is not uncommon to find that the way local events are portrayed back in one's *home country* are not the way they are perceived in the local situation. "Media" may also include friends on the ground. For example, Mustafa in Germany hears about an earthquake in Mexico City, so he gets on his Facebook account and quickly finds José, his friend who moved back to Mexico City, to ask if he was in the earthquake, if he is okay, and what it is like there.

The third culture brings multiple cultures into conversation and the media that one relied upon in the first culture are now examined in light of multiple perspectives. TCKs not only ask each other about what is in the news; they also ask each other which sources are preferred and why. At the same time, a sense of loyalty may hold TCKs to trust certain sources over others and maintain loyalties that potentially cause conflict. A recent example is the way students discuss the islands in the South China Sea.

> [While they are] known in the West as the "Spratly Islands" and named after a British explorer, it is not a surprise that China, Vietnam, and Malaysia all have different names for the islands and, along with the Philippines, lay claim to them. When the islands came up as a current events topic in an international school social studies class, the tenth graders became passionately involved in the discussion. Why?

> Because there were students representing all the invested
> countries except Vietnam. The news item came through the
> BBC and the article included whether or not the U.S. should
> be involved militarily. The students were processing the
> bias of the media, the historical claims, the financial invest-
> ments, and the political influence at stake. A U.N.-style battle
> took shape in the classroom, and no wonder!

While media can help us keep up with certain aspects of events and culture, they do not necessarily help TCKs understand the full dynamics of what is taking place in another part of the world. The result of the current access to vast amounts of media may be a false sense that expats really can keep up with home while not being there, and that TCKs know what is going on in their passport country and therefore will "fit" back in easily.

Sponsoring Organizations

In addition, many TCKs are not only shaped by the overall third culture experience, but also by the specific community, or *sector*, in which they live—e.g., missionary, business, military, diplomatic corps. Each of these groups also has its own subculture and clear expectations of behavior. In *Military Brats*, Mary Edwards Wertsch wrote:

> Certainly by the time a military child is five years old,
> the values and rules of military life have been thoroughly
> internalized, the military identity forged, and the child has
> already assumed an active stage presence as an understudy
> of the Fortress theater company [military].[13]

Whatever the rules are in any TCK's given subculture—be they matters of correct dress, correct faith, or correct political views—TCKs know that to be an accepted member (or child of a member) of that group, they must conform to those standards. Lois Bushong, a therapist and author of *Belonging Everywhere & Nowhere: A Guide to Counseling the Globally Mobile,* has an article written with Ruth Van Reken on her website called "The Powerful Impact of Systems on the Globally Mobile."[14]

Many of these sponsoring agencies have, or have had in the past, special behavioral or philosophical expectations of not only their employees, but also the employees' families. This is what Ruth Useem saw originally as TCKs having "representational roles." They often carried a responsibility far beyond their years and one that might not have happened if they had lived in more-traditional settings in the passport culture.

We also often forget to look at how the underlying dominant or national culture of the sponsoring agency itself may affect TCKs, particularly those who come from a different culture. They may make policies based on laws and time frames that work in India, but forget things might be different for their employees from Australia.

TCKs IN RELATIONSHIP TO SURROUNDING DOMINANT CULTURE

There is another aspect of cross-cultural living that has a significant influence on a TCK's life—the changing nature of how he or she fundamentally relates to the surrounding dominant or majority culture, be that the home or host culture. As has been said, one way we learn our sense of identity is as the world around us mirrors back to us who we are in that relational context. Because of mobility, those mirrors for TCKs are frequently changing and, thus, their identity is constantly being redefined in contrast or comparison to whichever world they are currently in. This is one of the key things we must understand in order to recognize how some of the "new normals" created by our globalizing world impact not only TCKs, but also children and families everywhere.

In the early 1990s, Barb Knuckles, a non-TCK friend of Ruth's, planted a vital seed in her mind. In a discussion of TCKs, Barb said, "I think there's a simple reason they have so many problems on reentry to their passport culture. In the host country, they are often seen as different. They can always console themselves that, yes, they are different, but it's because they aren't from this place. They see themselves as members of their passport country. The problem is when they go back to their passport country and still don't fit, what is their excuse?" Dave Pollock and Norma McCaig were already using the term "hidden immigrant" to describe this feeling of expecting to be alike and to fit in upon reentry and the frustration of finding that it was not so. Then Ruth met two TCKs with classic reentry experiences—but they were having them in their host cultures! On wondering why this was so, she realized the only common factor for both of them was that in their host cultures they physically looked like members of the dominant culture—just as most TCKs do on reentry. After Ruth shared her thoughts with Dave, they batted these ideas back and forth and wound up with the model shown in figure 4-3.

Cultural Identity in Relationship to Surrounding Culture

Foreigner	Hidden Immigrant
Look *different*	Look alike
Think *differently*	Think *differently*
Adopted	**Mirror**
Look *different*	Look alike
Think alike	Think alike

Figure 4–3: PolVan Cultural Identity Model

© 1996 David C. Pollock/Ruth E. Van Reken

Like Dr. Weaver's cultural iceberg model, this is another example of why the visible and invisible aspects of a person in relationship to culture matters. As Dr. Weaver said, the visible leads to expectations of who the person is in the invisible places. So for those who frequently move among different cultures, who people expect them to be (or who they expect themselves to be) compared to the reality of who they are can result in various outcomes listed in figure 4-3 and explained below.

- *Foreigner—look different, think differently.* In the early days of international mobility, most TCKs related to their host culture as foreigners, and many still do today. They differ from those in the dominant culture around them in both appearance and worldview. They know, and others know, they are not from this place. *What you expect is what you get.*

- *Hidden immigrant—look alike, think differently.* Norma McCaig and Dave began using "hidden immigrant" in the mid-1980s to describe the experience of TCKs returning to their passport culture. By now, we've realized that TCKs can also be hidden immigrants when they are growing up in countries where they physically resemble most of the citizens of that country. Internally, however, these TCKs—whether in the passport culture or host culture—view life through a lens that is as different from the dominant or majority culture as any obvious foreigner. People around them, of course, presume they share similar worldviews and cultural awareness because, from outward appearances, they look as if they belong to the group. No one makes the same allowances for the TCK's lack of cultural knowledge or miscues as they would an obvious immigrant or recognized foreigner. *What you expect is not what you get.*

- *Adopted—look different, think alike.* This category can literally relate to international adoptees and other immigrants who may not physically resemble members of the dominant culture but have lived there long enough to assimilate culturally to that place. This is, however, another common pattern of relationship for TCKs. Sometimes they appear physically different from members of the surrounding dominant host culture, but they have lived there so long and immersed themselves so deeply in this environment that their behavior and worldview are virtually the same as members of that culture. The TCKs may feel very comfortable and often more "at home" in this situation than in their passport country, and they feel wounded when others treat them as foreigners. This sense of being misperceived can also happen when ATCKs return to visit the place where they grew up. Suddenly they realize for the first time how "foreign" others see them to be when they feel this is, indeed, the world of their heart. Again, *what you expect is not what you get.*

- *Mirror—look alike, think alike.* This is the traditional pattern of those raised in a monocultural situation. While many TCKs feel there is nowhere in the world they fit as "mirrors," the truth is some TCKs grow up where they physically resemble the members of the dominant culture in the host culture. At times, they have lived there so long that they have adopted the deeper levels of that culture as well. No one would realize they aren't from this place unless they show their passports. TCKs who return to their home culture after spending only a year or two away or who were away only at a very young age may also fit in this category. Although they have lived abroad, their deeper levels of culture have remained rooted solidly in the home culture and they identify with it completely. And one other slight irony: perhaps in an international school where there is no standard of "look alike," TCKs find that they are mirrors to one another in the deeper places of culture where they reflect back to one another a shared understanding of what it is to grow up global. At any rate, this is a comfortable box to be in. *What you expect is what you get.*

Non-TCK children and adults also may fall into one or another of these boxes at any given time, but the difference for TCKs is that throughout childhood, usually because of physical mobility, they are constantly changing boxes depending on where they happen to be. They may be obvious foreigners one day and hidden immigrants the next. Many TCKs do not make a simple move from one culture to another; instead, they are in a repetitive cycle of traveling back and forth between home and host cultures throughout childhood. But why does that matter? Because as they move in and out of various cultures, TCKs not only have to learn new cultural rules, but more fundamentally, they must understand who they *are* in relationship to the surrounding culture. Each move is also a question of identity: *How do I fit in? Where do I belong?* Constantly changing who they are in relationship to those around them can add some challenges to developing a true sense of a core identity.

Here are some common reactions we see from TCKs as they try to sort out their identity issues, particularly when they are in the "hidden immigrant" or "adopted" box:

- *Chameleons*—those who try to find a "same as" identity. They hide their time lived in other places and try to conform externally through clothes, language, or attitudes to whatever environment they are in.
- *Screamers*—those who try to find a "different from" identity. They will let other people around them know that they are not like them and don't plan to be.
- *Wallflowers*—those who try to find a "nonidentity." Rather than risk being exposed as someone who doesn't know the local cultural rules, they prefer to sit on the sideline and watch, at least for an extended period, rather than to engage in the activities at hand.
- *Adapters*—those who just "are." They feel comfortable in their own skin and don't seem to have the need to either over-conform or super-rebel. By all appearances they slip right into the new place and move ahead. Neither are they angry with those who seem to struggle more.

Who can understand why some children react one way and others react in different ways? Or even why different children in the same family can have very opposite responses? Certainly there is no simple answer. What we have seen, however, is that while it is fine to go through these as "normal" defenses children or young people may use as they make various adjustments, these are not healthy strategies in the long term. Sadly we have met some ATCKs who are still living as chameleons, screamers, or wallflowers in their forties and fifties. When that happens, they remain behind protective walls that can encapsulate them and keep them from living in the freedom of being all that they were meant or made to be.

In the end, however, TCKs and their parents don't *always* share a common sense of national identity or a similar sense of "home." This can be distressing for some parents. In addition, throughout life, TCKs and ATCKs may encounter other unexpected or unrecognized cultural misunderstandings with teachers, peers at school or in the workplace, and their spouses or significant others. Why? Because, once more, who they appear to be outside, or by passport, isn't who they are in the invisible places within. We see in this experience what Weaver warned us would happen when he talked of the cultural iceberg—more confusion when what we expect of each other in the unseen layer is not what we get.

While cultural identity is far more complex than the simple model figure 4-3 depicts, we have seen in the many years since Dave and Ruth formed this model that it is at least a great starting point of discussion for many TCKs, ATCKs, and countless others of other types of CCK backgrounds to understand their stories. Some have suggested we add the matter of language to this graphic because that denotes another clue to who the person may be in the deeper level and can either add complexity to the person's identity or bring more clarity. If we did add it, perhaps the model would look something like this:

Identity in Relationship to Surrounding Culture

Foreigner	Hidden Immigrant
Look *different*	Look alike
Think *differently*	Think *differently*
Speak *differently*	Speak alike/*differently*
Adopted	**Mirror**
Look *different*	Look alike
Think alike	Think alike
Speak alike	Speak alike

Figure 4–4: The PolVan Cultural Identity Model, Expanded
©2006 Ruth E. Van Reken

As we saw in our iceberg model earlier, language is in the visible and invisible layers. It is how we identify others, but it is also part of our patterns of thinking and internal structure. In terms of how we relate to the surrounding dominant culture, again the places where expectation and reality do not necessarily meet are in the *hidden immigrant* and *adopted* boxes. If someone looks like the majority culture but then opens his mouth and speaks with a strong foreign accent, the language factor will identify him as a foreigner. If a person like a TCK is in that same hidden immigrant box and also sounds like the other citizens of this land, the impact of being different from expectations intensifies because she is seen as an *us* when really she is a *them*. But oddly, when someone is a hidden immigrant and can't speak the local language at all, others react with a particular type of disdain.

> While doing a seminar for an international school in Switzerland, Ruth asked her panel of students the usual: "What do you like best about growing up in this place and among many cultures?" and "What do you find the hardest?"
>
> A young white student from the United States responded, "The prejudice."
>
> "Prejudice?" Ruth asked. "What do you mean?"
>
> "When I get on the bus and someone talks to me in German and I can't understand them or answer back, they get mad at me and tell me I need to learn it."

Because of looking like the majority of the citizens of that country, the locals' expectation when seeing her in a public place was that they could speak German to her and she would understand and respond appropriately. They were annoyed when she didn't. But if she had appeared to be Asian or African, likely the same expectation would not have been there. And each time that type of rebuke happened, this young woman felt shame and then anger. Again, expectations based on appearance did not meet realities.

For those in the "adopted" box, the surprise goes in the opposite direction. Because others presume they will be speaking the local language with a different accent than the local one, when the person opens his or her mouth and sounds like others from that community, the surprise of the listener tells its own story. "Oh, where did you learn to speak Spanish so perfectly?" "Who taught you Japanese?" Ken Tanaka has a brilliant video on YouTube called "What Kind of Asian Are You?"[15] that tells this part of the story with humor but true insight.

Expanding Our Vision

If these are the most basic ways of looking at normal cultural identity development through the TCK lens, what happens for those in other CCK circles who are not traditional TCKs? The same type of questions TCKs ask or experience in regard to trying to understand their identity are ones we hear over and over from all other types of CCKs. We have found if we change the term "hidden immigrant" to "hidden diversity," it is more accessible. Ruth and Paulette Bethel defined hidden diversity as "a diversity of experience that shapes a person's life and worldview but is not readily apparent on the outside, unlike the usual diversity markers such as race, ethnicity, nationality, gender and so forth."[16] These questions of identity seem to be a unifying theme for CCKs of all backgrounds. In the last chapter of the book, chapter 19 ("Where Do We Go from Here?"), we will discuss more of these emerging stories in detail to show how this entire conversation about TCKs relates to countless others.

For now we proceed to the second main overlay of the TCK experience: high mobility.

Questions for Chapter 4

1. Do you or global children you know relate to Alex's feelings in the opening poem as "being an island and a United Nations"?
2. Can you give real-life examples of the distinct difference between making a cross-cultural move for the first time as an adult and growing up cross-culturally? Can you address how this has been with your family?
3. Have you had experience with a TCK who attends school in the dominant culture but goes home each evening to an entirely different culture?
4. Tell your story to the group using the Expanded PolVan Cultural Identity Model, figure 4-4. Please start with "When I was born, I was in (. . .) box; we moved when I was (. . .) and then I was in (. . .) box." Continue to trace the mobility patterns of your life through how they affected your identity as well.
5. How often did you go back and forth between these different identities? Which was the hardest experience? Please explain.
6. With which of these PolVan cultural identities do you identify most in your present situation? Please explain.

CHAPTER 5

Why High Mobility during Childhood Matters

I had adored the nomadic life. I had loved gallivanting from
Japan to Taiwan to America to Holland and onward. In
many ways, I had adapted well. I had learned to love new
smells and vistas and the mysteries inherent to new cultures. . . . I had conquered the language of internationalists,
both the polite exchange of conversation in formal settings and the easy intimacy of globetrotters. I was used to
country-hopping. To move every couple of years was in my
blood. In spite of the fact that foreign service life is one long
continuous meal of loss—loss of friends and beloved places—
I loved it. The warp of my life was the fact of moving on.[1]

—ATCK Sara Mansfield Tabor

Benefits of Mobility

Sara has written about some of the great benefits countless TCKs mention when
they reflect on their lives. Not only have they grown up cross-culturally, but most
have received a wealth of positive experiences from the mobility patterns of their
lives as well. For many TCKs and ATCKs, traversing time zones and datelines
while skipping from one airport to another is part of normal life. Sitting by the
gate waiting for their next flight to parts known and unknown feels something
akin to "home" at an experiential level. The amazing places they have seen, the
esoteric foods they have tasted, and the diverse cultural communities they have
witnessed are almost beyond belief for those who have not lived this way. And yet,
for them, as for Sara, it is normal. Learning that they can successfully navigate

their way in this wider world often adds to a particular type of confidence to try new things or take risks others might not dare to take. There is no question that this type of global mobility is a great gift. Few TCKs and ATCKs we have met would trade this part of their story for a less transient lifestyle.

Yet, as we have looked at the cross-cultural nature of the TCK experience in some detail, we have seen how the richness of the first overlay—growing up in a culturally diverse world—can also result in some real challenges along the way. What about the second main overlay of the TCK experience—high mobility? Are there equally significant paradoxes for TCKs that arise from this part of their lives as well?

The answer is "yes." Many TCKs and ATCKs discover that the very mobility that leads to such wonderful opportunities to see and explore our world also creates emotional and psychological responses that can have long-term impacts if not recognized and properly handled as they occur. Did you notice the phrase that Sara almost offhandedly tucks into her account of the joys of mobility? She acknowledges that this wonderful, highly mobile lifestyle is also "one long continuous meal of loss." Why? How does that play out long-term? And what happens when both aspects of this experience—the cross-cultural piece along with high mobility—are intertwined? These are all important questions we want to look at.

The Challenges of Mobility

In 1984, Sharon Willmer, an ATCK and therapist for TCKs, spoke at a conference about TCK issues and said that she had found two recurring themes among her TCK clients. The first was that they lacked comfort. The second was they lacked a sense of what it meant to be a person.[2]

In the ensuing years, we have come to see how profound her early insights were. Often when speaking at international schools, Ruth asks for a panel of students that represent the major groups attending that school—host national attendees, TCKs of all sectors, other types of CCKs, including those who return to a cultural environment at home each evening that is different from the cultural base of the school. When she asks these young people what they like most about their globally mobile lives or going to a school with peers from around the world, inevitably they talk of how much they love having friends from such a diversity of cultures and countries. Many mention how fun it is to travel and see the world. When asked what they find most difficult, the first response is, "Having to say good-bye all the time." Perhaps the next most common response is, "When someone asks me where I am from, I never know what to say."

The truth is, in 1984 Sharon had already identified the two greatest challenges these many panels of students talk about—dealing with grief and questions of identity. What is "Having to say good-bye all the time" about? The students are talking about chronic cycles of separation and loss, which lead to grief. What do we need when we are grieving? Comfort. When they struggle with explaining where they come from, what are they essentially saying? "I'm not quite sure how to name myself." These are questions of identity. Not only what does it mean to *be a person*, but what does it mean to be *this* person . . . me?

We definitely concur with both Sharon and the student panelists. When people ask us what are the *main* challenges that many TCKs and ATCKs face despite the obvious richness and gifts of a global childhood, we reply, "Finding a sense of personal and cultural identity and dealing with *unresolved grief*." For our purposes we define *unresolved grief* as grief that comes from recognized and un-recognized losses, but one that has never been mourned in a healing way. Often the residual effects appear as some type of lingering or episodic depression for no apparent reason, quick tempers for trivial situations or anger out of proportion to the event at hand, building protective walls in relationships, and so on. And the identity questions include not only the questions of "Who am I?" or "Where do I belong?" in relationship to surrounding cultures as we looked at in chapter 4, but also the more personal questions of "What does it mean to be *me*?" in a fundamental way that we will see in chapter 6.

We believe that the high mobility most TCKs deal with is at least a contribut-ing factor to both of these challenges. Many TCKs and ATCKs discover that the very mobility that leads to such wonderful opportunities to see and explore our world also creates emotional and psychological responses that can weigh them down at various points in life. But why? To begin, we need to take a closer look at mobility *per se*.

What do we mean by high mobility? What normally happens during any cycle of mobility? Are there factors that may intensify these normal patterns for TCKs? If so, what are they? And finally, how does understanding these matters help TCKs, ATCKs, and their families deal with issues related to mobility more effectively?

Defining High Mobility

People often ask how we can say that high mobility is one of the two main char-acteristics of virtually every TCK's life when it is obvious mobility patterns vary so widely among them. Some move to a different country every two or three years with parents who are in the military or diplomatic corps. We can see that their lives are highly mobile. Others live in one host country from birth to uni-versity, so mobility wouldn't appear to be an issue for them. The recent advent of short-term overseas assignments for the employee often means the family stays home for a particular posting. How can we say that each of these examples in-cludes high mobility as part of the story when the details of each TCK experience can be so different?

The fact is all TCKs deal with mobility at one level or another. Whether the family takes an annual leave for a month or stays overseas for a longer time and then takes leave for three to six months, each cycle of coming and going means saying good-bye to friends in the host country, hello to relatives and friends at "home," good-bye to those people a short time later, and hello once more to friends they previously left in the host country—if those friends are still there. When a parent takes a short-term assignment overseas and the family doesn't go along for a particular posting, there are still frequent and repeated cycles of separation within the nuclear family itself. Those from the military community have known this type of mobility for generations. In today's world, more and more families living overseas have experienced the unplanned mobility of having to evacuate due to political unrest. TCKs who attend boarding school have other major patterns of movement. Whether they go home once or twice a year or spend three months at school followed by one month at home, each coming and going involves more greetings and farewells—and more adjustments. Paul Seaman describes this pattern of mobility well.

> Like nomads, we moved with the seasons. Four times a years
> we packed up and moved to, or back to, another temporary
> home. As with the seasons, each move offered something
> to look forward to while something had to be given up. We
> learned early that "home" was an ambiguous concept, and
> wherever we lived, some essential part of our lives was always
> someplace else. So we were always of two minds. We learned
> to be happy and sad at the same time. We learned to be inde-
> pendent and [accept] that things were out of our control. We
> had the security and the consolation that whenever we left one
> place we were returning to another, already familiar one.[3]

Although Paul is writing about moving between home and boarding school environments, he expresses the paradox many TCKs feel even in moving between two equally familiar countries—that they can and do belong both "everywhere and nowhere."

Besides a TCK's personal mobility, every third culture community is filled with people who continually come and go. Short-term volunteers arrive to assist in a project for several weeks and then they are gone. A favorite teacher accepts another position a continent away. Best friends leave because their parents transfer to a new post. Older siblings depart for boarding school or university in another country. TCKs who are the "stayers"—remaining in one place while others move—still experience the effects of mobility. They are like a rock in the stream, thinking mobility isn't their story but forgetting the stream is moving on, carrying those they love away and they can't go with it. There are many complicated layers of movement often going on at the same time for TCKs. The totality of all these comings and goings—of others as well as TCKs themselves—is what we mean when we use the term *high mobility* throughout this book.

Why Mobility Matters

So why does mobility matter? Some say, "So why is that such a big deal just because they are TCKs? Lots of people move and they have to start over again too."

True. The reason we talk about mobility specifically for TCKs isn't because others don't experience the same thing; for TCKs it has to do with frequency and degree.

As psychologist Frances White says, "Because of the nature of their work, [third culture families] are particularly vulnerable to separations. They experience not only the . . . usual share of situational separations faced by the world at large but also a number of partings idiosyncratic to their profession."[4] In other words, because of the very nature of international living, TCKs generally go through chronic cycles of separation and loss far more often than the population at large.

TCKs not only experience these mobility cycles more often than most people, but usually their moves mean changing cultures as well as places. This increases the degree of impact from that experience as the issues related to what is commonly referred to as *culture shock* or *culture stress* are piled on top of the normal stresses of any move.

Certainly there are many positive outcomes from mobility. In part II we will look in detail at some of them, including:

- Great opportunity to travel
- Independence
- Lots of friends
- Many options
- Language acquisition
- Adaptability
- Sense of confidence

But, in our usual paradoxical TCK framework, these wonderful gifts don't cancel the challenges of mobility either. In reality, each mobility cycle is also a transition experience, a "passage from one state, stage, subject, or place to another."[5] Every transition experience includes loss despite whatever may be gained and with loss there is grief, conscious or unconscious. Even with an expected, welcome change like having a baby, the couple goes through a life transition cycle and may feel the loss of freedom and spontaneity and so experience some small grief despite their great joy in receiving this child. Chapter 13 discusses in detail Dave Pollock's transition model, which includes the predictable emotional/psychological stages of *involvement, leaving, transit, entry,* and *reengagement* that we go through when change comes for any reason and we have to adapt internally.

The more we love whatever we have lost, the deeper will be our feelings of loss and our grief, even if we are not consciously aware that we are grieving. Some ask why we talk about grief when it feels so terrible. Why not focus on happier things? But if you think about it, grief is an affirmation of the good, not a negation. We don't grieve for the loss of things, places, events, and relationships we don't care about or love. Again, it doesn't mean there are not good days and wonderful new things, places, events, and relationships ahead. It means that something precious has been lost and there needs to be a time to mourn that loss in order to move on more fully to the good of the present.

So what does grief look like? Does it mean we are sitting around and crying our eyes out all day? Maybe. But it can appear in many other forms as well.

THE GRIEF CYCLE

Any grief, whether big or small, triggers a well-defined grief cycle described by the late Dr. Elisabeth Kübler-Ross. She explained the behaviors and emotions of denial, anger, bargaining, depression, and acceptance through which we express grief.[6] The intensity of this process is related to the intensity of the loss. As we said, the more you love something, the greater you will feel its loss.

We don't go through these stages of grief in a linear fashion. Pam Davis, a counselor who works extensively with third culture families, developed the model shown in figure 5-1 to demonstrate the often wagon-wheel patterns of the grief cycle.

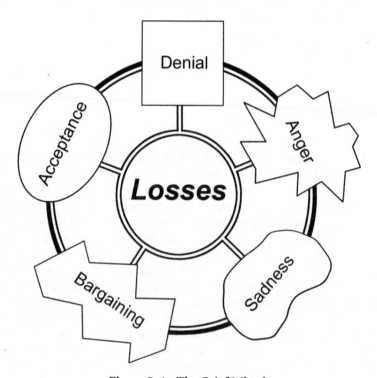

Figure 5–1: The Grief Wheel

© 2003 Pamela Davis. Used by permission

Going through one type of reaction like anger and moving into another does not mean you won't be angry about that loss again sometimes. That's one reason transition can become quite complicated for families. Not only is everyone in the family going through the overall transition process at different rates and in response to various perceived losses, but each person may be at a different stage of this grief cycle in relation to a specific loss or the overall loss within that larger journey on any given day. For example, one morning Justin may be angry about leaving his beloved dog behind, but Zoey may be sad about not being able to play with her friend next door, while Mom is busy setting up the house, denying that it is any big deal to move and scolding Justin for being so cantankerous this morning and Zoey for being so moody. One day it seems everyone is finally "well-adjusted" and the next day anger erupts from a family member at the slightest provocation. This uneven process can leave families in transition wondering if they will ever make it through or what is wrong with them or those around them.

Considering all the above factors, it's not hard to see that there might be significant periodic cycles of loss and resultant grief in any TCK's life. So many of these cycles of transition include losing the wonderful worlds they have seen and known as well as the countless friends they have made all over the world.

ATCK Alex Graham James describes these feelings better than anyone we know in her iconic poem "Mock Funeral":

> There was no funeral.
> No flowers.
> No ceremony.
> No one had died.
> No weeping or wailing.
> Just in my heart.
> *I can't . . .*
> But I did anyway,
> and nobody knew I couldn't.
> *I don't want to . . .*
> But nobody else said they didn't.
> So I put down my panic
> and picked up my luggage
> and got on the plane.
> There was no funeral.[7]

> —"Mock Funeral" by Alex Graham James

It's not hard to understand the grief. But the question remains: Why is *unresolved grief* such a major challenge for many TCKS and ATCKs any more than it might be for others?

REASONS FOR UNRESOLVED GRIEF

Remember our definition of unresolved grief says it is grief that comes from recognized and unrecognized losses a person has experienced that he or she has never mourned in a healing way. Here are five reasons we believe this grief is often unresolved for and by TCKs:

- Lack of awareness
- Lack of permission to grieve
- Lack of time
- Lack of comfort
- Lack of understanding

Lack of Awareness

One of the biggest reasons for unresolved grief is simply that the losses creating the grief are *hidden losses*. Everyone's life is filled with tangible and intangible things. What is it that makes a house a home? Surely it is more than the furniture or the color of the rug. Yet the tangibles are part of the intangible. The old fading recliner reminds us of Grandma and when we sat on her lap listening to her read us stories. We see the chair and feel a twinge of nostalgia for days that are no more. In that moment, the tangible and intangible mix and we know we are home.

Though third culture kids have a wealth of tangible and intangible realities that give their lives meaning, many of the worlds they have known are far away. Therefore, what they loved and lost in each transition remains invisible to others and often unnamed by themselves. Even concrete losses such as a grandparent's death have special challenges in this lifestyle because no one in the local community knows the one for whom the child is grieving because that person lived an ocean away. Such losses create a special challenge. Hidden or unnamed losses most often are unrecognized, and therefore the TCK's grief for them is also unrecognized—and unresolved. It's hard to mourn appropriately without defining the loss.

In recent years we have heard the term "ambiguous loss" coined by Pauline Boss.[8] Although the concept is similar to hidden loss, they are not quite the same. Ambiguous loss relates to more overtly difficult physical or psychological situations. For example, is a wife still married to her soldier husband who is missing in action? Does she mourn for his death or hope for his return? How does a person mourn the reality that his mother who has Alzheimer's is no longer the same mother he once knew? How does a TCK mourn the loss of a country and friends if they *might* be moving back there again next year? The loss stays "ambiguous" because they don't know if it is yet a real loss. In those moments, the concept of ambiguous loss relates to TCK experience as well. There is an uncertainty of how or what to grieve for. The recent technology revolution that allows us to connect to diverse people and distant places immediately and in real time also creates ambiguous loss. If I say good-bye and get on a plane but can still talk with you daily with video on my phone, what have I lost?

The difference with hidden loss is that often it is so nestled within the good of the experience that it isn't even visible. It may be that a lack of awareness of the loss comes from a focus on the positive aspects of the changes and the child avoids looking at or acknowledging the losses because they are painful or because they are distracted by the good. To admit how sad it was to leave Grandma in the home country would hurt and feels like a denial of how glad they are to return to their friends in the host country, so the child focuses somewhere else.

It is helpful to give the TCK the opportunity to recognize and name the loss: to be aware of it. Mourning a loss doesn't mean the mourner isn't recognizing the good in the present and future. But, as a funeral does, it gives permission to look at the loss consciously and acknowledge what has been lost, as we discuss in chapter 17.

Let's look at some specific hidden losses TCKs often experience.

Hidden Losses

These hidden losses also are likely to be recurring ones. The exact loss may not repeat itself, but the same *types* of loss happen again and again, so the unresolved grief accumulates. These hidden losses vary from large to small and include:

Loss of their world. With one plane ride the whole world as TCKs have known it can die. Every important place they've been, every tree climbed, every pet owned, and virtually every close friend they've made are gone with the closing of the airplane door. The sights and smells of the market, waves of people walking, darting between honking cars as they cross the streets, store signs written in the local language—everything that feels so familiar and "home" are also gone. TCKs don't lose one thing at a time; they lose everything at once. As they move from one world to another, this type of loss occurs over and over.

Loss of status. With that plane ride also comes a loss of status. Whether in their passport or host country, many TCKs have settled in enough to establish a place of significance for themselves. They know where they belong in the current scene and are recognized for who they are and what they can contribute. Then suddenly not only their world but their place in it is gone. As they travel back and forth between home and host country, this loss is repeated.

Loss of lifestyle. Whether it's biking down rutty paths to the open-air market, taking a ferry to school, buying favorite goodies at the commissary or PX, or having dependable access to electricity and water—all familiar habits can change overnight. Suddenly, traffic is too heavy for bike riding and stuffy buses carry everyone to school. Local stores don't have the items they want. Electricity and water can go off for three days at a time. All the comfortable patterns of daily living are gone, taking with them the sense of security and competency that are so vital to us all. These are major losses and also happen more than once. Definitely a sense of cultural balance is lost in these moments.

Loss of possessions. This loss doesn't refer only to possessions of monetary value but also to the loss of things that connect TCKs to their past and, again, their security. Because of weight limits on airplanes, long-loved toys or books are sold. Favorite clothes are left behind as being inappropriate in the new place. Tree houses remain nested in the foliage waiting for the next family. Evacuations during political crises mean all possessions are left behind. For those leaving to go to school, there are limits on what can be taken or would be appropriate. And so it goes.

> At one conference, TCKs were asked to name some of their hidden losses. All sorts of answers popped up.
> "My country" (meaning the host country).
> "Separation from my siblings because of boarding school."
> "My dog."
> "My history."
> "My tree."
> "My place in the community."
> "Our dishes."
> Dishes? Why that?
> "We'd lived in Venezuela the whole eighteen years since I'd been born. I felt so sad as I watched my parents sell our furniture. But when we got back to England and my mom unpacked, I suddenly realized she hadn't even brought our dishes. I said, 'Mum, how could you do that? Why didn't you bring them?'
> "She replied, 'They were cracked, and it's easier to buy new ones here.' She didn't understand those were the dishes we'd used whenever my friends came over, for our family meals, for everything. They were not replaceable because they held our family history."

The lack of opportunity to take most personal possessions from one place to another is one of the differences in international mobility compared with mobility inside a particular country. If someone moves from Amsterdam to Rotterdam, usually a mover comes, loads up the furniture and dishes along with everything else, and drives the truck to the new home. Although the house and city are different, at least familiar pictures can be hung on the wall, the favorite recliner can be placed in the living room, and some sense of connectedness to the past remains. In international and intercontinental moves, however, shipping the entire household is often impossible. Shipping costs much more than the furniture is worth. Instructions come from the organization (or parents) to keep only those possessions that can fit into a suitcase. Many things are too big or bulky to pack. It becomes simpler, more efficient, and more economical to start over again with new items at the next place.

Loss of relationships. Not only do many people constantly come and go in the TCKs' world, but among these chronically disrupted relationships are those that are core relationships in life—the ones between parent and child as well as with siblings, grandparents, aunts, uncles, and cousins. Dad or Mom may go to sea for six months. Grandparents and other extended family members aren't merely a town or state away—they're an ocean away. Educational choices such as boarding school or staying in the home country for high school can create major patterns of separation for families when the children are still young. Many ATCKs of former generations who went to boarding school at age six or returned to their home countries for secondary school grew up as strangers to their brothers and sisters who remained with their parents in the host country during those same years. Boarding schools remain an option for some TCKs to this day depending on specific situations, but they are not as common as in the past. The bottom line, however, is that the hidden losses in this type of separation are real, but the recognition of what they are or were may only show up years later.

> Until Ruth (Van Reken) was thirty-nine and started writing the journal that turned into *Letters Never Sent* (the story of her own TCK journey), she had no idea that the day her parents and siblings returned to Nigeria for four years and left her in the United States was the day her family—as she had always known it—died. Never again did all six children live with two parents as a family unit for any extended period of time. As she wrote, Ruth allowed herself to experience for the first time the grief of that moment twenty-six years before—a grief almost as deep as she would have experienced had she gotten a phone call that her family had been killed in a car wreck.

Loss of role models. In the same way we "catch" culture almost instinctively from those around us, we also learn what to expect at upcoming stages of life by observing and interacting with people already in those stages. Watching parents and those a few years older than us navigate these waters well ahead of us shows us how things will be and how we are to act or react when we "grow up."

In a gathering of older ATCKs, we again asked the question, "What are your hidden losses?" One gentleman answered, "Role models." He had only recently realized that during his twelve years in a boarding school from ages six to eighteen, he had not observed a model for a father who was involved in his family's life. Although he was a successful businessman, he had been married and divorced four times and was estranged from his adult children.

From our role models, we decide what and who we want to be like when we become adults. While living overseas as teenagers TCKs aren't around peers and slightly older adolescents from their passport culture, such as college or the career-beginning age group, so they are deprived of role models for young adulthood if they plan to repatriate and live in that culture as adults.

Loss of system identity. As mentioned before, many TCKs grow up within the friendly (or unfriendly, as a few might say) confines of a strong sponsoring organizational structure, which becomes part of their identity. They have instant recognition as a member of this group. Then at age twenty-one the commissary card is cut up, the support for education stops, invitations to organizational functions cease, and they are on their own as "adults." TCKs understand this change and probably maintain personal friends within the original system, but their sense of loss of no longer being part of that system is real. In fact, some TCKs have told us that this "graduation to adulthood" from their organizational system felt like their own families disowned them. Too often, however, they tell themselves these feelings are "silly" because mentally they do understand why this happened. It is interesting to note, however, how many ATCKs follow their parents footsteps back into similar careers in the military, missionary, or foreign service establishment where they once knew they belonged.

Loss of the past that wasn't. Some TCKs feel deep grief over what they see as the irretrievable losses of their childhood. ATCKs from the pre-jet-set days remember the graduation ceremony parents couldn't attend because they were a continent away. Other TCKs wish they could have gone to school in their native language. Some regret that they had to return to their passport country with their parents; they wanted to stay in the host country.

> Chris, a Finnish TCK, returned to Helsinki after a childhood in Namibia. While living there, separation from extended family seemed normal. All the other TCKs she knew had done the same. But that hadn't been the experience for her Finnish relatives. One evening, just after Christmas, Chris listened to her cousins reminisce about their childhood in Finland. They talked of family Christmas traditions, summer vacations at the family cottage on the lake, birthday celebrations and weddings when the family gathered. Suddenly, Chris felt overwhelmed by what she had missed

growing up. Later, in a gathering of TCKs from various countries, Chris spoke of how living overseas had robbed her of knowing the closeness of her extended family back home.

Loss of the past that was. While some TCKs grieve for experiences they missed, other TCKs grieve for the past no longer available to them. People who live as adults in the same country where they grew up can usually go back and revisit their old house, school, playground, and church. In spite of inevitable changes, they can still reminisce "on-site," but a highly mobile TCK often lacks this opportunity. But for many whose host countries have experienced the devastation of war or great political turmoil, the world they knew will never be accessible again, even if they physically return. This is a great loss.

In any of the hidden losses we've just mentioned, the main issue again is not the grief, per se. The real issue is that in these types of invisible losses, where the tangible and intangible are so inextricably intertwined, no one actually died or was divorced, and nothing was physically stolen. They were all surrounded by so much good. Contrary to obvious losses, there are no markers, no rites of passage recognizing them as they occur—no recognized way to mourn. Yet each hidden loss relates to the major human needs we all have of belonging, feeling significant to others, and being understood. The majority of TCKs are adults before they acknowledge and come to terms with the depth of their grief over any or all of these areas of hidden loss.

Hidden losses and fear of denying the good aren't the only reasons for unresolved grief, however. Even when losses are recognized, other factors may prevent a healthy resolution of grief.

Lack of Permission to Grieve

In her article "Refusing to be Erased," TCKidnow.com's current CEO, Myra Dumapias writes:

> Most people would not scoff at matters close to another person's heart or stories out of someone's struggles, battle scars (literal or metaphorical) and victories. Yet, for some odd reason, there still seems to be a point that some people doubt, minimize or challenge: the Third Culture Kid (TCK) identity and/or experience.
>
> Throughout the years, I have heard the responses below that minimize the impact of a globally or culturally mobile childhood and adolescence, the first three of which I heard before I knew the term TCK:
>
> "Yes, but I'm talking about real childhood struggles, like about money, gangs, or drugs, not just emotions."

"Maybe you're affected this much about (best friend) leaving because you don't have brothers or sisters."

"But what does moving frequently have to do with romantic relationships?"

"You sure it's not because you're single?"

"Oh, I always wanted to travel and you're complaining because you travelled so much?"

"You're just being nostalgic."

"Isn't it just abandonment issues?"

"But I know some military brats and they didn't complain."

It is as if the cause of what many TCKs experience as adults cannot be due to growing up as a global nomad or in a mobile family. The cause always has to be something else: being overly nostalgic, sensitive, single, sheltered, abandoned[9], . . .

Sometimes TCKs receive a very direct message like this that lets them know it's not okay to express their fears or grief. Colonialists' offspring were encouraged to "keep a stiff upper lip." Many others are asked to be "brave soldiers," perhaps particularly in the military and missionary context. In *Military Brats*, Mary Edwards Wertsch wrote of a girl who came down the stairs one morning and asked her mom, "What would happen if Dad got shot in Vietnam?" The mother's instant reply was, "Don't—you—*ever*—say—that!"[10]

Also, when parents are serving noble causes—saving the country from war, representing the government on delicate negotiations, or preaching salvation to a lost world—how can a child admit grief or fear? Children would feel too much shame for being selfish, wrong, or not spiritual or patriotic enough if they acknowledged how much it hurt to leave or be left. In such situations, TCKs may easily learn that negative feelings of almost any kind, including grief, aren't allowed. They begin to wear a mask to cover those feelings and conform to the expectations and socially approved behavior of their family or the community.

TCKs who grow up in a missionary community may face an added burden. Some mission people see an admission of painful feelings as a lack of faith. TCKs who want to keep their faith often believe they can't acknowledge any pain they have experienced. Conversely, other TCKs from such communities take the opposite tack; they believe that in order to deal with their grief, they must deny the faith they've been taught. They, too, have forgotten (or never grasped?) the paradoxical nature of the TCK experience we mentioned earlier.

Discounting grief. As TCKs and their families prepare to board the plane, Mom and Dad admonish them not to cry by saying, "Don't worry. You'll make new friends quickly once we get there." In discounting the pain involved in the good-bye, they communicate the hidden message that their son or daughter *shouldn't* be sad. *What's the big deal about saying good-bye to these friends when they can be so easily replaced?* is how it can sound emotionally to the TCK. Somehow, though, the TCKs still feel sad and end up thinking something must be wrong with *them*. After a while there is nothing to do but bury the pain.

Comparing grief to a higher good. When TCKs express sadness at an approaching move or loss, adults may try to cheer them up with the reminder that the reasons behind this lifestyle—and thus the losses involved—are of such importance (defending or representing the country, saving the world, earning enough money to pay for the child's later educational bills) that the TCKs *shouldn't* complain about a few paltry hardships along the way. Unfortunately, this noble reasoning is not comforting; in fact, it is shaming. Generally, TCKs already understand—and often agree with—the reason why their parents have a particular career and lifestyle. Most TCKs aren't asking their parents to change. All they're trying to say is that, in spite of what they *know*, it still hurts to leave friends and a place they love dearly. They need to talk about it and have it acknowledged and validated—often several times over the coming months.

Denying grief. It's not only TCKs who may deny their grief; adults around them often do the same. To comfort another person, to say, "I understand," is to admit there's a reason for grieving. Adults who busily mask their own sense of loss by denial can't afford to admit they understand the sad TCK. If they did, their own internal protective structures might tumble down and leave them quite unprotected. Instead of crying in front of or with their children, allowing the children to see that sadness is okay when you have lost something you love, they deny their own grief and force their children to deny their grief. The children would not understand that sadness is okay when you have lost something you love.

One therapist asked us if anyone had ever done a study on how parents react or reacted when they knew they must send their kids away to school at age six. Bowlby and others have written about how early separations between parents and children affect a child's ability to attach later to those parents or others, but we know of no official study regarding how the parents cope.[11] In asking ATCKs for their thoughts on this, a number have told us how their parents stopped hugging them in their early years so their children wouldn't *miss it* (the hugs) when they left for school at the age of six. Surely this was a loss for both parent and child.

Lack of Time to Process

Unresolved grief can also be the result of insufficient time to process loss. Any person who experiences loss needs a period of time to face the pain, mourn and accept the loss, come to closure, and move on. In the era when most international travelers went overseas by ship, the trip could take weeks, providing a built-in transition period that allowed time for the grief process. In today's world of jet travel, however, there is no transition time to deal properly with the inevitable grief of losing what has been left behind. A world disappears with the closing of the airplane door, and when the door is opened, the receiving community is excited to welcome the returnees. How can TCKs mourn losing the world they've loved when, unlike a funeral, the community surrounding them has no idea of the depth of their loss? In fact, they can become impatient if these TCKs are not ready to move on immediately into the many wonderful plans prepared for them.

Sometimes events require that we move on for the moment, and many TCKs learn to put those losses in an internal box in order to face the task at hand. If events keep moving quickly and the person does not create a space to mourn, the losses pile on top of each other.

Lack of Comfort

The presence or lack of comfort is another huge factor in whether grief is resolved or not. But to understand why people need comfort and why it's often missing for TCKs, we must first look at what comfort is and isn't and how it differs from encouragement.

Merriam-Webster's Collegiate Dictionary defines *comfort* as "consolation in time of trouble or worry."[12] Comfort doesn't change the situation itself, nor can it take away the pain, but it relays the message that someone cares and understands. Comfort validates grief and gives permission for the grieving process, or mourning, to take place. For example, when a person walks up to a widow standing by her husband's casket and puts an arm around her shoulder, that gesture, with or without words, is comforting. It can't bring the husband back to life or stop the tears or the pain, but it lets the widow know her grief is accepted and understood. She's not alone in her sorrow. So it is for the TCK who has just lost his world as the airplane takes off to the new place. A hand on the knee, or pat on the arm, or a hug—depending on the child—can say it all.

Unfortunately, in our very efforts to help another person "feel better," it's easy to confuse comfort with encouragement and end up giving neither. Encouragement is an attempt to change the griever's perspective. It may be a reminder to look at the bright side of a situation instead of the loss or to think about a past success and presume this present situation will turn out just as well.

Obviously there's a time for both comfort and encouragement, but what happens when the two are confused? If the grieving widow is told that it's a good thing at least her husband had a substantial life insurance policy, how does she feel? Neither comforted nor encouraged! If the leaving child is told, "Stop crying because tomorrow we're going to Disney World on our way to this new place," he too is neither comforted nor encouraged. When encouragement is given *before* comfort, the subtle or not so subtle message is, "Buck up, you *shouldn't* feel so low." It becomes a shame message rather than an encouragement. In fact, offering encouragement—no matter how well meant—when comfort is needed is another common way that permission to grieve is taken away. Perhaps because a TCK's losses are far less visible than the widow's, this mix-up between comfort and encouragement can more easily happen and prevent TCKs from being comforted or having the legitimate space to mourn their loss.

Lack of Understanding of How Children Grieve and Mourn

A fifth reason for unresolved grief has been suggested: parents often don't understand the grief process when they see it in their children. We need to realize that initially children don't have vocabulary for feelings. Julia L. Simens, international school counselor and author of *Emotional Resilience and the Expat Child*, says, "The ability to label emotions is a developmental skill that is not present at birth—it must be learned. Children who successfully handle transitions still need to have support and understanding from their parents that transition takes effort to be successful, even if you are used to moving."[13]

They certainly have feelings, but without adequate language to name their feelings, how can they let parents know? Perhaps they said it indirectly or by asking what seems to be a random question. "Mommy, do you think I'm going to die?" Mommy might address the question directly and think that the issue is resolved when she says to the child, "Of course not. You're healthy and young. You aren't dying!" But the child may instead be trying to express feelings about a recent death or loss. Children may think immediately of themselves, and they may act out what they feel in ways that are not considered appropriate, leading to a reprimand. This happened to Ruth as a child.

> When Ruth was eight years old and back in the U.S. for a year, the Bobby Greenlease kidnapping case made headlines for days. A woman had falsely presented herself as an aunt and taken Bobby from his school. As that case waited for resolution, the adults in Ruth's home sat around talking of many other high-profile cases through the years, notably the son of Charles Lindbergh. For his kidnapping someone put a ladder up to the side of the house and climbed through the window. For the rest of their time in the U.S., Ruth either asked to sleep on the floor at night (presuming any kidnapper coming could not see her) or slept with all the dolls she could gather to both hide behind and because she had heard stories of soldiers who were shot but the bullet hit a coin or some other object in the pocket over their hearts and they weren't killed. In her child's mind, she figured if someone did try to shoot her from the window, at least the dolls would take the blows. Of course, her parents didn't understand her behavior. They often questioned why she preferred the floor over the bed, or even tried to sleep on the floor in the closet! "Aren't that many dolls crowding you out?" they asked.
>
> Ruth said she preferred the floor and liked her dolls. Fortunately they didn't force her to change. But one day Ruth asked her mom, "How much money would you pay if someone kidnapped me?"

Her mom laughed and said, "No one is going to kidnap you because we don't have any money."

Well, that made it worse!!!! Now what if the kidnappers made a terrible mistake and took her by mistake? She was a goner for sure. Ruth tried once more.

"But, Mommy, if they made a mistake and did kidnap me, how much money would you pay to get me back?"

At that point, it seems her mom understood this was more than an informational question, gave Ruth a hug, and said, "We'd give everything." Given her mom's first comment, perhaps that shouldn't have been so reassuring, but for some reason it was. If this happened to her, her parents would figure out a way to rescue her. Whew!! That was all she needed to know.

Attention span is also a factor, and children will often "seem fine" and circle back to process later. When adults don't understand the way a child processes grief at a particular age, it is important for them to become learners by considering what their child might be asking. If a young child shows signs of ongoing sadness, it can be time to talk to a professional for additional insights.

As we said, the biggest problem is not grief itself. That is a normal, human response to the loss of anything we love. The biggest problem is *unresolved* grief. Grief that is not dealt with directly emerges in some way—in forms that are destructive and that can last a lifetime. That's *bad grief*, and it needs attention and resolution. How can people recognize if it has already gotten its foothold in their lives?

Expressions of Unresolved Grief

Unresolved grief will always express itself somehow. Often it will be in ways that appear completely unrelated to feelings of grief and apparently focused on totally different events. As we said earlier, the typical reactions of acute grief include denial, anger, bargaining, depression, and acceptance, but not always in linear or even obvious fashion. But how does it look perhaps many years later if it remains unresolved? We start with Dr. Kübler-Ross's grief cycle up to the acceptance stage and then add our own observations for other behavior we believe the basic grief responses can grow into. All of them create major defensive walls in an effort to continue to block out the conscious pain. The problem then is that the behavior can, in itself, create more pain for the ATCK and all around. Here are some examples of common reactions we see as TCKs try to deal with or reduce the pain of their losses.

DENIAL

Some TCKs and ATCKs refuse to admit to themselves the amount of sadness they have felt. "It didn't bother me to leave my parents for boarding school when I was six. I was so excited to go that once I got on the train, I didn't even think about them anymore." While this may be their conscious recollection of events, they forget that if a six-year-old *doesn't* miss Mommy and Daddy when he or she leaves for months at a time, something must be fundamentally wrong with that relationship—or they have already disconnected. Grief is normal when separating from those we love.

Others admit these separations were painful but claim to have gotten over them. Yet, as we've already seen, they continue to live lives that wall out close relationships to others—including spouses and children.

ANGER

The most common responses triggered by unresolved grief are defensiveness and a quick, flashing anger totally out of proportion to what are seemingly small circumstances in anyone else's mind. These types of responses can have devastating consequences in every context: marriage, work, social relationships, and parenting. For some, the anger is sublimated and eventually finds expression when TCKs take up a "righteous cause." They can defend the need for justice, environmental matters, civil rights, political reform, or religious practices with adamancy and vigor because no one can argue with their sense of outrage on such matters. Those who try will, of course, be seen as fools. This is not to say TCKs and others shouldn't be involved with such issues, but there is often a level of intensity that seems to go beyond the cause itself.

In any of these situations, people complain about how difficult the angry TCK is to live, work, or deal with, but few try to understand the pain behind the anger. Somewhere along the way the TCK decided the pain was simply too much to bear and replaced grief with anger as anesthesia for the pain. Unfortunately, anger ultimately increases the pain as the TCK's world becomes more isolated and lonely; no one wants to be near such an angry person.

SADNESS/DEPRESSION

Kübler-Ross called this stage depression; others prefer to call it sadness to differentiate this normal occurrence from a more chronic depressive condition. Either way, a feeling of sadness and lack of interest or energy is another manifestation of grief. This may be the time when TCKs listen to sad songs on the radio, don't have much energy to complete school or work assignments, and may not even want to contact old friends, let alone make new ones. This stage is when the reality of the loss hits. We can no longer deny what is occurring, the anger wasn't enough to stop it, the bargaining made us realize we can't outsmart or outrun it, and it seems we are left powerless. No wonder we are sad.

But in that powerlessness, the anger against the circumstances turns back against ourselves and it can, in fact, turn into a true depression if the grief gets bottled up for too long. We have met far too many ATCKs who have struggled for years with major depression because they never found a way through this stage. Just remember: sadness and depression (as well as denial, anger, and withdrawal) are normal in any grief process and must be respected as such. The problem, however, comes when TCKs, ATCKs, or anyone gets stuck here because they have never been able to name the grief and mourn the loss in healthy ways.

BARGAINING

Once it becomes clear that a loss is inevitable, we begin to try to figure out ways to deal with it that might ameliorate the intensity of what is ahead. We are beginning to accept the reality of what we can't change, but can't yet accept the finality of all this loss may entail. For TCKs or ATCKs, it may manifest in mentally planning how "one day" they will return to the land they are leaving or have left. Friends set up Facebook accounts to form groups with others to reminisce about the joys of the past. These can all be fine strategies as long as they don't live only in the past glories of how life was rather than moving into the present and future as well. As Pam Davis, counselor for TCKs, says for all the stages, "Bargaining is OK. It's a part of the process." It's a beginning step for how to deal with the losses productively.

WITHDRAWAL

Withdrawal is another way that both the anger stage and/or sadness are expressed as TCKs attempt to avoid feeling the pain of their losses. It can be through drugs or alcohol as they withdraw into another reality. For some, physical and emotional withdrawal can be part of grief turned into a true clinical depression. If withdrawal becomes severe, with the TCK isolating from everyone and virtually everything, professional help needs to be sought with someone who understands the TCK experience. Sadly, we know of TCKs who have ended their lives or finally lashed out at others following such despair.

But other times, withdrawal is simply another way to avoid their own pain. Some TCKs refuse to make contact with anyone from the past. They write infrequent emails home from university. Phone calls are rare, and text messages are brief. On the other hand, we have also seen TCKs use this as a conscious or unconscious way to strike out at parents and hurt them for "dragging me away from the place I love"—be it home or host country.

Emotional withdrawal as a protective mechanism can continue in some situations for many years. We've heard story after story from parents of ATCKs whose adult children were in the midst of a life crisis but told their parents, "Don't come. You can't do anything." Parents are often confused, not knowing what to do. They fail to recognize that their children may have emotionally withdrawn and denied their need for support rather than risk being disappointed that, once again, no one will be physically or emotionally present in their times of crisis.

REBELLION

If the normal anger felt in any grief situation isn't dealt with, it can easily take the form of extreme rebellion. Whatever the TCKs know the parents dislike, they will do. These are the screamers to the extreme, in behavior, language, dress, and values. For some, rebellion takes an inward, silent form; for others, it's blatant and loud. Either way, rebellion becomes the nearly impenetrable shield behind which the pain is deeply hidden. Each time a new circumstance comes that threatens to break through the fragile protection and expose the pain, it's like something inside the TCK metaphorically grabs a trowel and more plaster to reinforce the shield. Until he or she is willing to let the protection be gently removed so the wound can be exposed to light and air, however, healing cannot begin. Too often, it winds up in the forms of delayed adolescent rebellion we will talk about in Chapter 12. One sad fact: we have yet to meet an outwardly defiant, rebellious TCK or ATCK who, when talked to long enough, doesn't have a place of deep wounding or profound loss within. Yet, sadly, that TCK's protective behavior has too often been punished before anyone stopped to see what the wound or loss might be, and the original wound goes deeper.

VICARIOUS GRIEF

Transferring the focus from personal grief to others is another way to express unresolved grief. A TCK might sit at an airport weeping as he or she watches total strangers say good-bye. Some TCKs go into professions where this vicarious grief finds a more active, long-term expression.

> As a child, ATCK Joan spent twelve years in boarding schools. On a conscious level, she remembered the fun of game nights, the senior banquet, and the lifelong friends she had made. She denied any particular sadness from these years of family separation, outside of the initial tears of farewell in first and second grades.
>
> After college, however, Joan found herself working in a day-care center. She explained her choice of career by saying, "I just want to help kids whose parents must work not to feel lonely. I like to sit and hug them all day so they know they're wanted and loved. Kids need to be nurtured."

Joan realized after several years that she was excessively involved with every child under her care, trying to protect each one from emotional pain. Her anger sparked against parents who forgot to bring their child's favorite teddy bear. She fought with other workers if they sharply reprimanded a child.

Finally, Joan began to recognize that her deep involvement with these children reflected more than a normal concern for them. It stemmed from the extreme loneliness she had felt when separated from her own parents during her years at boarding school, which began when she was six. Instead of directly dealing with the loss of day-by-day parenting she had experienced, Joan had unconsciously tried to deal with her own grief by making sure no child under her care would feel that same pain.

Even ATCKs who don't express their grief through a profession often become the "rescuers" of the community. For whatever reasons, they are the unofficial dorm counselors, the ones who befriend the lonely people around, who may take in the homeless. All of these can, in fact, be noble and positive gestures, but if their activities are really a substitute for working out their own grief, their behavior eventually will become counterproductive. They may be so involved in rescuing others that they may never rescue themselves.

DELAYED GRIEF

TCKs may go through life without showing or consciously feeling any particular sadness and then suddenly find to their great surprise that a seemingly small incident triggers a huge reaction.

For ATCK Dan, it was the first day his son, Tommy, went off to kindergarten. Dan should have been happy that Tommy was starting this new phase of life. School was only one block away, so Dan walked Tommy right to the door, said good-bye, turned around to walk away—and found himself unable to see the sidewalk for the tears that filled his eyes. Once back home, his body sagged against the door as he sobbed uncontrollably. His wife couldn't imagine what had happened. "Is everything all right? Is Tommy okay?" Dan could only shake his head as his body continued to shudder with pain.

Dan was experiencing delayed grief. As he left his son at school, he suddenly had a flashback of his own departure for first grade. But the picture was different from how his son was beginning school. For Dan, the new picture put him inside a small, one-engine plane with four other school kids as it took off from a grassy airstrip. He could still see his parents standing on the edge of the forest waving to him. The memory of what he had felt while returning their farewell wave hit like an engulfing tide as he turned away from Tommy that morning.

Often the people most surprised by the delayed grief are those feeling it. What amazes so many ATCKs is that the grief from losses they have never consciously defined often seems to hit them hardest between the ages of twenty-five and forty. The first glimmerings of their unrecognized grief frequently begin when they have their own children. Sometimes that's when they first ask themselves, "If my parents loved me as much as I love this baby, how could they have ever let me go away?" Or they must face the fact they aren't the perfect parents they expected to be and wonder why they have outbursts of anger toward their children that surprise them.

Even without children, many ATCKs in this stage of life begin to realize that there's a good chance that the rootlessness, withdrawal from close relationships, or whatever they're experiencing isn't going to change no matter how much they change their circumstances. At that point, it's easy for ATCKs to think that if they had lived a "normal" life, they wouldn't have problems. They begin to blame others. Family and friends are shocked that this ATCK who "never had any problems" seems suddenly to be conjuring up all sorts of fantastic painful experiences. Finally, most ATCKs begin to face the fact that some answers for their reactions to life reside inside themselves rather than in outside events and situations. At this time, many finally examine some of this unresolved grief, work through it with a counselor or writing or art, and move on in productive, adult ways, using what they have learned from having gone through the grieving process. Chapter 16 suggests specific ways ATCKs can help themselves and be helped in this process.

Part III on transition offers many concrete suggestions for TCKs and their families dealing with the losses of transition as they happen, so grief does not need to accumulate in the ways it has for so many TCKs in the past.

Expanding Our Vision

Because everyone in this world experiences loss, everyone also experiences grief. Without doubt, what we have discussed here can be applied to life transitions of all varieties—death, becoming an empty-nester, dealing with chronic illness, etc. For other CCKs, however, some may find the specifics of the losses they feel or the ways they cope have much in common with traditional TCKs. Immigrant children may withdraw from any connection to their parents' mother tongue or passport country, both in their attempt to be "the same as" but also because it is too hard to keep connecting with and losing the past. International adoptees often seem to be "doing just fine" throughout their school years, but in young adulthood and into their midthirties want to discover more of their past and find themselves grieving for parents and a culture they may never know—even while being happy and contented in their current scene. Mixed racial heritage CCKs may silently grieve the loss that within the family they have no "mirror." The list could go on and on.

We hope that understanding the dynamics of issues related to mobility will help all TCKs/ATCKs and other groups of CCKs/ACCKs—including their families and all who work with them—find ways to work through the challenges so they can enjoy the adventures of life even more fully. But we also trust that understanding matters such as the hidden losses of life, the way lack of permission to grieve or discounting of grief can unintentionally happen, will allow people of all backgrounds—TCKs/CCKs or not—to translate these principles back to their own stories and find new language and understanding for their journeys too.

Now we will look at one more challenge many TCKs and ATCKs face that emerges out of what we have already discussed about the effects of cross-cultural mobility in chapters 4 and 5. This relates to discovering a strong sense of *personal* identity as well as cultural identity while growing up with high mobility among many different cultural worlds.

Questions for Chapter 5

1. Consider your story. Did you grow up with a highly mobile life? If you stayed mostly in one place, did the people around you move?

2. What were/are some gains you experienced if you have lived in a community of mobility, whether you were the leaver or the stayer? If you grew up in a more traditional less mobile community, what are some gains of that experience?

3. What are some losses you experienced if you had a highly mobile lifestyle while growing up? If you were a "stayer" or grew up more traditionally, did you also experience loss? Please explain.

4. How did you relate to the discussion on unresolved grief? Have you personally experienced any of the realities mentioned in reasons why grief may stay unresolved? Please explain.

5. When you consider some of the losses potentially mentioned in question 3, have you found positive ways to mourn these losses? If so, please share any helpful strategies with others. If not, what do you think has hindered that process for you?

6. Are there any suggestions you would make to those who are currently living with high mobility in how to build on the gifts of this while taking care of the challenges?

CHAPTER 6

Why Cross-Cultural Mobility during Childhood Matters

Sometimes I think the cement of my being was taken from one cultural mould before it was cured and forced into other moulds one after the other, retaining bits of the form of each but producing a finished sculpture that fit into none. At other times I think of myself like the fish we caught [while we were] snorkeling off Wewak. My basic shape camouflages itself in the colours of whatever surroundings I find myself in. I am adept at playing the appropriate roles. But do I have a colour of my own apart from those I appropriate? If I cease to play any role would I be transparent? To mix metaphors, if I peeled away the layers of the roles I adopt would I find nothing at the centre? Am I after all an onion—nothing but the sum of my layers?

—ATCK Sophia Morton[1]

In her powerful essay "Let Us Possess One World," Sophia reflects on one of the major questions many TCKs and ATCKs face: "Who am I—really? With all the pieces of my life scattered in many directions and places, who is the real me? *Is* there a real me?"

And those are questions many TCKs struggle with as they seek to put the disparate parts of their stories into some cohesive whole and discover what, indeed, it means to be a person. Therapist Sharon Willmer defined that as one of the key challenges she saw among her ATCK clients.[2]

Keys to the Challenges

In 1984 when I (Ruth) heard Sharon Willmer talk about personhood, something in my heart stirred. I knew it was important, but I couldn't wrap my head (maybe more my heart) around it. Sometime later, however, I picked up my pen and thought back to Sharon's seminar. *So what does it mean to be a person?* I wondered. I remembered that Sharon had begun with the term "relational" so I put that down first and added to it. Maybe you have other thoughts to add.

WHAT DOES IT MEAN TO BE A PERSON?

We as human beings (or persons) are:

- Relational—we are social beings
- Emotional—we have feelings
- Creative—we can think/make new things
- Volitional—we have the ability to choose
- Physical—we have a body
- Spiritual—we have a non-material spirit
- Significant—we have value
- Integrated—all these parts work together

A year or two before I made this list, my first book (now *Letters Never Sent*) had come out. While many readers resonated with my story and wrote to say they understood my feelings because they, too, thought they were the only ones crying at boarding school when the lights went out, there were others essentially patting me on my figurative back and saying, "Well, Ruth, if you hadn't been such an emotional person, you would have been just fine." (Pat-pat, as they walked away.)

During those years, and partly as a result of these criticisms, I began talking in general terms during a seminar about this basic idea of how easy it was for TCKs to feel guilty for somehow not measuring up to others' expectations of who they should be.

> After one such presentation, a gentleman whose first name, James, is all I remember, came up to me and said, "Ruth, you know what you're talking about isn't guilt."
>
> "Then what is it?" I asked.
>
> "It's shame."
>
> Having no idea what that meant, I asked him what he was talking about. "What's the difference?"
>
> "Guilt is for what you *do* that is wrong in the sense of morally wrong. There is a healthy shame for that, but the antidote for guilt is forgiveness. Shame is for who you *are*.

The only antidote for that is grace. When we mix up the two, we may not ask for forgiveness when we need to or we try to be forgiven for who we *are* when that's not what we need. We need grace to seek to understand ourselves and who we are and who we are not."

I confess I can be a bit slow. I heard him but I couldn't quite *get it* yet.

"Sorry, I still don't know exactly what you mean. How can you figure out the difference practically? In other words, what does shame look like?" I asked.

Did I just hear an internal sigh? I wondered. *Oh, dear. Now I'm feeling shame that I'm so dumb!*

"Ruth, think about all the 'I should' and 'I shouldn't' messages in your life. Things like 'I should have remembered to call him yesterday.' Or 'I shouldn't have bought that blouse for my friend's birthday. I can tell she thinks it's ugly and is just saying thanks to be polite.' (*And while he's talking I was still thinking that I 'should' be able to understand what he is saying!*) These are not moral failures. They are just part of being human and finite. There is no way we can get and be and do everything right. Sure, if you knew what you knew afterwards you might have done something differently, but believe it or not, you aren't God!"

Well, for someone whose husband says I should have been a pathologist because I always dissect things after they happen to see what went wrong or what I "should" have done better in whatever the situation is I'm thinking about, this was a bit of a revelation!

So back to my personhood list. When I read again the first two characteristics, it hit me. I had been feeling *shame* all this time for who I *was*—"too emotional"!! Not for what I had done.

But if at my core I am a relational being, then no matter the reason—good, bad, for a reason I understand, for a reason I don't—any time a relationship is broken, for whatever reason (including mobility), it is a big deal. Something at the core of me is severed. It's why death is so hard. It cuts to our soul as relational beings.

That meant there was nothing "wrong" with me as others had intimated (or at least as I had perceived their statements) because I felt sad to be away from my parents at boarding school when I was six. If Mom and Dad were my most basic place of relationship at that point in my life and that relationship was broken for an entire school year in terms of not being together day by day, it was, in truth, a pretty big deal. And, if the next characteristic about being a person—any person, not just me—was true and I was emotional as part of my being, then the truth also was I would feel pain from that separation and loss. Period. Not because I was "too emotional" but simply because I was a normal human.

When I saw that connection between being human and the feelings of grief I had uncovered from my past, a load lifted—the load of shame I had, in fact, been carrying not only as I listened to others' judgments of how I *should* or *shouldn't* feel or be now but from childhood when I didn't know why I couldn't be braver and not cry so much at times of separation.

And then the next light came inside me. "Wow! My sorrow is an affirmation of being human, not a statement of weakness. What kind of family would I have come from if I didn't miss my parents when I went to boarding school 300 miles away at age six?"

WHAT NEEDS DO HUMANS HAVE?

Because of my "Aha!" of understanding that my grief at missing my family was based on my needs as a person not being met, not a negation of them or myself, I made a list of needs that I believe all humans have—me included—based on the very essence of who we are. Here it is. As before, feel free to add your thoughts.

- *Because we are relational beings*, we need relationships that are close, on-going, and where we can truly feel known and also know others. We need to find a deep sense of being accepted and belonging to a place, person, and group.
- *Because we are emotional beings*, we need the opportunity to feel and express the full range of our emotions—from joy to sorrow and everything in between.
- *Because we are creative beings*, we need a place to express that specific creative part of ourselves—whether it be artistic, mechanical, mental, musical, sewing, or whatever our specific form of creativity is.
- *Because we are volitional beings*, we need a place to make meaningful choices for matters that affect our lives.
- *Because we are intellectual beings*, we need space and time to think and have others around with whom we can bounce off our ideas and questions.
- *Because we are physical*, we need a place and sense of safety and a way to take proper care of their bodies—exercise, healthy food, rest.
- *Because we are spiritual beings*, we need a time and space to contemplate the mysteries of life and an opportunity to explore what faith means to us.
- *Because we are significant beings*, we need a sense of purpose—that "who I am as this particular person called 'me' and what I do in this world matters."
- *Because we are integrated*, we need a sense that all the various parts of our personality, background, and experience work together in what we do and who we are.

I had looked at the TCK experience through the lens of cross-cultural mobility, but what if I stepped back and focused more directly on the K of TCK—what it meant to be a kid who is, of course, a person? Would that shed more light on some of the common things we know TCKs deal with—particularly the two main issues of identity and unresolved grief? How does the TCK lifestyle intersect with this core human identity? For one quick example, think about the needs listed. If it is true that as relational beings we need to be known and to know others, what happens to our sense of being known and knowing others when we suddenly move halfway around the world? And what if that mobility also takes us to another culture? We move to the next place where we may know no one or how life works in that place and we have to begin trying to establish relationships all over again—and then we may well be moving once more. When that happens time and again, something in our core is definitely affected.

Then the next "Aha!" came. Although I started by looking where people are alike, it is also true that no one is *the same*. H-m-m-m-m, again. If the list above is everyone's story, it is also no one's story if there is nothing more. We would exist merely as a vast sea of humanity with no differentiation. But that's not who we are. The mystery is that we are unique individuals as well.

FROM LIKENESS TO UNIQUENESS

Somehow, within the likeness that connects all humans, the fact of being "different from" or unique is equally important. Part of our sense of being significant is that "*I* matter. I am not a clone." Each of us wants and needs to know what it is that makes us not just *a* human but *this* human—the one others call Joe or Fatima or Musa or Mikail or Bronwyn or Ai Xia or any other person by name. We are not switchable beings.

"All alike yet all unique in the likeness," popped into my brain. Wow! How can that be? But it is. Everyone can think, but our thinking styles can be totally different. Everyone is physical, yet no two of us look exactly the same, and we have different ways our bodies work. Some are ballerinas, others are sports stars, others are in wheelchairs due to nerve destruction of some sort. Everyone is creative, but no one creates in the exact same way or the exact same things.

While intuitively it seems that to discuss personal identity, the starting place would be uniqueness, ironically our sense of true personal identity must begin with likeness before it proceeds to uniqueness. If we *begin* defining ourselves by "difference," then we have to maintain that difference in an alienating, "me/you" or "us/them" kind of way to keep our sense of identity. This can lead to what Janet Bennett calls a sense of "terminal uniqueness,"[3] a syndrome she has noted with TCKs and others who feel they are so different no one else in the world can understand them. That is a very lonely place to be. If, instead, we *begin* with likeness, we can understand why the TCK/CCK story is so universal in terms of the response. In fact, in working on this chapter one more "Aha!" came to me. If we begin with this premise of shared human needs we can see:

- The gifts of the TCK experience are often expressions of our needs as persons being met

- The challenges of the TCK experience are often expressions of our needs as persons *not* being met
- Cultural practices are, in essence, ways that people find to meet these fundamental human needs

On the other hand, although we start with likeness, it is true that how each person—TCKs included—responds to his or her experience is not uniform (see chapters 7–12). It is also true that each culture shapes how individuals express the essence of being human in specific ways, (e.g., styles of greetings, communal traditions, etc.). In the end there is no question that we must also look at our story as it has happened to us as a unique person.

How do we keep a balance between these two seemingly paradoxical realities? How do children develop that sense of "This is me!" as a unique person within the healthy context of the likeness that connects them to others and prevents a sense of terminal uniqueness? Explaining to them, "By the way, did you know you're a relational, emotional, volitional being who is alike and unique?" at age five isn't going to help much!

Personal Identity Formation

Barb Knuckles has developed a series of illustrations to show how children learn a sense of personal identity in relationship to what she calls "anchors and mirrors" (see figure 6-1). In this double metaphor, family, community, and place are anchors—the things that give us a place of grounding and strength. Yet, almost paradoxically, they are also mirrors—reflecting back the messages of who we *are* as seen by these entities.

NEEDED: ANCHORS

For children doing the developmental task of figuring out who they are, these anchors of family, community, and place might be likened to a tent where the anchors are the stakes to which the ropes are tied that hold up the tent.

Initially the ropes are short and the tent is a bit small as the children learn to navigate around it inside, but after they learn how life works in that smaller tent, the ropes are extended and the space inside becomes bigger. It is still a safe and protected environment and the children learn to operate in this wider space. This process repeats at regular intervals: first half-day at nursery school, first full day of school in primary school where teacher is constant through the day, moving into secondary school where there is a new teacher for each class, graduation, moving out of the home and on into life.

Personal Identity Formation: Identity Anchors

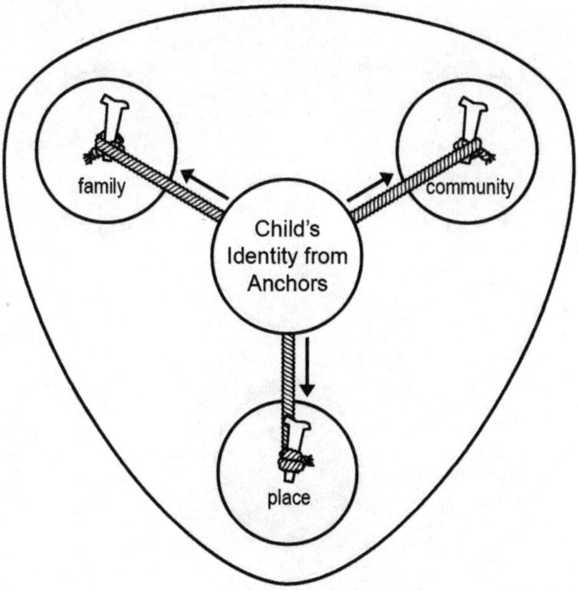

Figure 6–1: Identity Anchors
©2017 Barbara H. Knuckles. Used by permission.

When the anchors hold strong and steady, each stage may feel a bit scary to move into initially, but because the space is safe, children dare to try. As they do, the children learn about themselves—that they are competent, capable human beings who can dare to face the challenges that lie ahead in adulthood. Because they have figured things out before, they know they can again, and so forth.

NOT ONLY ANCHORS, BUT ALSO MIRRORS

But these three entities serve as more than anchors. Family, community, and place are also where children look and see a reflection of how each of these mirrors define them.

It's as if the stakes being used as anchors have mirror overlays on the top of them. It is here the reflections come back to children of how they are seen by this particular anchor in their lives.

When we put them together into a composite picture, we see one more thing: These three factors don't work in isolation from each other. (See figure 6-3.)

Personal Identity Formation: Identity Mirrors

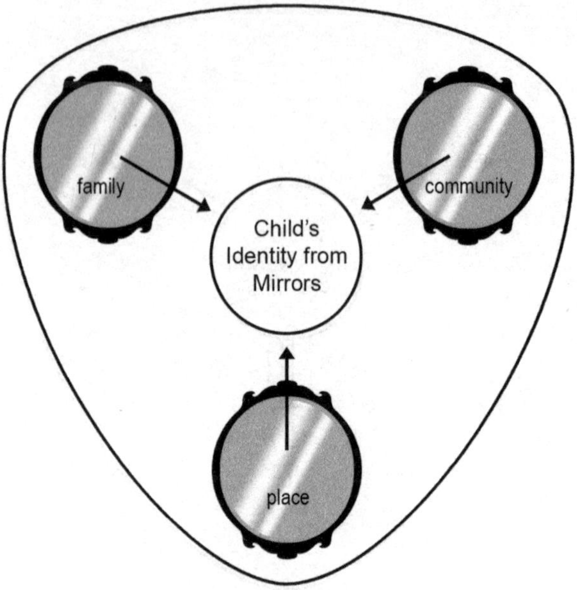

Figure 6–2: Identity Mirrors
©2017 Barbara H. Knuckles. Used by permission.

Part of the messages children receive about who they are comes from how these three entities interact with each other. When parents have high status in the community, the children internalize the message that they are significant as well. If, instead, the parent has a lower status or is even despised by the community, the children easily assume their value as a person is less than others. From the reactions and responses of the people in their lives as well as how those people interact with each other in the context of the physical space around them, children ultimately come to define who they are within this social context as well as who they are as a particular person—the likeness and uniqueness we have been discussing.

When the anchors and mirrors are steady and the messages received are hopefully consistent and positive, children don't have to waste energy in figuring out conflicting messages about themselves but can move ahead to always be discovering more of themselves and how life works.

The Ugly Duckling gives a great picture of how this works. The anchors of family, community, and place were there initially, but the mirrors overlaying them reflected only rejection. Instead of providing a safe place, the anchors and

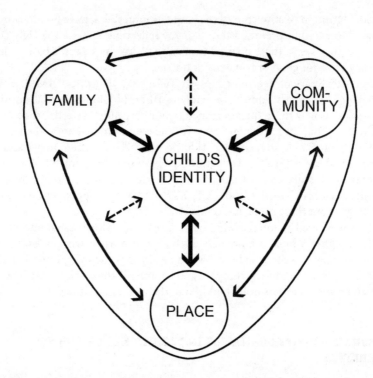

Figure 6–3: Identity Formation, Anchors and Mirrors, Traditional
©2017 Barbara H. Knuckles. Used by permission.

mirrors did the opposite. Not only did his family and community reject him, but how could he live in this place when the message clearly came that he did not belong? Sadly, when the duckling left the physical place of interacting with these anchors and mirrors, he took with him the messages already instilled. "I am ugly." "I am incompetent." "I am worthless." "I don't belong." It wasn't until he saw the beautiful community of swans and then his own reflection in the pond that he saw who he really was. As long as his identity was only *different from*, he felt *terminally unique*. When he looked first at other swans and then looked at himself, he could see both likeness and uniqueness. And this happened in the context of new anchors (community, place) and mirrors. Maybe in time, some swan family also adopted him!

Of course, this process is not unique to TCKs or other CCKs. This is the human story across nationality, social class, economic status, race, gender, and all the other categories by which we divide ourselves into groups. Children who, like the Ugly Duckling, are in the process of trying to discover who they are as individuals and in relationship to the world around them, have no filters to understand how to interpret the validity of any reflection. As with the Ugly Duckling, what they see in these mirrors turns into "I am" messages, a basic belief of who they are—for good or bad, true or untrue.

But after years of hearing countless TCKs ask, "How do I find a sense of belonging?" "Where is home?" or "How can I build long-term relationships?" the question is why these themes related to our core human needs are so repetitive for this group in particular. Why are the common benefits and challenges listed in chapters 7–12 so recurrent? Why do some TCKs seem to thrive and others struggle deeply? (See the Transition Matrix model in chapter 14 for further thoughts on this question.) Lastly, for all the changes in technology, mobility, and "global culture," why are today's TCKs still writing in the chat rooms and on their blogs about these same questions?

This is where the intertwining of mobility and culture come into play for TCKs. Let's take a look at how these anchors and mirrors work when they are often in flux. First, we look at how these same anchors and mirrors work in a traditional childhood and then compare and contrast that experience with the one most TCKs and countless other children in the world now know.

PERSONAL IDENTITY FORMATION IN TRADITIONAL CHILDHOOD EXPERIENCE

We define "traditional childhood experience" as the one most children in past generations knew. Here the basic anchors and mirrors stayed steady and relationships were long-term, as the children and those around them often lived in that place for generations, perhaps traveling to go on vacations but always returning "home." Figure 6-3 shows the child in the center of this basically steady world. (Note: We recognize that unexpected events from outside—such as death, divorce, natural disasters, or abuse—might shift some of this steadiness. We also realize even in traditional childhoods sometimes the mirrors in a particular child's life might reflect different messages than our examples, but for our purposes we are looking at the hypothetical "ideal" experience of identity formation for children in a "traditional childhood.") What are the reflections that affirm both likeness and uniqueness for the child in such an environment? How does it all work? In each example we give in the next sections, we follow with a reference back to a human need that is being met or unmet with this message to try to emphasize how this relates to our basic needs of personhood.

Family

Children look at parents who get up at 2:00 A.M. to feed them, read them stories day and night, kiss their "ow-ies" to make them all better after a fall, and attend every school concert or play that the children are in. What important "I am" messages do children receive about who they are when they are securely anchored here and looking at the family mirror? Here are a few examples of what those messages might be:

- *I am known.* Parents meet their needs even without language. "Here you go, sweetie. Take some milk. I know how hungry you must be." (Need for relational beings—"being known"—*met*).
- *I am okay when I express my emotions.* Even more, parents' interactions are how children learn to name their emotions. "Oh, did you fall off your bike? That must really hurt. Here, let Mommy kiss it. Do you want to choose a plaster (BAND-AID) to cover it?" (Need for emotional beings—"feeling and expressing emotions"—*met*)
- *I am able to choose what I would like.* "Which book shall we read tonight?" "Which plaster shall we use?" They are not robots or victims who have no say over meaningful things in their lives. (Need for volitional beings—"able to make choices"—*met*)
- *I am noticed.* Hearing the cheers of their parents from the stands or knowing they are in the audience listening as these children recite their lines. (Need for significant beings—"I matter"—*met*)
- *I am spiritual.* Families are usually the first place that lessons of faith are taught, and where children learn about the mysteries of life. (Need for spiritual beings—"I can wonder and believe"—*met*)

For children the world over, in the village, in the mansion, the family anchor/mirror is the most elemental place of learning a sense of personal identity. Even as adults, they know forever this family unit is where they belong and these affirming relationships continue.

Community
But while our personal identity development begins with the family, the community also matters—or more truthfully, the subcommunities all children have of school, youth groups, places of worship, sports teams, etc.

From the community, children hopefully see reflected:

- *I am part of a group.* Here they learn how to live in relationship with a larger world outside their family alone. Coaches teach them to be good sports. Teacher don't let them interrupt another student who is speaking. (Need for relational beings—"I belong"—*met*)
- *I am able to do some things well, some things not so well.* From the community children learn what their gifts are and are not. Do they get picked for the starring role in the play or only a walk-on part? Do they get straight A's in school, struggle to barely pass, or get a mixture of grades? Did they enjoy the

painting class offered in their local community center? (Need for significant beings—"Who am I as *me*, not just anyone"—*met*)

- *I am known.* Community members may not know them as intimately as parents, but they know the children by name and abilities. (Need for relational beings—"I am known in this place"—*met*)
- *I am valuable.* Folks in the community can give helpful mentoring and guidance. The children know that these others in the community believe they, the children, are worth investing time into them. (Need for significant beings—"I matter"—*met*)
- *I am understood.* The community members also know the cultural context in which these children are living without them having to explain it and vice versa. How life works here is understood by all. (Need for relational being—"I am known and I know them"—*met*)

In the end, community is also critical in forming a sense of personal identity. Here children discover their uniqueness even as they find their "belongingness" as well. They are not left alone to try to figure these things out.

Place

Traditionally, a *sense of home* (and thus, of identity and belonging) is attached to physical place. From their ground-breaking research on TCKs and place, Anastasia A. Lijadi and Gertina J. Van Schalkwyk from the University of Macau write:

> Place-identity, as a salient component of identity, develops as people identify with the place where they live and where a sense of belonging and emotional connection is fostered particularly in the earlier years of development . . . Place identity is important for maintaining a personal and social identity and for emotional well-being.[4]

Perhaps this is one of the most stabilizing anchors of all as it remains a place to return to even as adults.

It remains steady no matter the changes in family or community. It also grounds children in a historical context and connects them to those who went before and lived in this same place. Why do we have historical markers announcing this is where some president or prime minister or famous sports hero was born or grew up? It is like a "conferred" identity. "I belong to them because we both come from here." Although not tied together personally, pride of belonging to the same places somehow matters.

In some almost magical way, places hold our history. We look at the school building where we spent our first days of formal education and smile inside— how amazing we were once so young! We drive by the house where we once visited Grandma and wish we could do it just one more time. Walking by a street vendor in some strange city and smelling the curry that is flavoring the meat on his cart brings back memories of walking through a village years ago where this same smell permeated the air. Or, conversely, we receive an invitation to our secondary school's tenth reunion and shut it quickly. Why would we want to stir up memories associated with that time and place when all it does is remind us of bullies who harassed and teachers who demeaned? The feelings of rejection and sadness are not ones we wish to revisit.

But how is place part of identity formation per se? In a traditional childhood, from the anchor/mirror of place children (hopefully) see reflected:

- *I belong to a physical place.* They are not homeless or rootless. When strangers ask "Where are you from?" no matter how long it has been, no matter where they are, this is where they are and will always be from. (Need for relational/physical beings—"belonging and having a physical place for safety"—*met*)
- *I am competent.* Children are in cultural balance and feel confident about living in this place. How to dress for the local weather, what sports teams are important, which storefront shop carries a needed rice cooker, and how people think in this place are all known to them. (Need for integrated beings—"I am able to use all of who I am in this place"—*met*)
- *I am whole.* Here in this place, the different aspects and relationships of their lives flow together because all are also gathered in this place they know. (Need for integrated beings—"all of me works in cohesion"—*met*)

Altogether, this is literally and figuratively a good place to be!

IDENTITY FROM RELATIONSHIP OF ANCHORS AND MIRRORS

So why is it important to look at how family, community, and place relate to each other as part of identity formation? In the illustration, the child is protected in the middle of this overall process. These relationships are another key anchor/mirror in forming a child's sense of identity.

Family to Community

As children watch how their family interacts with others in the community, there is another type of mentoring going on. From the interaction of family to community and vice versa, children learn:

- *I am part of a tribe.* Tribes have traditions that occur for members of the tribe to gather and celebrate these things communally. Going with parents to ceremonies such as bar mitzvahs, confirmations, graduations, and national holidays are important. (Need for relational beings—"I belong"—*met*)
- *I know where I fit.* How parents relate to the community and the community to them determines in large part the children's social, economic, or other status. Children can be locked into a long-term sense of either entitlement or

despair because of it, even in a traditional community. (Need for significant beings—"I matter"—*met/unmet*)

Family to Place

Part of learning a deep sense of cultural balance is feeling competent at negotiating the life skills needed for survival and full participation in how life operates in a particular place. From the interaction of family to place, children internalize more messages about themselves, such as

- *I am physical.* In each place, survival skills are needed if we don't want to die. Children learn these skills first by watching their parents relate to this place—how to dress for the weather, how to plant and grow crops to eat, what immunizations to take against local disease. (Need for physical beings—"I know how to safely survive"—*met*)
- *I am creative.* Parents who involve the children in learning how to build a fishing net out of local vegetation, or create a beautiful bouquet from the flowers raised in the backyard prove that new things can be made from what is in the environment. (Need for creative beings—"I can make something new"—*met*)
- *I am able.* Children watch their parents make plans for where they will buy a house, or how they will finance a new car, or who and what they will vote for at the next election. (Need for intellectual beings—"I can think and figure things out"—*met*)
- *I belong.* There will never be a question for most children who grow up in this traditional way of *Where is home?* This place holds their history. (Need for relational beings—"I belong"—*met*)

Community to Place

Communities will do different group events, social functions, or cultural celebrations depending on what place they are in. It is not only parents who show a child how life is anchored and works in this place; those in the community do as well.

From the interaction of community and place anchor/mirror, children see more beautiful images of who they are both collectively and individually:

- *I am needed.* They are part of the construction—damming the creek for a swimming hole, whitewashing the temple. (Need for significant beings—"I matter"—*met*)
- *I am wanted.* They are included and welcomed into public space (the commons of New England or the public parks of China). They are participants in events on location (the water festival in Thailand). (Need for relational beings—"I belong"—*met*)
- *I am part of something bigger than me.* Children become part of the collective memory and stories. They belong to something beyond this moment in

history and time. They visit the nearby castle and know the kings in history books once walked here. (Need for significant/relational beings—"I matter/I belong"—*met*)

To sum it up, the point is that not only do we have basic anchors and mirrors from parents, community, and place to tell us who we are, but as they join and make a circle around the child, it's a warm and safe place in which to grow because the child is literally cocooned by and in it.

Identity Anchors and Mirrors after Moving

Physical mobility can interrupt the process of identity formation for all children, even when it is not cross-cultural, because with any mobility, potentially everything changes. When we add the cultural piece it becomes even more complicated. See figure 6-4 for a look at what happens to these most basic places of identity formation in the process of mobility.

Personal Identity Formation after a Move

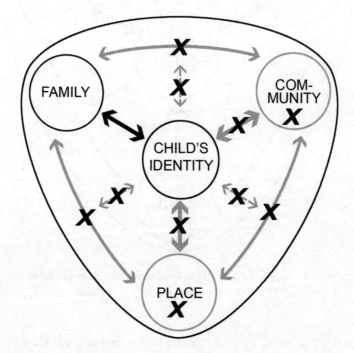

Figure 6–4: Identity Formation: Disrupted Anchors and Mirrors
©2017 Barbara H. Knuckles. Used by permission.

And so the move is made. The old world is essentially gone. Again, quoting Dr. Anastasia Lijadi and Gertina J. Van Schalkwyk, "The most exasperating experience in moving to a new place is to lose the sense of self and to lose touch with the people closest to us."[5] What anchors and mirrors will be left? Which new ones will come into play? How/where will the child find the new anchors and mirrors to continue learning? Will they give the same or different messages from the ones they had before? These questions can be for all moves, cross-cultural or not. But if the move is a move within the same culture, perhaps the anchors and mirrors remain at least culturally as circles—close to what the family has known before. They have to get to know new people, but they and those they meet don't have to try to understand each other's cultural lenses.

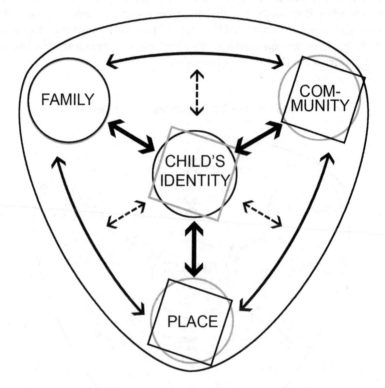

Figure 6–5: Identity Formation: Replacement Anchors and Mirrors
©2017 Barbara H. Knuckles. Used by permission.

For this discussion, however, we will look at mobility and these changing anchors/mirrors from the grid of a cross-cultural move. What's *right* and what's *wrong* can totally switch. Here the rules for how life is to be lived can totally change overnight. The anchors no longer feel secure and the mirrors may reflect totally different images of who the child is. We as humans are not only alike while unique, but our likeness and uniqueness are expressed through and in the context of culture. So which culture children are in and the specific messages they receive become part of their shaping. Because people in each culture do seek to have their basic human needs met through different culturally appropriate ways, there is a lot for children to learn—from food to dress to greetings to relational styles. It may be a while before all of the anchors feel secure again or the mirrors reflect any messages of belonging.

In the model, the new community and place have a different shape than the former place (figure 6-5). What about the family and child? Here they remain the same, but sometimes even family anchors and mirrors change through or during mobility. Are there different messages from squares than circle anchors and mirrors? Or vice versa? How will these different shapes now learn to interact? Will those interactive patterns complete the safe circle as before? Only time will tell. Let's see what kind of reflections and anchoring messages might be in this new place. Each category will have a "best-case scenario" and a "worst-case scenario" for the messages these changed anchor/mirrors reflect back to the child.

Family

The nuclear family can be the most stabilizing unit of all in any move because it usually stays intact, unless part of the mobility/change includes such things as divorce, a sibling going away to university, or death. But considering the family unit may be the only constant at all for children when they move, it is interesting—and perhaps not surprising—how many TCKs define home in terms of relationship to the family.

Best-case scenario: With mobility, children can look in the family anchor/mirror and see:

- *I am known.* Whether or not they have moved, parents still know their children well enough to understand where they might be hurting in the move or what special things they find will delight their children. (Need for significant beings—"I matter"—*met*)
- *I am safe to feel.* In any move, and particularly cross-cultural, parents can be listeners and comforters—before they encourage too much! (Need for emotional beings—"feeling and expressing emotions"—*met*)
- *I am able to choose what I like.* Parents continue to ask "Which book shall we read tonight?" "Which plaster shall we use?" Children with no choice about the move can still make choices such as what color to paint the room or what to eat for supper tonight. (Need for volitional beings—"able to make meaningful choices"—*met*)

Worst-case scenario: With mobility (and the stress it causes everyone), children can look into that same anchor/mirror and see:

- *I don't matter. What I want doesn't matter.* Children try to say why they want to take a certain toy and parents brush them off. Forgetting it might be a true "sacred object," parents refuse to pack it or give them that extra moment they need to say good-bye to someone or some place. (Need for significant/ volitional beings—"I matter/I can choose"—*unmet*)
- *I am not supposed to cry.* Parents are often going through their own stress during a move and become impatient when children are sad for their own good-byes. This is when the "lack of permission" parts of dealing with grief and why it is unresolved often begin. (see chapter 5) (Need for emotional beings—"feeling and expressing emotions"—*unmet*)
- *I am not able to choose what I want.* Not only was the move unstoppable (if that was what the children preferred) but parents are often in "efficient" mode. They make the plans for going, for finding a house, for getting it ready for the kids, for what will and won't be taken. They forget to ask their children's opinions. (Need for volitional beings—"My choices matter"—*unmet*)
- *I am insignificant.* Culture shock or career demands often leave little time or energy to spare for the kids. The message for kids is pretty clear, "You really don't matter." Questions such as "Am I loved?" "Do I belong" "Do I matter as much as my parents' work or the local people here?" start to grow. (Need for significant/relational beings—"I matter/I'm known"—*unmet*)

But still, for most children, the nuclear family is a major stabilizing force amid the chaos of change of any move, including a cross-cultural move. Countless TCKs and ATCKs tell us that their families have been the place where they have felt grounded no matter where in the world they move. Once they are in the friendly confines of the family, they know they belong no matter how different everything else is outside. Chapter 9 clearly shows how that sense of belonging to family amid the chaos of change remains a key factor even in our Internet age. Chapters 13–16 contain many tips for how parents can keep the family unit strong even during the challenges of cross-cultural mobility.

Community

With a physical move, everyone in the local community (and the subsets thereof) changes overnight. If the move is within the same country/culture, it can be a highly stressful time as the family members try to establish new relationships. But still, when they shop, the same money works. In town, the same flag still flies and those in the different segments of this community speak the same language. They and their new community don't have to explain these parts of their cultural selves to one another

But in a cross-cultural move, it's not just individual relationships that have to be established. It's building a foundational place of understanding for how this community works or doesn't work compared to the previous place. Establishing new relationships also requires the community to understand something about the newcomer's past cultural context as well.

Best-case scenarios: With mobility, the children may look into the community anchor/mirror and see:

- *I am competent.* As children realize some of their old ways of forming relationships or taking local transportation aren't working, people in the community come alongside to help them understand how life works there. The child pays attention and starts to thrive. (Need for intellectual beings—"I can think and figure things out"—*met*)
- *I am more than I knew!* Since they don't have a history here, they aren't as locked in to how the old community may have defined them. Now they can volunteer for the play and no one says (or thinks) "You're not good at that" so they are given a chance and do well! (Need for integrated beings—"I am able to use all of who I am in this place"—*met*)
- *I am the same here as before in what I believe.* Moving to a place where different faiths or forms of spirituality exist can be part of the process of evaluating and stabilizing their core values and beliefs, which they keep no matter where they go. (Need for spiritual beings—"I can wonder and believe"—*met*)
- *I am not alone. I belong to a new group.* Some TCKs are surprised to find there is language for their experience. Moving into another country and meeting other TCKs may mean they discover for the first time that they do have a name and a tribe to which they belong. (Need for relational beings—"I belong"—*met*)

Worst-case scenarios: With mobility, the community anchor/mirror produces the following messages to children:

- *I am unknown.* Unlike a more traditional community, no one here knows their name. If they go out for a sport, the coach calls out "Hey, you!" They feel both invisible and anonymous. (Need for relational beings—"I am known in this place"—*unmet*) (Need for significant beings—"I am *me*. I am not interchangeable"—*unmet*)
- *I am alone.* Others don't understand them or the cultural context from which they have come, or seem interested in finding out. (Need for relational beings—I am understood—*unmet*)
- *I am a stranger here.* And they are. The feeling is often worst during reentry to a land where they presumed they belonged. Older first-time TCKs can also feel this. Their peers have lived this internationally mobile lifestyle for a lifetime but it is new to them. They do not identity with others as TCKs as the community expects. (Need for relational beings—"I belong"—*unmet*)

When someone is moving, and particularly between cultural worlds, the messages being reflected back by the community anchor/mirror can be vastly different in one place than another. These fluctuating judgments of who they are can leave many children wondering, *Am I this competent, choice-making self, or am I totally stupid and invisible in my community?* This is one reason why personal identity as well as cultural identity becomes a difficult thing to sort out for many TCKs.

Place

One great gift of a TCK childhood is the many places most have seen and where they have lived. Amazing memories relate to place in their stored memory banks—again, a strong anchor for many. In a wonderful book called *The Worlds Within*, an anthology of today's TCKs under the age of twenty-seven, nineteen-year-old Monica Nelson, who has lived in the United States and Cote d'Ivoire, shares a story of such a memory in her essay, "Mango Rains," where she begins telling of how hot and dry it was in her boarding school dorm in Africa. Suddenly she sees some clouds in the sky and runs to her friends.

> "What is it?" she asked, not daring to hope. "Rain?"
> "Mango Rains!" Stephanie answered.
> "Mango Rains? But it's dry season."
> All cruel words forgiven and forgotten, Michelle listened as Stephanie explained how every year, just when dry season seems too much to bear, God sends a week of rain to wake up the mango trees and tell his people that there is always hope. As the girls talked, the rains began to fall. It was a heavy African rain that beat down on the thin tin roofs, deafening but exhilarating the students.[6]

Those of you who have also experienced lying in bed in one of those first storms of rainy season in Africa and heard the sound of the rain on the tin roof most likely smiled, at least internally, as you read this. You felt Monica's joy and perhaps were transported back to a moment in your life where you felt that same "whatever that sense is" that goes with listening to such a sound. Yes, for some, rain on a tin roof IS the sound of home, for it takes the person back to those moments of childhood. How special to remember when it was a "deliciously scary" sound—all that noise, all the pouring rain outside, but being tucked safe in bed with Mommy and Daddy in the next room. What memories places make!

With moving, many intangibles from the previous place are lost. The next move has only clay roofs, no more tin roofs for nights such as this. These undefinable senses of being *at home* can't go along nor can they be easily revisited if they are an ocean away. So what identity messages does the anchor/mirror of place reflect back to the child after a move?

Best-case scenario: With mobility, children's messages about themselves may become:

- *I am adaptable.* Some who move have a high spirit of adventure and exploration. They love to take on the challenges of figuring out how to use the new transportation system, or learn basic words needed to read signs or greet people. (Need for integrated beings—"I can use who I was before in this place too"—*met*)
- *I can learn new things.* New places offer new opportunities to learn new skills. There is a tremendous sense of success and an *I can do* attitude that can be another positive awareness of who they are that carries through life. (Need for intellectual beings—"I can think and figure things out"—*met*)
- *I am interested.* Instead of viewing others in this place with fear or disdain because they dress or behave differently from themselves, many seek first to understand how these differences may relate to survival here as well as part of culture. (Need for relational beings—"I want to know others and be known"—*met*)

Worst-case scenario: With mobility, children's reflection from the place mirror may tell them:

- *I am stupid.* Everyone else can read the signs. Everyone else knew "rubber" didn't mean an eraser. How does everyone else find their way with no street signs? (Need for integrated beings—"I am able to use all of who I am in this place"—*unmet*)
- *I am homeless.* Not in terms of a physical shelter but in relationship to a permanent locale. This is where the feelings of being rootless and restless that we talk about in chapter 10 are born. (Need for relational/physical beings—"belonging and having a physical place for safety and rest"—*unmet*)

RELATIONAL IDENTITY ANCHORS AND MIRRORS AFTER MOVING

What happens to the interactions of these three basic anchor/mirror components after a move? Again, quoting Dr. Anastasia Lijadi and Gertina J. Van Schalkwyk, "The most exasperating experience in moving to a new place is to lose the sense of self and to lose touch with the people closest to us."[7] Dr Lijadi, who has studied this topic of TCKs and place as a major research project, adds this.

> "A high mobility lifestyle may result in insufficient time for TCK to learn the important intricacies and nuances of the local culture, such as behaviours, language, and social skills. The TCK are constantly exposed to problems of nostalgia, disorientation and alienation. Even though the high

mobility individuals flourish in a new country, their cogni-
zance and memory of home could be irrevocably altered,
contributing in different ways to their construction of place
identity. The TCK were longing for a safe, secure and, in
some cases, an idyllic place where they can be in a norm-
free context, free of the demands of having to adapt and
adjust to yet another place.[8]

How and why, then, does any change in these interactions affect the child's
sense of self and personal identity? What human needs are impacted in one way
or another during this time? Here are a few examples. Add more as they come to
your mind.

Family to Community

Best-case scenario: the family-to-community interactions offer back positive
reflections to children:

- *I am protected.* Parents walk them to school the first days to make sure they
  don't get lost. They make sure social opportunities are safe and get good
  references for anyone they hire for child care. (Need for physical beings—
  "having a physical place for safety"—*met*)
- *I am important.* When parents take such care, or perhaps find mentors
  for their children, the children know that they matter. If not, why would
  parents go to all of this trouble for them? (Need for significant beings—"I
  matter"—*met*)
- *I am not a victim.* Instead of complaining about having no friends in the
  community, parents proactively invite others over who have similar age children or just to learn more about the new community. Choices are made to
  change situations proactively rather than hoping they will magically change.
  (Need for volitional beings—"I am not powerless"—*met*)

Worst-case scenario: the family-to-community (and vice versa) interactions
may reflect back the following messages to children:

- *I am my parents' keeper.* Children can be thrust into a reverse role with parents. They learn the local language faster and become interpreters at school
  and in the community. The children become cultural interpreters for parents instead of vice versa. (Need for relational beings—"Parents will take
  care of me"—*unmet*)
- *I don't matter.* Parents may have no status in this new community at all. They
  are unknown. This can be a major change at reentry if parents had a position in their company or third culture community overseas before returning to live in a local community where they blend into the masses with no

particular status. (Need for relational/significant beings—"I belong/Who am I as *me*?"—***unmet***)

- *I am confused.* In this new world, parents who always guided their children as mentors for how life worked in their community no longer know the way themselves. Who can help lead the way now? (Needs for relational/integrated beings—"I am known and I know them/All of me works together here"—*unmet*)

- *I am better than others.* Sadly, in new cultures sometimes parents (perhaps in culture shock themselves) constantly berate the local people and how life works here. This can lead to true arrogance and false sense of self. The children also miss out on learning true cross-cultural competence and skills. (Need for relational beings—"I know who I am"—*unmet*)

Family to Place

In relationship to place, when the move is to a similar place, once the basics of how to get around are done, the family can still participate in the types of sports or cultural events they knew before. When, however, the family moves to a totally different place where climate, architecture, sports, language, are all different from before, how can they guide their children where they have not yet learned to function?

Best-case scenario: The family-to-place (and vice versa) interactions may reinforce the following messages to children about who they are:

- *I am capable of many things.* Despite the differences in place the family learns together the needed skills to function here, building on skill sets from before. This keeps life from being divided into disparate pieces. (Need for integrated beings—"I am not many selves but one person in a different place"—*met*)

- *I am part of something bigger than me.* Wise parents will help their children explore the history as well as the present realities of this place. As a good friend once said to Ruth, "We are the place in history where the past flows through to the future. If we ever forget that, we lose our sense of self." (Need for relational beings—"I belong"—*met*)

Worst-case scenario: The family-to-place (and vice versa) interactions may mirror back the following messages to children:

- *I am a victim.* When parents can only complain about this new place and everything is compared to the idealized place they came from, children learn to be passive "victims" rather than seeing where choices to change things might be helpful. (Need for volitional beings—"I can make choices that can significantly affect my life"—*unmet*)

- *I am stupid.* Local people have many skill sets that make life operational here. They know how to crack open a fresh coconut, peel (and eat!) the local durian, and get around on buses when all the signs are in another language. Parents coming from elsewhere are unable to teach children these basic things so it impacts the children too. (Need for intellectual beings—"I can think and figure things out"—*unmet*)

Community to Place

Every community has events or traditions that are specific to its locale—perhaps a great rivalry with a nearby soccer team or a particular type of coffee or food for which they pride themselves. How does being in the place of the anchor/mirror of these interactions between community and place shape a child's sense of self?

Best-case scenario:

- *I belong.* As the newcomers begin to learn which professional sports teams are lauded in this place, or what foods are favorites at local festivals, they jump in and try these new things. Soon they begin to feel a sense of belonging once more. *This is 'us' and I am part of it.* (Need for relational beings—"I belong"—*met*)
- *I am curious.* Watching how life is in this new place and how others interact with the opportunities this climate or topography offer can spark a sense of interest and adventure rather than pulling back. (Need for emotional beings—"I can have joy!"—*met*)

Worst-case scenario:

- *I am alone.* Activities of the community are guided in large measure by the place. Children who grew up in Togo may not easily participate in social events in Kazakstan centered around skating and skiing. (Need for relational beings—"I am included"—*unmet*)
- *I am an outsider.* Local foods fill the markets where the community shops, but the foods familiar to the child's sense of home and comfort are gone. Many local foods are unrecognizable or inedible to the child. (Need for relational beings—"I belong"—*unmet*)

Bottom line, it's not hard to see why cross-cultural mobility affects a sense of personal identity. When anchors and mirrors are constantly changing and the dynamics of life are in flux, it is harder to keep a steady definition answering the question, "Who am I?"

And what about when the moves are multiple and frequent? How many times do the anchors and mirrors change for some TCKs and other CCKs? Barb drew a couple of other models to help us get the sense visually for how it often feels inside for the child.

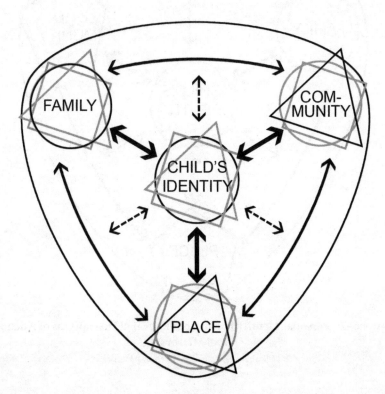

Figure 6–6: Identity Formation: Second Disruption of Anchors and Mirrors
©2017 Barbara H. Knuckles. Used by permission.

With the next move, the process we have just described starts all over again. But now there are triangles instead of only squares and circles. How different is this culture from the one they just left? Or the one they lived in before? The family and child are still primarily circles but they are also changing. Who will they become? Figure 6-6 represents that second move. The layering of messages from anchors and mirrors is increasing.

As we said in chapter 5, the issue for TCKs and other CCKs is that often their cycles of mobility are repetitive and ongoing. In the TCK world of yesteryear, many TCKs like Ruth only went between two countries. For her, it was Nigeria and the United States. In today's world, the number of cultures and countries children live in is growing, sometimes seemingly exponentially (see figure 6-7).

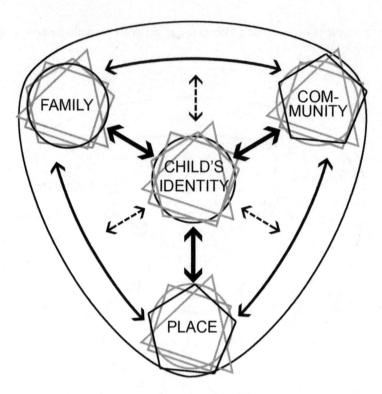

Figure 6–7: Personal Identity Formation: Repeated Disruptions of Anchors and Mirrors

©2017 Barbara H. Knuckles. Used by permission.

Halima knows about multiple moves. Here is her story, used with permission as she wrote it.

> My name is Halima. I'm thirty-six years old and I was born in U.S. and also lived in Gabon and Venezuela. My passport country is Nigeria and I have been living there for twenty-eight years now. However, I still feel disconnected. I feel like I just arrived yesterday! I arrived [in] Nigeria when I was nine years old. Went back to U.S. for a while and came back again.
>
> As a kid it was so easy to blend in with the folks and just play and be kids. But at age nineteen I started feeling restless and confused, asking myself "who am I really?"
>
> And I remember all I wanted to do was leave and head back to the States. Connecting with friends I grew up with here was gradually becoming difficult as I was realizing parts of myself I never knew I was.

> I became alienated and had to often "switch modes" (switch to Hausa mode! Hausa is the language spoken in the northern part of Nigeria). And then I lost myself! Constantly "switching modes" left me with some sort of split personality. I sometimes mistakenly speak with an American accent to folks and end up with blank stares! But years of therapy helped me get back in touch with my true authentic self, build my self-esteem, and live with much love and gratitude for my TCK experience and identity.
>
> It's still hard sometimes, dealing with the "where do I feel I am from?" question, and the itchy feet as well as never being able to fully integrate or blend in with the folks around. Being a hidden immigrant when everyone around assumes you are "one of us."
>
> That is the greatest challenge I face presently. So I am planning to move to Spain as soon as I can. I've been feeling more *Spanish* lately!

Notice what is beginning to happen to the child's circle as the circles, squares, triangles, and pentagons all begin to layer on one another in figure 6-7. Even though different shapes are on top in the community and place anchor/mirrors, behind them lie the messages from the previous anchors and mirrors likely embedded in the child underneath the one he or she is dealing with in the present. Parents may remain as steady mirrors, but by now the various relationships with community and place in different moves are shaping them within as well. Right now, the child is no longer exactly like any of the other shapes.

In the end, figure 6-8 may look extreme, but for TCKs or those who have made multiple cross-cultural forays, this is pretty well their experience. This illustration gives a visual feel for a child's potential inner state after high mobility among different cultures. Such a life creates a childhood filled with anchors and mirrors that are frequently changing and all potentially reflecting different messages about who that child is. It's not hard to understand why the "normal" TCK questions of "Who am I?" "Where is home?" "Where do I belong?" are real.

But, most interestingly, while for some TCKs it feels infinitely chaotic, others find ways to use this high degree of cross-cultural mobility. Doni knows this type of mobility well. Think about her anchors and mirrors as you read her story here (and more of it in chapters 12 and 19).

> As an ATCK who identified with seven cultures on five continents before adulthood, it's come to my attention that I pretty much raised myself. Not entirely, but very much so in terms of garnering social cues from immediate family and static culture from community. My life was THAT full of mobility from place, to people, to family, and more.

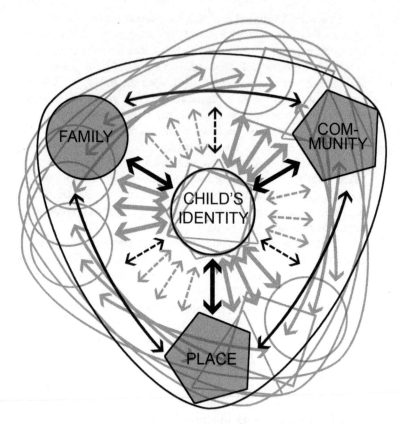

Figure 6–8: Identity Formation Model in Relationship to Multiple Shifting Anchors and Mirrors

©2017 Barbara H. Knuckles. Used by permission.

It created an identity that indeed is culturally complex. What you see is not what you get when you look at my outward appearances (accent, skin color, dress, etc.). I can almost guarantee when others think they can guess what I'm thinking—because of my *extreme* mobility—they miss the mark. Why? Because my thinking, value system, way of being, and how I present myself is a complex web of where I've been, ideas to which I've been exposed, and the myriad cast of characters with whom I spent time. Sounds simple—that's the same formula for everyone. The difference is the levels and layers of mobility I experienced while growing up led to a shifting foundation that taught me how to effectively straddle culture—but truly left few cues for those around me to accurately assess who I am beyond what they see on the outside.

Growing up, I felt confident and comfortable in my ability to straddle culture—THAT was my identity. It made me understand different people, places, underlying communication cues and provided me with the ability to translate meaning between and among others. I'm not sure that I knew there were parts "missing" from my upbringing, but that didn't matter—because I felt at "home" in all the places in which I'd grown up because I created a firm foundation for myself wherever I landed.[9]

In chapter 19 you can read when and why Doni did have a bit of an identity crisis along the way, but hers is also a great story for how TCKs can use repeated cross-cultural mobility to great advantage. Notice, however, in the first paragraph, her anchor/mirrors changed so frequently she felt she was, in essence, left to raise herself. And, yes, with her personality or for whatever other reasons, Doni is one who took on the potential chaos of so much mobility and has harnessed it for use in her many roles in life including TV personality, writer, *Culturs* magazine founder and CEO. She is on the faculty at Colorado State University, Department of Journalism and Media Communications, and is director of marketing at the Lory Student Center there.

Barbara Schaetti, Ph.D., is another wonderful example of someone who had to work through the ramifications of excessive mobility across cultures during childhood but, in the end, has and is using it well as head of Transition Dynamics, intercultural trainer, and so much more. In her article "Phoenix Rising," she summarizes some of her findings from the first Ph.D. dissertation on global nomads/TCKs and identity and tells her story.

Though I was raised to consider myself American, my core identity was formed by peoples and places, sights and sounds and smells, from all over the world. My father is Swiss by birth, my mother American; both were born in India. I was born in the U.S. but left at the age of fourteen months. I lived in ten countries on five continents by age eighteen and moved internationally twelve times by age twenty-two. I first attended schools in the French system and then the British and finished my secondary education in international schools. We used words of Urdu, Tamil, Swiss, and Arabic in our family's private language. We were evacuated out of Algeria during the war of independence from the French. I celebrated Guy Fawkes day when we lived in

> England; was given the full series of rabies shots when we
> lived in Morocco; participated in the naming ceremony for
> my batik teacher's son when we lived in Singapore.[10]

You can see she knows about multiple mobility cycles with changing anchors and mirrors all around her! Barbara goes on to talk about how terrible her initial reentries were to the United States and how she felt what Janet Bennett, CEO of Summer Institute of Intercultural Communications, calls "terminal uniqueness"—that sense we referred to earlier where individuals feel they are so different that there is no one else in the entire world who can understand them. But as Barbara grew in her understanding of culture and what it meant to be a "cultural marginal" in constructive ways, things began to change for her.

> Cultural marginality is in and of itself neither bad nor good
> although the experience has the potential to be both. It is
> characterized by the potential for, on the one hand, feeling
> at home nowhere and, on the other hand, feeling at home
> everywhere. Whether our cultural marginality hinders us
> or helps us depends on what we do with it. We can allow
> ourselves to become "encapsulated," trapped by it, or can
> learn to use it "constructively," as a strategic advantage. . . .
> *We owe it to ourselves and to one another to encourage the*
> *constructive experience of cultural marginality. There is so*
> *much power, so much to celebrate in the positive expression*
> *of the global nomad experience!* (italics ours)[11]

Over and over this message of hope is clear for TCKs, ATCKs, CCKs, ACCKs, and all other human beings. Often the first thing needed to move from a sense of terminal uniqueness or encapsulated marginality is understanding the reason for the common responses and reactions a globally mobile childhood can bring. Hopefully, part I has offered that understanding.

After understanding, it's important to remember what the Ugly Duckling did: He had to relook at the messages he had internalized about himself and see what was true or not. How can TCKs/ATCKs do that? One way is to begin with the basics of likeness and see what shame messages might be coming from simply being a human in the way Ruth discovered at the beginning of this chapter. Then it's easier to see how some of those core characteristics or needs are expressed in the uniqueness that has also been shaped by, and lived out in, the various surrounding cultures experienced (figure 6-9).

How does this work in helping us discover more about ourselves? First, we can start to listen more closely to our *self-talk* and see what we say about ourselves—particularly when we have a surprising reaction to somebody or some event. What are the messages we hear? Things like "I am a social misfit"? Or

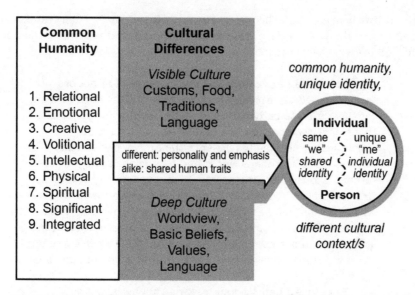

Figure 6–9: Identity Formation Likeness and Uniqueness Shaped by and Expressed in Culture

©2017 Barbara H. Knuckles. Used by permission.

"I am so dumb"? Or "I never get to do what I want"? Or "I will never belong anywhere"? Second, we must assess whether or not that internalized message is true in light of who we know for sure we are as persons. Then, we must decide, as did the Ugly Duckling, what messages are true and which ones are not. In other words, if we are relational beings at our core but feeling like no one wants to relate to us, might we consider that perhaps it's not really all about us? Maybe it's simply a matter that we just don't know yet how life operates here. Since we are intellectual beings and can think, then we should remember that stupidity is different from ignorance. We may not yet know about this thing, but we can learn. If we are volitional beings, then what is the choice we can make even within the context of this feeling of despair? Again, since we are relational beings, it's no shame to need a place of belonging nor to look for a community that reflects who we are and where we know we belong. It's what we need. In another part of her article "Phoenix Rising," Barbara Schaetti talks about the importance of giving children language for their experience, such as *global nomad*, *cross-cultural kid*, or *third culture kids*. It prevents a sense of terminal uniqueness and allows the richness of the story to grow as well.

Of course, we must remember that often our self-talk is invisible because we have assumed it as such a part of our identity that we don't recognize it. This happened to Ruth when she first made the personhood list. She got as far as "We are creative beings . . ." and her mind stopped. "H-m-m-m . . . I don't think that counts! I've always known I was out of line when the creative gifts were passed out." Here's what happened next:

> My whole life I have accepted the message "I'm not cre-
> ative." Why? My anchors/mirrors took the artwork in front
> of them and, to be honest, they were right when reflecting
> back "not so good." No one had to say it, but I could see it
> for myself when the teacher put the artwork of the day
> on the walls and there was mine . . . stick drawings where
> others had real-looking people. When we had to carve soap
> into figures, I had lots of pieces of soap in my hand while
> those around me had dogs, or houses, or something quite
> recognizable they had made. It was so shameful and often
> my grade in art kept me off the honor roll. I wasn't wrong
> to say I didn't have much artistic skill in anything physical
> or visual.
>
> But since I had started making this list about the
> likeness all people share, when I wrote, "We are creative
> beings," and the internal response was to deny that fact for
> myself, I decided I needed to stop. If I was human, I must
> create somehow. If that was so, where did I create?
>
> Then it hit me. I love ideas! And I love trying to put
> them together and create something new I haven't seen
> before. My mind often feels like a big internal jigsaw puzzle,
> always trying to find the next place where a new piece
> might attach. It felt almost silly to realize I hadn't thought
> about mental creativity before because I had predefined the
> word to mean only physical creativity. But starting with
> likeness, I saw the lie that I had accepted about myself—that
> I was not creative. And then I discovered the truth of how,
> in my uniqueness, I do create! I wasn't wrong that I couldn't
> draw—I couldn't. But I was wrong that I wasn't creative.
> Those were two different things.

The point of this story is in identifying likeness, Ruth could consider how that likeness was expressed in her uniqueness. It's important to know who we are rather than trying to be who we are not!

After all of this discussion about anchors, mirrors, and identity, what's the bottom-line point? The fact is that cross-cultural mobility during childhood does add extra strains and stresses for a child trying to figure out personal as well as cultural identity. The more stability TCKs can be given in any or all of the anchor/mirrors, the more opportunity they will have to catch a more accurate reflection of their likeness and uniqueness. But when the anchors and mirrors do shift, as they will, this is for sure:

- By starting with baseline likeness, there is a fundamental, fall back place of belonging. No TCK—or anyone—can be "terminally unique" despite claims to the contrary.
- By knowing the fundamental needs all people have, TCK, ATCKs, and those who care for them will have a clearer vision to understand *why* the tips and strategies for how to help in parts III and IV of this book are important. They are essentially ways to help meet these basic needs every person has.
- Remember all suggestions are just suggestions—ideas to be applied in a living, flexible way, not as rules—giving space for the uniqueness of each person in each family to thrive.
- By combining likeness and uniqueness, TCKs can affirm their place in the human experience with all others while celebrating the particular and life-shaping experiences their lives as TCKs has given them.

While you read The TCK Profile in part II and see the common responses many TCKs have, consider how various aspects of personhood are reflected in these benefits and challenges. You might be surprised!

Expanding our Vision

Personhood is everyone's story—not just a TCK's. For all who read, no matter your story, likely there are places in your lives that the anchors didn't hold steady and the mirrors weren't accurately reflecting who you are. For other CCKs and ACCKs, consider how and when your anchors and mirrors changed and who/what replaced them. What messages have you internalized from your story and the mirrors around you? Consider which ones are true and why, and then which ones are not. What are your particular areas of strengths and weaknesses as well? Knowing yourself in both is helpful and healthy! And for all who read this, as you process how these things apply to you, may you find at least one little nugget of gold about yourself you weren't aware of before!

Questions for Chapter 6

1. This chapter lists some shared human characteristics. Can you think of other universal dimensions of being human?
2. Make your own list of any additional needs you see coming from the characteristics of being human listed or from the other things you listed earlier.

3. When you consider your childhood, what reflections about yourself did you receive from family, community, and "systems" that were affirming? Which reflections felt discouraging?
4. Have you been able to replace any negative messages you internalized (such as Ruth's "I am too emotional" or "I'm not creative") with new reflections? Please explain how that happened.
5. What are some specific ways you see the intertwining of culture and mobility shaping you or those you know who have grown up as TCKs or other CCKs who also had mobility as part of their story?

Part II

Describing the TCK Profile

In part I we focused primarily on defining third culture kids and explaining their world. Now we want to look in depth at the specific benefits and challenges of this experience. Some benefits and challenges are seen most clearly in the shorter term; some become more obvious with time.

Then we will examine the character traits this lifestyle fosters along with how it affects interpersonal relationships and developmental patterns. While we most often use the term TCK alone for simplicity's sake, these are characteristics that often become even more visible in adulthood for ATCKs. Because this is a group profile, not every characteristic will fit every person. But the "Aha!" moment of recognition, which we have seen among countless TCKs and ATCKs, tells us these characteristics are valid as an overall representation of their world. For CCKs who may not also be TCKs, read along and see what you can apply to your story as well.

CHAPTER 7

Benefits and Challenges

Besides the drawbacks of family separation and the very real adjustment on the permanent return to the [home country], a child growing up abroad has great advantages. He [or she] learns, through no conscious act of learning, that thoughts can be transmitted in many languages, that skin color is unimportant . . . that certain things are sacred or taboo to some people while to others they're meaningless, that the ordinary word of one area is a swearword in another.

We have lived in Tulsa for five years. I am struck again and again by the fact that so much of the sociology, feeling for history, geography, questions [about] others that our friends' children try to understand through textbooks, my sisters and I acquired just by living.[1]

—Rachel Miller Schaetti

Introduction: The TCK Profile

The often paradoxical benefits and challenges of the TCK Profile are sometimes described as being like opposite sides of the same coin, but in reality they are more like the contrasting colored strands of thread woven together into a tapestry. As each strand crosses with a contrasting or complementary color, a picture begins to emerge, but no one strand alone tells the full story. For example, the high mobility of a TCK's life often results in special relationships with people throughout the world, but it also creates sadness at the chronic loss of these relationships. That very pain, however, provides the opportunity to develop a greater empathy for others. A TCK's expansive worldview, which enriches history classes and gives perspective to the nightly news, also makes the horror of the slaughter of Syrian citizens in Aleppo a painful reality. That same awareness can be what motivates a TCK's concern for solving those kinds of tragic problems. And so it goes.

Some of the characteristics—as well as the benefits and challenges—are primarily a result of the cross-cultural nature of the third culture experience. Others are more directly shaped by the high mobility of the lifestyle. Most of the profile, however, is this weaving together of these two dominant realities.

We begin by discussing some of the most common general benefits and challenges we have seen among TCKs and ATCKs, but before we do, let us make it clear once more that when we use the word *challenge*, we purposefully do not imply the word *liability*. A challenge is something people have the choice to face, deal with, and grow from. A liability can only be something that pulls someone down. Some may say we concentrate too much on the challenges, but if that criticism is valid, it is for a reason. We have seen the benefits of this experience enrich countless TCKs' lives, whether or not they stop to consciously define or use them. Many have also found unconscious ways to deal with the challenges and make them a productive aspect of their lives in one way or another. We have also seen, however, that for some TCKs (and those around them) the unrecognized challenges have caused years of frustration as they struggle to deal with matters that have no name, no definition. In the process, a few have lost sight of the benefits they have also received. It is our hope that in naming both the benefits and challenges, and then offering suggestions in parts III and IV on how to build intentionally on the strengths and deal productively with the challenges, many more TCKs will be able to maximize the great gifts that can come from their lives and live out with joy the richness of their heritage.

EXPANDED WORLDVIEW VERSUS CONFUSED LOYALTIES

Benefit: Expanded Worldview

An obvious benefit of the TCK experience is that while growing up in a multiplicity of countries and cultures, TCKs not only observe firsthand the many geographical differences around the world, but also learn how people view life from different philosophical and political perspectives. Some people thought of Osama bin Laden as a hero; others believed he was a villain. Western culture is time- and task-oriented; in Eastern culture, interpersonal relationships are of greater importance. The TCK's awareness that there can be more than one way to look at the same thing starts early in life. We listened to these rather remarkable stories during a meeting in Malaysia with TCKs ages five to twelve who were all growing up in Asia.

> "You know, last year we had to hide on the floor for four days because of typhoons."

"We couldn't go out of our house for a week when everybody in town started fighting."

"On our vacation last month we got to ride on the backs of elephants and go look for tigers."

"Well, so did we!" countered another seven-year-old from across the room. "We saw six tigers. How many did you see?"

Eventually New Year's Day came up as part of a story. Ruth thought she was asking a simple question: "When is New Year's Day?" Instead of the simple "January 1" that she expected, many different dates were given—each young TCK trying to defend how and when it was celebrated in his or her host country. Ruth knew that if she had asked most traditional groups of five- to twelve-year-olds in the United States about New Year's Day, this discussion wouldn't be occurring. Most of them probably would have no idea that New Year's Day could be dates other than January 1.

This awareness that New Year's Day can be celebrated in different ways and on different dates according to where in the world it is happening may seem like a small detail. Already, however, these children were learning how big and interesting the world they live in is and how much there will be to discover about it all through life. Many readers may not know that Henry Robinson Luce was an ATCK born and raised in China until he first set foot in the United States at age fifteen. He founded *Time* magazine in 1923 and *Life* magazine in 1936. He couldn't find enough international news in local publications, so he decided to fix the problem by starting these publications.[2] Interestingly, many of today's commentators in print and on cable news channels are also TCKs or other versions of CCKs with global childhoods. Fareed Zakaria, born in India, spent time as a foreign student, and ultimately immigrated to the United States. He has become an award-winning author and commentator on international relationships and policies. In a column he wrote for *Newsweek*, Zakaria states:

I've spent my life acquiring formal expertise on foreign policy. I've got fancy degrees, have run research projects, taught in colleges and graduate schools (see p139) I couldn't do my job without the expertise . . . [but] my biography [of living my formative years in countries outside my own] has helped me put my book learning in context, made for a richer interaction with foreigners and helped me see the world from many angles.[3]

Zakaria goes on to talk about the need to develop deeper understandings of countries other than your own and concludes by saying, "There are many ways to attain this, but certainly being able to feel it in your bones is one powerful way."[4]

Challenge: Confused Loyalties

Although their expanded worldview is a great benefit, it can also leave TCKs with a sense of confusion about all sorts of things. Most TCKs know the pull of watching the flags come in during the Olympics and wondering which country's team to cheer for—the one from the country they knew best as a child, or the one their passport says is their own. ATCK Benedetta Agnoli confesses, "The soccer world cup is always a nightmare." Why? Because she is Italian but born in Brazil!

But while feeling conflicted on team loyalties in sports is real, divided loyalties for TCKs and ATCKs often include such complex things as politics, patriotism, and values. Should they support the policies of their home country when those policies are detrimental to their host country? Or should they support the host country even if it means opposing policies of their own government? What about when they are around friends who are bad-mouthing their other country? Maya Butovskaya is one who often finds herself torn between her two worlds, Russia and the United States. She moved to the United States when she was sixteen and has lived between the two worlds since then. These are her thoughts on how her loyalties can be swayed in any given moment, time, or place:

> The two countries I consider my home [Russia and the United States] have always had opposing camps. Culturally and politically they sometimes feel like two different planets, which makes the culture shock when visiting one and coming back to the other that much more severe. When a friend shares their criticism of the political situation in Russia or a social or cultural aspect, I may agree with the criticism completely, but I still feel offended. And it goes both ways. When thinking of a negative political move in the U.S., it's also the same country that gave me amazing education and all the work experience and lifelong friends. When criticizing a social aspect in Russia, it's also the country where I grew up, [the] country with all my childhood memories and [the country with] very kind people who may not smile at a stranger but will help a stranger in time of need. My divided loyalty is rooted in feeling tied to both countries by deep life experiences that are hard to separate from specific instances.
>
> The other side of the divided loyalty coin is divided indifference. The feeling of "Why should I care, this is not really my culture," the darker side of not belonging to any culture fully. The feeling that I have many homes usually prevails and it's a positive one, but the indifference sometimes creeps up when feeling particularly torn. It's a difference between "Why can't you get along already; you are

both my homes" and "Okay, you may never get along and I can't relate to either anymore."[5]

This idea of indifference that Maya writes about makes sense but is not one we had considered before. Certainly the matter of divided loyalties is another type of experience many TCKs share despite the particulars of their story. Maya concludes with these thoughts:

> Boy, was I glad to find the TCK group and literature about it because it was a relief to read people's stories that are similar to mine. The setup is always different—I've read stories where someone moved [to] six or seven different countries— and while I only have two, the struggles are very similar.[6]

In *Homesick: My Own Story,* award-winning author Jean Fritz—a TCK before anyone knew there was language for such an experience—writes of her experiences as an American child in China during the 1920s. She attended a British school in China but defiantly refused to sing "God Save the King" because it wasn't *her* national anthem. She was an American, although she had never spent a day in the United States in her life. Throughout the growing turmoil that led to the revolution in 1927, Jean dreamed of her grandmother's farm and garden in Pennsylvania, fantasizing over and over about what it would be like to live and go to school in America. Finally, after what seemed like an endless boat ride and many struggles, Jean arrived at that long-awaited first day in an American school. Here's what happened.

> "The class will come to order," she [Miss Crofts, the teacher] said. "I will call the roll." When she came to my name, Miss Crofts looked up from her book. "Jean Guttery is new to our school," she said. "She has come all the way from China where she lived beside the Yangs-Ta-Zee River. Isn't that right, Jean?"
>
> "It's pronounced Yang-see," I corrected. "There are just two syllables."
>
> Miss Crofts looked at me coldly. "In America," she said, "we say Yangs-Ta-Zee."
>
> I was working myself up, madder by the minute, when I heard Andrew Carr, the boy behind me, shifting his feet on the floor. I guess he must have hunched across his desk, because all at once I heard him whisper over my shoulder:
>
> "Chink, Chink, Chinaman
> Sitting on a fence,
> Trying to make a dollar
> Out of fifteen cents."

> I forgot all about where I was. I jumped to my feet,
> whirled around, and spoke out loud as if there were no
> Miss Crofts, as if I'd never been in a classroom before, as
> if I knew nothing about classroom behavior. "You don't call
> them Chinamen or Chinks," I cried. "You call them Chinese.
> Even in America you call them Chinese."
>
> "Well, you don't need to get excited Jean," she [Miss
> Crofts] said. "We all know that you are American."
>
> "But that's not the point!" Before I could explain that it
> was an insult to call Chinese people Chinamen, Miss Crofts
> had tapped her desk with a ruler.
>
> "That will be enough," she said. "All eyes front."[7]

Which country had Jean's greatest loyalty and devotion—the United States or China? Did she know? All her life she had thought of herself as American, yet now here she was defending the Chinese. Certainly Miss Crofts and Jean's classmates couldn't understand why she would want to defend a people and a country halfway around the world from them—particularly at the expense of getting along with people from her own country. Because Jean physically looked like her classmates at that point, those around her had no vision for the fact that Jean had not spent her life studying about the Chinese culture and people but that, throughout her life, people from that world had been her playmates and friends.

While Jean Fritz may have been an early TCK who was misunderstood in her passport country for her past global experiences, it still happens in today's world. Paisley Callow, who calls herself a United States foreign service brat, recounts:

> I moved from Okinawa to the U.S. at age seven. My second-
> grade class was studying World War II and kids called me
> "the Evil Japanese Axis." Everyone avoided me until a U.S.
> Army brat moved from Germany. We became friends and
> giggled about how ignorant our classmates were.[8]

Fortunately for Paisley, the shame of being named in such a negative way turned into understanding when she met someone else who shared her experience, and together they could affirm their stories rather than receive the condemnation and shame.

Perhaps more difficult than the questions of political or patriotic loyalties, however, are the value dissonances that occur in the cross-cultural experience because TCKs often live among cultures with strongly conflicting value systems. One culture says female circumcision is wrong. Another says female circumcision is the most significant moment in a girl's life; it is when she knows she has become an accepted member of her tribe. One culture says abortion is wrong; another says it is all right for specific reasons up to certain points in the pregnancy. Still other cultures practice abortion based on the gender of the baby: males are wanted; females are not as desirable.

This expanded worldview and its resulting confusion of loyalties and values can be a greater problem for those who return to cultures that remain relatively homogeneous. In a study of Turkish TCKs during his master's degree program, Steve Eisinger discovered that "the statistics regarding public opinion . . . indicate that this expanded worldview may not be necessarily viewed as a positive characteristic."[9] Japanese researcher Momo Kano Podolsky describes how Japanese TCKs, or *kikoku-shijo*, were originally looked down on in the early days of their returning to Japan. While that opinion has now been reversed in Japan, the new ideas that the TCKs bring back, and their refusal to follow unthinkingly the cultural patterns of preceding generations, can sometimes make them unwelcome citizens in their own countries—whatever that country and culture might be.[10]

THREE-DIMENSIONAL VIEW OF THE WORLD VERSUS PAINFUL VIEW OF REALITY

Benefit: Three-Dimensional View of the World

As TCKs live in various cultures, they not only learn about cultural differences, but they also experience the world in a tangible way that is impossible to do by reading books, seeing movies, or watching nightly newscasts alone. It is because they have lived in so many places, smelled so many smells, heard so many strange sounds, and been in so many strange situations throughout their lives that when they read a story in the newspaper or watch it on TV, the flat, odorless images they see or the words they read magically transform into an internal 3-D panoramic picture show. It's almost as if they were there in person—smelling the smells, tasting the tastes, perspiring with the heat. They may not be present at the event, but they have a clear awareness of what is going on and what it is like for those who are there.

> Each summer Dave Pollock led transition seminars for TCKs. During one of these, he asked the attendees, "What comes to your mind if I say the word *riot*?" The answers came back: "Paris." "Korea." "Iran." "Ecuador."
> Next question. "Any details?"
> More answers: "Broken windows." "Water cannons." "Burned buses." "Tear gas, mobs." "Burning tires." (Burning tires. Who would think about burning tires except somebody who had smelled that stench?) "Tacks."

Anyone might think of guns in a riot, but why tacks? Because this TCK had seen tacks spread on the streets of Ecuador to flatten tires, so people couldn't travel during a riot. It makes sense, but probably only someone who had seen it would name it.

Having a 3-D view of the world is a useful skill not only for reading stories but for writing them. For TCKs who like to write, their culturally rich and highly mobile childhoods give them a true breadth of hands-on experiences in many places to add life to their work. Pearl S. Buck and John Hersey were among the first ATCKs who recorded in words the world they had known as children growing up in China. In a feature article for *Time* called "The Empire Writes Back," Pico Iyer gives an account of an entirely new genre of award-winning authors, all of whom have cross-cultural backgrounds.

> Authors from Britain's former colonies have begun to capture the very heart of English literature, transforming the canon with bright colors and strange cadences and foreign eyes. They are revolutionizing the language from within. Hot spices are entering English, and tropical birds . . . magical creations from the makers of a new World Fiction.[11]

Iyer goes on to describe the great diversity of each writer's background and then states,

> But the new transcultural writers are something different. For one, they are the products not so much of colonial division as of the international culture that has grown up since the war, and they are addressing an audience as mixed up and eclectic and uprooted as themselves.[12]

Without ever using, or perhaps even knowing in those early days, the term *third culture kids*, Iyer has conveyed vividly the richness of their experience. In the last few years, the ranks of TCK authors has swelled. Beside Pico Iyer and his book *The Global Soul*, the list now includes such best-selling authors as Khaled Hosseini (*The Kite Runner* and *A Thousand Splendid Suns*); William Paul Young (*The Shack* and *Eve*); Ted Dekker (*A.D. 33* and fifty-one other titles); and the many books of Isabel Allende, including *My Invented Country*.

Another growing genre where the TCK/CCK story rings out is in the film industry. The book *The Namesake*, by Jhumpa Lahiri, became a major movie. Lahiri was born in England to parents from India, and was later raised in the United States after her parents immigrated there. Throughout her childhood, there were frequent trips back to India as her parents tried to keep her attached to her roots. Her writing and movie clearly depict the tension of young people and families trying to keep the ways of the old country in the world while living in the new.

Challenge: Painful Awareness of Reality

With this three-dimensional view of the world, however, comes the painful reality that behind the stories in the news are real flesh-and-blood people—not merely flat faces on a TV screen. When an airplane crashes in India or a tsunami rips the coasts of Thailand, TCKs find it appalling that their local evening newscasters seem to focus mainly on how many citizens of their particular country died—almost as if the other lives lost didn't matter. As they watch an empty-eyed woman and desperate man search vainly for their child amid the rubble of an earthquake in China, ATCKs know the couple's loss is as painful as their own would be if they were in that situation. Many of them know that when bombs drop on Syria or a bomb goes off at the Boston Marathon, or terrorists attack a Nairobi shopping mall, people scream with fear and horror there just as they did on March 22, 2016, at the airport in Brussels.

Many TCKs have seen war or faced the pain of evacuation and its disruption. For some it has happened in their host cultures. In others, it has happened in their passport culture. Either way, with this global lifestyle, they are often an ocean or mountain range away from their families at times of great political and social upheaval or even natural disasters. A special hardship is that others around them may have no idea why a war or an earthquake drifting by on the scrolling news line on CNN makes such a difference to this TCK or ATCK.

> As a child, Samar grew up as a Lebanese citizen living in Liberia and attended a U.S.-based international school. Her father had a thriving business until the civil war in Liberia began. After her family fled back to Lebanon, more civil unrest hit that land and they then emigrated to France. In time, Samar and her family returned to Lebanon and lived amid the continuing tensions there. Eventually, Samar married her Lebanese sweetheart, Khaled, and they moved to the United States while Khaled finished a medical residency program. Samar made friends with local citizens as she pushed her new baby's stroller while walking with other young moms in the park. Within these social interactions, they all appeared to be living similar lifestyles.
>
> Then the unrest in Lebanon flared up once more. While the other moms continued talking about the color of their kitchen curtains and making playdates for their children, Samar suddenly lost interest in such discussions. Her life became centered on CNN and MSNBC, trying to figure out from the on-screen images how close the fighting was to her parents' home. Every thunderstorm made her want to hide, because it reminded her of the sounds of war in both Liberia and Lebanon. She found herself resenting her newfound friends for their seeming lack of interest in not only her family, but in all those others who suffered because governments had chosen to wage their wars where real people like her and her family lived.

This can be one of the loneliest times of all for those who grow up and live cross-culturally—when the reality of our grief is overwhelmingly real to us yet incomprehensible to those now around us who never knew us as we were before and have no personal ties to the country we called "home" or to which we at least feel very attached. This is where unresolved grief can begin to fester because these very real losses are totally unseen by others.

CROSS-CULTURAL ENRICHMENT VERSUS IGNORANCE OF THE HOME CULTURE

Benefit: Cross-Cultural Enrichment

TCKs and ATCKs usually have a sense of ownership and interest in cultures other than just that of their passport country. They set their Internet home pages to receive news from the places they've lived. They enjoy aspects of the host culture others might not appreciate. While the smell of the Southeast Asian fruit durian would precipitate a gag reflex in most of us, TCKs who grew up in Malaysia may inhale the scent with glee—it is the smell of home. Those who grew up in India use *chapatis* to pick up the hottest curry sauce. Still other TCKs and ATCKs sit cross-legged on the floor whenever they have a choice between that and a lounge chair. They consider these aspects of their lifestyle part of the wealth of their heritage.

Perhaps more important than what they have learned to enjoy from the more surface layers of other cultures, however, is the fact that most TCKs have also gained valuable lessons from the deeper levels. They have lived in other places long enough to learn to appreciate the reasons and understanding behind some of the behavioral differences rather than simply being frustrated by them as visitors tend to be. For example, while a tourist might feel irritated that the stores close for two hours in the middle of the day just when he or she wants to go shopping, most TCKs can understand that this custom not only helps people survive better if the climate is extremely hot, but it's a time when parents greet the children as they return from school and spend time together as a family. Many TCKs learn to value relationships above convenience as they live in such places, and it is a gift they carry with them wherever they may go later.

Challenge: Ignorance of Home Culture

The irony of collecting cross-cultural practices and skills, however, is that TCKs may know all sorts of fascinating things about other countries but little about their own.

> Tamara attended school in England for the first time when she was ten. Until then she had attended a small American-oriented school in Africa. In early November, she asked her mother, "Mom, who is this Guy Fawkes everybody's talking about?"
>
> Tamara's mom, Elizabeth, a born and bred English-woman, tried to hide her shock at her daughter's ignorance. Tamara seemed so knowledgeable about countless global

matters—how could she not know a simple fact about a
major figure in British history? And particularly one whose
wicked deed of trying to blow up the Parliament was decried
each year as people throughout the country burned him in
effigy? Elizabeth hadn't realized that while Tamara had
seen the world, she had missed learning about this common
tradition in her own country.

TCKs are often sadly ignorant of national, local, and even family history.
How many rides to various relatives' homes are filled with parents coaching
TCKs about who is related to whom? Many kids simply haven't been around the
normal chatter that keeps family members connected.

One major advantage TCKs have in today's world of the Internet—with
email, Facetime, Skype, blogs, Facebook, YouTube, and more—compared to
previous generations of TCKs is a better means of keeping up with pop culture,
including current movie stars, politicians, musicians, and other public figures,
as well as fads and trends. Many older ATCKs remember all too well the reactions from their peers to an innocent question such as, "Who's Elvis?" when they
reentered their passport culture after being away for years! Such questions could
lock them forever into the "Camp of Inner Shame."

There is, however, an important point to make here. In recent years, personnel directors, parents, and even some educators from international schools have
stated that with all the new technological changes, TCKs no longer have any cultural adjustment "problems." In fact, some have seemed almost dismissive. One
principal from an international school in the United States said emphatically
that his students had none of these TCK challenges because they went online every morning to read the newspapers from their passport countries. What he and
others forget or don't understand, however, is that while media provide one place
of cultural learning, knowledge of facts alone isn't enough to put someone in cultural balance. Cultural cues and nuances are picked up unknowingly from our
environment. Eleanor Nicolás learned this when she moved between Britain and
the U.S., where she, and others, thought she would have no language problems:

> My father caught me checking my ears one night in the
> bathroom. "Ellie, what on earth are you doing?"
> "My teacher told me to check my ears."
> He later saw a school newsletter which had a sec-
> tion "Check Your Errors!" I still remember him wheezing
> with laughter at the kitchen table, explaining what I had
> misunderstood.[13]

When people switch cultures, humor is another unknown. Jokes often
are based on a surprise, an indirect reference to something current, or a play
on words that have a double meaning specific to that culture or language. Few
things make people, including TCKs, feel more left out than seeing everyone else

laughing at something they can't understand as funny. Or, conversely, they try to tell a joke that was hilarious in their international school, but nobody laughs in this new environment. Such things are not so easily taught or caught on social media as when we live somewhere.

Probably most TCKs have some story about getting caught in an embarrassing situation because they didn't know some everyday rule of their passport culture that is different from their host culture. One TCK couldn't pay her bill because she had forgotten to mentally add the tax to the amount listed on the menu. Another was shamed by his visiting relatives because he came into the room and sat down before making sure that all the oldest guests had found their places. Not knowing cultural rules can also be dangerous.

> In the village in Mali where Sophie had grown up, passing anyone—male or female—on the street and not saying hello created instant social disfavor. In London the rules were different, as she learned in a police seminar on rape prevention during her first semester at university. "Never look a stranger in the eye," the policeman said. "After attacking someone, a man often accuses the woman of having invited him with her look." And Sophie had been smiling at strange men all over the city!

Expanding Our Vision

All these benefits and challenges are a mere beginning of the TCK Profile. And for the TCKs who are in multiple other CCK circles, these benefits and challenges can be amplified as they may be happening on a more frequent basis each time they switch cultural worlds within one of their subset worlds. And, of course, these are often characteristics of other groups of CCKs as well, particularly where they have international interactions, such as immigrant families, children from bicultural or binational families, children of refugees, or children from minority populations who interact with the majority culture on a frequent basis. We would love to hear these stories too. They could likely fill another book!

We continue our discussion by looking at common personal strengths and struggles many TCKs and other fellow CCKs may share.

Questions for Chapter 7

1. Have you experienced contrasting or conflicting loyalties built from your international life? How has this impacted your relationships? How did you navigate the challenge?

2. When have you experienced connection, whether a celebration or tragedy, with something abroad that wasn't felt the same way by people around you in your country of residence? How did it impact you, and how were you able (or not able) to share the experience with your peers?
3. What's one thing that you wish other people (either who have not been TCKs or who haven't lived in your mix of countries) knew about somewhere you have lived?
4. What anecdote or experience have you had in missing a pop culture reference in your country of origin (if any)?
5. Do you find yourself experiencing a different sense of national identity when abroad versus home?

CHAPTER 8

Personal Characteristics

The benefits of this upbringing need to be underscored: In an era when global vision is an imperative, when skills in intercultural communication, linguistic ability, mediation, diplomacy, and the management of diversity are critical, global nomads are better equipped in these areas by the age of eighteen than are many adults . . . . These intercultural and linguistic skills are the markings of the cultural chameleon—the young participant-observer who takes note of verbal and nonverbal cues and readjusts accordingly, taking on enough of the coloration of the social surroundings to gain acceptance while maintaining some vestige of identity as a different animal, an "other."[1]

—Norma M. McCaig
Founder, Global Nomads International

Norma M. McCaig, one of the true pioneers in raising global awareness of the existence and issues facing TCKs, was a business ATCK herself and worked extensively with international companies preparing employees and their families for overseas assignments before her death in 2008. In this chapter and the next we will discuss many of the characteristics and skills (their benefits and corresponding challenges) of the TCK that she mentions.

CULTURAL CHAMELEON: ADAPTABILITY VERSUS LACK OF TRUE CULTURAL BALANCE

Benefit: Adaptability

TCKs usually develop some degree of cultural adaptability as a primary tool for surviving the frequent change of cultures. Over and over TCKs use the term *chameleon* to describe how, after spending a little time observing what is going on, they can easily switch language, style of relating, appearance, and cultural practices to take on the characteristics needed to better blend into the current scene. Often their behavior becomes almost indistinguishable from longtime members of this group, and they feel protected from the scorn or rejection of others (and their own ensuing sense of shame) that comes with being different from others. A quote from the *Financial Times* after the inauguration of U.S. President Barack Obama in 2009 talked of how he benefited from his "chameleon power" to make a lot of different people feel he represents them.

Cultural adaptability may begin as a survival tool, but it also has immensely practical benefits. TCKs usually learn to adjust with relative calm to life where meetings may start the exact minute for which they have been scheduled or two hours later, depending on which country they're in. Partly because of the frequency with which they travel and move, TCKs can often "roll with the punches" even in unusual circumstances.

> Nona and her ATCK friend, Joy, waited in vain for a bus to carry them from Arusha to Nairobi. They finally found a taxi driver who would take them to the Tanzanian/Kenyan border and promised to find them a ride the rest of the way. At the border, however, the driver disappeared. Night was approaching, and travel would no longer be safe.
>
> As Nona watched in amazement, Joy walked across the border to find another taxi. She soon returned to the Tanzanian side, got Nona and the bags, and returned to a waiting driver who took them to Nairobi. Later, Nona complimented Joy: "If it was me by myself, I'd still be sitting at the border, waiting for that first driver to come back."
>
> Joy replied, "Well, there are times when all I can think is, 'This is going to make a great story in three months, but right now it's the pits.' But I always know there's a way out if I can just think of all the options. I've been in these kinds of situations too many times to just wait."

Challenge: Lack of True Cultural Balance

Becoming a cultural chameleon, however, brings special challenges as well. For one thing, although in the short term the ability to "change colors" helps them fit in with their peers day-to-day, TCK chameleons may never develop true cultural balance anywhere. While appearing to be one of the crowd, inside they may still be the cautious observer, the *wallflower* described in chapter 4—always a bit withdrawn and checking to see how they are doing. In addition, those around them may notice how the TCK's behavior changes in various circumstances and begin to wonder if they can trust anything the TCK does or says. It looks to them as if he or she has no real convictions about much of anything.

Some TCKs who flip-flop back and forth between various behavioral patterns have trouble figuring out their own value system from the multicultural mix they have been exposed to. It can be very difficult for them to decide if there are, after all, some absolutes in life they can hold on to and live by no matter which culture they are in. In the end, TCKs may adopt so many personas as cultural chameleons that they themselves don't know who they really are. Even when they try to be "themselves," they are often simply exchanging being chameleons in one group for the cultural chameleon version of them in another group.

> Ginny returned to Minnesota for university after many years in New Zealand and Thailand. She looked with disdain on the majority of her fellow students, who seemed to be clones of one another, and decided she didn't want to be anything like them. She struck up an acquaintance with another student, Jessica, who was a member of the prevailing counterculture. Whatever Jessica did, Ginny did. Both wore clothing that was outlandish enough to be an obvious statement that they weren't going to be swayed by any current fads.
>
> Only years later did Ginny realize that she too had been a chameleon—copying Jessica—and had no idea what she herself liked or wanted to be. She had rejected one group to make a statement about her "unique" identity, but she had never realized that among their styles of dress or behavior might be some things she did, in fact, like. Since she had totally aligned herself with Jessica, Ginny never stopped to think that some of Jessica's choices might not work for her. Was it all right for her to like jazz when Jessica didn't? What types of clothes did she, Ginny, really want to wear? It was some time before she was able to sort out and identify what her own gifts, talents, and preferences were in contrast to those she had borrowed from Jessica.

HIDDEN IMMIGRANTS: BLENDING IN VERSUS DEFINING THE DIFFERENCES

While virtually all TCKs make cultural adaptations to survive wherever they live, traditionally most TCKs were physically distinct from members of the host culture and easily recognizable as *foreigners* when living there. Even today, the child of the Senegalese ambassador in China would likely not be mistaken for a citizen of the host culture. As mentioned earlier in our discussion on identity, when TCKs are obvious foreigners, they are often excused—both by others and themselves—if their behavior doesn't exactly match the local cultural norms or practices. Based on their appearance alone, nobody expects them to be the same.

Only when these TCKs, who are easily recognized as true foreigners in their host culture, reenter their home culture do they face the prospect of being the hidden immigrants we discussed in chapter 4.

As we also mentioned there, a frequently overlooked, but important, factor is that in our increasingly internationalizing world, many TCKs are becoming hidden immigrants in the host culture as well. Asian American children may look like the majority of others when they are in Kunming, China; a Ugandan diplomat's child may be mistaken for an African American in his classroom in Washington, D.C. So why is this hidden diversity an important issue?

For one thing, being a hidden immigrant gives those TCKs who desire it the choice to be total chameleons in their host culture in a way other non–look-alike TCKs can't do. Once they adapt culturally, people around them have no idea they are actually foreigners, and the TCK may like this type of relative anonymity. A second reason to be aware of the potential for a hidden immigrant experience in the host culture is to recognize that some TCKs who prefer *not* to adapt to the surrounding scene will often find a way to proclaim that they are different from those around them, as other TCKs do upon reentry to their passport culture. This can result in some interesting behavior! Here are three different responses from TCKs who were hidden immigrants in their host culture.

Benefit: Blending In

The first is Paul, an international business TCK who was born in Alaska and then lived in California and Illinois until he was nine. At that time, his family moved to Australia, where his father worked for an oil company.

> My first year of school in Australia was horrible. I learned that Americans weren't very popular because of a nuclear base they'd set up near Sydney. People protested against the "ugly Americans" all the time. I felt other students assigned me guilt by association just because I was a U.S. citizen. Looking back, I realize the only kids who were good to me didn't fit in either.
>
> By the end of the first year, I'd developed an Australian accent and learned to dress and act like my Australian counterparts. Then I changed schools so I could start over and no one knew I was American. I was a chameleon.

As a hidden immigrant in his host culture, Paul made a choice an obviously foreign TCK could never make. Until he chose to reveal his true identity, no one had to know that he was not Australian. Theoretically, some might argue that he made a poor choice, but from Paul's perspective as a child, blending in to this degree gave him the opportunity not only to be accepted by others, but to more fully participate in school and social events while he remained in Australia. On the other hand, TCKs who choose this route also say they live with a fear of others discovering who they really are. Sometimes they feel as if they are living a double life; feeling one thing on the inside and projecting something else outwardly. They may wonder if they are a hypocrite.

Challenge: Defining the Differences

While Paul chose to hide his identity by becoming a chameleon, Nicola and Krista are TCKs who reacted in an opposite way. They became the screamers we mentioned before. Because they looked like those around them, they felt they would lose their true identity if they didn't find some way to shout, "But I'm *not* like you." This is how each of them coped.

> Nicola, a British TCK, was born in Malaysia while her father served with the Royal Air Force. He retired from the service when Nicola was four years old. The family moved to Scotland, where Nicola's father took a job flying airplanes off the coast of Scotland for a major oil company.
>
> At first, Nicola tried to hide her English roots, even adopting a thick Scottish brogue. In spite of that, by secondary school she realized something inside her would never fit in with these classmates who had never left this small town. She looked like them, but when she didn't act like them they teased her unmercifully for every small transgression. It seemed the more she tried to be like them, the more she was having to deny who she really was inside.
>
> Finally, Nicola decided to openly—rather defiantly, in fact—espouse her English identity. She changed her accent to a proper British one and talked of England as home. She informed her classmates that she couldn't wait to leave Scotland to attend university in England. When Nicola arrived in Southampton on her way to the university, she literally kissed the ground when she alighted from the train.

> Krista was an American business TCK raised in England from age six to sixteen. She attended a British school for six months before attending the local American school. We were surprised to hear her tell of how fiercely anti-British she and her fellow classmates in the American school became. In spite of the prevailing culture, they steadfastly refused to speak "British." They decried Britain for not having American-style shopping malls and bought all their clothes at American stores like The Gap and Old Navy during their summer leave in the United States. And why did everyone insist on queuing so carefully anyway? It looked so prim and silly. She couldn't wait to return to the U.S. permanently, where everything would be "normal."

The difficulty for Nicola and Krista, however, was that in trying to proclaim what they considered their true identity, they ultimately formed an "anti" identity—be that in clothes, speech, or behavior. Unfortunately, when TCKs make this choice, they also cut themselves off from many benefits they could experience in friendships and cultural exchange with those around them from the local community. In addition, as TCKs scream to others, "I'm not like you," people around soon avoid them and they are left with a deep loneliness—although it might take them a long time to admit such a thing.

PREJUDICE: LESS VERSUS MORE

Benefit: Less Prejudice

The opportunity to know people from diverse backgrounds as friends—not merely as acquaintances—and within the context of their own cultural milieu is another gift TCKs receive. They have been members of groups that include a striking collection of culturally and ethnically diverse people, and most have the ability to truly enjoy such diversity and to believe that people of all backgrounds can be full and equal participants in any given situation. Sometimes their unconscious, underlying assumptions that people of all backgrounds are still just that—people—can surprise others, and the TCKs in turn are surprised that this isn't necessarily *normal* for everyone else.

> A group of international students in China was traveling through the western part of the country, exploring parts of the Silk Road. Their teachers planned a day for them in an isolated village set aside for people with Hansen's disease. Biological, historical, and cultural understandings of the disease were studied, and the teachers were somewhat nervous about how the students would react. The bus pulled into the village, introductions were made, and the students began to pair off with villagers to tour, talk, and spend the morning together. As students literally reached out by moving close and even giving hugs, the villagers laughed, gasped, and some wept.
>
> Later when the group debriefed, some of the students asked why the reactions were so strong. The group leader, a Dutchman, choked up as he explained that many of the villagers had never been talked to or touched by an outsider before because of their disfiguring disease. The students simply saw fellow human beings.

TCKs who use their cross-cultural experiences well learn there is always a reason behind anyone's behavior—no matter how mystifying it appears—and may be more patient than others might be in a particular situation to try to understand what is going on.

> When ATCK Anne-Marie returned to Mali as a United Nations worker, she heard other expatriates complaining that the Malians who worked in the local government hospital never planned ahead. The medicine, oxygen, or other vital commodities were always completely gone before anyone reported that it was time to reorder. This had caused endless frustration for the U.N. workers.
>
> While listening to the usual grumbling during morning tea one day soon after she arrived, Anne-Marie interrupted the flow of complaints. "I understand your annoyance," she said, "but did it ever occur to you what it's like to be so poor you can only worry about each particular day's needs? If you haven't got enough money for today, you certainly aren't worrying about storing up for tomorrow."

Of all the gifts we hear TCKs say they have received from their backgrounds, the richness and breadth of diversity among those they truly count as friends is one they consistently mention among the greatest.

Challenge: More Prejudice

Unfortunately, however, there are a few TCKs who appear to become *more* prejudiced rather than less. There may be several reasons for this. Perhaps it is because historically many TCKs' parents were part of what others considered a special, elite group (such as diplomats or high-ranking military personnel) in the host country. The parents' position often brought special deference, and the children had little contact with the local population outside of servants in the home or the drivers who took them to school or shopping. In such situations, a sense of entitlement and superiority over the host nationals can easily grow.

> The movie *Empire of the Sun* gives a clear picture of what this privileged lifestyle has been for some TCKs. The story opens with the scene of a young British lad being driven home from school in the backseat of a chauffeured limousine while he stares uncaringly out the windows at starving Chinese children on the streets. As he enters his home, the young man begins to order the Chinese servants around as if they were his slaves.
>
> One day all is changed. When the British boy tries to tell the maid what to do, she runs up and slaps him. The revolution has come, and years of suppressed bitterness at his treatment of her erupt. It takes World War II and several

years of incarceration in a concentration camp before this
TCK finally understands that the world is not completely
under his control.

While this may seem like an exaggeration in today's world, when adults from
any expatriate community constantly speak poorly of the host culture residents
in their presence, TCKs can pick up the same disdain and thereby waste one of
the richest parts of their heritage.

DECISIVENESS: THE IMPORTANCE OF NOW VERSUS THE DELUSION OF CHOICE

Benefit: The Importance of Now

Because their lifestyle is transitory, many TCKs have a sense of urgency that life is
to be lived *now*. They may not stop to deliberate long on any particular decision
because the chance to climb Mt. Kilimanjaro will be gone if new orders to move
come through. Do it now. Seize the day! Sushi is on the menu at the shop around
the corner today. Better try it while you can. Some may fault them for impulsive-
ness, but they do get a lot of living done while others are still deciding what they
do or don't want to do.

Challenge: The Delusion of Choice

For the same reason that some TCKs seize every opportunity, other TCKs seem,
ironically, to have difficulty in making or feeling excited about plans at all. So
often in the past their desires and intentions to do such things as act in a school
play, run for class office, or be captain of the soccer team were denied when Dad
or Mom came home one day and said, "Well, I just received orders today; we
are shipping out to Portsmouth in two weeks." No matter how much the TCKs
thought they could choose what they wanted to do at school or in the neighborhood, it turned out that they had no choice at all. They weren't going to be there
for the next school year or soccer season after all. Off they went, their dreams
vanishing. In Portsmouth, or wherever their next post was, the TCKs asked
themselves, *Why even make plans for what I want to do? I'll just have to leave again.*

These preempted plans can lead to what some mental health professionals
call a "delusion of choice." In other words, a choice to act is offered ("Would you
like to run for class president next year?"), but circumstances or the intervention of others arbitrarily eliminates that choice ("Pack your bags; we're leaving
tomorrow."). Reality for many TCKs is feeling choiceless. The achievement of a
goal, the development of a relationship, or the completion of a project can be cut
short by an unexpected event or the decision of a personnel director. Military
brats may feel that their only choice is to obey protocol and please authority or
rebel and face consequences.

For some TCKs, decision making has an almost superstitious dimension: *If I
allow myself to make a decision and start taking the necessary steps to see it through,*

something will happen to stop what I want. For others, this delusion of choice is wrapped in a theological dimension: *If God finds out what I really want, he'll take it away from me*. Rather than be disappointed, they refuse to acknowledge to themselves, let alone to others or to God, what they would like to do.

Other TCKs and ATCKs have difficulty in making a choice that involves a significant time commitment because they know a new and more desirable possibility may always appear. Signing a contract to teach in Middleville might be a wise economic move, but what if a job opportunity opens in Surabaya next week? It's hard to choose one thing before knowing all the choices. Experience has taught them that life not only offers multiple options, but these options can appear suddenly and must be acted on quickly or they will be gone. Yet the very fact that one choice might preclude another keeps them from making any choice at all.

Chronically waiting until the last minute to plan rather than risking disappointment or having to change plans can be particularly frustrating for spouses or children waiting for decisions to be made that will affect the entire family. Holding open multiple options may frustrate and disappoint others when a last-minute decision means not attending an event where they are expected. Adult TCKs also may miss significant school, job, or career opportunities. It becomes such a habit to wait that they never follow through on leads or fill out necessary forms by the deadline.

One of the most disabling outcomes of this delusion of choice is that it can lead some TCKs and ATCKs to take on a *victim mentality*. They may fuss or complain bitterly about their circumstances, but seem unable to make the choices necessary to extricate themselves from the situation or change things even when they could. No matter what others may suggest to ameliorate the circumstances, the ATCKs always have a reason that person's suggestion won't work. Perhaps this is another way of avoiding one more disappointment in life: *If you don't hope, then you can't be disappointed*. It may also be that with choice comes responsibility, and another internal message is, *If you don't try, you can't fail*. It's simply safer not to try than to risk disappointment or failure. For whatever reason, this place of being seemingly unable to make even the simplest choice to begin to change unwanted circumstances is a sad reality for some ATCKs we have met.

RELATION TO AUTHORITY: APPRECIATIVE VERSUS MISTRUSTFUL

Benefit: Appreciative of Authority

For some TCKs, living within the friendly confines of a strong organizational system is a positive experience in their lives. Relationships with adults in their community are basically constructive and nurturing. There may be almost a cocoon atmosphere on their military base or embassy, business, or mission compound. The sense of structure under such strong leadership gives a feeling of great security. This world is safe. The struggles of others in the world can be shut out, at least for some time, and perks such as generators, special stores, and paid vacations are all part of a wonderful package deal. As adults, they look back on their TCK childhood and those who supervised their lives with nothing but great fondness.

Challenge: Mistrustful of Authority

Other ATCKs and TCKs feel quite differently. For all the reasons (and maybe more) mentioned under "The Delusion of Choice," they begin to mistrust the authority figures in their lives, easily blaming virtually all of their problems in life on parents or organizational administrators who made autocratic decisions about where and when they would move with little regard for their needs or the needs of their family. One of them told us,

> My parents finally got divorced when Mom said she wouldn't make one more move. The company had moved my dad to a new position every two years. Each time we went to a different place, even different countries—sometimes in the middle of the school year, sometimes not. My mom could see how it was affecting us children as well as herself. We would finally start to find our own places within the new group when it was time to move again. Mom asked Dad to talk to the managers of his company and request they leave us in one place while we went through high school at least. They said they couldn't do it as they were amalgamating their headquarters and the office in our town was being phased out. Dad didn't want to find a new job, and Mom wouldn't move, so they got divorced. I've always been angry about both my dad's decision and the company's.

In the end, some TCKs who have had their life unhappily affected because of decisions made by others tell us they would rather starve before risking the possibility that the direction of their lives will be so profoundly affected once more by the decision of someone in authority over them.

ARROGANCE: REAL VERSUS PERCEIVED

At times, the very richness of their background creates a new problem for TCKs. Once, after a seminar, a woman came up to Dave Pollock and said, "There's one issue you failed to talk about tonight and it's the very thing that almost ruined my life. It was my arrogance."

Unfortunately, arrogance isn't an uncommon word when people describe TCKs or ATCKs. It seems the very awareness that helps TCKs view a situation from multiple perspectives can also make TCKs impatient or arrogant with others who only see things from their own perspective—particularly people from their home culture. This may happen for several reasons.

- *A cross-cultural lifestyle is so normal to them that TCKs themselves don't always understand how much it has shaped their view of the world.* No one is without a worldview, including TCKs. They easily forget it's their life experiences that have been different from others', not their brain cells, and do consider themselves much more cosmopolitan and just plain smarter, or at least more globally aware, than others.
- *This impatience with, or judging of, others and their views can sometimes serve as a point of identity with other TCKs.* It becomes one of the markers of *us* versus *them*. It's often easy for a get-together of TCKs to quickly degenerate into bashing the stupidity of non-TCKs. The irony is that the TCKs are then doing unto others what they don't like having done unto themselves—equating ignorance with stupidity.

Sometimes TCKs and ATCKs appear arrogant because they have chosen a permanent identity as being "different" from others.

> Todd, an ATCK, was angry. His parents could do no right. His sponsoring organization had stupid policies, and his American peers ranked among the dumbest souls who had ever been born. Todd castigated everyone and everything. Mark, his good friend, finally got tired of the tirades and pointed out the pride and arrogance coming out in his words.
>
> "You know, Todd," Mark said, "it's your experiences that have been different—not your humanity. I think if you try, you might discover you are not as different from the rest of the world as you seem to feel. You know, you're a normal person."
>
> At that, Todd fairly jumped out of his chair. "The last thing I want to be is *normal*. That idea is nauseating to me."

This *I'm different from you* type of identity is often a defense mechanism to protect against unconscious feelings of insecurity or inferiority. It is another expression of the "screamer" we have discussed. But a *different from* identity has a certain arrogance attached to it. TCKs often use it to put other people down as a way to set themselves apart or boost their sense of self-worth. *I don't care if you don't accept me, because you could never understand me anyway.* TCKs chalk up any rejection they feel or interpersonal problems they have to being different, rather than taking a look to see if they themselves might have added to this particular problem.

At other times, however, what is labeled as arrogance in TCKs is simply an attempt to share their normal life experiences. People who don't understand their background may feel the TCKs are bragging or name-dropping when they speak of places they have been or people they have met or, in Benjamin Steets' case, they judged him simply for his fluency in different languages.

> My dad is German, my mom is Swiss. I was born in Eng-
> land, lived there for two years, then our family moved to
> Albania, where we lived for nearly ten years. While there I
> went to an American/British–based international
> school, where our curriculum and language of instruction
> were all in English. I learned to speak American English,
> Albanian, Swiss German, German, French, and Spanish
> during my first sixteen years of life. A few years ago my
> family moved (back?!) to Germany and I now attend the lo-
> cal gymnasium.
>
> All students in my school are required to take English
> as one of our subjects. Obviously, for me this is not a hard
> class as I am totally bilingual. But the other day I overheard
> someone talking about me and they said I was arrogant and
> a show-off. Why? Because he said that I think I am better
> than everyone just because I can speak English better. I felt
> very sad.

The problem for Benjamin is, unless he understands what is happening, his gifts from this experience can become a point of shame. Some TCKs then feel they have to hide the "real" them and lose the strengths they have due to others' judgments.

And sometimes there may be a mix of both real and perceived arrogance. The conviction or passion with which TCKs speak because of what they have seen and/or experienced makes them seem dogmatic and overly sure of their opinions. Is that arrogance? It's hard to know, as sometimes we are not sure of our own motives. A TCK wanting to join in a conversation about futbol in Venezuela and tell of the amazing goal his teammate scored does not necessarily *have* to mention that it happened when he was playing in Madrid. He might do so because it's a normal context for him, or, just maybe, it might also be a way to try and impress his friends.

Expanding Our Vision

Again, these are common characteristics of the more traditional TCK experience. What about those TCKs who are more culturally complex? Perhaps they come from minority situations, or are of mixed-racial heritage or bicultural backgrounds—or any other combinations of the CCK circles listed in chapter 3. Perhaps they are culturally complex CCKs who don't happen to be in the TCK subset, per se.

We have found that depending on the context of their particular stories, there are some individuals who live perpetually in the hidden immigrant category or the adopted situations of the PolVan model. Unless they are in a third culture environment (if they are traditional TCKs), where "the look" can be anything, they may never live in a mirror situation if judged by traditional definitions of belonging. A Haitian diplomat's child in Benin likely lives in a hidden immigrant situation in both home and host cultures. An Australian Chinese immigrant's child or now adult may be in the adopted category in Australia but a hidden immigrant if in China. And so it goes. The reality remains if we change "hidden immigrant" to "hidden diversity" as per our definition in chapter 4 that it is "a diversity of experience that shapes a person's life and worldview but is not readily apparent on the outside, unlike the usual diversity markers such as race, ethnicity, nationality, gender and so forth," the principles in this chapter can be applied in many places. In addition, the gifts similar to those we talk about for the traditional TCK experience are often similar for other CCKs, and our hope is that they can also be recognized and used more clearly.

Next we look at the benefits that Norma McCaig referred to that can develop into true life skills.

Questions for Chapter 8

1. Have you, or others you know, felt like a "hidden immigrant" or "adopted" at some point in life? Please share your story briefly and tell how you felt.
2. Did you, or the person you are thinking about, use any of the common responses mentioned (chameleon, screamer, wallflower, or adapter) to help get through that time? How did it work then? Is it an ongoing mechanism? If not, how/when did it change?
3. How do you relate to the discussion on "Delusion of Choice"? Are there other reasons making choices can be hard?
4. When/if you feel choiceless in a particular situation, how do you respond in the short term? In the long term?
5. What parts of the section on real and perceived arrogance did you relate to? Are there any stories like the one Benjamin experienced you would like to share?

CHAPTER 9

Practical Skills

> One day I poured out my bitter complaints to a senior mis-
> sionary. I could not understand why the mission imported
> thirty Canadian and U.S. young people to do famine work,
> when not one of the more than fifteen resident MKs [mis-
> sionary kids]—experienced in language and culture—had
> been asked to help. He told me to quit complaining and sign
> on. I did.[1]
>
> —Andrew Atkins

The feelings Andrew expresses reflect the fact that growing up as a TCK not only increases an inner awareness of our culturally diverse world, but the experience also helps in the development of useful personal skills for interacting with and in it. Some of these characteristics are acquired so naturally they aren't recognized, acknowledged, or effectively used—either by ATCKs or others—as the special gifts they are. At the same time, some of the skills also have a flip side, where a skill can become a liability in certain situations. We will look at both in this chapter.

CROSS-CULTURAL SKILLS

As TCKS have the opportunity not only to observe a great variety of cultural practices but also to learn what some of the underlying assumptions are behind them, they often develop strong cross-cultural skills. More significant than the ease with which they can change from chopsticks to forks for eating, or from bowing to shaking hands while greeting, is their ability to be sensitive to the more hidden aspects or deeper levels of culture and to work successfully in these areas. For ATCKs who go into international or intercultural careers, this ability to be a bridge between different groups of people can be useful in helping their company or organization speak with a more human voice in the local community and be more sensitive to the dynamics of potentially stressful situations in the international work environment.

> Before her untimely death in 2016, ATCK Nancy Ackley Ruth was a highly sought out cross-cultural trainer. In her seminars on the added value of TCKs in the workplace, she told the story of a corporation that wanted to branch out and begin doing business internationally. The CEO in the United States set up a conference call with potential new partners in the Middle East. When they did not join the call at the appointed time, he became frustrated. Next, the CEO could barely contain his impatience when these new business contacts at last joined the call but began what he termed "chitchat"—each one asking about the other's family, the weather, and so on. Finally, the CEO could take it no longer and interrupted the conversation to remind them that there was only a half-hour left to do their business.
>
> The voices on the other end of the call became strangely quiet as the CEO tried to proceed. A junior partner, Tom, sitting beside the CEO passed him a note that read, "You may not realize it but you were doing business. In that part of the world, relationships must be established before business deals can be done."
>
> In the end, the CEO almost lost the contract. It was only when Tom, who was an ATCK, urged the CEO to visit these potential business partners in person and to take him along as cultural interpreter that the business deal got back on track.[2]

Perhaps it's obvious from this story why an ATCK's experience in very different cultures and places around the world can be helpful in the global workforce. ATCKs often find themselves particularly qualified not only for the corporate world, but also when it comes to jobs or situations such as teaching or mentoring locally as well as internationally. In these days when developing "global awareness" among education majors is a strong emphasis in many universities, ATCKs who go into this field are already well equipped in this area.

> When a U.S.-based magazine for teachers asked ATCK Fran to write on global awareness in the classroom, she happily wrote about all the TCKs and other CCKs the teachers needed to consider as a hidden diversity among their students. After all, she had been doing many seminars for

teachers, helping them understand all the immigrants and CCKs in their classrooms.

The editor didn't reply for a few days. When she did email back, she said, "I'm sorry, but we didn't want you to write about the students, we wanted you to write about global awareness in the classroom."

Fran, of course, thought she had! In the end, she had to enlist the help of her copy editor friend, Sarah, who was born, grew up, and became a teacher in the U.S., to help her understand what it was the magazine wanted. When Sarah explained that they wanted to emphasize how it was good for teachers to travel so they could begin to understand that others had different outlooks, or to see the sights they were going to teach about, Fran had to laugh at herself. Talk about a cultural misunderstanding! She and the editor used the same words with totally different understandings of what they meant.

If worldview is the lens through which we see and interpret the world, then it was apparent they had two different lenses. Fran realized what they were asking for—that teachers needed to have a first-hand appreciation for other places and cultures—was so basic as part of her life experience, it hadn't occurred to her it was something teachers would have to learn! At that moment, Fran realized she might not be quite as automatically skilled as a cross-culturalist as she had assumed.

Why is it that this innate global awareness can be such an asset to ATCKs in a profession such as teaching? First, it helps them understand the students better. The fact that most TCKs have attended schools with a wide variety of cultural learning and teaching styles gives them firsthand insight into their students' struggles with language, spelling, and conceptual differences, whether those students are from a local ethnic subculture or have lived in another country. ATCKs, of all people, should be willing to allow for differences in thinking, writing, learning, and language styles.

Second, ATCKs can well use their 3-D view of the world. They have firsthand stories to augment the facts presented in geography or social studies textbooks. They may be able to bring life to the textbook's chapter on how the Netherlands reclaimed its land from the sea because they have walked on those dikes. Maybe they have seen the prison cells in the Philippines where American and Filipino POWs were held during World War II. From whatever countries where they have lived or traveled, ATCKs can bring their students fresh and personalized ways of looking at the world. The 3-D view may also include the ability to approach the material from multiple perspectives such as realizing that indigenous people fighting for political freedom often call themselves freedom fighters, while others call them agitators or worse.

Most ATCKs have gone to school in places where there were a large variety of races and cultures in their classrooms. As teachers, ATCKs can bring a vital understanding in helping their students see how they share common feelings and humanity with their peers from various backgrounds, even when circumstances may differ.

> Nilly Venezia, an ATCK who is founder and director of Venezia Institute for Differences and Multiculturalism, works with both Jewish and Palestinian children in the Gaza Strip. She has designed storybooks for children to help her students focus on their shared humanity rather than the political issues in their environment. The stories may be set in different cultural or geographical places reflecting where the students come from, but each story focuses on a theme to which all the students can relate, such as fearing a bully, visiting Grandma's home, or sharing jokes with friends. Nilly believes that "emotions are the universal language" and that if we can help children connect in areas where they are alike, we can go a long way to establishing positive relations between very different groups.[3]

Because of their own experiences, TCKs and ATCKs can be effective mentors for new students coming to their school or community from different countries or cultures or even other parts of their own country. They know what it is like to be the new kid on the block and how painful it can be if no one reaches out to a newcomer, and, conversely, how wonderful it is when someone does. In so many areas, they can effectively help others settle in more quickly—and less traumatically—than might happen otherwise.

Teaching and mentoring are only two examples of how a TCK background can be helpful later on. One friend told Ruth that a particular U.S. American pharmaceutical company had survived the buyouts of other companies because this company had thought about the international market ahead of the others. Why? The CEO of that company was an ATCK from a non-U.S. country. He believed that if his corporation wanted to do business globally, they needed to bring people from the other countries in which they were working to be at corporate headquarters. This ATCK/CEO wanted their insights in how to set up an effective business plan for their countries to be part of the decision-making process from the beginning. He knew these international business persons could give better input than a U.S. executive sent to that land who would give feedback based on a Western cultural lens.

Sometimes TCKs can be connectors or mediators between groups that are stereotypically prejudiced against one another.

Francisco is a black Panamanian TCK. At age six, he moved to the United States while his stepfather pursued a military career. Initially, Francisco lived in the predominantly white culture in the community surrounding the army base. Here he learned firsthand the shock of being the target of racist slurs and attacks. Later his parents moved and he went to a more racially diverse high school where he became a chameleon who apparently fit perfectly into the African American community. Eventually most of his friends saw him as Francisco and forgot, if they ever knew, that his roots were not the same as theirs.

One day, however, a heated discussion erupted among his black friends about why "foreigners" shouldn't be allowed into the country. Finally, Francisco spoke up and said, "You know, guys, what you're saying about them, you're saying about me. I'm not a citizen either. But foreigners have flesh and blood like me—and like you." Then Francisco pointed out how this kind of group stereotyping was why he and they as black people had known prejudice. Francisco reminded them that he—their personal friend, a foreigner—was living proof that people of all backgrounds, races, colors, and nationalities were just that: people, not statistics or embodiments of other people's stereotypes.

OBSERVATIONAL SKILLS

TCKs may well develop certain skills because of the basic human instinct for survival. Sometimes through rather painful means, they have learned that particularly in cross-cultural situations it pays to be a careful observer of what's going on around them and then try to understand the reasons for what they are seeing.

One TCK was branded "nerd of the year" when, after being home-schooled overseas, on his first day of going to public school "at home," he carried his books in a brand new briefcase—just like the one his dad took to work. The briefcase served a most utilitarian purpose—keeping books together in an easily transportable manner. But in this new school, a backpack slung over one shoulder (and one shoulder only) served the same purpose in a far more socially acceptable manner, and "nerd" was not something he wanted to be. On day two he arrived with a secondhand, scuffed black backpack that blended in perfectly.

Through such experiences, TCKs learn firsthand that in any culture these unwritten rules govern everyone's acceptance or rejection in a new setting. In addition, they have seen how behavior unnoticed in one place may cause deep offense in another. Something as seemingly insignificant as raising a middle finger or pointing at another person with your chin can have vastly different meanings depending on the culture. Mistakes in conscious and unconscious social rules—whether eating style, greetings, or methods of carrying schoolbooks—often send an unwanted message to people in the new culture. Observing carefully and learning to ask, "How does life work here?" before barging ahead are other skills TCKs can use to adapt more effectively. Unfortunately, there are times when there is no one available to ask and trial by error is the method of the day.

Mariella, a German ATCK who had grown up in India, took a job working for an NGO hospital in Ghana. It wasn't long before she heard complaints from the expatriate staff that the patients often threw their prescriptions away immediately after exiting the doctor's office. That seemed odd to her as well, so Mariella began investigating.

She soon noticed that when the new doctor from Germany dispensed these prescriptions, he always sat sideways at the desk. The patients were on the doctor's left side as he wrote notes on their charts using his right hand. Whenever the doctor finished writing the prescription, he would pick it up with his free left hand and give it to the patient.

This process probably would not have caused a second thought in Germany, but Mariella knew from her childhood in India that there the left hand is considered unclean because it is the one used for dirty tasks. Giving someone anything with that hand is both an insult and a statement that the object being offered is worthless. She wondered if that might be the case in Ghana as well and asked her new Ghanaian friends if the way a person handed something to another person made a difference in their culture. When their replies confirmed her suspicion that using the left hand in Ghana had the same connotation as she remembered from her childhood in India, Mariella understood why the patients didn't fill the prescriptions! She suggested the doctor turn his desk around so all the patients sat at his right, and that way he would naturally give out the prescriptions in a culturally appropriate manner. He followed her advice and the problem was solved—and the people valued and filled their prescriptions.

SOCIAL SKILLS

In certain ways, learning to live with the chronic change that often characterizes their lifestyle gives many TCKs and ATCKs a great sense of inner confidence and strong feelings of self-reliance. While not always liking change—and sometimes even hating it—TCKs do expect to be able to cope with new situations. Many have moved in and among various cultural worlds so often that, while they may not know every detail of the local culture, they can see beyond that to the humanity of the people in front of them.

> Jamie grew up in the Philippines and often traveled with his parents between the city of Manila and various fishing villages where they did research. After college he took a job selling insurance in the U.S. He talked easily with clients, looking the part in a jacket and tie.
>
> What they didn't know was that he was living out of his car and sleeping in a hammock on dry nights. When he met with a mentor, Pete, for coffee, Pete asked if everything was going okay and if he needed anything. Jamie laughed and said he was practicing for a trip. In a week he would drive his moped 1,300 miles to the coast, catch a boat to Honduras, and take work cleaning and doing simple maintenance in a hostel.
>
> He did just that! His blog posts filled up with tales of adventure and stories of meeting businessmen, officials, and trekkers alike from all corners of the globe. In his free time he volunteers at a local orphanage. This flexibility to connect to a variety of people in multiple contexts with confidence and apparent ease is not uncommon for TCKs.

It seems many TCKs and ATCKs can also generally approach various changes in their life circumstances with some degree of confidence because past experience has taught them that given enough time, they will make friends and learn the new culture's ways. This sense that they'll be able to manage new situations—even when they can't always count on others to be physically present to help in a crisis—often gives them the security to take risks others might not take.

This type of confidence comes out in various ways. It may involve believing you are able to work with others to solve the world's problems or it may come out in simpler ways. Helga, a Belgian ATCK, planned to go alone on a five-week trip to Australia and New Zealand. Some friends were shocked.

> "Do you know anyone there?" they asked.
>
> "Not yet," she replied.
>
> "Well, how can you just go? Aren't you scared to stay with people you don't know? How will you find them at the airport? What kind of food will you eat?"

> Actually, she hadn't thought of it. She'd just presumed one
> way or another it would all work out. As a teenager and
> university student, she'd often traveled halfway around
> the world alone to see her parents during school vacations.
> Customs and language barriers were no longer intimidating.
> Lost luggage could be dealt with. She had a great time.

But there is a flip side to this type of confidence as well. While TCKs develop feelings of confidence in many areas of life, there are other times or situations in which they may be so fearful of making mistakes they are almost paralyzed. Paul, the American TCK who grew up in Australia whom we mentioned earlier, moved once more as a teenager—a critical age when peer approval is vital. Here's what he said about that move.

> I changed worlds once more at age fourteen when my dad's
> company moved him from Australia to Indonesia. But the
> consequence of switching worlds at that age is you can't
> participate in the social scene. Everyone else seems to know
> the rules except you. You stand at the edge, and you shut
> up and listen, mostly to learn, but you can't participate. You
> only sort of participate—not as an initiator, but as a weak
> supporter in whatever goes on—hoping that whatever you
> do is right and flies okay. You're always double-checking and
> making sure.

Just as true chameleons move slowly while constantly checking which color they should be to blend in to each new environment, so TCKs can appear to be socially slow while trying to figure out the operative rules in their new situations. To avoid looking foolish or stupid, they retreat from these situations in such ways as overemphasizing academics or withdrawing in extreme shyness. Even those who have been extremely social in one setting may refuse to join group activities in the next place because they have no idea how to do what everyone else already can. Maybe they have returned home to Sweden from a tropical climate and have never learned to ice-skate, toboggan, or ski. They would rather not participate at all than let anyone know of their incompetence. We've even seen TCKs who play futbol as their lifeblood refuse to play in their passport country because the styles were so frustratingly different.

Insecurity in a new environment can make TCKs withdraw even in areas where they have knowledge or talent. It's one thing to join the choir in a relatively small international school overseas, but quite another to volunteer when you are suddenly in a school of 3,000 students. Who knows what might be expected? Who knows how many others are better than you? And so the TCK holds back to wait and watch, even when it might be possible to be involved.

While these TCKs are trying to figure out the new rules and if or where they might jump in, people around them wonder why they are holding back. If the

TCKs do jump into the fray, it's easy for them to make "dumb" mistakes and be quickly labeled as social misfits. This can lead to another problem. Because TCKs often don't feel a sense of belonging, they can, as did both Paul in this chapter and Ginny in chapter 7, quickly identify with others who don't fit in. Unfortunately, this is often the group that is in trouble with the school administration or one in which scholastic achievement is disdained. Later, if the TCKs want to change and make friends with those more interested in academic success, it may be difficult because they have already been labeled as part of the other group.

LINGUISTIC SKILLS

Acquiring fluency in more than one language is potentially one of the most useful life skills a cross-cultural upbringing can give TCKs. Children who learn two or more languages early in life, and use these languages on a day-to-day basis, develop a facility and ease with language in a way that is useful to them throughout life.

Bilingualism and multilingualism have advantages besides the obvious one of communicating with various groups of people. For instance, Jeannine Heny, an English professor, believes learning different languages early in life can sharpen thinking skills in general and actually help children achieve academically above their grade level.[4] Learning the grammar of one language can strengthen grammatical understanding in the next one. Research has also shown that bilinguals are better at ignoring interference, which may make them better at focusing at a specific task, for example in a noisy classroom.[5]

Strong linguistic skills also have practical advantages as the TCK becomes an adult. Some careers are available only to people fluent in two or more languages. One American ATCK works for a large international company as a Japanese/English translator. She learned Japanese while growing up and attending local schools in a small town in Japan. Another American ATCK works as an international broadcaster using the Hausa language he learned as a child in Nigeria.

Even if a career isn't directly involved with language, opportunities to take jobs in certain countries may require language learning. There's no doubt that a job applicant who already speaks the country's language will see his or her résumé land a lot closer to the top of the pile than those who will have to spend a year or two in language school. Even when the language required isn't one the ATCK already knows, the fact that he or she is obviously adept at learning more than one language improves job opportunities as well.

Along with the many advantages, though, there are some precautions to take in a multiple-language environment. Speaking another language, and knowing it well enough to think in it, are not the same, and that difference can be critical. During a seminar in Asia where many of the expatriates were in cross-cultural marriages, this issue of multiple languages in the home came up. A teacher from an international school told the following tale.

A few years ago, we had three children from the same family arrive at our school. To be honest, we thought they were all developmentally delayed. They spoke adequate English, but something didn't seem quite right. We eventually discovered that their parents were from two different cultures and neither of them spoke one another's mother tongue, so the family used English at home. Unfortunately, the parents' English wasn't very good, and therefore their children had never experienced any language deeply enough to think in it conceptually. Once the children were in an environment where they could learn language for concepts as well as facts, they did well in school.

The follow-up comment by the teacher who told that story was to point out the problem here was not that the parents had confused the children with multiple languages. The problem was that in not teaching either or both of their original languages to the children and only using a language neither of them knew well—English—their children had not developed the vocabulary and concepts deeply enough to think conceptually in that language. Dr. Ute Limacher-Riebold, expert on parenting bilingual (or more) children, offers a follow-up caution here as well.

Schools often assess children only based on the school language, which unfortunately gives a wrong idea about their overall linguistic proficiency. For example, if a trilingual child (mother speaks language 1, father language 2, at school the child learns language 3) seems to know and use 40 words in the school language, and the assessment is not done in language 1 and 2 as well, the words the child knows in these two languages are not taken into consideration. If a child of the same year group knows 80 words, the trilingual child is obviously considered "running behind" the monolingual peer, but in most cases, these trilingual children know even more words than their monolingual peers. But traditional assessments—like you can find in most monolingual schools all around the world—don't take this into account.

This leads to a misinterpretation that puts parents under a great pressure and leads teachers (and doctors) to advise parents to drop their family languages. This is a great mistake because we now know that this can lead to great struggles both academically and psychologically: these children get the message that their family languages are not worth learning; this means that their family cultures are not "good enough" and that they have to hide their origin and identity.[6]

Ute also shared with Ruth thoughts about the differences between children and adults when it comes to language learning.

> A child does learn the nonverbal clues faster and in a more intuitive way than an adult, but this is when a child acquires the language or learns it in a certain way. Adults can learn and acquire language as well; they can gain a nearly native fluency even if they learn the language later in life: it only requires more time![7]

Rita Rosenback, another language expert and author of *Bringing Up a Bilingual Child*, agrees.

> We should also remember that children have several years when they can fully concentrate on learning the language. They are also supported by adults who speak at an appropriate pace, repeat when needed and have a lot of 1-to-1 tuition. If adults had the same time and support, they would also learn a language quickly![8]

So the good news is there is hope for adolescents, young adults, and adults! However, often when learning a new language once we have started schooling, the thinking process of our mother language often superimposes itself on the second language—at least initially—which makes learning the new language more difficult. It also inhibits us from fully understanding the thinking patterns of those who use that language. When children learn languages, as Ute says above, they learn the nonverbal clues faster and more intuitively regarding how people in that culture think and relate to one another. Adolescents and young adults (and adults) often translate word for word and never gain an understanding of how the same word may have a different implication in another language. Ironically, however, learning the nuances for certain words in their adopted language can sometimes keep TCKs from fully understanding the nuances of the translation of that same word in their mother tongue. This happened to JoAnna.

> For years, American friends of ATCK JoAnna told her that she was the most guilt-ridden person they'd ever met. No matter what happened—if a glass fell out of someone's hand, a friend lost her notebook, or someone bit his lip—JoAnna always said, "Sorry."
>
> The instantaneous answer always came back. "What are you sorry for? You didn't do anything."
>
> JoAnna's equally instantaneous reply was also always the same. "I know I didn't do anything. I'm just sorry."
>
> For years this exchange was a point of significant frustration for both JoAnna and her friends. She couldn't get out

of the habit of saying sorry and her friends couldn't get over being irritated by it. None of them understood the impasse.

When she was in her forties, JoAnna went to live in Kenya for a year. During a hike in the woods with Pamela, another American, Pamela said, "I'll be glad when I get back to the States, where everyone doesn't say 'sorry' all the time."

JoAnna asked why that was a problem.

"It drives me crazy," Pamela said. "No matter what happens, everyone rushes around and says, '*Pole, pole sana*,' (which means 'Sorry, very sorry'). But most of the time there's nothing to apologize for."

For the first time, JoAnna understood her lifelong problem with the word "sorry." For Pamela, a U.S. citizen, sorry was primarily an apology. She had never realized in this African context that people were expressing sympathy and empathy rather than apologizing when they used that word. For JoAnna, in the African language she had learned as a child, and in the two she had learned as an adult, sorry was used as both an apology and as an expression of sympathy. It had never occurred to her that "sorry" was only an apology word to most listeners using American English. No wonder she and her American friends had misunderstood each other. They weren't speaking the same language!

Although the linguistic gifts for TCKs are primarily positive ones, there are a few pitfalls to be aware of. These include being limited in any one language, becoming a "creative speller," and losing fluency and depth in the child's native language. No matter how bright the child is, the specialized terminology needed for studying medicine (or fixing cars, discussing computers, studying science, etc.) may be missing if someone is working in many languages but not necessarily immersed in a particular language because of not living where it is normally spoken. Ultimately, he or she may never have time to learn the more specialized meanings and usage of each. JoAnna's story demonstrates how idiomatic expressions or nonliteral meanings of common words can also cause confusion in such situations.

Interestingly enough, it's not simply those who work or study in entirely different languages who may find themselves linguistically challenged. Perhaps for the very reason it seems so minor, TCKs who speak and write English find it very difficult to keep American and English spelling straight. Is it *color* or *colour*? *Behavior* or *behaviour*? *Pediatrician* or *paediatrician*? Even worse, how do you remember if it's *criticise* or *criticize* when *criticism* is spelled the same everywhere? While this may seem like a minor irritation, it can become a major problem when, for example, a student taught not only in Britain but in any of the former British colonies transfers to a school rooted in the U.S. American system if the teachers are not sensitive to this issue.

These differences in spelling provide a special challenge to schools everywhere that have a mix of nationalities among their students. Many solve the problem by keeping both an English and American dictionary available to check on the variations that come in on assigned papers. With a sense of humor, an understanding teacher, or a spell-checker appropriate for the current country, most TCKs weather this particular challenge successfully.

The most serious problem related to learning multiple languages at an early age, however, is that some people never become proficient in their supposed mother tongue—the original language of their family roots and personal history. Among TCKs, this occurs most often among those who come from non-English-speaking countries but attend international schools overseas where classes are predominantly taught in English. Fortunately, schools like the International School of The Hague (ISH) and others have begun developing some very strong programs to help students maintain fluency in their mother tongue. One example:

> When Ruth went to visit ISH, she sat in the guidance counselor's office and learned about the strong after-school clubs where children of various original languages could meet and work together in those languages. In addition, they had on file who on their staff spoke which languages. As Ruth and the guidance counselor sat and talked a teacher ran in, obviously very excited. She held a paper in her hand and explained how she had given a dictation assignment to her English class. The idea was to see if children knew how to spell and to punctuate their work. Unfortunately, a student had just arrived that day who didn't yet speak English—the language of instruction at ISH. How could she do this assignment? Fortunately, the teacher realized she could use the school's language speaker's list to call someone down to her class to translate the dictation a sentence at time. Here, in her hand, lay the result of that. A beautifully written, wonderfully punctuated essay. There wasn't a word of English in it, but it was obvious this child knew how to write and spell and punctuate in her original language. The teacher had offered this student a way to be successful on her first day in a new school instead of making her an instant failure.

Sadly, however, many national and international schools do not yet offer such programs. When that is a boarding school with little home (and thus language) contact for months at a time, language can become a major issue when the

TCK returns to his or her parents, with the supposed mother tongue becoming almost a foreign language. Families whose members lack fluency in a common language by which they can express emotions and profound ideas lose a critical tool for developing close, intimate relationships.

> Kwabena is a Ghanaian TCK who faced the problem of never gaining fluency in his parents' languages. His father was from the Ga tribe, his mother from the Anum tribe. Kwabena was born in predominantly English-speaking Liberia, where his father worked for several years. Eventually, the family moved to Mali, where French was the official language. The family could only make occasional visits back to the parents' villages in Ghana, where his grandparents spoke only the local languages. By the time Kwabena reached his teens, he sadly realized he could never talk to his grandparents and ask for the family stories all children love to hear because he couldn't speak enough of their language and they couldn't speak the English, French, or Malian languages he knew.

Most TCKs we know, however, count the benefits of having facility in two or more languages as another of their greatest practical blessings. What is more, it's just plain fun to watch a group of ATCKs at an international school reunion suddenly break into the greetings or farewells of the language they all learned in some faraway land during their youth. At that moment, language becomes one more marker of all they have shared in the world that now may seem invisible to them. It reminds them of the depth of experience and life they do, in fact, share with others of their "tribe."

And for parents who wish to know more on this topic of how to deal with multiple languages in a child's life, there are a growing number of resources, such as Rita's book *Bringing Up a Bilingual Child*.[9] We have listed more information on our Resources pages.

Questions for Chapter 9

1. When you read Andrew Atkins' quote at the beginning, did you relate? Have you ever felt you or a TCK you know have skills that don't seem to be recognized or used as fully as you would like? Explain.
2. Do you find yourself or others acting differently in social situations in different countries or cultures? If so, what are some of the differences?
3. Do you feel that the Internet has made it easier or harder for TCKs and others to develop social skills? Please explain.

4. How many languages can you speak? If more than one, at what ages did you learn them?
5. If you or others you know learned multiple languages as a child, what was your biggest asset from that? Any challenges along the way?
6. What do think might be effective strategies for helping children maintain the family's original language?

CHAPTER 10

Rootlessness and Restlessness

> I was born in Rio de Janeiro, so I'm Brazilian. I am Italian
> because my parents were both born and raised in Bologna,
> but I have never actually lived in Italy. My French is as flu-
> ent as my English because I grew up in Switzerland and Bel-
> gium—I also speak Italian and Spanish. Portuguese was my
> first language .... I am unlike most people who answer the
> question "Where are you from?" with just a few words or
> just one word. I can't .... I feel equally at home in Geneva,
> Brussels, London, Paris, Bologna, Venice, and New York. It
> always feels like I never left and I miss all of them all the
> time .... I would move to another country in a heartbeat if
> I had the chance.[1]
>
> —ATCK Benedetta Agnoli

While Benedetta's story is a shining example of the gifts of mobility for TCKs in that she has seen the world and is obviously very comfortable and confident to continue trying something new, two common characteristics that again can be both a benefit and a challenge are also embedded here—a deep sense of rootlessness and restlessness. Both are involved in what for so many TCKs is the most nagging, deep, heartfelt question of all, *Where do I belong?* The answer to that generally requires some sense of being grounded, along with stability. The issues of rootlessness and restlessness are such key aspects of the TCK Profile that they deserve a chapter of their own.

Rootlessness

There are several questions many TCKs have learned to dread. Among them are these two: "Where are you from?" and "Where is home?"

WHERE ARE YOU FROM?

Why should anyone dread such a seemingly simple question? Consider Erika again.

> Like most other TCKs, when someone asks Erika that question, her internal computer starts the search mode. What does this person mean by "from"? Is he asking my nationality? Or maybe it's, "Where were you born?" Does he mean, "Where are you living now?" or, "Where did you come from today?" Or does he mean, "Where do your parents live now?" or, "Where did you grow up?" Actually, does he even understand what a complicated question he asked me or care? Is he simply asking a polite, "Let's make conversation about something while we stand here with shrimp on our plates" question, or is he really interested?
>
> Erika decides what to answer by how she perceives the interest of the person who asked or what she does or doesn't feel like talking about. If the new acquaintance seems more polite than interested, or if Erika doesn't want a lengthy conversation, she gives the "safe" answer. During college she simply said, "Wisconsin." Now she replies, "Dayton." It's the "where I'm living now" answer.
>
> If Erika does want to extend the conversation slightly or test out the questioner's true interest, she throws out the next-higher-level answer: "New York"—still a fairly safe answer. It's where she visited during each home leave and where her family's roots are.
>
> If the person responds with more than a polite, "Oh," and asks another question such as, "Then when did you move to Dayton?" Erika might elevate her reply to a still higher level, "Well, I'm not really from New York, but my parents are." Now the gauntlet is thrown down. If the potential new friend picks up on this and asks, "Well, where are you from then?" the conversation begins and Erika's fascinating life history starts to unfold. Of course, if the newcomer doesn't follow up on that clue and lets the comment

go, Erika knows for sure she or he wasn't really interested anyway and moves the conversation on to other topics—or simply drops it altogether.

On days when Erika feels like talking more or wants to make herself stand out from among the crowd, however, she answers the question "Where are you from?" quite differently. "What time in my life are you referring to?" she asks. At this point the other person has virtually no choice but to ask Erika where she has lived during her life and then hear all the very interesting details Erika has to tell!

But it is not only Erika who feels this way. When people try to tell us that because of the Internet, the TCK Profile is "moot," that everything is different now, all they or we need to do is look at what is posted on the myriad of websites on or by TCKs and ATCKs, or visit their chat rooms on the web, and this one aspect alone belies those de-criers. If anything, the question of "Where am I from?" is more acute than ever. Why? Because the increasing mobility of so many TCKs leaves them not having to choose between two primary places as it would have been for TCKs of former generations, but now many have lived in a plethora of places. Benedetta's story is a perfect illustration of that growing "new normal." If to be "from" someplace refers to a geographical location, how can she ever choose one from among the many places where she has grown up and lived?

WHERE IS HOME?

While this question at first seems to be the same as "Where are you from?" it is not. In some cases, TCKs have a great sense of "at-homeness" in their host culture. As long as Erika's parents remained in Singapore, "Where's your home?" was an easier question to answer than "Where are you from?" She simply said, "Singapore." Both her emotional and physical sense of home were the same.

Other TCKs who have lived in one city or house during each leave or furlough may have a strong sense of that place being home. In January 1987, the U.S. ambassador to Ecuador spoke at a conference about TCKs in Quito and said, "I think every expatriate family should buy a home before going abroad so their children will have the same base for every home assignment. My kids feel very strongly that Virginia is home even though they've lived outside the States over half their lives." This is undoubtedly an excellent idea, and one to be seriously considered when at all possible.

For many families, we realize that buying a house in the home country isn't a viable option, but TCKs still develop a strong *sense of home* in other ways. Often TCKs whose parents move every two years rarely consider geography as the determining factor in where they consider home. Instead, home is defined by relationships.

When Dave Pollock asked Ben, a TCK from the diplomatic
community, "Where's your home?" Ben replied, "Egypt."
Dave was somewhat surprised as he'd not previously heard
Ben talk about Egypt, so Dave asked how long he had lived
there.

"Well," Ben replied, "actually, I haven't been to Egypt
yet, but that's where my parents are posted now. They
moved there from Brazil right after I left for university, so
when I go home for Christmas vacation, that's where I'll go."

Home May Be Defined by Relationships

The reality that home is often defined by relationships is underscored in a study
done by Alice Wu on how technology is impacting the TCK (aka global nomad)
experience. As far as we know, Alice, an intercultural communication consultant
and adjunct lecturer at Cornell University, is the first person to begin making
videos on the topic of TCKs. She filmed her first one in 1994 titled *Global Nomads: Cultural Bridges for the Future* (Wu and Clark, Bojer and Barzilay), which
we mentioned in chapter 2. At that point in time, students communicated with
friends and family basically by telephone or handwritten letters. Phone calls were
expensive, however, as those they contacted were often in other countries. The
TCKs' frequent moves resulted in some shared opinions about home.

> "I couldn't really consider anything home—that's in some
> ways very liberating," one commented, while another said,
> "Home has been my family—I've never really called Guate-
> mala, or Australia, or wherever, home."[2]

In 2001 Alice did another video, and called this one *Global Nomads: Cultural
Bridges for the New Millennium*. By this time, email had become a common practice, helping the TCKs stay in better touch with family and friends.

> "What contributes to one's sense of home is the people you
> grow up with," one student explained, describing how mov-
> ing to the U.S. and meeting friends from previous places felt
> like coming home. Technology contributed to this sense of
> home by providing more tools to communicate with friends,
> and this greater sense of connection helped alleviate some
> of the grief of leaving them: "I've found a real outlet for my
> roots through the Internet, and my roots are all over."[3]

However, students also described challenging transitions:

> "When I came to college, that was really difficult for me,
> losing the one thing that was stable in my life—my fam-
> ily; they were somewhere else." Since many global nomads

defined "home" as their families, this student may have felt
that he had lost his home.[4]

As you can see, the underlying definition of home as it applies to relationships is still coming through for these students. And while technology wasn't
the perfect solution for all, it definitely was a positive force for some because it
helped them stay more connected to their past, so their sense of having a home
also increased.

Alice did another video in 2014. In keeping with her theme, she called this
one *Global Nomads: Cultural Bridges in the Age of Technology*. By then, the world
had changed dramatically. Technology had become an essential part of college
students' lives and it certainly connected them more with family and friends:
When asked how it had changed a globally mobile experience, one student said:

> "I can't say what it was like without it, but I Skype with my
> parents at least once a week. I'm always up to speed with
> them."[5]

Alice offers several more interesting findings. Because technology helped
these TCKs keep better relationships with far-flung family, some students described feeling at home in more than one place, unlike students in the 1994 and
2001 studies when many students said they did not consider anyplace home. But
the conclusion in the end is remarkable:

> Finally, just as in 1994 when students mentioned how essen-
> tial their families were to finding home, twenty years later
> this was still true: "When I'm with my family, no matter
> what place in the world it is, I'm home. To me, home is wher-
> ever my family is."[6]

The point being: for all that has changed, some things have not; however,
technology seems to be very helpful in strengthening at least some TCKs' capacity to answer the question, "Where is home?"

Feeling "at Home"

Amel Derragui, whose husband introduces her as "an Algerian girl, born in India, raised in Serbia and Uganda, living in France who meets an Austrian guy
in Iran at a Turkish Party"[7] has written a wonderful blog on finding home both
through relationship and place—a new theme we are hearing from ATCKs as
they journey through life. After writing about her efforts to find a sense of home
in each of the places she had lived and never quite succeeding, she writes that
after meeting her now husband, that sense of homelessness changed:

> Having found this place in his heart and having made space
> for him to settle in mine, I can finally fully appreciate all
> the other homes I have, even if each one of them represents

only one portion of my whole identity . . . . Now I know that
home for me is the place I identify with, and I do identify
with more than just one. Each one of these homes completes
my identity and makes it so rich. I am homefull and I feel so
blessed.[8]

We are encouraged for the creative ways many TCKs and ATCKs are now
finding what it means to feel "at home" in many different ways and places. Sadly,
however, we still meet some TCKs for whom "Where is home?" is still the hardest
question of all. *Home* connotes an emotional place—somewhere you truly belong. There simply is no real answer to that question for TCKs who, for whatever
reason, do not find that sense of being at home totally in either their family situation or in the external environment. They may have moved so many times, lived
in so many different residences, and attended so many different schools that they
never had time to become attached to any. Additionally, for some their parents
may be divorced and living in two different countries. Denis tells his story.

When someone asks me, "Where is your home?" I tell them
I don't know and that I don't really have a home. The reason
is my parents got divorced when I was one year old and I
was a TCK with my mother. My mother is originally from
Taiwan but she now lives in London. "Home" should be
where my mom is, but she moved to a new country after I
stopped living with her. London isn't home.

My father has lived in Switzerland for about thirty
years now; I could call that home but I can't because I've
lived with him for about one year total. My conclusion is
that home is where I currently am.

So now my home is Luzern, Switzerland, even though I
don't speak a word of German and I've only been here for
eight months.

"Home" as Part of Your History

Another factor for some TCKs who have spent years in boarding schools is that
they may feel more bonded to the boarding school than they feel when thinking
of their parents' home. Paul Seaman writes,

"Home" might refer to the school dormitory or to the house
where we stayed during the summer, to our family's home
where our parents worked, or, more broadly, to the country
of our citizenship. And while we might have some sense of
belonging to all of these places, we felt fully at home in none
of them. Boarding life seemed to have the most consistency,
but there we were separated from our siblings and shared

one "parent" with other kids. As it grew colder, we could
look forward to going home for the holidays. We were always eager to be reunited with our families, but after three
months of separation from our friends, we were just as
eager to go back. Every time we got on the train, we experienced both abandonment and communion.

Another phenomenon we have noticed is an attachment that children will
make to a particular place in the collective family history that feels "homey" to
them. We encourage parents to ask their children what places feel like home to
them. It may be a relative's house, or a vacation spot that the family returned to
often. One mother began to laugh in a TCK seminar in China. "Do you know
what my kids have told us we can never sell?" she asked, "Our Volvo station
wagon with the leather seats. Whenever we return to Australia, we always drive
around visiting people and going on vacation. The kids say that feels like home!"

No matter how home is defined in terms of a physical place or emotional
space, the day comes for many TCKs when they realize it is irretrievably gone.
For whatever reasons, they can never *go home*. In our earlier editions, we said that
"Now when someone asks Erika where her home is, she simply says, 'Everywhere
and nowhere.' She has no other answer." That was then, but if you ask her now
(as we did!), she says it is still the same answer because she needs no other answer. For her, she is a world citizen. It is something beyond a single culture or a
physical place, but it is her sense of home. After moving to Europe and marrying
a man from England, giving birth to their son in The Netherlands, sending him
to primary school in Russia and secondary school in France where she now lives
with her husband and son, Erika, too, has found peace and *at homeness* in ways
others may not understand, but one that works well for her. The good news for
all is that as life emerges, for those who are willing to open up to new possibilities
outside of traditional ways of defining "home," the sense and place of belonging
can still happen.

Restlessness—The Migratory Instinct

ALWAYS READY FOR THE NEXT MOVE

In the end, many TCKs develop a *migratory instinct* that controls their lives.
Along with feeling rootless, they often feel restless as well. Did you notice what
Benedetta said in the story earlier in this chapter? After listing all the places she
has lived, she added, "I would move to another country in a heartbeat if I had
the chance." This type of restlessness often results in an internal dialogue for
TCKs and ATCKs that runs something like this: "Here, where I am today, is
temporary. But as soon as I finish my schooling, get a job, or purchase a home,

I'll settle down." Somehow the settling down never quite happens. The present is never enough—something always seems lacking. An unrealistic attachment to the past, or a persistent expectation that the next place will finally be home, can lead to this inner restlessness that keeps the TCK always moving or always wanting to be "on the move."

> Inika had waited for what seemed like forever to return to her host country, Guatemala. She finally found a job that offered her the prospect of staying there for many years, possibly even until she retired. Two weeks after arriving, however, Inika felt a wave of panic. For the first time in her life, there was no defined end point. Now she had to be involved with the good and bad of whatever happened in this community. She wondered why she felt like this so soon after reaching her goal. Then she realized that throughout her life, no matter where she had lived, any time things got messy (relationships with a neighbor, zoning fights in the town, conflicts at church), internally she had leapfrogged over them. There was always an end point ahead when she knew she would be gone—the end of school, the end of home leave, or something. Suddenly, that safety net had disappeared. For the first time in her life Inika either had to engage completely in the world around her or start forming another plan to leave.

Obviously, it is good to be ready to move when a career choice mandates it, but to move simply from a sense of restlessness can have disastrous effects on an ATCK's academic life, career, and family. Without question there are legitimate reasons to change colleges or universities. Sometimes TCKs who live a continent away must enroll in a university without having the opportunity to visit beforehand. After arriving, they discover that this school doesn't offer the particular courses or majors they want or the type of college is not a good fit for them. Perhaps they change their interest in what career they want to pursue and this school doesn't offer concentrated studies in that field. In such situations, there is no choice but to change. Some TCKs, however, switch schools just because of their inner migratory instinct. Their roommates aren't quite right; the professors are boring; the weather in this place is too hot or too cold. They keep moving on, chronically hoping to find the ideal experience. Unfortunately, frequent transfers can limit what TCKs learn and inhibit the development of their social relationships.

Once through with school (or after dropping out), a TCK who has moved often and regularly may feel it's time to move even when it's not. Some ATCKs can't stay at one job long enough to build any sort of career. Just as they are anticipating a position of new responsibility and growth, that old rolling stone instinct kicks in. They submit their letter of resignation and off they go—again always thinking the next place will be "it."

> Sylvia raced through life. In the ten years following her graduation from university, she acquired two master's degrees, had seven career changes, and lived in four countries. One day it struck her that while she had a vast amount of broad knowledge and experience, her career was going nowhere. And she wasn't sure she still wanted, or knew how, to settle down.

THE RESULTS OF MOVING WITH REGULARITY

Some feel almost an obligation to be far from their parents, siblings, or even their own children. When it is possible to live closer, these adult TCKs choose not to. They have spent so much time separated from family that they don't know how to live in physical proximity—or don't want to. Others, like Bernie, have learned to deal with interpersonal conflict, including family conflict, by separating from the situation. He said, "I loved growing up with high mobility. Every time there was a problem, all I had to do was wait and either the people causing the problem left or I left. I have handled all of my life's conflicts the same way." Camilla is another example of how this restlessness works.

> Camilla, a foreign service ATCK, attended twelve schools in sixteen years all around the globe. Now, every two years, an internal clock goes off that says, "This assignment is up. Time to move." She has either changed jobs, houses, cities, and—twice—husbands in response to that message.
>
> Unfortunately, her migratory instinct has affected Camilla's children. Although she has noticed their insecurities developing as she perpetually uproots them, Camilla appears powerless to settle down. The overt reason for change always seems clear. "I don't like the neighborhood we're in," or "My boss simply doesn't understand me," or "I have a nasty landlord." It never occurs to her that she is replaying a very old tape that says, "No place can ever become permanent. Don't get too attached." Or, "If you have a problem, just leave." Nor does she realize it might be possible to replace the old tape with a new one that plays a message that could serve her better in some of these situations—that she can also make a choice to stay.

For some, making that choice to stay against all the feelings to leave began life on another course.

ATCK Claudia had gone down a common path of changing universities on an annual, or even semiannual, basis until she finally managed to graduate. She had moved various places after graduation and had finally settled in one place long enough to get some public health training and had finally begun a "real job." One day in talking with a friend, Claudia told her she thought she would soon be moving.

"Why?" asked the friend.

"I don't know. It just seems like I need to."

The next day Claudia came back to that friend and said, "I thought a lot about the why question you posed. I realized I like my job, I like this city, I am near my grandparents, I have friends here. It occurred to me that for the first time I could make a choice to stay."

And she did. . . . long enough to get her master's in public health and in the end made a positive move with an NGO to work in Africa. At that point, she could use the gifts of her cross-cultural childhood positively because she had intentionally been willing to pause and complete her course so she had the possibility of doing this other job she came to love.

SETTLING IN ONE PLACE

Some TCKs have an opposite response to their highly mobile background. They have moved so many times, in so many ways, and to so many places, they swear they will find a place to call their own, put up the white picket fence, and never, ever, move again. Lakisha, a non-TCK married to an ATCK, told us:

When I met Antwayne, I think I fell in love with his passport as much as I did with him. I was intrigued with all the places he had been and everything he had seen. I envisioned a life of worldwide travel and living in all sorts of exotic places. Unfortunately, I assumed wrong. When my father surprised us with a lovely bungalow for our wedding present, Antwayne was thrilled. That was the first time he shared with me how he had always dreamed of finding a place to call his own and settle down. This was it. So I'm still reading my travel magazines and dreaming.

ATCKs sometimes share how difficult it is for them that adult life is a more static lifestyle, even when they have chosen it. There can be, as one described, "the feeling that the TCK tribe has moved on and I have been sidelined from the game because I chose to lead a monocultural life. The anecdotes of travel, and language and cross-culture are no longer my stories." And yet there is a desire for broader engagement and a sense of frustrated longing to bring the gifts of the mobile life to bear.

Enlarging Our Vision

A few years ago, one ATCK's father came to Ruth and said, "My daughter isn't rootless and restless because she's a TCK. She's rootless and restless because she's part of the Gen X generation." Of course, that got Ruth to thinking again of how and why these characteristics might be declared for an entire generation. Are there commonalities between what is going on in our world and this prototype we are looking at now? Perhaps it is possible that this is where we begin to see the reality of the global shift affecting people of all backgrounds. Even for those who never move, the realities of the past monocultural environments where roots were deep and strong and generational are disappearing as the world now comes to where people are. These are all things to think about! And "domestic TCKs" who have moved often and chronically within their home countries also tell us of a similar sense of rootlessness and restlessness so we understand, once more, that the issues we describe for traditional TCKs have many applications for others in today's world.

Next we take a further look at how the TCK experience, including this rootlessness and restlessness, shapes the patterns of their relationships.

Questions for Chapter 10

1. When people ask where you're from, what is your usual answer? Does it change? If so, when and why? If not, why not?
2. How do you literally tell your story? What's your "elevator pitch" (thirty-second speech) about your basic coordinates in life?
3. Is there a difference from knowing "Where is home?" and where someone can feel "at home"? Can there be more than one place? Please explain your response.
4. Whatever your story, do you relate more to the sense of wanting to have roots or to the restlessness? Please explain.
5. If you or others you know have struggled with the question of "Where is home?" and have found a sense of resolution to this question, please share your tips with others.

CHAPTER 11

Relational Patterns

> Multiple separations tended to cause me to develop deeper
> relationships more quickly. Also, when I was with family or
> friends, we tended to talk about things that matter spiritu-
> ally, emotionally, and so on. I still become impatient with
> [what I see as] superficiality.[1]
>
> —Response to an ATCK survey

Relationships are another area affected by the paradoxical nature of the TCK experience. The wealth of friends from so many places and backgrounds is often beyond measure, yet the chronic cycles of leaving add so much loss as well. It is true that some say because of today's Internet world, what we have written in the past about the TCK experience and challenges of dealing with these chronic cycles no longer applies. We agree that the Internet has affected the TCK experience in major ways, yet we continue to hear from TCKs asking for help in understanding or knowing how to change negative interpersonal patterns with which they struggle. So perhaps this is a good opportunity to look at what is and isn't different for TCKs and their relationships in today's technologically driven world.

As we've seen, TCKs past and present often define their sense of rootedness in terms of relationships rather than geography. Because of that, many TCKs will go to greater lengths than some people might consider normal to nurture relational ties with others—be they family members, friends with whom the TCKs have shared boarding school years, or other important members of their third culture community.

Unfortunately, the same mobility that creates such bonding can result in relationships being a source of great conflict and pain as well. In the past, the cycle of frequent good-byes inherent in a highly mobile lifestyle have led TCKs and

ATCKs to develop patterns of self-protection against the further pain of separations that may affect relationships throughout their lives (we will discuss these patterns later in this chapter). Many wonder if the Internet has changed that. Let's start by taking an overall view of TCKs and common patterns of relationships from both a past and current perspective.

Large Numbers of Relationships

TCKs usually develop a wide range of relationships with people from various countries and ethnicities as they or people around them habitually come and go. New friends enter their lives while old friends add to the number of contacts they have on social media.

"I could travel to almost any country in the world and stay with a friend," Tom bragged after one transition seminar. This may sound like an exaggeration, but for many adult TCKs, it's the truth. With friends from their childhood now in countless places, TCKs build a rich international network that is useful for all sorts of things—from finding cheap room and board while traveling to setting up business connections later in life.

In our first two editions, we talked about the practical difficulty of sustaining these relationships when address books for snail mail letters exceeded 900. Obviously, few people send out that annual letter via snail mail anymore, choosing instead some form of social media to stay connected—different media for different people at different times. But the question remains of how many of these relationships can be sustained over the long term at a meaningful level—even using social media.

These are questions for which the answers are constantly changing and still to be fully known. But without doubt, having the ability to keep up with more friends is far more possible today than before. In Alice Wu's *Global Nomads: Cultural Bridges in the Age of Technology*, students, who included a number of TCKs, shared experiences and insights about advantages and disadvantages of their mobile lifestyles, as well as the effects of technology. One remarked:

> "It's interesting to think that people even ten to fifteen years back didn't necessarily have these kinds of resources to reach out. We are the first generation to be reckoning with this, defining the way we go about relating to one another."[2]

This demonstrates how fast the world is changing. Today's TCKs likely can't imagine the past without these tools. In fact, when the authors asked a group of TCKs and ATCKs who frequent the Third Culture Kids Facebook page what they thought were similarities and differences between older TCKs and younger ones, ATCK Melissa Gatlin wrote:

> The only thing I find different between us early ones [TCKs]
> and those that became TCKs after the '80s—'90s is that
> most of my post-'90 TCKs keep in contact with more of their
> old friends due to Internet. Some of the really young ones
> I know were amazed that I have no contacts from my first
> eleven years . . . because they had Skype accounts since
> 2004 or had previously used email or social media to keep
> in touch.[3]

Other remarks from the TCK panel moderated by Alice Wu at Cornell University certainly substantiate this idea that it is not hard for today's TCKs to keep in touch with one another in a way never done before:

> "With Skype and all these things, it's literally feeling like
> we're still with each other . . . imagine without this, it's like
> you're just on a lonely planet."

> "Being able to send someone an iMessage—no matter where
> they are, they get that—or a Snapchat—no matter what
> you're doing, somewhere someone who's really far away
> can see what you're doing too. You come back and pick up
> exactly where you left off."[4]

There is no question that fundamentally it is far more possible for today's TCKs to keep in touch with friends of all backgrounds and from any corner of the globe. The TCKs attending Cornell reported that their transitions to university were also made easier since they could stay in close touch with their families and friends they had just left.[5]

But students also expressed concern. Some students also had reservations about technology and how the ability to be in constant contact with so many people could feel overwhelming. Others wondered whether social media, like Facebook, were good for active communication, or simply for providing information.

Their concerns have merit. For all the good ways technology helps TCKs (and others, of course) keep in touch with past relationships, it is true that this can lead to other types of stress. Feeling obligated to keep up with the past can, indeed, be overwhelming. With instant communication possible everywhere, these tweets and texts and messages can consume an enormous amount of the TCKs' time. And since their friends know they are available on the other side of this message, if they don't answer pretty quickly, the friend can feel ignored and angry. And so the pressure to keep up is high while the time to do so with this large number of friends is limited.

One other potential problem, however, is that keeping up with past relationships prevents some TCKs from moving into the present and future. Tina Quick, author of *Survive and Thrive: The International Student's Guide to Succeeding in the U.S.*, says this is a major issue for many international students at universities. She tells of a student whose roommate had lived in China, so she stayed up very late at night to chat in real time with her friends and family, then frequently slept through classes, and flunked out of school.[6]

> While today's communications technology can be such a blessing for staying in touch with friends and family around the globe, it can also be an incredible time ravager. With Internet social networking sites such as Facebook, Snapchat, Twitter, Instagram, and others that seem to be popping up nearly every day, students can find that they are spending more time on their cyber relationships than with the real thing. Or they may be spending more time on the computer playing games or watching movies than on their studying. Life can actually begin to revolve around mobile screen technology, even when real, physical people are present. And this is not just a TCK phenomena in the least.[7]

Parents also express concern as they watch their TCKs arrive at a new place and refuse to engage with people they are meeting at school or in the community. Instead, these TCKs prefer to rush to their rooms after school to connect to far-flung friends via the Internet rather than making new friends. Another reason some TCKs don't want to move on is they feel as if they are being disloyal to these past friends if they stop spending as much time on the Internet in order to more fully enter their present scene by finding new friends in their new location. One TCK who had tried that "past only" method in one move decided in her next move to refrain from using the Internet for two weeks after the move so she would be forced to get to know new friends and then go back to social media on a more measured basis. So perhaps the new challenge is how to teach a balance between the good of maintaining friendships while also building new relationships in the current place.

Deep and Valued Relationships

Presuming that the TCKs have found a "both/and" way for keeping past relationships while moving to the present, it seems there are particular challenges when those who have grown up in the third culture try to establish real-time relationships with those who did not grow up in this lifestyle. This seems to happen most often when the TCKs are in a "hidden immigrant" status, such as the time they return to their passport country or appear similar to the students in the host country. Or it may happen later when they enter the job market and bump into invisible walls they can't understand. Somehow it seems others are playing by a set of social rules they have missed.

If we go back to the cultural iceberg, it is true that in the unseen layer there are, in fact, unwritten rules for how people first meet and then process moving into deeper relationships. Ironically, TCKs may have instinctively learned these unspoken rules in whatever culture they were in before. The problem is if they play by these old rules when the rules have changed, there are these unseen cultural clashes Dr. Weaver warned about.

One common complaint from many TCKs is that they feel people in their home cultures are "shallow" or "don't care about me." Conversations with peers seem boring, and the TCKs long for the good old days with their international friends. Why is this such a common complaint?

The fact is that while there are undoubtedly different cultural rules for how to begin establishing relationships in different cultures and countries, each culture has them. People in different cultures not only enter but move through the various levels at different paces. Some cultures jump past small talk quickly and treat strangers like long-lost cousins, inviting them to stay the night, eat what they want, and come as often as they wish. In other cultures nobody bothers to go next door to say hello to the family that just moved in from who knows where. It might be interesting for someone to do a survey to see if this sense of others being "shallow" or "not caring" relates to the type of community around them. But regardless, over and over we hear this complaint from older TCKs and ATCKs.

JUMPING INTO DEEP LEVELS OF FRIENDSHIP

So what's the deal here? For various reasons, TCKs seem prone immediately to get into topics that fall into level three. In other words, while others are still at the "polite" stages, TCKs are offering opinions on and asking what others think about such topics as how the president's term is going, what the government should do on its immigration policy, or whether the United Nations should intervene in some new world crisis. Perhaps even more often, they are asking what others might perceive as a too-personal question for the time they have been together. When the new acquaintances either don't seem to care about (or may not even know about) these global issues, or don't want to express their opinions or share personal details, TCKs deem them shallow—and who knows what those others think of the TCKs? They may see the TCKs as brash, impolite, prying, or arrogant.

Why do TCKs and ATCKs often jump into supposedly deeper levels of communication faster than others? We offer several possibilities.

1. *Cultures define "deeper level" in different ways.* On an Internet chat group for TCKs, this matter of relational levels became a hot topic of discussion. An interesting response came from a Dutch ATCK, Ard A. Louis, who grew up in Gabon and now lives in New York. He wrote:

At least among educated Europeans, it's very common to discuss politics or other potentially divisive topics upon a first encounter. In fact, sometimes we look for something to argue about on purpose. Part of being "educated" is being able to talk about art, philosophy, politics, etc. . . . and argue your points if need be.

This is very different with Americans, who seem always to look for points of common interest. For example, how often when you meet someone do they ask where you're from and then try to find some point of commonality like "I've been there" or "Do you know so and so?"

Another very common topic of discussion is pop culture, especially movies/TV shows most people have seen. (Pop culture is the great unifying factor in the U.S.—and being well versed in its history helps tremendously in fitting in.) Thus, a very common first impression of Europeans arriving in the U.S. is that Americans are superficial because they seem to have no opinions about even their own political situation, let alone what's happening in the rest of the world.[8]

Ard's point is that, as we said earlier, the methods and styles of relating to one another differ from culture to culture according to cultural habit. Of course, when we don't know the expectations of a particular situation, we can unknowingly offend someone because topics TCKs talk about are also often seen as being in the third level already. Seth, a Scottish ATCK, found this out the hard way.

I'd never met this Israeli businessman before that evening, but during supper with a group of expats welcoming him to our community, I asked him how the political situation in Israel was doing.

Another person at the table, Carrie, was a U.S. American. She almost spit out her food and instantly changed the subject of conversation. When we finished that new topic, I went back to my original question. Carrie had the same reaction.

Afterward she told me how horribly rude I'd been to ask such a question of someone I barely knew. Frankly, I was stunned. Here was a guy with lots of firsthand information about key world issues and Carrie thought I shouldn't talk about it. I asked her why this was so bad. She told me in her family and culture you were never allowed to talk about religion or politics because that always caused trouble and I wondered: What else would you talk about?

Until I heard about these different levels of communication and personal relationships, I couldn't understand why
I shouldn't start with asking for simple information about
a political situation in another country. As a TCK, we were
always interested to know from people on the ground how
things were. By the time you read such news in any paper
or on the Internet, you aren't sure if it is how the people living there experience it, so why not ask? It blew my mind![9]

2. *Practice with conversations has taught TCKs to jump into deeper levels quickly
using questions.* Many TCKs know how to get into relationships fairly quickly
when they want to simply because they have had so much practice starting and moving through getting-to-know-you conversations. But it may be
more than that. A few years ago Ruth had an "Aha!" about how and why it
seems when TCKs and ATCKs meet, they often seem to begin their exploration of the *other* with questions beyond the polite clichés or discussion of
the weather.

For years, I have wondered why it seems when I meet new
people all over the world, I happily jump into asking various questions so I can (in my mind) get to know them. I find
people's stories fascinating and I always want to know more
of who this person is past the surface.

At the same time, I confess my frustration that often
when I do ask questions, I seem to hit a brick wall. A few
years ago I took a job at a nursing home and each mealtime,
I would ask the other employee sitting at my table questions
such as, "Are you from here?" "Yes/no," comes the reply . . .
(cut the meat while answering). If no, "Where did you grow
up?" "Ohio" (lift fork to mouth). "How long have you worked
here?" "Five years" (chomp chomp chomp). "Are you married?" "Yes/no" (lift glass for a quick drink).

Never once would these new acquaintances ask me back
a question as simple as the dreaded, "So where are you
from?" Even if it is the unanswerable question for many of
us, isn't it a common response people often use to extend the
conversation?

At first I chalked it up to different educational levels
or social/cultural styles. Then I attended a farewell dinner
for some professional people. Surely they would talk. The
process began: "Hi, Are you from here?" (maybe that would
work better than "Where are you from?") . . . and the entire
pattern of nonresponse to me replayed itself. This group was
actively engaged with each other, but not once in the entire

evening did anyone answer my inquiries with an inquiry in return.

This truly puzzled me. No wonder so many TCKs and ATCKs say, "No one cares about my story." It seemed to be the truth!

It wasn't until a few years later when Ruth attended a storytelling seminar and the leader asked participants to introduce themselves not by name or occupation but rather through a one-minute-or-less snippet of their story that her "Aha!" came. Of the six attendees, Ruth knew three. When they gave their snippet, she knew where to put that piece in the overall context of their story. Conversely, when the other three told their snippet, all it did was raise a host of questions in her mind. Why were they on this airplane? What forest were they walking through? Because she knew nothing about them, she had no place to hang this information. That's when she realized that due to the high mobility patterns of her life, she was constantly meeting people whose stories she doesn't know. Thus, in order to have some framework from which to understand them and their story, she had to ask questions.

For people who have grown up basically in one place, however, when they interact with their neighbors on a day-to-day basis—even as they meet new acquaintances—a simple answer tells the whole story. "Where are you from?" "Berea." And to one who knows Berea (because they've lived near Berea or heard about Berea), that word can give clues of class and economic and social status because "everyone" here knows that "if you are from Berea, then you are (fill in the blanks)." No more questions are needed. But if the TCK knows nothing about Berea, that is simply the name of a town and the TCK knows little more than before he asked the question.

So is one of the issues for those TCKs and ATCKs who don't feel others care simply a matter that in their lives they establish relationships by questions that help them find connections, both because they are interested and because they must ask more questions when "Berea" means nothing to them since they don't speak in the local *shorthand?* Often TCKs and ATCKs have no starting point without questions others may not need to ask, but when those others don't ask questions in return as another TCK/ATCK would do, it seems they don't care.

It's easy in that situation to forget that asking these questions may not be the local people's way of establishing relationships. A series of questions to them may be seen as prying. Because they are used to living in more-monocultural situations, they don't need to ask each other the type of questions TCKs and ATCKs might need to ask because the questions and the answers are within a known context. If the answer had to be explained, it's obvious the inquisitor isn't an *us*, and if they are not used to exploring *other*, then why bother to ask anything in return? Or worse, perhaps they simply see the TCKs and ATCKs as rude, and why would they want to connect with them anyway?

3. *What is normal content in one setting may not be normal, or appropriate, content in another setting.* The store of knowledge from the various experiences they have had feeds into many different topics, so TCKs often think they have something relevant to say. Because of their parents' careers, TCKs often grow up in homes where discussions on a current political crisis, starving children, religious views, or solutions to the economic woes of the country are standard fare. To express opinions on these topics is normal and people around them have asked their opinion or seemed interested because the TCK's firsthand insights might help those others understand the complexity of issues in the newspaper or on television that are happening an ocean away.

4. *TCKs feel a sense of urgency to develop a relationship.* TCKs may also jump into deeper levels of communication quickly because there is little time to develop a particular relationship. They understand that if something doesn't happen now, perhaps it never will. TCKs routinely meet people of incredible diversity who can teach them so much about their part of the world. Why waste time in small talk? In one sense, almost everyone can be an instant friend. Because they have connected at a relatively deep level, many of these quick relationships do become long-term friendships—or at least part of that electronic address book. Sometimes, however, this leads to the TCK being seen as an elephant and trampling over peoples' perceptions of the right approach to a friendship, or even a nice conversation!

MAKING NEW FRIENDS

In *Military Brats*, Mary Edwards Wertsch discusses the "forced extroversion" the military lifestyle fosters because time is too short to wait to make friends. She says one technique she used to break into new groups was the "confessional impulse." In quickly spilling family secrets (a fourth- or fifth-level disclosure), she sent a message that she wanted to invest in a new friendship. Often her confession was met by a similar confession from the new friend. Wertsch also says that military kids might be more willing to be open than their civilian counterparts because they probably won't be around to deal with any negative consequences from these confessions.[10]

Non-TCKs who are used to staying at the first or second level of relationships for relatively long periods may misread TCKs who jump in at a deeper level. This type of confusion happened at a camp where Dave Pollock served as a seminar leader.

> Several days after camp started, a group of tearful, non-TCK young women sought Dave out. They felt completely confused by actions of the TCK males. A young man would

engage one of these young women in, to them, deep and meaningful conversation, and she would think he was interested in her. But the next day he would do the same with someone else. After three days the young women were confused, angry with each other, and angry at the young men.

When Dave spoke to the guys, they were shocked that these girls thought they had even considered anything more than a friendship for this week at camp. The TCK young men said they had no romantic presuppositions whatsoever. They just wanted to get to know these young women, find out what they thought about life, the world, their faith, and other assorted interesting topics. It seemed like a perfect chance to understand more about non-TCK Americans. But the seriousness of the conversation communicated a level of warmth and relationship that meant something quite different to the young women.

TCKs usually place a high value on their relationships—especially those from their TCK world. Often the style and intensity of friendship within the international third culture is quite different from the types of friendships they have in their home country. Most expatriate families live far from relatives and tend to reach out to one another as surrogate families in times of need. When there is a coup, it's the friends in this international community who are together in the fear, the packing, the wondering, and the leaving. Without a doubt, a great deal of bonding that lasts a lifetime takes place at such times.

FINDING SOMEONE WHO REMEMBERS

Relationships—both with friends and family at home as well as with friends from their third culture world—are also valued because they give the TCKs a sense of connectedness. These relationships are the one place TCKs can say, "Do you remember when . . .?" and someone actually does!

A TCK's wedding is usually quite a sight. When Robin Shea married Kevin McGee, her high school sweetheart from boarding school, you would have thought you were in Africa rather than in New York. Papier-maché palm trees framing a painted mural of a tropical beach decorated the reception hall. Kevin and his groomsmen all wore flowing robes from Sierra Leone. Robin's dad wore a chief's robe as he walked her down the aisle. Friends came from far and near, filling the pews with equally colorful attire. The wedding had turned into a minireunion. Watching these TCKs chatter unceasingly throughout the reception was like watching

long-lost family members reunite. There was no question
about how they viewed their relationships from the past.

Effects of Cycles of Multiple Losses on Relationships

While many TCKs jump into relationships with both feet, others approach any
new relationship with caution. In a 1986 survey of 300 ATCKs, 40 percent of
the respondents said they struggled with a fear of intimacy because of the fear
of loss.[11] Too many close friends had moved away. Frequent, painful good-byes
make some TCKs unwilling to risk emotional involvement again.

Often these TCKs are labeled as quiet or shy. They never take available opportunities to be deeply engaged in their schools or communities. Even TCKs
who are regarded as gregarious, open, and friendly because of their skill at jumping into the second and third levels of communication often refuse to move on to
the fourth and fifth levels of true intimacy. They manage to erect walls, usually
without realizing it, to keep out anyone trying to come closer.

When Fiona became engaged to Jack, she couldn't believe
that someone would actually be with her for the rest of her
life, so she prepared for what seemed the inevitable loss by
presuming Jack would have a fatal car wreck before their
marriage. When that didn't happen, she feared it would
happen on their honeymoon. After safely returning from
their honeymoon, Fiona worried whenever Jack was a few
minutes late coming home from work. On their first anniversary, he was over two hours late due to an electrical failure
in the mass transportation system. By the time he got home,
she had started crying with an "I knew it would happen"
despair, had begun to plan his funeral, and wondered how
long you had to be married before you didn't need to return
the wedding gifts.

Although Jack is living to this day, for a long time after
the wedding Fiona couldn't understand why she always
seemed to fuss over insignificant details—like whose turn
it was to take out the garbage—just when she and Jack
felt especially close. She finally realized that deep inside
such closeness terrified her because she still feared losing
it. Fussing was her way to keep up a wall of safety. Fiona
had been losing people she loved dearly since first separating from her parents at age six when she left for boarding
school, and it took a long time for her to let her guard down
and dare to believe Jack would be staying.

As we will see in our discussion on the stages of transition (chapter 13), people try to protect themselves from the pain of losing a precious, or at least valued, relationship in various ways. TCKs are no different. Here are three common ways it happens.

1. *Refusing to care.* Some try to limit their vulnerability to impending grief by refusing to acknowledge they care for anyone or anything. In the end, however, they know a pain of loneliness far greater than the one from which they are running. The independence they have been so proud of turns into a profound isolation that keeps them prisoner until the day they become willing to once more feel the pain of loss in order to know the joy of closeness.

2. *Quick release.* A second common response for people trying to avoid the pain of losing a relationship is called the "quick release." This is a form of the "leaning away" we discuss in chapter 13 as part of the leaving stage of transition. When friends are about to leave, or when TCKs think they themselves might be leaving, their response is frequently to let go too soon. Friends stop calling each other and don't visit, play together, or go out for lunch. Each wonders what he or she did to upset the other one. A "quick release" also happens at points when some kind of temporary separation is about to occur. Many ATCKs talk of how easily they have an argument with a spouse the night before one of them is leaving for a short business trip the next day—an unconscious attempt to protect against loss based on past patterns rather than the reality of the moment. Some ATCKs who themselves have commonly used anger as part of their quick release (or had it used by those they were separating from) may see any type of anger as a precursor to separation and emotionally detach at the first sign of it.

> Garth and his new bride had their first argument. He told us later, "I knew right then she was going to leave me." Inside, he went stone cold toward her. *Let her leave. I don't care. I don't know why I married her anyway,* he thought. When he finally realized his wife had no intention of leaving, he began to think through his reaction and what had happened. He remembered frequent arguments with his parents just before he left for boarding school, probably each of them unconsciously trying to make the leaving easier. Garth began to realize that because of that previous pattern, he subconsciously made automatic assumptions that any conflict meant the impending loss of a relationship.

3. *Emotional flattening.* Refusing to feel the pain is another common response of TCKs to the multiple losses due to the high mobility of their lives. Even when TCKs feel intensely about leaving a friend or relative, some refuse to acknowledge the hurt to others or themselves. It's almost as if they will themselves to be emotionally flat—feeling neither great joy nor great pain.

They say they don't like messy good-byes and, in fact, refuse to say them. Becky and Mary Ann were two ATCKs caught in this pattern.

> Becky and Mary Ann had met at a Global Nomads International conference. For both of them, it was the first time they had consciously reflected on how their pasts as TCKs had affected them. Each had basked in the joy of discovering another person who understood her deep, inner, secret places. They had laughed together, cried together, and talked incessantly. Suddenly the conference was over, and that inevitable moment of saying good-bye had come.
>
> Becky and Mary Ann stood by the elevator as Mary Ann prepared to leave for the airport. Chances were great they would never see each other again; they lived an ocean apart. As they looked at one another, each knew she had let the other into a space usually kept off-limits. What did they do now?
>
> After a brief, uncomfortable stare, both broke into wry smiles of understanding.
>
> "So what do we say?" Becky asked first.
>
> "I guess there's not much to say but the usual," and Mary Ann paused, bent her right arm up so the palm of her hand faced Becky. Like a windshield wiper making one sweep across the windscreen, Mary Ann moved her forearm from left to right while saying "Byyee."
>
> "I guess you're right, Mary Ann. So byyee," and Becky mirrored the perfunctory farewell wave Mary Ann had just made.
>
> Then they laughed. For some, this might have seemed an incredibly cold way to say good-bye after they had shared their lives so intensely. For them, however, it was a moment of recognition, of understanding how each had learned to avoid painful farewells. They simply didn't acknowledge them! But, in another way, it also represented the sum of all they had shared that needed no verbal explanation.

Unfortunately, however, not all who exercise the protective mechanism of emotional flattening realize it as poignantly as Mary Ann and Becky did at their moment of parting. Even more unfortunately, this flat emotional response can be transferred from avoiding the pain of farewells to all areas of life. Sometimes what is praised as confidence and independence among TCKs may actually be a form of detachment. In his book *Your Inner Child of the Past*, psychiatrist Hugh Missildine cites the work of John Bowlby and says that whenever there is a prolonged loss of relationship between parent and child, for *whatever* reason, children go through grief, despair, and, finally, *detachment* in trying to cope with that loss.[12] Historically, many TCKs have known profound separation from their parents at an early age when they went to boarding schools around the age of six. While this practice has changed markedly and relatively few TCKs leave home this early, attachment can still be a huge issue for the ATCKs who did leave home at a young age. In addition to going away for schooling, however, the chronicity of separating so repeatedly from friends and other relatives can lead to a habit of detachment for many TCKs, whether they went to boarding school or not. They simply refuse to let themselves care about or need anyone again. The sad thing is, when pain is shut down, so is the capacity to fully feel or express joy.

This detachment response can be devastating in a romantic relationship or marriage. The ATCK's partner feels rejected because there are too few external demonstrations of love from the ATCK. Conversely, no matter how many romantic gestures are offered to the ATCK, nothing seems to spark a warm response.

It can be equally painful for the child of such an ATCK. Some ATCK parents seem genuinely unable to delight openly in the pure joy of having a child, of watching that child grow, of playing games together, or of reading stories at bedtime. Not only do the children miss the warmth and approval they long for, but the ATCK parent also loses out on one of the richest relationships possible in life.

We have seen TCKs' lives enriched when they learn to deal in healthy ways with the cycle of relationships they face. They do, in fact, have a wealth of experiences to share and rich diversity among those they have met, and they have every possibility for making truly deep friendships that last across the years and miles. As TCKs become skilled at going through the process of transition in the healthy ways discussed in later chapters, they can learn to enjoy each relationship they have, whether it be a long- or short-term friendship. Because all people lose relationships at one time or another, they can share the transitional skills they've learned for themselves to help others cope during their own life transitions.

Expanding Our Vision

Again, many of these patterns appear in the TCK experience not primarily because they are TCKs, but because they are human beings who are all in the process of negotiating relationships and connections with others—and they are trying to protect themselves from being hurt. Surely refugees who have known incredible, wrenching separations from family and country must build up some form of protection to survive for a period of time. Within families, and particularly families with parents from different cultural heritages, finding the places of connection is important. For CCKs and people of all backgrounds, taking a look inside their relationships will, hopefully, open a broad discussion about the multiple layering of cross-cultural relationships and the growing complexity of our world in general, and how that affects relationships.

Questions for Chapter 11

1. Would you say in general it's easy or hard for you when you meet new people to begin a conversation with them? How do you usually handle those first moments—either way?
2. What would you say is the pattern for how people establish relationships in your passport country/culture? Have you lived where the cultural rules for relationships were quite different? If so, how did that feel and what did you do?
3. What do you think the biggest challenge is for long-term relationships for TCKs/ ATCKs? What is the biggest gift?
4. How would you say these challenges and gifts are the same as or different from those with other CCK or even non-CCK backgrounds? Please explain.
5. What are lessons you may have learned by this point in life to overcome the challenges and enjoy the gifts more?

CHAPTER 12

Developmental Issues

I missed many social cues that I would rush to remedy, lest anyone think I purposely intended to offend—seemingly inconsequential things like saying, "Nice to meet you," at introductions, the tradition of purchasing graduation gifts for friends. . . . Funny enough, through all the changes, I had been placed "ahead" in school—missing sixth and seventh grade—when I was in New York City. Because of our travel, school officials were unsure of what grade I should be placed in, and subsequent testing placed me two grades further. As the years passed, when I missed what should-have-been an obvious social cue in my home country of the United States of America, I attributed it to having skipped the grades where my peers learned these norms. It wasn't until my late thirties that I realized it was my entire upbringing, not those supposedly essential two years, that caused the gap.[1]

—Doni, Publisher
Culturs: The Global Multicultural Magazine

Doni is one of the more amazingly culturally complex ATCKs we have met, an ATCK who identified with seven cultures and lived in five countries before adulthood. Doni describes herself as "being a United States Citizen, with a decent foundation of the country's cultural norms, an Afro-Latina Caribbean heritage and global mobility along with the potential to carry three passports." In chapters 4 and 6, we discussed how various patterns of moving in and between different cultural worlds can be a challenge as TCKs try to develop a clear sense of their own identity. But Doni's story is one more proof that for many, the ways of the past where this developmental process happened relatively easily and naturally when most communities were stable and fairly monocultural are gone. That often leads to another developmental reality lurking in the shadows that is also evident in this snippet of Doni's story: It is the matter of *uneven maturity*.

In matters related to a global awareness or interacting with adults, historically, at least, TCKs have often seemed far older than their years. Notice how the educators at times advanced Doni in school beyond her years, yet she had just mentioned missing all the social clues. Like Doni, in relationships with peers in their passport cultures, they may sometimes seem quite clueless as to what is appropriate and thus appear immature. People often say, "I can't believe you're only fourteen (or whatever age). You seem much older." Equally often (and probably behind their backs), these same or other people marvel at the TCKs' lack of sophistication or social skills. Some TCKs feel this discrepancy too and start to wonder which person they really are: the competent, capable, mature self or the bungling, insecure, immature self? In many ways they're both; that's part of the problem in trying to figure out who they are. Why is uneven maturity such a common issue for many TCKs?

UNEVEN MATURITY

To understand why TCKs seem to face such an uneven task while moving into true maturity, let's stop and remind ourselves of some fundamental developmental tasks we all face on our path from infancy to adulthood. Figure 12-1 gives us some clues about how and why maturity develops unevenly for many TCKs.

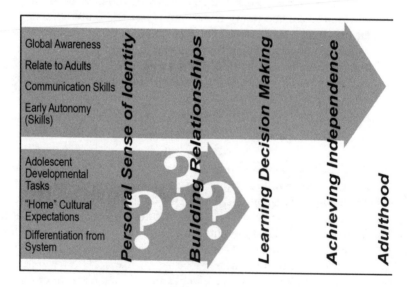

Figure 12–1: Uneven Maturity for TCKs
©2008 Barbara H. Knuckles. Used by permission.

Looking left to right across this model, we see five emotional and psychological developmental tasks every child must navigate to move in a relatively smooth manner from dependent infant to a mature, responsible adult:

- Developing a sense of personal identity
- Building strong relationships
- Developing competence in decision making
- Achieving independence
- Moving into adulthood

When looking top to bottom in the smaller print, there are aspects of the TCK lifestyle that may accelerate the normal developmental process. The last three show where the same TCK experience can slow it down a bit. We'll look at the normal stages first, then at factors for the early maturity and the others for late maturity, including prolonged adolescence.

Developmental Tasks

From birth, children of every race, color, creed, or background begin to perform various developmental tasks. They move from rolling over to sitting, crawling, standing, walking, and, finally, running. Each task is sequential. If a broken leg keeps a child from learning to stand, he or she must still learn to stand when the leg heals before learning to walk and eventually to run. Although we all use and build on these foundational accomplishments throughout life, when they happen as expected, we take them for granted. This is what life "should" be. However, if a child isn't walking by age two, something is out of sync. Pediatricians call it *delayed development* and begin to investigate the reasons for this delay. But how does this relate to the TCK experience?

While learning to run and talk are two early physical developmental tasks, there are other important steps in every child's growth from infancy to becoming a mature adult, including these critical emotional and psychological developmental processes.

1. *Establishing a personal sense of identity.* This begins early on as children begin to differentiate their sense of self from their parents (think "terrible twos!"). It's also a process of discovering, *Who am I? What makes me me? Where do I fit in my family and group?*
2. *Establishing and maintaining strong relationships.* Young children initially bond to their immediate families, but during their teenage years relationships with peers become critical before they can move on into adulthood.
3. *Developing competence in decision making.* Competent decision making is based on the assumption that the world is predictable and that individuals have some measure of control. In ideal situations, children and adolescents learn to make decisions under the protection of the family before moving on to make their own choices.

4. *Achieving independence.* When we have the stability of knowing what the rules of the family and culture are and have learned to make competent decisions, we can begin moving toward the independence of adulthood.

5. *Moving into adulthood.* With the first four stages complete, adolescents are ready to move on into adulthood. They have established a sense of "otherness" from parents and families of origin and are confident, ready, and able to take responsibility for their decisions and actions.

Traditionally, most people moved through these developmental tasks while living in one physical place or one primary culture group. In that context, the world stayed constant. There was a solid place to test the rules and know decisions made could have a relatively predictable outcome. This kind of psychological and emotional development happened as normally as learning to walk and talk does for most children. No one thought much about it. This traditional world, however, is not the one in which TCKs grow up. As a result, these developmental tasks are often being interrupted or expedited. It is from that process we see both early maturity and prolonged adolescence. Here are some reasons for both among TCKs. Refer to figure 12-2.

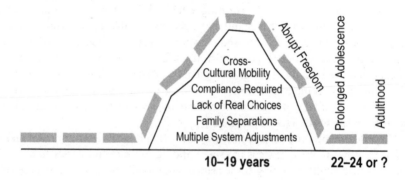

Figure 12–2: Prolonged Adolescence for TCKs

©2008 Barhara H. Knuckles, updated 2017. Used by permission.

Early Maturity

It's not only others who see TCKs as "more mature." They often feel more comfortable with older students rather than fellow classmates when they begin college back in their passport countries. Others are amazed with their confidence to travel the world alone or how well they communicate with adults. There are several reasons for these places where they seem "ahead of the game."

1. *Broad base of knowledge and global awareness.* TCKs often have an "advanced for their years" knowledge of geography, global events, and politics in other countries and are interested in topics not usually discussed by younger

people in their home cultures. Many TCKs have learned unusual practical skills at a very young age as well—such as how to set up solar energy panels to keep computers running for translation work in the Amazon jungle, how to or how to pilot a single engine plane, or breed rabbits for a meat business.

2. *Relationship to adults.* TCKs generally feel quite comfortable with adults because they have had lots of experience with them. Generations usually mix much more in third culture communities than in the home country. Why? Because, at least traditionally, many expatriate communities live within relatively defined parameters: kids attend the same school; most of the parents appear at the same international or organizational functions; families may go to the only international church in town; and they bump into one another frequently in the one or two grocery stores that carry foods imported from their particular homeland. Since the children may already be friends through school, families visit as families rather than as adults only. In certain situations—such as homeschooling—some TCKs spend more time with adults than children, which makes them come across almost as "mini-adults."

3. *Communication skills.* Children who speak two or more languages fluently also seem like mini-adults. How could they have learned to speak like this so soon in life? Multilingual TCKs generally feel at ease using their languages to communicate with quite diverse groups. In fact, TCKs often serve as translators for their parents—again, a task usually reserved for adults. All this continues to increase their exposure to, participation in, and comfort with a world of culturally diverse adults as well as other children and gives them an unusual air of maturity.

4. *Early autonomy.* In many ways, TCKs have an earlier sense of autonomy than peers at home. By their early teenage years, TCKs literally know how to get around in the world and enjoy functioning in quite diverse ways and places. This may be the result of traveling alone to boarding school or having the opportunity as young children to explore their surroundings freely by trikes, bikes, and hikes. A reliable, safe public transportation system in some countries adds to that sense of autonomy. Many TCKs in Japan take the train for two hours each way to school—even in early elementary grades. When one TCK lived in Australia, he took a ferry and a bus by himself to school every day at age eleven, while his friends back in the United States waited at the corner of their street for the school bus to pick them up.

These are some of the reasons why TCKs are often told, "You seem so much older than your age." But what about the three other factors on this list:

- Adolescent developmental tasks
- "Home" cultural expectations
- Differentiation from system

How might they contribute to this uneven maturity? Let's see.

Prolonged Adolescence

Ironically, while in many ways TCKs seem advanced for their years, there are also many ways they seem to lag far behind. In a 1993 survey of nearly 700 ATCKs, Ruth Hill Useem and Ann Baker Cottrell observed that it wasn't unusual for TCKs to go through a prolonged adolescence, often between the ages of twenty-two and twenty-four, and sometimes even later.[2] TCKs who have never heard the expression "prolonged adolescence" have still sensed that they are definitely out of sync with their peers at times but can't figure out why.

What exactly does this term mean? In the past, we have used the term "delayed adolescence" to speak of this psychological phenomenon but have now come to realize that this is a medical term for the physical delay of adolescence. So we return to the term "prolonged adolescence," which Dr. Ruth Useem and Dr. Ann Baker Cottrell used in their landmark survey of ATCKs.[3] And why is it a characteristic of many TCKs? Let's first define adolescence itself. Here's one definition we found before our first revision in 2009:

> Adolescence essentially begins when physiologically normal puberty starts. *It ends when the person develops an adult identity and behavior* [italics added]. This period of development corresponds roughly to the period between the ages of 10 and 19 years.[4]

Interestingly, this is no longer the standard for the parameters of adolescence! Around 2013, new guidelines came out from various professional organizations who specialize in child and adolescent psychology saying that adolescence is now considered to be extended to age twenty-five.[5] This, then, raises a question: Shall we simply scrap this part of our book and say that TCKs are now in what is considered the normal range for adolescence and let it go? Or shall we at least share what the early researchers noticed about TCKs in this regard as early as the mid-1980s? Dave Pollock included this characteristic in every seminar he did by the mid- to late-1980s and on. This may be one of the first actual "proofs" of Michigan State University sociologist Dr. Ted Ward's statement in 1984 that TCKs were the prototype citizen of the future.[6] The question some current researchers might wish to consider as they look at some of the reasons earlier researchers on the TCK phenomenon believed might be the cause of this prolonged adolescence (compared to what was then the norm): Are there parallel reasons in what was observed about TCKs in earlier years that might be happening in a different context for virtually everyone in today's world? Is this one place where researchers can dig more deeply into studying the TCK experience as a concentrated form of what is becoming the "new normal" for so many across the globe? We believe it might be so.

For that reason, and because all TCKs and their families didn't yet get the memo that normal adolescence has now been extended for the general public, they may continue to wonder, What is wrong with me? So let's go back to basics.

What is prolonged adolescence as the TCK community has observed it for many years now? We realize we were comparing TCKs to the normed developmental standards derived from studying children from monocultural childhood patterns of the past.

Simply stated, prolonged adolescence means it often takes TCKs longer than what has been traditionally considered "normal" to complete the emotional and psychological developmental tasks that move people from infancy to adulthood. The tasks we listed earlier—developing a sense of personal identity, building strong relationships, developing competence in decision making, and achieving independence—are all part of that process of ultimately moving into adulthood. Prolonged adolescence doesn't mean TCKs can't complete these tasks. It simply means it may take a bit more time. Don't forget: a child who breaks a leg before learning to walk will, in fact, walk in the end, but not as soon as others.

But the question remains: Why has prolonged adolescence (compared to past norms) been so common for many TCKs—long before it was noticed for the population as a whole?

Adolescent Developmental Tasks

Cross-cultural mobility in developmental years disrupts the flow of tasks adolescents complete as they mature. We go back again to yet another reason why cross-cultural transitions and high mobility *during developmental years* are so significant.

As we've said before, part of completing the developmental tasks of building a personal sense of identity, building relationship, learning decision making, and achieving independence on the way to adulthood involves a testing of the rules, values, and beliefs learned in childhood during these adolescent years. One common way teens test is through direct challenges, something parents of teenagers around the world know only too well: "Why do I have to be in by midnight?" "Who says I can't wear my hair like this?"

After the testing is a period of integrating the cultural practices and values we decide (often unconsciously) to keep. We then use these to make decisions about how we will live as autonomous adults rather than continuing to live as children guided by external, parental rules alone. When the cultural rules are always changing, however, what happens to this process? This is, again, why the issues of cultural balance and mobility—and the age or ages when they occur—become very important. Often at the very time TCKs should be testing and internalizing the customs and values of whatever culture they've grown up in, that whole world, its familiar culture, and their relationships to it can change overnight with one plane ride. While peers in their new (and old) community are internalizing the rules of culture and beginning to move out with budding confidence, TCKs are still trying to figure out what the rules are. They aren't free to explore their personal gifts and talents because they're still preoccupied with what is or isn't appropriate behavior. Children who have to learn to juggle many sets of cultural rules at the same time have a different developmental experience from children growing up in one basically permanent, dominant culture that they regard as their own.

1. *Extended compliance required.* Some TCKs experience prolonged development because of an extended compliance to cultural rules. In certain situations, TCKs are not as free as peers at home might be to test cultural rules during their teenage years. For instance, some TCKs need to comply with the status quo in a given situation for their own safety and acceptance. Instead of freedom to hang out with friends in shopping malls or on the street corners, many TCKs find themselves restricted, perhaps for safety reasons, to the military base or missionary compound. If they don't want to be kidnapped or robbed, they must obey regulations that might not be necessary in the home country. Also, some TCKs' families belong to organizations with fairly rigid rules of what its members (and their families) may and may not do. An embassy kid doing drugs or a missionary daughter who gets pregnant can result in a quick repatriation for the family. In such cases, not only might the parents lose their jobs, but the TCKs might well lose what they consider to be home. This adds pressure to follow community standards longer than they might otherwise.

2. *Lack of opportunities for meaningful choices.* In the situations just mentioned, when TCKs aren't as free as their friends in the home country might be to make some of the decisions about where they will go and what they will do, they don't have the same opportunity to test parental and societal rules until a later period in life than usual.

   In addition, as we saw in the discussion of the delusion of choice in chapter 8, the fact that life is often unpredictable makes it hard for many TCKs to make decisions. It's difficult to make a competent decision if the basis used to decide something is always changing. A TCK's lifestyle in many third culture communities is frequently dictated by the sponsoring agency. If the U.S. Navy assigns a parent for a six-month deployment, it doesn't matter what the TCK does or doesn't decide about it—that parent will be going. For these reasons and probably more, some TCKs don't learn to take responsibility for the direction of their lives. They are more prone to just "letting it happen."

3. *Family separations.* TCKs who are separated from their parents during adolescence may not have the normal opportunity of challenging and testing parental values and choices as others do. Some who were separated in early years find themselves wanting to cling to parental nurture and make up for early losses. They don't want to move into adulthood yet. Still others who have spent years away from home may idealize their parents in almost fantasy form. To challenge anything about their parents would call that dream into question. In situations such as these, we've seen many TCKs delay the

normal adolescent process of differentiating their identity from that of their parents until their late twenties or even into their thirties.

"Home" Cultural Expectations

Operating between different cultural systems causes the adolescent to be confused about norms and expectations in each culture. Incompatible educational and social factors also contribute to at least the appearance of prolonged adolescence. The Danish TCK who graduates from an American-based international school may return to Denmark and discover that she must do two more years at the secondary level before going to university. Suddenly she is grouped with those younger than herself and treated as their peer. This is especially traumatic if she's become accustomed to being seen as older than her years. The social slowness discussed earlier can contribute to prolonged adolescence by severely impeding the normal developmental task of establishing and maintaining strong relationships—particularly with peers and members of the opposite sex. Judith Gjoen, a Dutch ATCK who grew up in Indonesia and is now a clinical counselor in Norway, wrote about the difficulties Europeans face on their return home after attending a predominantly international school.

> Dating is very American. Scandinavian ways of interrelating between the sexes are much more informal. There is much more flexibility in the sex roles. All boys learn to knit; all girls learn carpentry. Furthermore, a young person's identity is not so strongly connected to "dating status." From a Scandinavian perspective, the American way can be slightly overdone and hysterical. You are not prepared for the European way of being together [males and females] when you have been socialized into an American system.[7]

The development of other social skills may also be delayed by not knowing the unwritten rules in the TCK's age group back home or in the new culture. How loudly do you play music? How long do you talk on the phone? When do you engage in chitchat and when in deeper conversations? How do you behave with a friend of the opposite sex? When the rules around them have changed, TCKs sometimes retreat into isolation from others rather than try to cope.

Sometimes the very maturity noted earlier coupled with the sometimes more hidden prolonged adolescence may lead to unforeseen problems. The initial attraction of a young TCK to older, more mature people may result in the choosing of an older marriage partner. Unfortunately, while the "early maturity" of the TCK may make such a match seem like a good idea, the deeper delay in development may scuttle the relationship later on. Sometimes the TCK isn't as ready for the responsibility or partnership of marriage as he or she appeared to be because the issues of personal identity, good decision making, and ability to build strong relationships haven't been resolved. Other times, as in any marriage, when the younger partner goes on to develop a deeper, truer maturity, the older spouse doesn't always continue to grow at the same rate. This can leave the younger partner disappointed, disillusioned, or dissatisfied.

Differentiation from System

TCKs who grow up in the subculture of the parents' sponsoring organization have a few extra factors to deal with in this process of establishing a sense of identity. Although in reality these issues are extensions of what we have already discussed, it's important to understand how growing up in what is often a fairly structured community can be one more factor in a TCK's developmental process.

There can be many benefits to living in a carefully defined system. In many situations, the whole system of the sponsoring organization serves to some extent as both family and community. It provides materially as a good parent might, with air travel paid for, housing provided, and perhaps special stores made available. In many cases, as mentioned earlier, it also provides specific guidance or regulations for behavior.

An organizational system is one of the places where the need for belonging can truly be fulfilled because there are clear demarcations of who does and doesn't belong. Some TCKs have a deeper sense of belonging to that community than they will ever have with any other group and feel secure within the well-ordered structure of their particular system.

Other TCKs, however, feel stifled by the organizational system in which they grew up. They may be straining at the bit to get out of what they see as the rigid policies of the system. They realize that they have had almost no choice in countless matters that have deeply affected their lives—such as when and where their parents moved, where they could go to school, how to behave in certain common circumstances, or how they could express their inner passions. They see their organization as an uncaring nemesis and feel intense rage at a system that requires conformity to rules and regulations regardless of individual preferences. Some blame the system for ruining their lives.

Certainly anyone who grows up in a clearly defined system is very much aware of how the group expects its members to behave. Failure to conform brings great shame on the TCK or the whole family. In many cases, the rules of these systems are a higher priority than the rules of the family, superseding decisions parents would normally make for their own children—such as when and where the children go to school.

What might make the difference in how or why an organizational system seems so positive for one person and restrictive for another? At the risk of oversimplifying, and recognizing that there are many differences in how each agency may be run, figure 12-3 outlines the basic ways TCKs relate to the system in which they grew up—from the perspective of their own personal makeup, gifts, and personality. Understanding this perspective can help us answer the preceding question.

Not Fit Keeps trying to conform *win/lose*	Not Fit Neither conforms nor resists but quietly does own thing *lose/win*
Fits Internal match *win/win*	Not Fit Continually resists system *lose/lose*

Figure 12–3: Barbek Model: Identity in Relationship to the System

©1988 Barbara H. Knuckles. Used by permission.

1. *A TCK who doesn't fit the system but attempts to conform.* Some children, by personality, gifting, or whatever, simply aren't a good fit for this particular system. Secretly, they prefer rap music while others around are denouncing it as junk. They long for color and beautiful decor but live in a plain, brown, adobe-type home within a system that feels it isn't spiritual to focus on worldly beauty. They find crowds of new people frightening, but they paste on a smile and act cordial to the dignitaries at the never-ending receptions. They have learned not to reveal their feelings or desires, because they learned early on that it was *wrong* to feel or think that way. Instead of being able to explore the mystery of their own personality and set of gifts, they feel ashamed of this secret longing and try harder and harder to be what they perceive the system says they should be.

   The major problem for members of this group is that their sense of identity comes almost totally from an external system rather than from the unique mix and validity of who they are deep within. If this type of conformity doesn't change at some point, people in this group may become more and more rigid over the years in adhering to the system that now defines them. They fear that if they let any part of it go, they will lose themselves because they don't know who they are without this structure to hold them together. Secretly they often feel shame that they are not able to be as they "should" be. In this scenario, the individuals lose the chance to live fully as they were made to live, but the system wins as there is no challenge to it.

2. *A TCK who fits the system.* Feeling comfortable is relatively easy for those whose personality and interests pretty well fit within the structure or rules of the system under which they have grown up. It might be an easygoing military kid who never seems to question authority, a pragmatic missionary kid who doesn't see the point of the fancy accessories in a Lexus, or a diplomat's kid who is an extrovert and thrives on meeting new people. They can go along with how life works in this system and it doesn't conflict with how they

think, what they like to do, what they want to be, or, most importantly, who they are by their very nature. There is room in this system to express who they are at this core. It's a pretty good match. Both the individuals and the system "win" because the individuals are living true to themselves internally but in doing that, there is no attempt to rock the system's metaphorical boat.

3. *A person who doesn't completely fit the system but doesn't realize (or at least seem to mind) it.* People in this group go ahead and listen to whatever kind of music they want—not to be rebellious, but because they like it. It doesn't occur to them—or worry them—that others might disapprove. If told that, in fact, others might disapprove, they would likely respond, "That's okay. If they do, I'll use my earphones." They stay in their rooms and read—not because they're rejecting the social scene, but because they love to read. They make decisions that don't quite match those of everyone else—not for the sake of being different but simply because they prefer the way they've chosen. They don't feel compelled to be exactly like everyone else but are happy to join with others when they do share an interest. Perhaps they have the inner security to be independent because many of their foundational needs of relationship and belonging have been well met in early years within their family. Maybe it just happens to be one of the attributes of their personality. Either way, they are discovering and operating from who they are inside rather than letting their environment define them. Here the individuals "win" as they go ahead with how things are for them internally but the system "loses" in that they do not do all they can to defend or support it . . . nor to destroy it. It is what it is, and they are who they are. Here, as in the people described just above, they are living in congruence with who they are made to be internally.

4. *A person who doesn't fit the system, knows it, and spends years of his or her life proving it.* People in this group like to think of themselves as members of the group just discussed, but they're not. For whatever reasons, they learned early on that at least parts of them didn't fit the system. Perhaps they cried their first night at boarding school and were told to be brave—but they couldn't stop crying. Maybe they honestly wanted to know why things should be done one way rather than another but were given the unsatisfactory reply, "Because I said so." Still, the burning question inside wouldn't go away. Unfortunately, as they keep bumping into something that doesn't fit them inside, some TCKs finally decide—consciously or unconsciously—to throw out everything the system stands for. They'll be anything but that system. The irony is that these outwardly rebellious TCKs actually get their identity from the very system they're rejecting. People who are determined to prove who they are not rarely go on to discover who they are. In this scenario, both the individuals and the system lose. Often there is a secret shame in this identity as the individuals live life as a permanent screamer but don't know how to find a way to a positive identity anymore.

It's important to remember that it's not wrong to be part of a strong organizational system. An organization is an efficient and necessary way of forming a community into functional groups, usually for the purpose of accomplishing a common goal. We can relate to it, be part of it, and even have some of our core needs of belonging met by it. But it's not, by itself, who we are. Once that's understood, figure 12-2 shows what can happen when TCKs and ATCKs can take a better look at their group and determine which parts of the system do or don't fit with who they are, keeping in mind that they don't have to reject or retain an entire system. It may be there are parts of the system the ultimate screamers would like to espouse once more, but they feel if that happens, they would have to embrace the whole again. Since they know they can't do that because there are also parts they will never want to be again, they don't know what else to do but reject the whole.

Delayed Adolescent Rebellion

A prolonged adolescence is painful enough for the TCK who keeps wondering why he or she can't be like others, but even more painful—not only for TCKs, but for their families as well—is a delayed adolescent rebellion: when the normal testing of rules either starts unexpectedly late or becomes exaggerated in an all-out, open defiance of nearly every possible convention the family and/or community hold dear and extends far beyond the adolescent years. Obviously, this type of rebellion also occurs in families that don't live abroad, but we want to look at a few specific reasons for a later rebellion in some TCKs and then at why it often continues past the normal teenage years.

1. *Extension of prolonged adolescence.* In any journey to adulthood, there are always those who in the process of testing the rules of their upbringing decide they will avoid adults' expectations, no matter what. For whatever reasons, they assume an "anti-identity." This process of rebellion is often an offshoot of normal adolescent testing of cultural norms. When that normal process is prolonged for all the reasons mentioned earlier, the rebellion that often comes during that time will be delayed.
2. *End of the need for compliance.* Sometimes it seems that young people who have been forced to comply to a fairly rigorous system throughout their teenage years decide to try everything they previously couldn't do once they are finally free from those external constraints. Rather than the usual process of testing rules a few at a time while still under a parent's watchful eye, they go off to university and seemingly "go off the deep end."

    This form of rebellion may actually be a positive—though slightly misguided—move toward independence. In these situations, parents and others may need to understand the reason for the behavior and be patient in the process, while also pointing out (when possible) that some of this behavior may be counterproductive to the goal of the independence they seek.

3. *Loneliness.* Sometimes the rebellion is a plea for help. We have met many TCKs who have tried to express to their parents that they need a home base; that they feel desperately lonely when vacation time comes and everyone else goes home and they stay in the dorm because their parents are still overseas and relatives in the home country seem like strangers; or that they are struggling in school and want to quit. But the parents never seem to hear. Instead, they send email messages with platitudes like "Cheer up," "It will get better," or "Trust God," or they explain once more why they need to stay in the job they're in.

Eventually, some TCKs finally scream through their behavior the message they have not been able to communicate verbally: "I need you to come *here*—to be near me." When they get arrested for drugs, or get pregnant, or try to commit suicide, they know their parents will come—at least for a short period. Unfortunately, the parents who didn't hear the earlier verbal or nonverbal messages often don't understand, even at this point of major rebellion, the deep loneliness and longing their child is experiencing. They judge the rebellion without understanding the reason, and a deeper wedge than ever is driven between parent and child.

At that point, the TCK's behavior may become more extreme than before, and whatever form the rebellion takes—drugs, alcohol, workaholism, some esoteric cause—becomes a way in itself to numb the pain of longing for some type of security and home base. The sad thing is that until the loneliness and longing are addressed, the TCK will stay walled off, often in very destructive behavior, fulfilling the worst prophecies made about him or her.

4. *Anger.* One of the common manifestations of unresolved grief, anger, may erupt in this time of rebellion and intensify it. The anger may be directed at parents, the system they've grown up in, their home country, God, or other targets. Unfortunately, once again people don't always stop to find out what's behind the explosion. The judgment and rejection of the TCK's experience increases the pain and fuels further anger and rebellion.

There is another situation that may be the cause of anger. TCKs who have spent many years physically apart from their parents by being away at a boarding school or back in the passport country, or perhaps even when one parent is away on deployment or frequent short-term assignments, may, as we said, unrealistically idealize them. As young adults, these TCKs begin to discover their own imperfections, realize their parents aren't perfect either, and not only become angry at the loss of their fantasy but also begin to blame their parents for the lack of perfection in *themselves.* "If I'd just lived a normal life or had better parents, I wouldn't be struggling the way I am now." While anger against parents for imperfections in ourselves is probably a normal part of the developmental process for everyone, TCK or not, when parents remain overseas, working through it can be difficult for all concerned.

The bottom line is that no matter what the reason for the anger, it's often turned against the parents and may be expressed in an almost punitive rebellion—the TCKs want to hurt those whom they feel hurt them.

A major problem with delayed-onset and then prolonged adolescent rebellion, however, is that rebellion in the mid-to-late twenties may have a destructive effect far beyond that of teenage rebellion.

> Pierre was a diplomat's son from Switzerland who grew up in four different South American countries. During his early twenties, when friends asked how he had liked his nomadic lifestyle, he always replied, "Oh, I loved it! It never bothered me to pack up and move. We always knew there was something very exciting ahead. I've lived in nine different countries."
>
> After marriage and three children, however, the story changed. Certain job situations didn't work out. He became tired of trying to find ways to support his wife and children. In the end, he became totally disenchanted with family life and the attendant responsibilities and simply walked away from everything he'd apparently valued before. "I've spent my life," he replied to those who questioned him, "doing what everyone else wanted me to do and I'm tired of it. Now I'm finally going to do whatever I want to do."

We stress that this type of rebellion is neither desirable nor necessary. The TCK as well as parents, family, and friends are all wounded in this process. Being aware of some of the reasons delayed rebellion occurs may sometimes prevent it, or it may help the family deal with prolonged adolescence in its early stages, so they and their TCKs aren't held prisoners to destructive behavior. Perhaps the best preventive measure parents and other adults can take against this type of rebellion is to make sure, even in situations where their TCKs are raised in a strong organizational (or family) system, that there are opportunities for the children to make real choices in matters that don't compromise their safety or the agency's effectiveness. This says to the child, "I am listening to you. Your needs are heard. You don't have to scream to get my attention." Most importantly, TCKs and ATCKs who read these lines and recognize themselves need to know they have the choice to take responsibility for their own actions and find help for their behavior rather than continuing to blame others for how awful their lives have been or have become. (See chapter 16 for further help in this area.)

We've talked a lot about both the benefits and challenges of growing up as a TCK, but sometimes we wonder how the young people can put it all together. Dirk is a TCK who has learned how to use his whole life well. He is a German

TCK who grew up in Taiwan and went to university in the United States. He says he learned to live with the challenge of many cultures and places by living fully in whichever one he is currently while not denying the others are also part of his life. He uses a computer metaphor to describe this phenomenon.

> I just build windows. I know that all my windows are open, but I have to operate in the one that's on the screen. When I'm in America, I activate the American window. When I'm in Germany, I activate the German window and the American window goes on the back burner—and so do the people in it.

PARADOXES OF UNEVEN MATURITY

In summary, when thinking about TCKs' identity and development issues, don't forget the interweaving of challenges with great benefits. Uneven maturity offers almost paradoxical benefits and challenges, as do all other TCK characteristics. The very reasons for some of the delays in adolescence are rooted in the greatest benefits of the third culture experience. Once they are aware of and understand the process, however, TCKs and/or their parents can be alert to and guard against a certain smugness or sense of elitism they sometimes exhibit about how "mature" they are, while at the same time not panicking about areas where they still need to catch up.

TCKs find in their experience numerous opportunities for fulfilling their basic human needs in the most profound ways of all, and they often emerge with a very secure self-identity. We have seen that TCKs who dare to wrestle through the hard questions of life can develop a deep and solid sense of purpose and values that goes deeper than those who are not forced to sort through such questions to the same degree. In addition, the exposure to philosophical, political, and social matters that are almost part and parcel of the TCK experience means there is every potential for substantive intellectual development. By its diversity alone, a TCK's world creates questions to ponder. This is one aspect of personhood that has every potential to be filled to overflowing for TCKs.

Of all the TCKs we have met or worked with, very few would ever exchange the richness of their lives to avoid the inevitable challenges they have faced along the way. Given time, the maturity process will sort itself out into a more even flow as they, like others, move on through adolescence—prolonged or not—into adulthood. In the end, through this very process of having to figure some of these matters out with conscious thought rather than an unconscious process, many TCKs and ATCKs find themselves with a very clear and strong sense of personal identity in the end. Perhaps some of their process is only defined as "uneven" because it is judged by models that may not be as standardized as once thought in these days of changing cultural patterns around our world.

Expanding Our Vision

As the psychologists and other child care experts wrestle with what is happening to young people in our globe, they wonder why there are so many boomerang kids—those who go off to university or a job and then return home to live with parents. This is unlike the generations before who usually went off and never came home again to live. Perhaps a closer look at the TCK developmental experience might shed light for not only other CCKs, but also all those growing up in a world where the stability of former years seems like only a dream. While the brain research is saying that adolescence extends past previous assumptions, it is also possible one reason so many young people don't "launch" at the ages they did before is simply that in our globalizing world, as in the TCK world, cross-cultural mobility or interactions in their countless forms is making the path less smooth.

Questions for Chapter 12

1. Have you or others you know experienced uneven maturity? Did any of the factors mentioned here play a part? Explain. Are there other factors you consider that might have led to early maturity?
2. As you read about prolonged adolescence, do you identify with any of the reasons listed for you or others you know? Do you think some of these reasons might, in fact, apply to what is happening for others in our world? Please explain
3. If you or others you know grew up in a strong system, which of the "system identity" boxes in figure 12-3 do you relate to the most personally or see for your friends? What do you think of the idea that the one who most adamantly refuses to conform to the system is being defined by it?
4. Have you seen/experienced the impact of "uneven maturity" on relationship and dating issues? In what ways?
5. Is there anything else you would like to comment about that struck you while you read this chapter?

Part III

The TCK Journey

Part I explains the context of the TCK Journey—the *why's* of this story. Why does it make any difference when children grow up with a high degree of cross-cultural mobility compared to more traditional childhoods? Why does the growing cultural complexity of both traditional TCKs and other groups of CCKs make understanding the context of this experience more important than ever?

Part II describes the classic characteristics TCKs, past and present, often exhibit. This is the "what" of the story—what happens as children grow up as part of the highly mobile, cross-cultural tribe described in part I.

Part III takes us in a slightly different direction. This is where we begin the "what to do" sections of the book.

Chapter 13: The Transition Experience. This includes the Transition Model David Pollock created in the 1980s. As a true pioneer, Dave often opened his transition seminars saying, "I'm likely not going to tell you something you don't know, but you just don't know you know it yet." Sure enough, as he spoke, the lights went on in people's hearts, and often the tears ran down their cheeks. Building on the core of Dave's model included in the first two editions of *Third Culture Kids*, his son Michael has added insights and many practical tips from his nine years as principal and student development director of an international school in China and his ongoing involvement with TCKs through his organization, Daraja.

Chapter 14: Coming "Home": Reentry. This continues the discussion about doing transitions well but focuses specifically on reentry and how TCKs can survive and thrive in that often challenging time. Don't miss Michael's Transition Challenge Matrix, which gives new ways to measure what factors may help or hinder a smooth reentry.

Chapter 15: Enjoying the Journey. Starting with the advice Ruth's dad gave her to "unpack your bags and plant your trees," these are short, fun tips shared from Ruth's own journey as a TCK and a mom of TCKs.

Chapter 16: Adult TCKs: There's Always Time. This chapter is for adult TCKs (ATCKs) who didn't have language for or awareness of their TCK story as it happened. Some wonder if it's too late to deal with things in their lives they now recognize may stem from this experience. Now may be the time for healing and learning to use your gifts. Included are insights and practical tips for the ATCKs as well as those who love and work with them, such as parents, friends, and therapists.

CHAPTER 13

The Transition Experience

All the world feels caught in these goodbyes, goodbyes that
bruise and hurt, yet remind us that our hearts are still
soft and alive. As we tell our stories we realize that these
transitions and moves are all part of a bigger narrative, a
narrative that is strong and solid and gives meaning to our
lives. As we learn to tell our stories, we understand not only
the complexity of our experience, but the complexity of the
human experience, the human heart. So we learn to tell
our stories—because your story, my story, and our stories
matter.[1]

—ATCK Marilyn Gardner
Between Worlds: Essays on Culture and Belonging

In these few words, Marilyn powerfully expresses the paradox of repeated transitions—the bruising of the good-byes, yet the magnificence of the story also being shaped through it all. Transitions are a human experience. No one can opt out of them, but for TCKs and their families, they become a way of life.

Iranian author and poet Mimi Khalvati wrote a lyrical metaphor describing the process of transition itself. The poem is called "The Soul Travels on Horseback." In this piece, Mimi paints a stunning picture of how we as humans *experience* cultural and geographic moves in today's world. She describes how the soul follows the body, but slowly, on the back of a horse from one place to another in the midst of change. In a world where the rate of change is picking up to supersonic levels, we are left breathless. Yet she reminds us that in such a world, where the way for the horse is "beset by obstacles and thorns," we also have time to wait and process in the in-between world of an airport lounge.

This is a powerful picture, not only because of the reference to the airport lounge as a place of reorganization, but because in this metaphor change is different from transition. So what's the difference between these two words—*change* and *transition*?

Change and Transition

Change is the *physical or external process* of moving from one location or state of being to another. It's what happens outside or *to* you. "To become or make someone or something different," is the way the Merriam-Webster dictionary defines it. Transition, defined by experts, is the "passage to the change." It focuses on the *psychological* and *emotional changes* people go through to arrive at the new place.[2] In other words, transition is the process of adapting to the changes we experience.

Change and the need for transition happen for many reasons. Going from health to a chronic illness, from singleness to a married state, from falling asleep in a peaceful country and waking up to the aftermath of a terrorist attack are all examples of changes of state where there is no physical motion. This chapter will focus on the impact of change and transition through the lens of a global move, a dis-location if you will, and all that comes with it.

Change is often fast—an external event or series of events—while transition is a more internal and time-consuming process. While change is inevitable, transition, at least a strong and healthy transition (stable, comfortable, and self-assured), is not guaranteed. None of us can avoid change, but the question is what happens in the chaos that often comes with change. That needs to be figured out. But the rate of change is increasing exponentially and it seems impossible to keep up. Although humans are adaptive creatures, the soul does indeed need time to catch up.

Ironically, because change and transition are so common for TCKs, some people figure the kids are used to it, so it's not a problem. Blogs and Facebook posts often contain comments that question or even belittle the TCK experience with an attitude or words expressing, "What's the big deal? We all have difficulty in transitions," or "Life is hard, get over it, and get over yourself." When TCKs read those things, it's easy for them to wonder if those postings are right and ask themselves why, in fact, they can't just "get over it."

If a healthy transition is the ability to adapt and adjust to change in a positive way, then it stands to reason that factors that complicate and hamper or slow the adjustment process need to be understood and addressed. Missing or misunderstanding the compounding effects of the TCK's transition can leave some folks wondering why attention should be given to children privileged enough to traipse around the globe.

But anyone who has read this book from the beginning knows better. Chapters 4–6 already looked at the results of the high mobility TCKs face—their own and others'. Chapter 5 specifically focused on the issues of unresolved grief that can arise for many reasons, including the multiple layers of grief that often occur during TCK transitions. The adjustments that an individual makes in transition are multidimensional, just as each person has multiple facets. Here are just a few possibilities:

- The physical body must adapt to time zone and climate. Jet lag is real.
- Our thinking (cognition) must adjust as language and culture change.
- Emotions are in flux as both loss and excitement co-exist.
- Our social lives tilt and remix in new ways.
- Our spiritual dimension is also likely to feel stretched as our beliefs and inner identity get bumped about.

There are other dimensions of change on a sliding scale of intensity, and chapter 14 covers them. Global relocation change involves loss no matter how great the gains. During the transition process, remember that each person in the family will not go through these stages at the same rates nor in a simple forward direction. Some will feel more disoriented and lost than others in the process; knowing some landmarks can help the traveler gain confidence in this journey. Also, don't forget that loss is experienced on both sides of the equation—the leavers and those being left—and grief is a result.

Now it's time to look at what actually happens to us as human beings during our transitions and develop strategies to deal well with the inevitable challenges. As with the grief cycle, there are clearly defined stages most of us pass through during a transition experience. Take a look at what they are and why they matter.

The Stages of Transition

An essential part of building a strong foundation for TCKs includes making sure highly mobile families and all who work with them learn to deal well with the entire process of transition. When we understand the process, we are not caught off-guard (even though we can't stop how we feel) and can make plans to deal well with each stage. There are at least two important reasons for learning the art of good transitions: to help TCKs (and their families!) normalize their experience so that they understand they are neither isolated nor emotionally unhealthy, and to help TCKs avoid long-term unresolved grief that can happen as a result of these losses. They need to know "You are not alone," "You are not crazy," and "The grief will subside in time—even if it never completely disappears."

Chapter 5 briefly lists the five stages of the transition experience David C. Pollock first identified during the 1980s in his classic model (with one small adaptation in stage 3 from "transition" to "transit"):

1. Involvement
2. Leaving
3. Transit (In Motion)
4. Entering
5. Re-Engagement

This chapter discusses the stages of typical transition and explores some common psychological and sociological experiences, showing in each stage what happens to the person/family leaving and to those left in the community. Suggestions for healthy ways TCKs and their families can navigate through this normal process will follow. For practical purposes, the story is written from the perspective of those doing the move, even though change and transition affect the stayers too. The assumption is that this is indeed "our story" as we use the universal "we," even while remembering that as individuals or within a family, each of us may experience it in different ways.

The Transition Experience

INVOLVEMENT STAGE

Our Response

We don't even know we're in a stage! Life seems too normal to be a *stage*. We feel settled and comfortable, knowing where we belong and how we fit in. Hopefully, we recognize we are an *intimate* part of our community and follow its customs and abide by its traditions so that we can maintain our position as a valued member. We feel a responsibility to be involved in the issues that concern and interest our community. Basically, we're focused on the present and our immediate relationships rather than thinking primarily about the past or worrying about the future.

When we are involved in a place, our affiliations are often multiple: we belong to clubs, classes, associations, faith communities, and sports teams, and feel affirmed in our roles. We feel secure and safe. As Dr. Doug Ota says in his book, *Safe Passage*, "In terms of foundations there is no more fundamental foundation than feelings of emotional safety and belonging."[4] In a healthy experience, both time and emotional resources are available to be curious, creative, learning-focused, and empathetic toward others.

Community's Response

Involvement is a comfortable stage for those around us as well. People hear our name and instantly picture our face, form, and function. They know our reputation, history, talents, tastes, interests, and where we fit in the political and social network. In the ideal involvement stage the members of our community know us, trust us, and are committed to us. They are comfortable with us and respond in kind to our joys, sorrows, and needs.

Strategies for Healthy Involvement

This is the time when life proceeds "normally." Parents can concentrate on helping their children develop particular gifts such as music, sports, performing and visual arts, or how to fix the car or broken plumbing. Because children usually feel more settled and confident in how life works here, they have the energy to think about more than basic survival skills. When strangers come, we are the ones who welcome them and can be mentors and a bridge to the local community. Involvement is a nice place to be!

LEAVING STAGE

Then the time comes when things begin to change. While some families may carefully think through the pros and cons and make a decision to move, many others have the decision made for them by circumstances or their organizations. With that decision or announcement, each member of the family moves from the comfortable transition stage of involvement to the leaving stage. Whether this move is between countries or even to a new location in the same country, leaving is a critical stage for everyone to navigate well.

Our Response

Once we learn we are leaving, deep inside we begin to prepare and often start to disengage internally from the world around us. At first we, and those around us, may not realize what's going on—especially if the departure date is more than six months away. With shorter warning, however, this mostly unconscious leaving process starts immediately. We may begin loosening emotional ties, backing away from the relationships and responsibilities we've had. We call friends less frequently. We don't start new projects at work. Our involvement and commitment to the present circumstances may wane. In Western cultures, during the last year before graduation from high school or university, this "leaning away" is called "senioritis."

While it may be normal—and perhaps necessary—to begin detaching at some level during this stage, it is often confusing both to us and our friends. This detachment can produce anger and frustration in relationships that have been close or in how we handle job responsibilities in work settings.

> During one transition seminar, Dave Pollock talked about this loosening of ties as part of the leaving stage. Soon he noticed a general buzz in the room. One gentleman sat off to the side, blushing rather profusely as others began to laugh. When Dave stopped to ask what was happening, the blushing gentleman said, "Well, I guess I better confess. I'm the

manager here, and just yesterday those working under me asked to meet with me. They complained about my recent job performance and told me I don't seem to care; I take far too much time off; I'm unavailable when they need me, and so on. As you've been talking, I just realized what's been happening. Last month, my CEO told me I would be transferred to a new assignment, so mentally I've already checked out."

"That's pretty normal," Dave said rather sympathetically.

"I know," he replied. "The only problem is I'm not due to leave for two more years. Maybe I'd better check back in again!"

We may not upset an entire office staff as this man did, but unless we consciously choose to maintain and enjoy relationships and roles as long as possible, at some point everyone will back away in one form or another. It's an unconscious part of the process. In *Safe Passage* Ota writes of the biology behind our avoidance by pointing to a Ronald Friedman and Jens Forster study demonstrating that what motivates our transition process affects a person's brain significantly.

A simple task of helping a mouse complete a maze was differentiated by an owl hovering over the maze of half the subjects and a slice of cheese at the end of the maze for the other half. The perception of "avoidance" or escape from the owl for the one group was juxtaposed against the perception of "approach" or the search for cheese from the other group. Given a test for creativity directly after the maze, the results were stunningly 50% higher for the participants in the group whose "approach systems" were activated by the cheese as opposed to those whose "avoidance systems" were activated by the owl. Ota draws this conclusion, "The loss of familiar friends and predictable environments activates our biologically-based attachment systems, making our behavior tend in the direction of caution and avoidance."

To drive the seriousness home, Ota cited studies by Naomi Eisenberger whose functional magnetic resonance images (fMRI) revealed that social isolation stimulates the same areas of the brain as physical pain.[5]

Our brains and bodies change in response to the stress of moving! So it is thoroughly understandable that anticipating the upcoming changes, particularly if we have experienced previous moves, creates a pain-avoidance and fear-caution response, leaving us no energy and creativity.

Other forms of self-protective denials or avoidance behaviors may surface as well:

Denial of feelings of sadness or grief. Instead of acknowledging sadness, we may start to think, *I don't really like these people very much anyway. My coworker takes way too much of my time with all her problems. I'll be glad when I'm out of here and she can't text me every ten minutes.* Some people also deny their sadness at leaving by focusing only on what is anticipated. Their sense of time is in the future. They talk about the wonderful things they will do, eat, and see in the next location and make a mental leap over the *process* of getting there.

> One Canadian ATCK began to weep at this point in a transition seminar. Later she said, "Dave, I feel terrible. I grew up in a remote tribe in Papua New Guinea (PNG). When I left to return home for university, I could only think about how much I'd enjoy having Big Macs, TV, and electricity. I looked forward to new friends. When my PNG friends came to say good-bye, they started to cry, but I just walked away. Now all I can think about is them standing there as my little plane took off. They thought I didn't care. I want to go back and hug them one last time. What should I do?"

Of course, there was nothing wrong with this TCK developing a positive view of the coming move, but when she didn't acknowledge the losses involved in the leaving, she had no way to deal with them. Denying our feelings may get us through an otherwise painful moment, but the grief doesn't go away, and we simply hold on to it into the next stage of transition.

Denial of feelings of rejection. As friends plan for future events (e.g., next year's school play or the annual neighborhood barbecue night), we suddenly realize they are talking around us. No one asks what we would like to do or what we think about the plans. We (or a member of our family) seem to be invisible. Of course, we understand. Why should they include us? We'll be gone. In spite of what we know, however, we can still feel intense rejection and resentment. If we deny those feelings and push them aside as ridiculous and immature behavior (obviously I *shouldn't* feel like this), then that underlying sense of rejection and resentment may produce a seething anger, which results in almost unbelievable conflicts—especially with those who have been close friends and colleagues. Failing to acknowledge that we are beginning to feel like outsiders (and that it hurts) only increases the chances that we will act inappropriately during this stage. On the other hand, this can be a two-way street. We can hurt others too.

> "I'm accepted to two schools in the U.K. and can't wait to get back to Britain!" Nala gushed with excitement at a predeparture event for TCK high school students in Brazil. The leaders watched some of her friends physically create more space for her in the circle.

Later as they all processed, the fellow students shared how they were glad for Nala, but also felt stung that their school choices did not seem as prestigious. One friend, Gabriela, in particular was hurt because Nala seemed to have forgotten that they were previously planning to go to university together. Now here she was all excited to be off somewhere else. Even though Gabriela knew that there were logical reasons the plan for a mutual university experience hadn't worked out, it still didn't feel good that Nala was acting so happy about other plans! So far, they hadn't had time to reconcile. Sadly, the physical space they created was a physical representation of what Gabriela and her fellow "stayer" friends felt.

Separation is a complex process whether we feel we are being left out of plans or others feel we are leaving them out . . . even though consciously we all know we won't be together when any of those plans happen! Still, somehow it hurts because exclusion is a real type of pain, registering in the same receptors of our brain as physical pain.

Denial of "unfinished business." The closer we come to separation, the less likely we (or family members) are to reconcile conflicts with others. We talk ourselves out of mending the relationship, unrealistically hoping that time and distance will heal it, or at least remove the broken pieces to an irrelevant corner of our reality. Once more, the difficult truth is that we arrive at our next destination with this unfinished business clinging to us and influencing new relationships. Bitterness in one area of life almost always seeps out in another.

Michael shared this reality in a retreat on transition with college students and stopped as a Nigerian TCK put her face in her hands.

"It's so TRUE! Oh, my gosh! Now I get it!" and she began to share with the group how she had left Nigeria with an unresolved relational issue. Not only had the issue itself resurfaced through social media, but she also found herself distracted, edgy, and judgmental in her dealings with fellow students in her New England high school. When she returned to Nigeria on a planned vacation, she finally faced the issue and resolved the conflict. After returning to the U.S. for the rest of the school year, things went infinitely better.

Denial of expectations. To prevent disappointment or fear, we may deny anything we secretly hope for. "It doesn't matter what kind of house I get; I can live anywhere." It's easy to deny we hope someone will give us a nice farewell. We figure if we have no expectations, we can't be disappointed. In reality, however, everyone has expectations for every event in their lives. When our expectations are too high, we are disappointed. When expectations are too low, we create fear, anxiety, or dread for ourselves.

Community's Response

We may not consciously realize it, but as we're loosening our ties to the community, the people in our community are loosening their ties to us. Not only do people forget to ask our opinion about future events, they begin giving what we consider "our jobs" to others. They choose someone else for committees and announce the name of the teacher replacing us next year. (Ouch!) *The same types of denials we may use are being used by them!* Suddenly our flaws as a friend or co-worker seem glaringly obvious and they secretly wonder why they've maintained this relationship for so long as well.

But often they also give us special attention. There are ceremonies of recognition—a watch presented for years of faithful service or a plaque given to say thanks for being part of a team. Graduation ceremonies remind those graduating that this school will never be the same without their shining presence. This special attention and recognition help the person leaving to forget for a moment that even though there are promises never to forget each other, already there is a distance developing between the leaver and those soon to be left behind.

Strategies for Healthy Leaving

Involve the kids: Some parents have asked us when is the best time to let the kids know of an impending transition. A few tell us they don't want to let their children know at all. This can be a cultural decision about what is more kind: to shield children from coming pain or to prepare them ahead of time.

> At an international school seminar, a Korean mother asked Michael if he thought it would be a good idea to let her children know about an impending move or to wait. She did not want to cause them distress, or throw off their academic focus. Then the mom shared how they had given their children some days' notice before the last move and how the children had been distressed. "Wouldn't it be better to just wait until the last minute?" she wondered.

Michael asked when the move was coming and she said, "Two weeks or so; it depends on the company." For sure, he encouraged her to tell the children right away! No matter when the children discovered they were moving, it would be hard for them, but it would be a thousand times worse if they never had a chance to say good-bye to the world where they now lived. And the impact on the children's ability to focus, learn, and study could be deeply compromised on the far side of the move as well.

We believe that once parents know a move is on the horizon and it is okay for it to be public knowledge in the community, children should be told. Older children who can be trusted with knowledge a corporation or embassy may not yet want public about a parent's assignment may, of course, be told when the parents first know. As we said earlier, knowing in advance gives everyone a good opportunity to do the necessary process of both closure in the present environment and proper anticipation of the new.

Leaving right is the key to entering right. This leaving stage is a critical one to do well if we want not only to make the current transition as smooth as possible, but also to help children grow in the process rather than become stuck in some of the challenges already mentioned. Since denials—of ourselves, parents, TCKs, or those of friends around us—and moments of special recognition, such as graduation or farewell ceremonies, don't change the ultimate reality of this leave-taking, it's essential that all involved—parents, TCKs, teachers, friends, others in the community—face and deal with the normal grief inherent in leaving a place and people we love. Doing this rather than running away from it will allow a healthy transition process to continue. We also need to look ahead realistically and optimistically. How can we face our approaching losses squarely while still looking forward with hope? The best way is by making sure we go through proper closure during this leaving stage. Without that, the rest of the transition process can be very bumpy indeed, and settling on the other side will be much more difficult. Yes, leaving right *is* a key to entering right. So how do we best do that?

Building a "RAFT"

The easiest way to remember what's needed for healthy closure is to imagine building a RAFT. By lashing four basic "logs" together, we will be able to keep the "raft" afloat and get safely to the other side.

- Reconciliation
- Affirmation
- Farewells
- Think destination

Reconciliation

Anytime we're facing a move from one place to another, it's easy to deal with tensions in relationships by ignoring them. We think, *In two weeks I'll be gone and never see that friend again anyway. Why bother trying to work out this misunderstanding?* Children can do the same in their own ways, particularly if they have begun to withdraw emotionally from the current place. We cannot overstress how vital it is to address any relational issues in need of repair and healing.

> An experiential exercise Michael uses is to have a student put on a backpack and try to walk, then run, away from it, which is obviously impossible and brings the point home

with humor. Additionally, with fifth-graders heading to middle school in the international school, he and the teachers designed a three-day outing on the Great Wall of China dubbed GWU (for Great Wall University). As the students hiked the wall they learned and practiced, experientially, aspects of being a TCK, including how to leave well.

One assigned task was to pass a large sack from hand to hand up a particularly steep section of the wall. The sack was filled with rocks and there was a great deal of moaning until the momentum flagged and the bag stopped, fifty yards from the top. The leaders reminded them of the task: "You must pass the bag, hand to hand, until it reaches the top."

Suddenly it clicked for one of the Korean boys and he began undoing the tie on the sack and pulling the rocks out as classmates yelled, "Nooo, you can't do that!" But as the adults just stood smiling, the other students joined in, emptying the sack, so that moaning turned to laughing and cooperation as they quickly completed the task.

The metaphor is apt. Reconciliation is like taking the rocks out of the sack. If we don't address unresolved relational issues before moving, instead of taking them out, we're taking the rocks in the sack with us. The difficulties don't go away after the move. Instead, in leaving, we carry along the mental and emotional baggage of unresolved problems. This is a poor choice for three reasons:

- Bitterness is never healthy for anyone.
- The old discontentment can interfere with starting new relationships.
- If we ever move back to this same place or meet up with these people again elsewhere, it will be much harder to resolve the issues then. Some ATCKs refuse to attend school reunions because they still don't want to meet certain people who hurt them or whom they know they hurt. What a sad memory to carry throughout a lifetime!

Reconciliation includes the need to both forgive and be forgiven. In Michael's seminars he stresses that forgiveness does not mean "forgetting" as if the offense did not happen, but it requires two steps:

1. Relinquishing the desire or right for revenge.
2. Agreeing to live with the consequences of the other person's behavior. In this way, the wound is acknowledged and the decision is made not to wound back, and then we set about tending to the wound to see it healed. This freeing process is not natural and must be entered as a conscious choice.

How forgiveness happens may vary among cultures. In one culture, it might mean going directly to the person with whom we have a conflict and addressing the issues. In another culture, it may mean using an intermediary. Obviously, true reconciliation depends on the cooperation and response of the other party as well, but we as humans all need to at least try to do all we can to reconcile any broken relationships before leaving.

Finally, it's important to remember that sometimes the woundings and wrongs that are received or given may be illegal or potentially dangerous to the well-being of others. In these cases, it is necessary that information be shared with the appropriate trusted authorities. Forgiveness never means hiding criminality or a potential threat to self or others.

Affirmation

Relationships are built and maintained through affirmation—the acknowledgment that each person in this relationship matters. Again, styles or customs of affirmation vary from culture to culture and may be expressed differently according to the age of each child, but in every culture, in every age bracket, an important part of closure is to let others know we respect and appreciate them. There are many concrete ways people do this:

1. Have the children identify their special teacher or other favorite adults in the community and suggest they create something tangible to share with that person as an expression of gratitude.
2. Encourage children to think of gifts they might like to give various friends, perhaps an item that belongs to them that has meaning for the friend, too.
3. As a family, invite families with close ties over or go out to dinner and prepare questions that encourage stories of shared adventures, challenges, and laughter.
4. When leaving family members behind, help children write out specific reasons they appreciate being that person's grandchild, niece, nephew, or cousin and then deliver the note with some flowers the children help to pick out.

Obviously, there are countless other ways to show affirmation. The point is that acknowledging others helps us as well as those we affirm. It not only solidifies our relationships for future contact, but in expressing what they have meant to us, we are reminded of what we have gained from living in this place. Part of good closure is acknowledging our blessings—both to rejoice in them and to properly mourn their passing.

Another way to affirm relationships and to create important "relational bridges" is to plan together how we will communicate in the future and when we plan on seeing each other again. Even if plans change along the way, the process affirms that our friends will not be "out of sight and out of mind."

Farewells

Saying good-bye in culturally and age-appropriate ways to people, places, pets, and possessions is important to keep from having deep regrets later. Noting "lasts" can help, such as "last time to visit the beach" or "last time to eat at a special restaurant." Children will need reminders when it is the "last time" to see certain friends and relatives. Prompts going into a visit can help children consider how they want to leave. Schedule time for these farewells during the last few weeks and days.

> One woman forgot to take into account that in the local culture everyone must come to the departing friend's house on the last day to bid a final farewell. In order not to offend the countless people who streamed in all day long, she visited with each one in turn. By the end of the day, her bags still weren't packed and she literally missed her flight!

Saying farewell. Here are some suggestions for how to say farewell in these four key areas. We recommend making lists as a family and giving children a time to think things through themselves as we decide whom or what to include in our farewells. Sometimes parents are surprised to learn who and what are or are not important to a child.

- *People:* Farewells to significant people in our lives are crucial. Parents should take special care to help their children say good-bye to people with whom they have had meaningful relationships in the past as well as the present, including those from the local community who may have been caregivers. Helping kids say good-bye may include baking cookies with them to give to that special person. Brave parents sometimes schedule a party or overnight when their children can have a final chance to say good-bye to close friends. When times are planned for intentionally saying farewell, anticipating those special times can go a long way to helping children avoid the excessive pulling away that can lead to the long-term consequences we mentioned earlier.
- *Places:* Everyone has places that evoke an emotional response. It may be a spot tied to a special moment in our lives (our engagement, for instance) or where we go when we are upset or where certain events always occur. These are the places we come back to visit and show our children years later. Part of healthy closure includes visiting such sites to reminisce and say farewell. This is particularly important for TCKs who may be losing their whole world with next week's plane ride. Many TCKs mourn for the favorite tree they used to climb years after they have left the land of their childhood. People say good-bye to places in different ways. Some plant a tree that will grow long after they are gone, symbolizing a living, ongoing connection to this part of their lives. Others leave a hidden secret message or "treasure" to look for in case they should return. Some just want to sit and reflect or repeat a fun activity. We also take pictures in our mind, which help ground us later.
- *Pets:* Pets aren't equally important in every culture, but they can be significant when it comes to good-byes. TCKs need to know how their pets will be cared for and who will love them. If the pet must be put to sleep,

everyone who cares for that pet, particularly children, should say good-bye. Some TCKs tell us how devastated they were after parents promised their pet would be happy in a new home, only to find out months or years later that the dog was euthanized or the chicken given to someone for food. As difficult as it may be, honesty is best, even if it causes tears. Finding a new home for a pet can also take time, so this process is best begun early.

- *Possessions:* One problem (some might say blessing!) international sojourners face is that they can rarely take all their possessions with them when they move. Parents may delight in the chance to throw out a child's dirty rock collection, never realizing how precious those rocks were to their child. Certainly, we realize part of life is letting go, but parents should talk with their children about what to take and what to leave as they pack. Everyone in the family needs to carry some treasured items to the new location. These become part of the collection of *sacred objects* that help connect one part of a global nomad's life to the next. But sometimes even treasures must be left behind. When that happens, it's important to part with them consciously. Placing a precious object in the hands of someone else as a gift or finding a friend or family member to store it are two ways to say good-bye to an inanimate but important object. Laia Colomer Solsona is an archaeologist who is interested in the artifacts globally mobile people carry as part of their history. She has a fascinating Facebook group called "The archaeology of a mobile life," where she displays many of the pictures and stories others have sent her, sharing the stories of what the objects mean and why the people have carried their objects literally around the world![6]

Rituals of farewell: These include rituals commonly associated with certain types of transitions, such as graduations or retirement parties. They are another important part of building this RAFT. Taking the time for "rites of passage" and celebration gives us markers for remembering meaningful places and people and helps nail down the reality that we are, in fact, leaving.

This normal pattern can be complicated for internationally mobile families. Some permanently return to their home country after the oldest child graduates from secondary school abroad. The graduating TCK goes through the rites of passage—the graduation ceremony, and maybe the "wailing wall" afterward, where all line up and say good-bye to one another. However, the needs of the younger children for the same types of closure when they leave for the passport country are often overlooked. This can later add greatly to the younger child's sense of "unfinished business," while the older TCK in the same family is off and running once he or she gets to the homeland.

Remember, *every* member of the family needs to build the RAFT during any leaving process. While we are driving that point home, it is also important to note that the RAFT is a good process to use even before leaving for "short visits" such as summer holidays or long vacations. Even if the four steps are done in shorthand fashion, it makes a difference to live with short accounts in a world that is quite unpredictable. The bottom line is once we know the steps of the dance we should practice them often—they are good for us.

Think Destination

Even in the midst of saying the good-byes and processing the sad reality of those good-byes, we need to think realistically about our destination: Where are we going? What are some of the positives and negatives we can expect to find once we get there? Will we have electricity and running water? How will we learn to drive on the other side of the road? Do we need to take a transformer with us to keep our 110-volt appliances from burning out on a 220-volt electrical system? What kind of Internet connections can we expect? What type of cell phone service or providers operate in this new place? How frequently can we expect to keep in contact with friends and relatives in the place we are leaving?

This is also the time to look at our external (e.g., finances, family support structure) and internal (e.g., ability to deal with stress or change) resources for coping with problems we might encounter. What resources will we find in the new location and what will we need to take with us? Who can help with adjusting to the new culture when we get there? If this is a move back to the passport country, what kind of expectations do we have for how we or our children will adjust based on the shorter periods of leave we have taken to this point? This is the best time to figure out if someone will meet us at the airport or if we should expect to call an Uber or local cab. Where will we stay until housing is located, and what will that housing be like?

While these are primarily the concerns parents need to consider, thinking destination is equally important for children. Practical things such as maps, pictures of the next house or school, details of the upcoming itinerary, and places that may be visited along the way are all helpful tools parents can use to help children think and plan ahead. Increasingly, there are workbooks for children to use in this process. *The League of Super Movers* and *My Family Is Moving* are books Beverly Roman has written for preteens and young children in this leaving stage. Reading through stories such as *B at Home* by Valerie Besanceney, or *A Ball, a Book, and Butterflies: A Story about International Transition* by Anna Barratt and Sally McWilliam will give parents ways to discuss and normalize what their children are feeling as they talk about the characters in the story. Some organizations are creating their own materials that help kids through the specific issues involved in military, missions, state department, etc., moves. If at all possible, this last phase of building the RAFT is also a great time to try to make contact with other families or children who are in the new place or already attending the new school so that mentors are already being put in place and that crucial step of creating "relational bridges" begins.

Neglecting to think through some of these issues will mean the adjustment for all members of the family may be rockier than it needs to be once we arrive at the new destination. If we are expecting too much, we'll be disappointed. If we don't expect enough, we may not use the resources available, thereby making life more complicated than necessary. Of course, nobody can ever have a perfect picture of what life in the new place will be like. And, again, always recognize that each member of the family will go through the stages of transition at a different pace, but doing our best to prepare beforehand can prevent a lot of problems later on.

After all of this thorough preparation in the leaving stage, it's time to move into the transit stage itself.

TRANSIT STAGE

At the heart of the transition process is the *transit stage*, in which we experience any number of sensation combinations. Emotional storm, rational calm, limbo, purposeful progress, relief, and excitement are all part of the chaos. Again, paradoxically, it can also offer a sense of adventure that includes quiet contemplation and rushing through adrenaline-soaked action. *Where will this next step take me? I can't wait to find out!* The transit stage begins the moment we leave one place and ends when we not only arrive at our destination but make the decision, consciously or unconsciously, to settle in and become part of it—to take hold again. We could also call it the "in motion" stage. Nothing is quite settled.

The late Norma McCaig, founder of Global Nomads, always said the transit stage is a time when families moving overseas become at least temporarily dysfunctional, even when they look forward to the adventure. This dysfunctionality doesn't have to last, but it can be painfully discomfiting at the time. Even if we built our RAFT perfectly in the leaving stage and enjoy observing the new world around us, this is when we often begin to mourn most acutely—and often unexpectedly—the loss of things and people left behind. The permanence of the move and the irretrievability of the past stare us in the face and we sometimes wonder if we've made a terrible mistake.

The sense of chaos mentioned above is often the common theme. Schedules change, new people have new expectations, living involves new responsibilities, but we haven't yet learned how everything is supposed to work. A person who jumps into an airplane for a business or vacation flight to another city cannot truly understand the impact on a family moving across the globe, bags and weight balanced and maxed out, sleep patterns wrecked, struggling through airports in Beijing, Paris, Chicago, or Rio. The stress of the chaos makes it a time of significant vulnerability as well.

It is no wonder that an analogy from the world of circus performance comes to mind. The experience of the "in between" can be dizzying. We become like the trapeze artist who has let go of the first bar and is gliding through space, hoping to successfully grab the second. This is the perfect picture of the concept of *liminality. Liminal space is the space between things, the neither here nor there and neither this nor that.* What the trapeze artist experiences is very similar to global transition: the pace is fast, there is not much margin for error, and feelings of excitement, happiness, anxiety, terror, and wonder weave all together. Some TCKs have written about this stage as producing a kind of addiction; the stress and resulting adrenaline creates a "junkie" effect, causing them to crave it from time to time. With what we are learning of the brain, we agree: it's real. One does not need to be an adrenaline junkie to learn to appreciate the "neither here nor there" aspect of liminality:

> "I'm happiest in an airport or on a plane," wrote one travel-seasoned twelve-year-old. "Even if I'm sad about leaving a place, I'm excited about where I'm going . . . and I haven't been able to be disappointed yet."

> Marilyn Gardner writes: "Being able to travel is one of life's greatest gifts. It simultaneously keeps one humble and fully alive. And for me the gift and magic begin at the airport. The airport is a place where I don't have to try. It's where I can be fully comfortable between worlds."[7]

Charles La Shure described liminality in the context of communal rituals for initiation:

> The initiate (that is, the person undergoing the ritual) is first stripped of the social status that he or she possessed before the ritual, inducted into the liminal period of transition, and finally given his or her new status and re-assimilated into society. Viewed in a positive light, liminality provides freedom of movement, but the flip side of that coin is a lack of stability. Being betwixt and between means that you don't belong anywhere. As social animals, few humans can survive for long without belonging somewhere, at least to some extent.[8]

Many TCKs can relate to the "stripping away" aspect of the transition experience and this liminal space. While this "stripping away" can be painful, paradoxically the possibilities and the opportunities of liminal space can be valuable. It is a rare time of being unencumbered, with space for reflection, self-assessment and new perspective. There can certainly be a sense of freedom in the "move and wait" ebb and flow of "in between" travel. Responsibilities are often simpler and more straightforward: stow our luggage in the overhead bin, fill out the arrival card, don't lose our passports, watch for the metro stop, etc.

There can also be a comfortable feeling of anonymity, like moving in a bubble of private space. That is why suddenly meeting an acquaintance in the plane or train terminal can be disorienting; we are suddenly thrown back into the category of a "known quantity," and that can feel both reassuring and disconcerting. Being "known" can also mean having a past one would like to forget or at least let go of for a time, with the resultant freedom from connection.

> While Zach stood in the immigration line in London, weary
> from an overnight flight from Malaysia, all he wanted to do
> was to get through this routine part of international travel
> and catch the underground to his final destination and rest.
> The official asking the usually banal questions looked at
> his monitor and suddenly said, "Ah, you are the one with
> the sandwich." Jet-lagged confusion led to silence until the
> official added. "You once came through customs with a
> sandwich."
>
> And suddenly the memory gate opened on a scene years
> previously, of irate customs and border protection officials
> discovering an undeclared, half-eaten Kuala Lumpur chicken
> sandwich that a family member had placed in Zach's bag on
> the flight. "Oh, great!" he thought, "now they track every-
> thing and that stupid sandwich will be on my record for-
> ever." Sometimes being unknown is a gift.

In the circus, the far side of the trapeze, the "catch," is followed by a swing to
the platform or a return. This seems an apt analogy, since each person, even in a
couple or family, may have a different experience. A parent may transfer to another country and/or culture and start working, but the family arrival will come
later. A family may arrive together and the mother begins her job immediately
while the rest of the family is still in a type of limbo. Housing, schools, and even
jobs for some family members may be up in the air while one family member
begins new routines, as in the following true but composite story:

> By the time the rest of the Costa family, (the mom, a high
> school daughter, twin boys in middle school, and a dog) ar-
> rived in Catania, Italy, from Brazil, their father had already
> been working with his corporation for six months. The com-
> pany did an excellent job providing for the basic needs of the
> family. However, as the father went off to work each day,
> the rest of the family were left at loose ends with language,
> culture, and local geography to figure out and a month and
> a half before school began for the children. Immersed in
> challenges at the plant, Dad did not have much time to bring
> the family up to speed. With a career in refugee work on
> hold, Mom's work search wouldn't even begin until after the
> children were settled. She began with where to find grocer-
> ies and the mound of paperwork needed to retrieve their dog
> from quarantine.

In the transit stage we are hit most strongly with contrasts and comparisons
as multiple geographic and cultural worlds are experienced in close proximity
and sequence to each other. We can still be heading to our next destination as

weather changes from subzero and snowy to blazing summer sun; bangers and mash becomes tandoori chicken and basmati rice; dinner at 5:30 or 6:00 P.M. becomes dinner at 9:30 or 10:00 P.M.; and driving our own car becomes catching buses, the metro, and taxis.

Our Response

The key aspect in our response stems from the vulnerability of our situation. We have cast off our normal moorings and support systems at this point. Suddenly we aren't relinquishing roles and relationships—they're gone! We've lost the comfort they gave but haven't formed new ones yet. We're not sure where we fit in or what we're expected to do. We have entered uncharted territory and this chaos leads to a strong impetus for change, to fight or flee. Common responses include:

- *Being more self-centered than normal.* We worry about our health, finances, relationships, and personal safety to a far greater degree than usual. Problems that aren't generally a big deal are exaggerated: headaches become brain tumors and sneezes become pneumonia. The loss of a favorite pen causes despair. We know we'll never find it again because the usual places we would look for it are gone.
- *Reacting out of proportion to circumstances.* Our own reactions can jump out of all proportion: we panic over an overdrawn account, parents become hypervigilant over safety and real or anticipated dangers for their kids, we misplace our cell phone and are sure it has been stolen. We can be more irritable or prone to tears and waves of emotions.
- *Forgetting to take time for normal routines.* Parents who are focusing on their own survival often forget to take time for the routines that soothe their children, giving them safety and security, such as reading stories; stopping to pick them up; sitting on the floor with them for a few minutes; or checking in conversationally about friends, homework, or the book they are reading. Children wonder what's happening and can feel unsettled and invisible. The insecurity of each family member contributes to the chaos for everyone. Family conflicts seem to occur for the smallest reason and over issues that never mattered before.

Outside of the home environment the enormous change between how the old and new communities take care of the everyday aspects of life—banking, buying food, cooking—can create intense stress. To make matters worse, we may be scolded for doing something in the new place that was routine in the old one.

> TCK Hanna grew up in an area of chronic drought in East Africa. The local adage for flushing the toilet was "If it's yellow, let it mellow. If it's brown, flush it down." Breaking that rule meant serious censure from her parents or anyone else around.

> Unfortunately, Hanna's grandma in the United States
> had never heard this wonderful rule. At age thirteen,
> Hanna visited her grandma. Imagine Hanna's chagrin and
> embarrassment when Grandma pulled her aside and scolded
> her for not flushing the toilet.

A severe loss of self-esteem may set in during this transition stage. Even if we physically look like adults, emotionally we may feel like children again. Sometimes we get scolded for things about which we "should have known better," but, particularly in cross-cultural moves, it seems we have to learn life over practically from scratch. This can be especially hard for TCKs who are still trying to understand exactly who they are and where they belong. Probably nothing strikes at a person's sense of self-esteem with greater force than learning language and culture, for these are the tasks of children.

Suddenly, no matter how many decibels the voice is raised, people around don't understand what the transitioning family member is trying to say. The person discovers gestures he has used all his life have very different meanings now. The person may become functionally illiterate. Cultural and linguistic mistakes not only are embarrassing, but make the TCK or his family member feel anxious and ashamed of being so stupid. Often anger erupts over little things, we become upset with ourselves for our responses, we may make bargains with those in the family for how we plan to do better, but all of that can turn to depressive moods as the enormity of the change hits us. That enormous shift also requires huge amounts of internal energy—glucose, in fact—to feed the prefrontal cortex of the brain to keep us in control and on an even keel. That is energy not available for other functions like learning and being creative. This can be exhausting and cause us to be irritable as we try to adjust, especially if we are trying to "keep up" with our normal tasks and pace.

Some people turn to social media at this point to fill in those gaps and may find just the right amount of support to be encouraged and to keep pressing on. Alternately, some may find that their friends are impossibly busy and have little time, or they can spend so much time connecting with old friends that they avoid committing to the adjustment process in our new locale.

Community's Response

Initially the community may welcome us warmly—even overwhelmingly. But in every culture the newcomer is still exactly that—and newcomers by definition don't yet fit in. Our basic position in the new community is generally one of *statuslessness*. We carry knowledge from past experiences—often including special knowledge that has no use in this new place. No one knows about our history, abilities, talents, normal responses, accomplishments, or areas of expertise. Sometimes it seems they don't care, which can be because they really don't care or because they don't know how to begin to show us they care. For TCKs entering a new school, it can be particularly devastating when their teacher makes an inaccurate comment about a country they've lived in and won't listen when the TCK tries to give their perspective. These experiences make us question whether our achievements in the previous setting were as significant as we thought.

One type of exception to the "statusless" rule occurs when we enter carrying with us something inherently valued by the community and news has preceded us. A celebrity or diplomatic family may not experience statuslessness, even in the transition stage. Sometimes students entering the third culture have found that they have "superstar" status because they are "fresh" from a place whose customs, trends, fashions, and language are popular.

Generally, people may now see us as boring or arrogant because we talk about things, places, and people they have never heard mentioned before. We feel the same way toward them because they talk about local people and events about which *we* know nothing. Often we don't know the rules of small talk, the items and issues that are taboo or controversial, and may be clueless as to the nuances of how people in this place make friends.

Circles of relationships among the community are already well defined, and most people aren't looking to fill a vacant spot in such a circle. As someone told Ruth's daughter after one move, "People are like Legos. They only have a certain number of links where they can attach to others. If their Lego block is already full when you come, then they simply don't have room for you." Even when we understand this, it's easy to become resentful and begin to withdraw. *Fine,* the TCK (or anyone) may say inside, *if they don't need me, I don't need them.* Rejection (or perceived rejection) and withdrawal can become a social death spiral leading into greater isolation, loneliness, and anger.

The transit stage itself can be tough because it includes keen feelings of disappointment. The difference between what was expected and what is being experienced can trigger a sense of deep resentment or even panic. All connection and continuity with the past seem gone, and the present isn't what we had hoped it would be. How can we relate the different parts of our life into a cohesive whole? Is the orderliness of the past gone forever? We look longingly to the future— hoping that somehow, sometime, life will return to *normal.*

Strategies for Healthy Transit

When people ask how they can avoid chaos and confusion during the transition process, the answer is, "You can't." They can, however, keep in mind that it's a normal stage and will pass if they hang on long enough. Also, there are a few steps we can take to help us maintain some sense of equilibrium and connectedness with the past and to smooth the way for the future stages of entry and reengagement.

On a practical level, the things Michael and his teachers used for grade-school field trips apply.

- Have your checklists and organizers handy.
- Keep track of your important documents.

- Safety first: look both ways twice.
- Look out for your buddies, hold hands, and stick together.
- Bring good snacks and share.
- Have fun, take pictures, and keep a journal.

And if the snacks don't work, here are some more-serious suggestions for this time.

Sacred objects. One way we stay in balance is through the use of sacred objects—those mementos we mentioned earlier that specifically reflect a certain place or moment of our lives. That's why the choice of which possessions to keep and which to give away is so important during the leaving stage. A favorite teddy bear pulled out of the suitcase each night during the travels from one place to another reminds the child that there is one stable thing in his or her life amidst the general chaos. At the same time, Mom or Dad may be reading a treasured book they brought along, which reminds them of other times and places where they have read those same inspiring or comforting words.

Other sacred objects are worn. Did you ever look around a group of TCKs or their parents and see how many were wearing some article of clothing or jewelry that connected them to their past? It might be a Tuareg cross hanging on a gold chain or a Peruvian Chankas Warrior bracelet. Perhaps they're wearing a sari instead of a sweater. Often an ATCK's home is quite a sight to behold—with artifacts gathered from around the world, all proving that "I was there! It's part of my history." Each sacred object serves as a good reminder that the current moment or scene is part of a bigger story of our lives.

Pictures. They are another important way we connect with special moments and memories in our past. One ambassador asked each staff member to list what he or she would put in the one bag allowed for an emergency evacuation. Photographs headed the list for every person, far above things with much more monetary worth. Why? Because each picture reminds us of some relationship, an experience we have had, a place we have visited. Pictures add a value to our lives that money alone can't buy. A small picture album with photographs representing significant highlights of our past life and location gives us a lovely place to visit when we need a few reflective moments in the middle of this sometimes turbulent stage. Pictures can also be helpful for letting people in the new place know something more of our history.

Of course, we recognize that everyone we would like to show these pictures and sacred objects to may not see the same value in them that we do. (And often it's vice versa when they try to show us theirs!) Why don't most people particularly enjoy another person's PowerPoint or video show? Because friends who weren't there can't see anything interesting in a skinny cow walking down the middle of a road; it seems rather bizarre to them. And they certainly don't want to hear a twenty-minute story about the man with the shaved head in the back row of a group picture. For the person who was there, though, that picture or video segment brings back a flood of memories, and every detail is fascinating. That's why globally nomadic people should make a pact to look at each other's slides or home videos. It's how they can affirm their experiences!

"Stop and smell the roses." Often we are flying from one spot to the next, suddenly living amid strange customs and languages, and forget to take the time to enjoy where we are. While the transit stage can be overwhelming, it can also be seen as a wonderful time of exploration. We may not feel ready to settle in yet, but surely we can at least be interested observers. There is much to learn, and to help TCKs learn, about the cultures and places in which we are living on any given day during transition.

Even if we built our RAFT perfectly in the leaving stage and have done all of the above to maintain stability, transit is the stage where we often begin to mourn more acutely the loss of things and people left behind. If we think back to the grief cycle we discussed in chapter 5, up until now we have likely been in the denial and bargaining stages, maybe with some anger along the way—but even there, the anger is often directed at those we are leaving behind as part of our preparation for the upcoming separation. Transit is the stage where sadness and possible depression can hit. We feel unbearable emptiness when we realize we can't call our best friend to meet us for a cup of coffee. We miss the comfort of knowing everyone in our factory or office by name. The permanence of the move and the irretrievability of the past stare us in the face, and we wonder if we've made a terrible mistake.

During the leaving stage we knew these losses were coming, but now their reality is here. This is a critical moment and one that can affect any or all members of the family for years to come. Parents must decide what to do with their own grief as well as the grief that they see in their children. Will they deal with it or try to pack it away—out of sight, out of mind? In particular, will they choose to comfort their children at this point or only try to cheer them up?

Sometimes the chaos of the moment is so great we simply can't afford to deal fully with the reality of what we are losing, and our only choice to survive seems to be to ignore those feelings. But if we aren't willing to look at our own losses, we can't help others, including children, with theirs. Some children may not be able or ready to do anything but block out the past and survive at this point. That is a common means of getting through this part of transition, and that is okay in the short run. But since it is important to mourn for what we have lost as well as celebrate what we have gained, let's look at what we mean by mourning.

Mourning the Losses. What, in fact, is mourning? How is it different from grief? Professor of philosophy and ATCK Jim Gould says that loss always produces grief, consciously or unconsciously, and that it will come out one way or another whether we intend it to or not. Because of that, he believes those living these globally nomadic lifestyles need to develop better rituals of mourning to help in that process of dealing with grief intentionally rather than suppressing it.[9]

Before we consider what some of these rituals might be, let's make sure we understand better the difference between grief and mourning.

> Grief is an emotional reaction/response to loss. Grief tends to follow a common pattern of emotional states, such as shock, confusion, denial, anger, sadness, rage, depression, isolation, to name a few, and not always in that order. If grief is experienced fully and allowed to unfold naturally, the process gradually leads one to some sort of acceptance and peace with the matter. . . . While grief is the emotional reaction/response to loss, mourning is the process one undertakes to deal with the void that is now left. Mourning is the process of acclimating to living a life without this special someone or something. It is a period of adapting to the changes created by this loss.[10]
>
> —Jade Kramer
> Ascension Healing Therapies

Grief counselor and therapist David Fireman also says this about the difference between grief and mourning.

> Grief is the natural psychological, behavioral, social, and physical response which is the beginning part of mourning. . . . In other words, one can mourn but not be in acute grief. Therefore, by definition, mourning is a more encompassing phenomenon that involves more than grief . . . adapting to the new world without the deceased [or other losses of mobility].[11]
>
> —David Fireman, LCSW
> Center for Grief Recovery and Therapeutic Services

In other words, mourning is a conscious decision to look at the grief, face it, and go through a process of moving from the loss to the next stage of life.

If we think about it, many of the suggestions we offered for helping build the RAFT might also be cited as part of these rituals of mourning. Taking time to consciously say good-bye to people, places, pets, and possessions is, in many ways, like standing before a casket and saying good-bye to a loved one who has died. Giving thanks and affirmation for the good is what eulogies are about. Resolving conflicts is what people often try to do before someone they love dies. Thinking ahead to prepare for how life will be after the losses of this transition is also part of long-range mourning. This is why building that RAFT is so critical to an ultimately healthy transition.

In some ways, this transit stage is like the morning after the funeral. We wake up and all the busyness of going to the hospital to visit, or having a hospice nurse help at home, or getting ready for the funeral is gone. Now the reality sets in that this person and life as we knew it with them is forever gone. And so the mourning continues. Tears come again. Here are some other things to do to help us mourn in healing ways.

- Acknowledge the losses and even take time to list them, particularly the hidden losses (see chapter 5).
- Expect the grief and name the stages as we feel them: anger, denial, sadness, etc.
- Let ourselves cry; this is the body's way of purging sadness.
- Don't force the grief, or feel guilty if we are on an even keel, even if other people are feeling it and we are not. Everyone has their own time line, and happiness is a gift.
- Find a physical way to have a "funeral" or "memorial service" for hidden losses, (e.g., flowers laid on a picture or sacred object representing the loss).
- Allow others to mourn with you by telling your story or share in your "memorial service."
- Give the comfort of listening and just being present to others who are grieving.
- Find creative expressions for what we are experiencing: poetry, photography, painting, or composing/playing music. Find a club or an empty beach and dance, pray, or sing.
- Be thankful for everything—even the difficult experiences—as they "grow us up."
- Keep wonder and laughter alive.
- Seek and create art that gives expression to our experience and also lifts us beyond ourselves—beauty and creativity, design, humor, and truths that remind us of another paradox of life. We can celebrate life even while mourning loss.

ENTERING STAGE

"Welcome, Marcus, we're glad to see you've made it!" a resident director (RD) of an East Coast college in the U.S., boomed.

Inside himself, Marcus winced a bit. Did this person have any idea of what he was saying? Did he know the journey Marcus had been on before he "made it" to this campus? He knew the RD was most likely assuming he had just traveled 1,000 miles from Minnesota where, presumably, he had grown up. Certainly Minnesota was a lot farther away than his roommate had come. The roommate had "made it"

from the next town. But did this RD have any idea of the
magnitude of the odyssey Marcus had taken to get there?
Probably not.

Marcus had been accepted to this university eighteen
months earlier while attending high school in Singapore but
deferred his enrollment. He spent Christmas in Tanzania
with his sister, who was studying on extension, and spent
time in a Maasai village where he purchased a colorful
shuka. He finished his semester in Singapore and after
graduation took an adventure and service trip to western
China for almost a month. After the service trip he returned
to the States and took a train 380 miles north to meet his
parents, then drove 800 miles visiting relatives before moving into a large house with generous friends in Maryland
from July to January. Marcus was not finished moving.

After working at a local camp, getting a driving permit,
taking a community college class, and enjoying the holidays,
Marcus, *shuka* in hand, took a flight for Hong Kong to spend
five months at a volunteer-run NGO. When Marcus returned
to the U.S., it was to help his family pack and move from
Maryland to Minnesota, where, due to real estate complica-
tions, the family was functionally homeless for seven weeks,
camping and relying on the hospitality of total strangers.

Marcus celebrated moving into his family's new home
the night before he and his dad got into the family car to
drive 1,300 miles to his college. It had been a long journey
indeed!

Throwing his colorful *shuka* on the bed and stowing
his school supplies, he said, "Well, I guess I'm pretty much
settled in . . ." After twenty months of motion, Marcus had
stepped into the Entering Stage.

Simply arriving at our destination does not mean we are going to be in the
Entering Stage. It begins that day we consciously decide we are going to move
toward this new place: the past is gone but there is still much good that we experience in the present. Or, perhaps, it is the day when we have a surprising "Aha!"
that we are, after all, beginning to feel at home once again—at least in some moments and places in our new environment.

Our Response

During this stage, life is no longer totally chaotic. We begin to accept that this
is where we are and have made the decision that it is time to become part of this
new community—we just have to figure out how to do it. Although we very much
want to move toward people in this new place, we still feel rather vulnerable and

a bit tentative. What if we make a serious social faux pas? Will others accept us? Will they take advantage of us? We often deal with these fears through an exaggeration of our normal personality traits as we begin to interact with others in our new location. People who are usually shy, introverted, or quiet may become more so. Normally gregarious or outgoing individuals may become loud, overbearing, and aggressive. Then, of course, we're mad at ourselves for acting so "dumb" and worry even more that people won't like us.

Sometimes TCKs who feel a bit lost in all of this may be more likely to take risks in this period, trying to find a way to connect, or even to avoid their feelings of loneliness. This may be necessary to a degree, but it can lead to dangerous, harmful, or illegal behaviors if unchecked.

The entering stage requires the building or rebuilding of trust between us and the others in our new community, that necessary element in human interaction. We wonder how much of our story to share and easily make the mistake of telling too much (to the glazed-over face across from us), or too little, scuttling our own history and potentially losing a chance to spark interest and a fresh connection.

> When Marcus' dad asked how he would answer his fellow students about where he was from, he quickly replied that he would tell them he was from Minnesota. That way, he reasoned, he would not be "shuffled off into a marginal group of internationals, sitting by themselves and eating sashimi off of batik tablecloths."
>
> And how would he handle the "fellow Minnesotan" who would be excited that they were from the same state, but curious as to why he didn't know anything about it? And what about meeting that other TCK who grew up all over South America, but who now says, "Yeah, I'm from Texas," and a potential connection is lost?
>
> He would figure that out, he said, but clearly, he just wanted to be part of the "normal college experience"—which completely made sense.

It is normal to struggle through the balance of the extremes during the entering stage, making mistakes along the way as we seesaw back and forth; ambivalence is a common emotion. We start to learn the new job or the rules at school, feel successful on a given day, and think, *I'm glad I'm here. This is going to be all right.* The next day someone asks us a question we can't answer and we wish we were back where we knew at least most of the answers. Our emotions can still fluctuate widely between the excitement of the new discoveries we're making and the homesickness that weighs us down. When we say *boot* and *bonnet* instead of *trunk* and *hood* (or vice versa), everyone laughs and tells us how funny we are. We laugh with them, but inside there is that feeling that nobody thought this was strange in our last place. There we were "normal," not funny. On the other hand, tomorrow we catch ourselves just before saying the wrong word and use the local term instead. When it passes without a flicker from those around us (in spite of how strange it sounds to our ears!), we realize we are actually beginning to learn how life works here. In the process, we can feel and act in ways that confound ourselves and others.

> When Michael teaches, he often describes this part of transition as being similar to a fish who has been hooked by a fisherman. There are a number of forces and instincts at work, symbolized by the line, the flow of water, and the urge to "get off the line." He makes the point that "a fish with a hook in its mouth does NOT act like a fish without a hook in its mouth."
>
> He tells the story of a first-grade student who began exhibiting some extreme behaviors such as rolling on the floor and biting things. Teachers and the guidance counselor did some assessments and Michael, as principal of the school, had to decide how to tell the parents that the child was exhibiting strong signs of textbook autism.
>
> Then the guidance counselor asked how long the student had been "in country." Inquiry found the boy was fresh from Korea and had not known he was moving until the day before he left his friends, midyear. The counselor advised giving the boy at least two more weeks before bringing up the suspected condition and, sure enough, the boy's behavior leveled out quite quickly; he did not have Asperger's—he was reacting to transition.

Eventually, we too will begin to level out. We may go to the noisy, busy, local market and actually recognize someone from our new community and be able to call that person by name. We drive to the other side of town, down quiet streets with signs we cannot yet read, without anyone telling us where to turn—and we find the house we are looking for! Someone calls with a procedural question at work and this time we *do* know the answer. Hope begins to grow that we will, in fact, one day have a sense of belonging to and feeling of competence in this community.

Community's Response

Of course, this entry stage is a bit uncomfortable for members of our new community as well, although they may have been eagerly anticipating our arrival. Before we came, everyone's roles were clear. Relationships—whether positive or negative—were established. Life functioned without explanation. We show up, and life changes for them too. Now *everything* seems to need an explanation. There may also be resentment if we act like we know how everything should work before we really take time to listen and see—and this is especially so if we have the power to make changes right away, and use that power.

The community also has to adjust their social order at least slightly to help us find our way in. In the end, however, people in the community begin to re-member our names, include us in the events going on, realize we are here to stay rather than simply visit, and start to make room for us in their world.

At the same time, there are in each society the equivalent of "free radicals" in the molecular world, who for one reason or another are missing an element that makes them ready to bond. Scientists describe these atoms or groups of atoms as "unstable and highly reactive." The same can be true in a new social setting where folks who are marginalized because of behavior are looking for new friends. The results can be disastrous. By the same token, just as free radicals can link up with other atoms to create a stable molecule, so many people who are also new in the community, or have experienced a change in their social status, may be ready to include others in a healthy way. Some risk and discernment is required on both sides of the equation.

Strategies for Healthy Entering

Enter positively. This is the stage where the results of building the T of the RAFT—Think Destination—well become clear. The more we have thought ahead about this time and what we and our family will need to make a positive entry into this place, the sooner and smoother we can begin to positively move into our new life. It's important for everyone involved, however, to recognize that they don't have to wait around helplessly for the new community to reach out and receive them. There are many ways to proactively help ourselves in this process. So how, then, can we (and the new community) move from the desire to establish ourselves in our new community to actually accomplishing it?

In communities with chronically high mobility, there are two interesting, though rather opposite, responses to newcomers. Some have designated people to help new members get oriented. There are maps of the town with the key places to shop marked and instruction guides for dealing with the local host culture—all tucked in a basket of goodies. One person is specifically assigned to take the new family around, and the whole system of orientation goes like clockwork because it has happened so many times. It's great when we relocate to such a community.

On the other hand, members of other highly mobile communities are so tired of seeing people come and go, they basically don't do much at all for the newcomer. Their thought process goes like this: *What's the use? These people will just be gone again,* or, *Why bother getting to know them? I've only got three months left here myself.*

Such an attitude makes it more difficult, of course, for us as newcomers, and we can then begin to feel very angry and withdraw from or wall off others too. But we do not have to remain there. With some understanding of why oth-ers may seem cautious, and with some patient persistence to reach out to new acquaintances, or by inviting families with children of like ages over for an evening, in time we will find even in these communities it is possible to find a way into a positive sense of belonging to this new place.

Choose and use mentors. One of the main keys to successfully negotiating the entry stage, particularly in an international or cross-cultural move, is to find a *mentor*—someone who answers questions and introduces the new community to us and us to it. These mentors function as "bridges" and can smooth our way in, significantly shortening the time it takes for us to get acclimated to the new surroundings, and help us make the right contacts. They can also give tips for the unspoken and unseen "do's and don'ts" that are operative in this new community and culture. Whether we are conscious of this need for a "mentor" or not, in the entry stage we are at least unconsciously looking for and finding, in some way, such people.

The problem, of course, lies in finding the *right* mentor, both for parents and children. If this person is our "introducer," then who we meet, what attitudes we pick up in the local community, and even how others see us, are shaped by this mentor. If we are guided well in this introductory phase to a new place and community, our chances for success rise. "It's hard to make a first impression a second time." If, on the other hand, we learn negative attitudes about this place and, unknown to us, the mentor is already one of the fringe people as far as others are concerned, we will likely wind up with a very different feeling and experience in this place. Even worse, if the chosen, or self-assigned, mentor has a bad reputation in the community, others may put us in the same category and avoid us as well.

This issue of finding the right mentor is particularly critical for TCKs as they move into a new place. At the very time when they are in the position of being "outsiders," often those who are also on the fringes of the receiving community will be the first to introduce themselves to a newcomer. They, too, may be looking for friends while others belonging to the "in" group already have their cadre of friends nicely established and may not be interested in adding more. TCKs or any new arrivals to a school or community are, of course, so happy *someone* has reached out to them that they can easily jump into a new relationship before understanding what the ramifications of such a relationship might be.

How can any newcomer know who is or isn't trustworthy as a mentor? How can all members of the family make a wise decision at this point?

Our suggestion is to be appreciative and warm to all who reach out a helping hand during this entry time, but inwardly to be cautious about making a wholehearted commitment to this relationship before asking a few questions: Is this person one who fits into the local community or is he or she definitely marginalized in one way or another? Does this person exhibit the positive, encouraging attitudes we would like to foster in our family, or does this person make negative remarks and display hostile attitudes about almost everything? Beware of the latter!

When we take a little time to evaluate a potential mentor, we may discover that this person who greeted us so warmly is, in fact, one of those wonderful people who belong to the heart of any organization, school, or community and has the great gift of making newcomers feel almost instantly at home. That person could well go on to be the best possible mentor in the world for any particular member of the family and be a great friend. If, however, we find out that this person who is so eager to befriend us, or our TCKs, is a marginal member of the community, then we must ask the next question: Why do they want to befriend us?

Some are marginal simply because they, like us, are relative newcomers and are still looking to establish new friendships. While they may not yet be members of the inner circle, they have learned the basics of how life is lived in this place and can be most helpful. In fact, they often have more time to spend orienting newcomers than those whose plates are already full with well-defined roles and relationships. Relationships that start like this often turn into lifelong friendships.

If, however, we find out that the first person who approaches us, and particularly our TCKs, so invitingly has been intentionally marginalized from the community, we need to be cautious about adopting this person as a mentor. Such people are often in some kind of trouble within the community. Perhaps they rebel against the accepted standards of behavior, break laws, or defy teachers, and they often want to recruit naïve newcomers for their own agenda.

Besides using our common sense in situations such as these, there are other ways to try to find good mentors. We can make use of any active mentoring programs already in place. Some agencies or corporations set up "matching families" for those coming to their community. One potential problem is that an organization may have a mentoring program for the adults in the family, but the children's need for a mentor is forgotten. In such cases, parents may need to be more proactive and ask those in the human resources or employee care departments of their organization if they can give the names of possible families to contact in the next posting. Many international schools have set up a "big brother/big sister" program, with good mentors already identified, to help new students through their first few weeks at school. Getting involved with such things as parent/teacher groups can be a way for parents to meet other parents and help to find informal mentors if no formal mentoring programs are available.

In some places, mentors are simply hard to find for various reasons. At such a time, parents can look for mentoring programs such as SeaChange Mentoring, where founder Ellen Mahoney matches adult TCKs with current TCKs not only to help them navigate transition but also to develop and use the gifts they are acquiring in their life story. Transition coaching, such as Michael Pollock's Daraja (meaning "bridge" or "stepping-stones"), is also becoming an increasingly helpful resource to think through the process of healthy transition.

Special Challenges of Cross-Cultural Entry

Most of this discussion on the entry stage applies to any kind of move. But there are extra stresses recognized by experts around the world for those trying to enter a completely new culture—which is the nature of most transitions for third culture families. Lisa and Leighton Chinn, a couple who have been working with international students for almost three decades, have outlined four stages of cultural stress that occur during this phase: Fun, Flight, Fight, and Fit.[13] It's important to acknowledge these extra stages, because they often happen in spite of all we have done right to prepare for our move and can make us feel that none of our other preparations mattered. The process can go something like this—sort of a second transition cycle within the larger first transition process.

As we have looked ahead, we have developed a sense of anticipation and excitement for our new assignment. We decide it will be *fun* to explore the new environment, learn its history, and enrich our lives through meeting new people. The first few days after arrival, we busily engage with all we meet and feel excitement that we can actually answer the greetings in this new language we tried to study before we came, and all seems well. We think, *What fun!*

A few more days pass, however, and things aren't quite as exciting. We don't like not knowing how to get to the store on our own because we haven't learned yet how to drive on the "wrong" side of the road (or keep taking the wrong bus), we're tired of not being understood past simple greetings by those around us, and we wish we could go "home"—back to that place where we knew how to function and where we fit. This is the *flight* stage and is in reaction to the frustration or fear that we experience in the new situation.

Soon, however, we may get tired of feeling so useless or out of place. We are tired of dodging and avoiding and begin to get angry. After all, we used to fit. We were competent individuals where we used to live, so it can't be our fault that we feel so lost and insecure. We begin to blame everything and everyone in this new place for our discomfort. If they would only do things "correctly" (meaning the way we used to do them), everything would be fine. Internally, and sometimes externally, we begin to *fight* the way things are being done here—perhaps even expressing anger at those trying to help us adjust.

Over time we begin to get in the swing of things and experience less frustration and fear and more success and ease; we discover that we *fit*. As with any model for experience, the curve from fun to fit is not necessarily a smooth one at all—ours could very well look like a tangled fishing line! Frustration can give way back to fun when we learn to laugh at our own mistakes and give ourselves a break for not knowing all we need to know. Fit can slip back into fight when we think we have figured something out and hit a new snag or nuance.

> Damien moved to Taiwan as an international school elementary principal and found in moving into his new position that he had inherited an administrative assistant. For months he struggled with unmet expectations in Xiao Ling's

performance. Internally he fumed and could be outwardly snappish.

He finally scheduled a meeting together with a Chinese administrative colleague to address the issues. Through dialogue he learned that many times when his assistant said, "I know," she really didn't understand what he was saying at all. She thought it was more professional to know, so therefore claimed she did—and she did not want him to "lose face" for being unclear.

Relieved that the cultural hurdles had been cleared and feeling cheery, Damien ended the meeting. At that point his Chinese colleague dismissed the assistant and shut the door. "You realize that this is not just cultural, right?" No, he didn't. "She is hiding her incompetence behind her culture. We will find you a new assistant." Several months and some more gray hair later, this is indeed what happened.

Knowing these reactions might happen doesn't necessarily stop them, but it can help us to anticipate what is coming and recognize it as normal. Expecting these responses can also help us to mitigate the strong feelings with more reasonable action.

These are the moments we need to remind ourselves that entry also takes time, to remember that in six months to a year we can presume that if we keep learning humbly, we'll be driving comfortably, we'll have discovered where the stores are for the things we want to buy, figured out how to keep our organization moving forward, learned how to conduct business, and most likely, made new friends. At that point, once again we will *fit*.

REENGAGEMENT STAGE

The light at the end of the proverbial tunnel is that in any transition, cross-cultural or not, a final, recognized stage of reengagement is possible. Although there have been moments of wondering if it will ever happen, given enough time and a genuine willingness to adapt, we will once again become part of the permanent community. And then the day finally comes. We settle into our new surroundings, accepting the people and places for who and what they are. This doesn't always mean that we like everything about the situation, but at least we can start to see *why* people do what they do rather than only *what* it is they do.

Reinvolvement, or reengagement, is not the same as feeling "at home" because home can prove to be an elusive concept. Pico Iyer, author of *The Global Soul*, said in a TED talk that 220 million people live outside their birth countries today and are "taking pieces of many different places and putting them together into a stained glass whole" because, as he adds later, "home is less a piece of soil than a piece of soul."[12] Perhaps "home" is actually a *peace* of soul, for home is safety, belonging, contribution and growth; for this to happen, we must commit to others and them to us. And, in the end, many who grow up globally feel "at home" in many places!

Our Response

We accept our new place, role, and community. Depending on the degree of difference in this new situation, we may still feel alien from time to time, but overall, we feel settled again. We may not be native to this community, but we feel we can ultimately belong. We have a sense of intimacy, a feeling that our presence matters to this group and we feel secure. We can still feel like the newcomer or outsider at times and will still have to make some surprising adjustments, but time again feels present and permanent as we focus on the here and now rather than hoping for the future or constantly reminiscing about the past.

Technology, especially social media, enables people to make choices about social relationships as never before. While Skype, Instagram, Facebook, Twitter, and a host of other platforms allow people to connect over distances and time zones, social media also play a role in creating barriers to reengagement. One way to check our progress in reengagement is to examine how we see people around us. Cross-culturalist Jerry Jones suggests our getting acquainted with people in a new community is a progression from *scenery* to *machinery* to *persons*. He says first we see other people in a new place as part of the landscape and we feel curious and observant. Next we get to know them for what they can do for us—taxi drivers, salespeople, food vendors—and we feel satisfied or frustrated with them. Finally, we get to know those in our new community as people and our feelings range from cautious to empathetic to delighted. We take on new responsibilities and develop a reputation.[14]

Community Response

Others in the community again see us as part of the group. They know where and how we fit. Once more, people hear our name and instantly picture our face and form. They know our reputation, history, talents, tastes, interests, and where we fit in the political and social network. They let us in on the news of the day, ask our opinion, and count on us for community events. Our neighbors and colleagues consider us in their plans, seek our friendship, and respond to our needs. It is a great place to be—until the contract runs out, the visa is not renewed, the political landscape changes, or our commander reassigns us . . . and the process begins again.

Strategies for Healthy Reengagement

Once more, we feel involved in our situation. This time, however, perhaps we don't take it for granted. Hopefully our experience in needing a mentor when we arrived helps us to volunteer formally or informally to help other newcomers settle. We realize it is time to refocus on helping our children develop to their fullest potential. Once more there is time and space for that (we hope!). But another great gift to give children as they begin also to settle is to remind them they don't have to give up the past to settle into this present and move to the future. When everyone has done the journey well, it is a time to celebrate that they can have a sense of belonging and love for "all of the above" places and people they have known instead of having to choose just one. It is indeed a good place to be!

However, there is one caveat. Some children have moved so many times and to so many places that they never wind up in this place of reengagement in any place they go. Sadly, some have felt they were outsiders their entire life because of how many times they have moved. Adjusting the quote from Charles La Shure, we are humans who simply cannot thrive without belonging somewhere and to some people. That is why, as we saw in chapter 6, it is important to remember that building a strong *sense of home* in relationships, particularly in the family, is key to keeping the foundation strong even when geography frequently changes. In coaching and seminars, Michael refers to these relationships as "relational anchors." These are people with whom children can feel fully invested and involved no matter the geography or culture. The people who are "anchors" may also be in the role of "bridges" who have experienced several places and contexts that the TCK children have experienced and can both relate and validate the "both/and" of the child's experience. Refer to chapter 6 for the discussion of "mirrors" and "anchors." When life brings us to a liminal space, or we choose it, strong relationships become the "catch" where we are secure and connected.

This is the normal process of transition. Knowing about the various stages doesn't keep them from happening, but it does help us not to be surprised by what happens at each stage, to recognize we are normal, and to be in a position to make the choices that allow us to gain from the new experiences we encounter while dealing productively with the inevitable losses of any transition experience.

Expanding Our Vision

The lessons from the TCK transition experience apply not only to other types of CCKs, but to every living person. All of us go through multiple types of transitions as life requires each of us to manage change. Although Dave Pollock developed his transition model from observing TCKs and mobility, there are many applications for the concept. Glenn Taylor makes one such in his book *Pastors in Transition*, applying the principles to another fairly mobile community. The overlay with Dr. Elisabeth Kübler-Ross's stages of grief we mentioned in chapter 5 makes sense when we remember that in most changes we lose as well as gain, and grief will certainly follow. The trick is to remember that the process of change in our lives is not a "loss" or "gain" dichotomy, but a combination of losses and gains. It is imperative that we balance both sides of the equation as we relocate around the globe, addressing the challenges and maximizing the benefits.

Perhaps one more paradox of the TCK experience is that learning to transition well through change and ensuing loss becomes a great asset in a TCK's life for themselves and others. Having language and concepts to understand this basic process gives cohesion and further clarity to situations that would otherwise seem completely unrelated.

> ATCK Latasha told us that during her bout with breast cancer, knowing about the transition cycle was a key in helping her deal with the cancer. She realized with the initial news of the diagnosis, she began the "leaving" phase—moving from life as it had been to life in the world of chemo and radiation cycles she didn't yet know. As she faced the prospects ahead, she saw how she needed to deal not only with her potential loss of life, but the many hidden losses also entailed in such a time as this: the loss that she could not be involved in the day-by-day activities of life with her friends as she was used to doing; the loss that her record of near-perfect health was now forever gone; the loss of her sense of identity—that when others saw her bald head, they would see "cancer patient" rather than Latasha.
>
> She found the knowledge of the transition cycle extremely helpful as she went through the differing feelings of her treatment phases of chemo and radiation. She could name this as the transition stage—the old world was gone but what lay ahead remained unclear. Survival was the goal for each day, knowing another stage was coming.
>
> At the end of her treatments, she realized she had moved into the entry, or perhaps reentry, phase. Life had gone on without her in her former world—how would she find her way back in? "With intentionality"—meaning it was up to her to reach out to others as well as expecting them to reach out to her. She did so, and feels totally re-involved at this stage.

Latasha's story demonstrates that learning to deal constructively with the challenges of the TCK experience translates into strengths for other changes and transition in our lives. As TCKs and others continue to understand this basic human process, they can understand why they no longer have to shut down their emotions or shut out relationships. Instead, all of us—TCKs, other CCKs, adults of all backgrounds—can risk the pain of another loss for the sake of the accompanying gain because we know how to bridge the distances. Learning to live in this kind of open hopefulness turns each challenge into one more strength.

Questions for Chapter 13

1. Did you have any "Aha!" moments while reading about the common responses of leaving—"leaning away," denying the grief, etc.? What are your normal responses and strategies as you leave a place? Please explain.

2. The chapter speaks of the importance of building a RAFT: Reconciliation/ Affirmation/Farewells/Think Destination. Have you knowingly or un- knowingly built any part of a RAFT in past moves? How did building or not building a RAFT help or hinder your transition?

3. As you read about mourning, are there things you do already that might be considered "rituals of mourning" to deal with loss in a healing way?

4. Forgiveness and reconciliation are identified as key actions in the healthy leaving/entering cycle. Do you agree or disagree? Why or why not?

5. How have you experienced the liminal space of the transit stage as a gift, a burden, or both? Please explain.

6. Share an example of culture shock you experienced. How did you respond? Did it fit one of the stages mentioned of fun, flight, fight, or fit?

CHAPTER 14

Coming "Home": Reentry

Culture shock is a peculiar thing. It feels as if all your
guideposts have been turned upside down, as though the
words you read were unexpectedly printed backwards, as if
the air you took for granted with every breath was suddenly
scented in a strange and unfamiliar way. I looked around
at the people I went to classes with: I looked like them; all
of us wore jeans and T-shirts, we spoke the same language,
though some of us had different accents. We had similar
interests, similar callings. We were intelligent, we were
young, we were finding our paths, defining our interests. Yet
the very way the other students walked in the world, viewed
their place in it, and approached others made me feel like
a stranger, and there were times of intense longing for the
familiarity of home.

—Nina Sichel
Unrooted Childhoods: Memoirs of Growing Up Global[1]

And now we have come full circle. After all these years of careful planning
to make the most of the years in a host culture, to deal positively with the
transitions along the way, to make good school choices, and to enjoy the
journey among many worlds, the time has finally come for the family, or at least
the TCKs themselves, to go "home." Although it does not always work out that
way, one of the factors that distinguishes the TCK experience from that of a true
immigrant is the full *expectation* that there is some kind of expiration date on the
overseas life. Presumably, after living for "a significant period of their developmental years outside their passport culture," the day will come when most TCKs
make a permanent, or extended, return to that country and culture.

Oddly enough, for many TCKs this is one of the most difficult transitions they go through, no matter how many other moves they have already made. Commonly called *reentry*, for a great number of TCKs this process more closely resembles an entry. Additionally for children who are new to their "home country," parents are often going through reverse culture shock themselves, suddenly disoriented by the things they thought they knew but don't know. These TCKs lack parental stability to help them through the landing. College-aged TCKs returning alone or with one parent repatriate without the cocoon of family comfort.

Why is reentry often so hard?

Reentry Stresses

Some reasons for reentry stress are simply extensions of the many factors already talked about, particularly the normal challenges of any cross-cultural transition: the grief of losing a loved world, the discomfort of being out of cultural balance, and the struggle to find a place of belonging in a new place with new people.

The above are normal for all of us. But TCKs often have other potential layers in the experience of reentry. Young adult TCKs, in particular, are going through the usual changes of moving from childhood into adulthood (often referred to as adolescence). The dimensions of change can become confusingly layered. One attempt to understand the complexity is the set of models here.

Figure 14–1: The Big Three and the Soup
©2014 Michael V. Pollock

It reflects the importance of the major challenges of TCKs in terms of understanding who they are, where they belong, and what to do with their lives. Over and over TCKs express fear of being "trapped" by circumstances. Reentry is often the point where decisions are made that will impact the TCK's life outcomes: studies and training, friends and partners, geography and connections. Running through those questions are the impacts of mobility and loss that with the resultant grief create the "soup" that swirls through the other themes.

In terms of the TCKs' overall developmental process, we see **four core dimensions** in flux during reentry (see the circle within the square in figure 14-2):

1. *Cross-Cultural:* Returning to their own country means that those who have grown up in the third culture have to decide what part of each of their cultures to keep and how much of the new culture to assimilate.

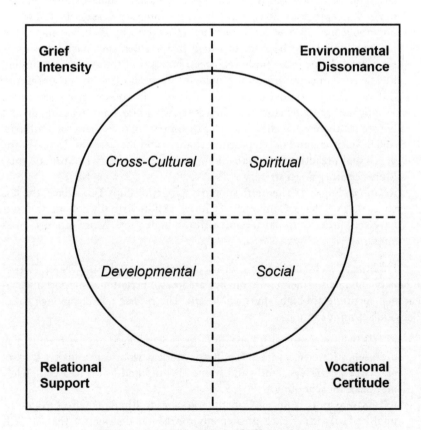

Figure 14–2: Transition Challenge Matrix
©2013 Michael V. Pollock

2. *Spiritual:* Adolescents and young adults have the task of examining what they believe and answering existential questions for themselves for full ownership.
3. *Social:* The young adults may be socially adjusted to people older than their peers and yet be behind peers in certain tasks.
4. *Developmental:* Current research suggests that brain development, particularly in the prefrontal cortex area responsible for logic, control of the emotions, organizing, and planning is still developing until age twenty-five.[2]

All four dimensions listed are adjustments that every person goes through, but the tasks become more complex with **four factors** that happen over and over in the TCK community. Each of the four factors has a sliding scale of intensity as we relate them to the TCK experience (see factors outside the circle but in the square):

- *Grief Intensity:* How much loss and grief TCKs have had and how well they did or didn't process it determines their grief intensity. Less grief = less stress.
- *Environmental Dissonance:* If the place TCKs grew up is similar in geography and climate to the place to which they reenter, they have lower environmental dissonance and lower stress; however, if the two are dissimilar, their environmental dissonance increases in proportion to the amount of differentness. More environmental similarity = low dissonance = less stress.
- *Vocational Certitude:* How sure they are of what they want to be and do and how to get there intensifies or lessens the impact of the other cross-cultural, social, spiritual, and developmental changes and increases or decreases the depth and breadth of the transition. Each person's story is a unique mix. More certainty = less stress.
- *Relational Support:* The more supporting relationships TCKs have, the less stress they will have. Conversely, TCKs who know virtually nobody and thus have very little relational support will feel high stress. More support = less stress.

Looking at each factor on a sliding scale makes the picture clearer. If grief intensity and environmental dissonance are low and relational support and vocational certitude are high, *stress will be low.* The reverse will create *high stress.* Let's look at some examples.

- A TCK who reenters with her family to a town where she has friends may experience lower grief intensity than a student who feels a higher level of grief when he leaves family and friends behind and heads to a completely new place for schooling.
- A TCK returning from the Canadian Rockies to Rio de Janeiro (geography unalike) will experience greater environmental dissonance than a TCK moving from Mombasa, Kenya, to Abidjan, Cote d'Ivoire (geography alike). In other words, if TCKs return to a place that feels a lot like "home" because

of its particular type of geography (and climate), their "environmental dissonance" will be low. If, on the other hand, they return to a place that is totally different from where they have been growing up, it's going to feel a lot less like home than they might expect. They will experience high environmental dissonance.

- A TCK may reenter into a large circle of family and friends or may know no one in the new community. Lots of built-in support from family and friends lessens the stress. However, if the TCK goes to a college where he doesn't know anyone, he will feel high stress due to few or no relationships to support him.

- Finally, TCKs who know exactly what they are going to study and how their training will proceed for the intended job or career have high vocational certitude, which results in lower stress. TCKs who have absolutely no clue what to study or do with their lives will have low vocational certitude, which results in high stress.

When the four core dimensions (cross-cultural, spiritual, social, and developmental) are overlaid with and multiplied by the intensity of the four factors (grief intensity, environmental dissonance, vocational certitude, and relational support), the resulting layered challenges create high stress that can overload the TCK's bodily systems and result in compromised mental and physical functioning and even illness. At the same time, if the stress is not all that great, reentry is usually easier. Many TCKs navigate these turbulent waters successfully. Often it is because they have been previously gifted with awareness and tools. Some have a solid foundation to navigate the normal process of change in the four dimensions, and some may experience lower change impact between the factors.

Michael's "Aha!" moment that caused him to create this model came while considering why TCKs can have greatly different responses to reentry. Compare the vast differences in how Ted and Trisha experienced reentry in their lives.

> Ted is U.S. American ATCK. While he grew up between Mexico and Texas, he now lives in Asia, where he works as an international art dealer. His children attended a local international school, and when Ted heard there was to be a seminar on TCKs, he decided as a parent to come.
>
> When Ted heard Michael speak on the difficulties of reentry and how important it was to prepare kids, he came up afterwards to share that while he understood what Michael had said, he didn't relate or feel he had experienced any real struggle at reentry time.
>
> When Michael asked Ted about his story, Ted explained that he had grown up between Texas and Mexico, as his family was part of a group working on developmental projects in Mexico. His parents' organization established "rotating communities" so that while one group of families worked

in Mexico, the other lived in Texas, and then they switched. When the project ended, his family and the others stopped rotating and life went on with his friends and community intact because now all of the families stayed together in Texas.

Adjusting to college in Chicago was as difficult as it would be for any Texan, he figured. Ted missed his Mexican friends and wondered if he would ever return to visit. He reasoned that if he wanted to, it wouldn't be that difficult, but the truth is that, for whatever reason, he had never yet tried. For Ted, reentry didn't seem to be a big deal.

Think about Ted's story.

- He had low grief intensity because he moved with his peers and the same families through childhood, and they stayed together after the project ended. (low stress)
- He had high relational support as the core of his closest relationships moved with him. (low stress)
- He had low environmental dissonance since the landscape, weather, and climate of Texas and Mexico are very similar. (low stress)
- He wanted to be an artist and curator and followed that path directly through school, so experienced high vocational certitude. (low stress)

All four of the factors were on the low stress end for Ted; therefore, the transition did not seem so difficult. Perhaps the loss of connection to Mexico and his friends there might show up as grief later. Certainly there are some TCKs who insist that they did "just fine through their process, thank you," and then go on to list the hurts, scars, and pain they are still enduring in mid- to late life. But in Ted's case, based on the Transition Challenge Matrix, reentry had not been traumatic for him in the way others have experienced it, allowing him to move quite easily into college life.

On the other end of the spectrum, take a look at Trisha's poignant story.

Trisha looked like a happy college freshman. Petite and outgoing with blonde hair and blue eyes, you wouldn't guess that she felt quite out of place on a U.S. campus, but she had grown up in a remote area of Siberia. Her parents had been doing translation work and community development in a small ethnic group of East Asians. As an eleventh-grade student in a small international high school that mixed local and expatriate children, she was part of a close community.

During the summer break her parents announced that they were taking a temporary leave from their work in Russia to receive marital counseling as directed by the mission.

She and her brother packed hurriedly and were only able to meet up with a few friends to let them know of their plans and tell them they would be back in the fall. The rest they contacted on social media.

After two months of counseling in the U.S., her parents announced that they would not return to Russia and were getting a divorce. In the moment it took to break the news, the children's lives changed drastically. Trisha's pain accumulated in the loss of parent relationship, loss of the home they knew, loss of friends in Russia, loss of possessions left behind when they thought they were only leaving for the summer, loss of mission membership, loss of faith community, and loss of plans and expectations for the future. The greater part of her universe was lost, unexpectedly and instantly.

For Trisha, good-byes, closure, and managed change were not possible. Her world was now upside down. She cried easily, felt anxious, depressed, and sometimes angry—really angry—even though she did not always know where to direct that anger.

After a year of upheaval, a new school, cross-cultural adjustment to life in California, divorce proceedings, and custody battles, Trisha left her new "home" for college. She arrived on the campus of a small midwestern college surrounded by cornfields. She was a hidden immigrant, looking like everyone else, but with layers of differences and unprocessed grief that made transition seem akin to scaling a 500-foot cliff.

Her grief was very intense and her stresses covered almost everything about her life.

- Trisha had extremely high cross-cultural differences and environmental dissonance as well between Russia and California and again between California and the Midwest, producing layers of stress. (high stress in both the cross-cultural dimension and the environmental dissonance factor)
- Because her parents had been missionaries and their organization did not allow divorced couples to continue serving in that mission, Trisha was totally cut off from the mission system—her previous place of belonging. The shame of her parents' situation caused her to cut off others in her faith community, so processing her own faith became harder. This situation also kept her from having the relational support she was used to having from the mission, her faith community, and her parents. (high stress and grief intensity in the spiritual dimension and relational support)

- Outwardly, she appeared socially adjusted, but because of her vast cultural differences, inside she felt like a hidden immigrant. (high stress cross-culturally, lots of grief over lost culture and friendships)
- Although her personality was warm and welcoming, underneath she struggled to understand her peers or relate to them much of the time. (high stress socially)
- Those around her didn't understand she wasn't as comfortable in social situations as she seemed on first impression. At nineteen, her brain was still developing its capacity for organization and impulse control. (high stress developmentally)
- And her relational support was extremely low, considering all her parents were dealing with in their personal lives, relationship (loss of) issues, and reentry issues—and there is no mention of other relatives or friends who reached out to help her.

This is a story of layer upon layer of stresses, and it's not hard to see why reentry was so difficult for her.

UNREALISTIC EXPECTATIONS

Expectation of a "dream world." In today's world, many TCKs go back and forth between home and host cultures at fairly regular intervals. When they tell us they "know what it's like" to live in that passport country based on those visits, they forget that going for vacation is different from living somewhere longer term. When TCKs return for a limited time, relatives plan special events and parents may indulge their children (and themselves) with various "goodies" they have missed overseas—a favorite ice cream flavor, or a trip to Disneyland. It's easy for TCKs to begin to think of all this attention and special privilege as normal for life in this country. When it turns out they have to settle in and no one seems to notice they are "special," it can be a shock.

Expectation of "sameness." Reentry stress is often connected to the unconscious expectations of both the TCKs and those in their home culture of how they will relate to one another. Chapter 4 describes how most TCKs have been recognized as foreigners while living in their host culture. Some have lived there as hidden immigrants, and a few fit into either the adopted or mirror category. When TCKs return to their passport culture, however, almost all are hidden immigrants. Now everything Gary Weaver talked about in his model of the iceberg and how that relates to cultural expectations and stress starts to make even more sense. People at home take one look at these returning TCKs and expect them to be in the PolVan "mirror" box illustrated in figures 4-3 and 4-4—those who think and look like the home country "locals." Why wouldn't they expect this? After all, these TCKs are from the same racial heritage, ethnic, and national background as those "at home" are.

TCKs look around them and they, too, often expect to be in the mirror box. For years they've known they were "different" but excused it because they knew they were Asians living in England, Africans living in Germany, or Canadians living in Bolivia. That justification for being different is now gone, and they presume they will finally be the same as others; after all, these are their own people. Wrong.

Take another look at Krista and Nicola, our look-alike TCKs in chapter 8 who let their host culture peers in England and Scotland know how eager they were to return to their home countries where they "knew" they would finally fit in and belong.

> When Krista first returned to the United States, she felt euphoric at finally being "home." It didn't take long, however, before Krista realized to her horror that she couldn't relate to her American classmates either. Somehow she was as different from them as from her English peers.

> The same thing happened to Nicola when she returned to England. After literally kissing the tarmac when she disembarked from the plane in London, a strange thing soon happened. Nicola found herself increasingly irritated with her English peers. Their world seemed so small. Internally, she began resisting becoming like them, and within a year, virtually all of her friends were international students and other TCKs. She wondered why she could never completely fit into the world around her, whether it was Scottish or English.

Both Krista and Nicola's disappointment was greater because they had always presumed that if they could only make it "home," they would no longer feel so different from others. The type of scorn or anger both Krista and Nicola felt toward their peers *at home* happens when expectations don't match reality. A British TCK in Burkina Faso did not expect her friends there to know where Reading (England) was, but in Reading, she can't believe her friends don't know where Ouagadougou is.

Expectation of "one-way change." Sometimes TCKs return to a passport situation with images, accurate or idealized, based on where they lived before or people they have visited through the years. They give lip service to "Yeah, I know it will be different," but deep down expect that what they left behind is still how it is. The reality of how different it is can come as a big shock—not unlike what Rip Van Winkle experienced when he returned home after being asleep for a hundred years. They are shocked when remembered landmarks may be gone, friends have moved or died, and the house that was so big in their memories is now a tiny bungalow. The cause is that like two motorcycles driving away from each other in opposite directions; the distance apart is multiplied by at least two. A person who left friends behind three years ago has experienced three years of changes while the friends left behind have done the same. Six years of difference have occurred between them. In the age of social media, it's easy to forget that what a person posts, tweets, and pins on an e-board doesn't give a true picture of what that person is like in person, in 3-D flesh and blood.

REVERSE CULTURE SHOCK

TCKs who expect "sameness," or think they are already up to speed culturally through the Internet, almost laugh when they hear about reverse culture shock—experiencing culture shock when returning to the passport country rather than a foreign land. They, and often their parents, promise it will not be so—which can make it worse.

In fact, many TCKs have similar experiences to those of Krista and Nicola, where all seems well at the beginning of reentry. Relatives and old friends welcome the TCKs warmly, while the school bends over backward in its efforts to assess how transcripts from some exotic foreign school relate to the local curriculum. Soon, however, unexpected differences begin to pop up. Classmates use slang or idioms that mean nothing to the returning TCKs. Everyone else is driving a car; they only know how to ride a bike. If they do drive, they learned to drive on the other side of the road. TCKs never had to pump their own gas when they could still call it petrol and others would understand what they meant. Friends, relatives, and classmates are shocked at the TCKs' ignorance of these most common practices necessary for everyday living.

Their "hidden immigrant-ness" comes into play big-time here—particularly at the deeper levels. Cultural dissonance lurks beneath the apparently similar surface. A TCK whose parents worked in Uganda with the AIDS patients in refugee camps accepts an invitation to join friends at McDonald's for a hamburger. The TCK fresh from Uganda can only think about how many people could eat for a whole day or week in that refugee camp for the amount of money this one meal cost. Even worse, he watches people throw out leftover food and can't help expressing his shock and horror. The friends who invited him out for lunch feel this TCK is ungrateful at best, condemning at worst.

And so the problems may continue to mount. TCKs who have grown up in a culture where there's a commitment to honesty and respect accompanied by orderliness and quiet find entry into a confrontational, loud, self-centered home culture quite offensive. Those who've grown up in a boisterous, activity-centered, individualistic culture may find people from their own country docile and self-effacing. Often TCKs begin to realize they don't even *like* what is considered their home culture. And those in that home culture may soon realize they're not so sure they like the TCKs either. But no one stops to think how these reactions are related to their original expectations of one another. Reentry is, in fact, reverse culture shock. Soon the fun stage is gone and the fight and flight stages appear.

Common Reactions to Reentry Stress

This is when the four common ways TCKs respond when changing cultural worlds can appear: adapting as a chameleon and basically trying to hide the difference; becoming a screamer and making sure to define the difference; retreating as a wallflower to hope others don't notice the difference; and adapting, like Ted, to go with whatever flow is there.

For the TCKs who become chameleons, screamers, or wallflowers during reentry, there are often unseen reasons guiding these coping mechanisms. While coping mechanisms work for a while, they can be crippling in the long term. Let's look at some things potentially lurking behind the behavior others see.

ELEVATED FEARS

Fear of being disloyal to the past. Some TCKs unconsciously fear that allowing themselves to repatriate totally means being disloyal to their host country. "If I allow myself to like it here, it may mean I really didn't like it there," or "If I adjust and fit in, I may lose my memory of and commitment to return to that place where I grew up." Such fears can make them lose the delight in their present, which is as much a part of their life experience as their past has been. They haven't yet learned to live in the great paradox of a "both/and" world.

Fear of losing their identity. When the foundation of the cultural ground beneath is badly shaking, even those who thought they had a clear sense of personal identity may begin to shake with it. All they have left is this memory of who they were, the life they had before, and that there was once a place they felt truly "at home." They subconsciously wonder: If I let go of the place and the people where I have always identified most and fit in best to align myself with my home country and culture, will I lose some important part of me? Marilyn Gardner says it well.

> Perhaps our unspoken fear is that if we learn to sing songs of joy in this new place, this new land, then we will forget the old, we will lose our identity, all that we know, all that is familiar. As one person put it: "I wanted to preserve my identity, to hold dear the soil in which my roots are settled, to Never Forget Who I Am. After all—my identity has come at such a high cost."[3]

A SENSE OF ELITISM OR ARROGANCE—TRUE OR PROJECTED

Reentry is a key time when the potential arrogance or sense of elitism ascribed to TCKs comes up, but in an odd way. Some TCKs seem disdainful of those who do not share their experience. The idea in the TCK description that TCKs relate to others of shared experience turns into, "I can *only* relate to other TCKs." Perhaps this is part of the screamer saying, "I'm not like you, so don't expect me to be," but it certainly appears to others (and is, in fact!) an arrogance that further isolates the TCKs from many rich friendships they might otherwise have.

Arrogance might also be the charge laid at the feet of the TCK who returns to her passport country as the "worldly traveler" who has seen and done so much more than her peers that they should simply sit at her feet for instruction and stories—if she can tolerate them.

The fear of losing identity or betraying the past can show up in another form of arrogance—longing only for the past, which was obviously so much better than this world of the passport country. There is no one or nothing here of enough interest to pursue.

Self-centeredness during transition can easily cause TCKs to feel upset that no one wants to know their story. Often the truth is they didn't ask the other people to tell their story either. Forgetting that others who didn't live overseas also have a story to share is another type of elitism.

EXCESSIVE ANGER AT "HOME" CULTURE AND PEERS

Ironically, TCKs can often be culturally tolerant anywhere but in their own passport culture. In a "foreign culture," most TCKs will usually keep quiet about their opinions or only express them to fellow TCKs or expatriates. These rules seem to change, however, on reentry. Suddenly some TCKs feel free to express every negative opinion they have about their home culture, no matter who is around. While chronic put-downs may be an unconscious defense for the TCKs' own feelings of insecurity or rejection, such remarks further alienate them from everyone around them. But, like it or not, they *are* (usually) a member of this group by birth and citizenship. In affirming one part of their experience and themselves, they reject another.

DEPRESSION

Even though a "wallflower" response of withdrawing to assess the scene is a common reentry response, it can also reveal or, ironically, mask depression. Common withdrawal patterns that can initially be within a normal range and then move toward true depression might include TCKs having a hard time getting out of bed, not pursuing activities that normally bring satisfaction and joy, or sitting in their rooms using smart phones, tablets, or laptops all day rather than joining any activities at school, trying to make friends, or looking for interesting community groups. Withdrawal can have less obvious forms, however. Some students retreat into their studies and earn straight As—but who can fault them for that? Others spend hours practicing their favorite instrument and winning every musical contest they enter. While everyone congratulates them for their honors, no one realizes this is another form of escape or even depression. Mobile screen devices may create an alternate social reality in which a person has a "social life" consisting of only what is chosen, edited, and posted or in which only past relationships are continued through video and text chat. Any of these scenarios can mask an inability to move into the new social reality.

While anger or depression may be an initial coping mechanism, if either of these extends beyond six months to a year or creates a danger to the TCK or others, professional help may be needed. Obviously, there are many reasons for depression, but in looking at the biographies of many of today's young people carrying out violent attacks, many are CCKs of one sort or another. One of the Columbine shooters, Eric Harris,[4] was a military TCK whose family had moved to Colorado when his father retired six years earlier, but he never felt he fit into the culture there. In each story, there are the warning signs retrospectively of anger and depression, but always the surprise from those who knew them that they wound up doing what they did.

The sad thing is, for a few TCKs, when they find out that even at "home" they don't fit, the depression can become a serious and life-threatening issue. Psychiatrist Esther Schubert, an ATCK herself, has done research among TCKs and reports that suicide rates go up among TCKs after their first year home when it seems they give up hoping they will ever fit. For them, it's the ongoing struggle to fit in rather than simply the initial reentry that leads to despair.[5] This isn't the common pattern, but one of which to be aware. If TCKs or ATCKs are reading this and feeling this despair even now, please seek some help from trusted friends or counselors.

Helping in the Reentry Process

While there are no foolproof ways to ensure a perfect reentry, it's an important time and all involved should pay attention to it. The basic key for all concerned is first to understand what the normal process is about. Normalizing this part of the TCK experience is as important as it is for so many other facets. Barbara Schaetti, an American Swiss ATCK who did her Ph.D. dissertation on identity development among TCKs/global nomads, offers this advice.

> Introduce your children from their earliest years abroad to the terms "global nomad" and "third culture kid." They may not be interested at the time, but when they start searching for how to make meaning of their internationally mobile

lives, they'll know there's this particularly relevant subject that people have written and spoken about.[6]

It's also helpful to talk with others who have already been through it and to attend (or send your TCK to) seminars, which are often offered, especially in the transition between high school and college. Blogs, websites, e-zines like Denizen, and books for third culture families abound, including *Homeward Bound* by Robin Pascoe, *The Global Nomad's Guide to University Transition* by Tina Quick, or *The Art of Coming Home* by Craig Storti. (See the Resources in the back of this book for specifics.) Here are practical steps that can also help.

Make plans to stay in touch with others before leaving the host country. Rosalea Cameron, an Australian ATCK, did her dissertation research on TCKs. She discovered a major positive link between TCKs who had managed to keep a sense of continuity between the different phases of their lives and those who developed into leaders.[7] Hopefully, before the family leaves the overseas experience, each member has built a strong RAFT (chapter 13) and made concrete plans to keep the thread of connection going between where they've been and where they will be. This connectivity or bridge from past to present/future is vital for smoothing the way during reentry as TCKs affirm the truth of "both/and" in their lives, realizing they can and will maintain connections with the past as well as make new friends in the present. This does not mean those relationships will remain static but does provide a root for them to be nourished.

> Growing up in Kenya, Michael's best friend was Chris Bransford. For three years, minus a short hiatus while Chris' family lived in the Seychelles, the boys could be found everywhere together—up on the railroad tracks, deep in the forest, skateboarding down hard-packed dirt trails, or playing marbles in the schoolyard.
>
> When Michael repatriated to the U.S. at age twelve, the boys exchanged gifts and promised to keep in touch. The problem was that Chris' U.S. home was on the West Coast and Michael moved back to the Green Mountains of the Northeast—at best there would be 3,000 miles between them. Still, they wrote on blue aero forms, keeping up now and then until Michael had the opportunity to revisit Kenya in his junior year of high school.
>
> What a reunion as they laughed at Chris' extra four inches of height and caught up on sports, adventures, other friends, and dating! At the end of the week they said good-bye again, this time with a more mature understanding of how long the separation might last. Chris headed to college in California and Michael to western New York, but by then email had taken hold and they remained in touch, if sporadically,

until Chris announced he was planning to attend Michael's college on consortium for a semester in his senior year. Dismayed, Michael relayed to Chris that he was heading to Kenya to student-teach and would live with Chris' parents. Even so, they overlapped by two months, playing intramural soccer and visiting Toronto together.

And the friendship continues: The pattern of gaps and reunions has repeated through thirty years of surprise meetings, including weddings. In the last "coinciding," which happened several years ago, Michael met two of Chris' four sons at boarding school in Kenya, playing soccer on the same pitch above the elementary school, "Titchie Swot," where he and Chris had played as children.

The point of this story is to never give up on those core relationships, even if the ties are irregular and the distances are great. As TCKs, our friends are scattered like shells on seashores around the globe. With the world interconnected by technology, unless the Internet goes away, those meetings don't have to be so random. We smile when we see a tweet or post saying some equivalent of, "I'll be in Tel Aviv May 6–15. Will anyone else be there?" and then the replies begin to come in and warm embers are blown to flame again. TCKs are nomads who don't often travel together, but with work and a little providence, our dispersed connections can still ground us.

Reentry is another instance of entering a "foreign culture." The implication is that they need to apply all the things that a person does for any transition to adjust well into the second and third culture to the return journey. (See chapter 13 on transition and apply it for reentry.) The mantra should be "There are always reasons people do what they do, and my job is to sleuth out that reason!"

Reentry seminars can be a great help in this process. Our recommendation is that the training include at least one or more mature ATCKs who have successfully made that adjustment and who can explain the differences between assimilation (adjusting to the culture at the cost of losing your own practices and values with the purpose of conforming to or becoming a member of that culture) and integration (exchanging characteristics while maintaining integrity to become an equal but different part of the culture). Many reentry programs also teach practical skills like using a local library, applying for a job, opening a bank account, and connecting with services in an emergency. (See the Resources for ways you can participate in counseling or a seminar online.)

Learn how to make new friends or reconnect with old ones. This is another important emphasis. Learning how to make new friends or reconnect with old ones can be a challenge if not approached again from an understanding of the dynamics of the third culture. TCK specialists Heidi Tunberg and Libby Stephens have worked with hundreds, if not thousands, of students making the transition back to North America and developed a model for how the friend-making process works and what principles to keep in mind for those entering the U.S.[7] The specifics may differ according to where TCKs repatriate, but it is important to pay attention to relational styles no matter where you repatriate.

The premise is deceptively simple, the applications many, and the resulting "Aha" moments of young adult TCKs confirm the principles. In the United States, in the "introducing stage" people decide if someone they've just met is interesting and basically safe. While we know we shouldn't "judge a book by its cover," we cannot get to know everyone we encounter, so it is natural and necessary to size others up and decide on whether to introduce yourself and what to say or not say about where you are "from." If things go well initially, then you enter the "testing stage" to see if you have enough in common to become friends.

This reality is why Michael recommends that every TCK develop their answer to "Where are you from?" before entering a situation where introductions are taking place, because, in part, stammering and shifting your eyes after such a "basic" question may raise doubts about whether you are a stable person, even though on the inside you may be asking, "Do you really want to know? What aspect of 'from' are you asking about: birthplace, passport, where I was yesterday?" So let this be a quick guide. TCKs need to prepare a 5/15/Coffee answer. (This is "timed" for U.S. northern culture; in the south, you get a little more time, and TCKs should adjust for the speed that people usually answer the question.)

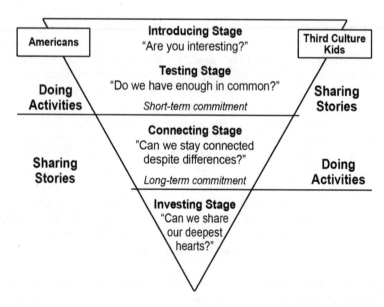

Figure 14–3: Libby Stephens and Heidi Tunberg Friendship Model
©2012 Libby Stephens/Heidi Tunberg. Used by permission

- Have a five-second answer that gives the basics of the places your family has called home. For example, "I mostly grew up in Southeast Asia." Neat and quick, followed by, "What about you?"
- If the person asks a follow-up question, have the 15-second version ready, with a little bit of detail such as, "We're a military family, so . . ." or "My parents are from Zimbabwe and the U.S. and I grew up . . ."
- If the response is positive and interesting, make a date for coffee, and make sure to ask the other person all about his or her growing up as well.

If introductions go well, we may proceed to the "testing stage" to explore if we have enough in common to become friends. This is where things get interesting for TCKs. For reasons discussed in chapter 12, those who grow up globally often jump into the stories of their lives quickly, looking for common ground (or one-upmanship?!) in adventures, beginnings and endings, languages, foods, funny culture stories, and global experiences. The stories are framed in the geography of place, throwing out city and country names like a commercial fisherman putting out a multihook longline. Common points of connection may be people and places, favorite street foods, or experiences on public transportation, and the banter goes back and forth. TCKs rely heavily on stories to discover connections because time is a precious commodity and we want to invest it in people to whom we feel connected.

By contrast, people who have spent many years in one place or culture are accustomed to getting to know each other over time. They prefer to invite prospective friends to share activities; through doing things together, they slowly discover whether a new acquaintance is trustworthy and if they feel comfortable enough to go deeper and share their stories. Neither approach is wrong, but the differences can create misunderstandings. It is during this stage that TCKs may judge those who primarily lived in one place to be shallow and uninteresting because they initially steer clear of personal conversations. Those who have grown up and lived in one place all of their life may, in turn, misinterpret the storytelling and more personal conversation topics favored by TCKs and consider them braggarts, emotionally needy, or romantically interested. If they can successfully navigate this stage, however, a friendship is forged and the "connecting stage" begins.

In the connecting stage patterns are reversed as the question becomes, "Can our connection survive our differences?" Here TCKs, having found connection through stories, are now willing to invest time doing things together, and local non-TCKs begin sharing stories with the people they have come to trust through spending time together. Both cultural styles are heading in the same direction; both are answering the questions: 1. *Will this relationship go the distance?* and 2. *Can I trust this person with my deepest heart?*

TCKs who reenter and misjudge the way friendship is created have much to lose. TCKs need to remember that it is our shared humanity that drives our desire to know and to be known, not culture. Our culture simply dictates the normal way a particular group seeks to meet this common need. Don't miss the humanity in each other that arrives by different pathways, but seek to understand the paths and perhaps cut through the forest to walk with each other.

The foundation stones of the TCKs' lives can never be taken away. When TCKs fear losing the past by moving to the future, remind them that a building set on a firm foundation doesn't lose that foundation when it gets bigger. No one can ever take away one experience or depth of understanding or breadth of how they see the world.

Foundations are meant to be built on. While no one can take away any foundation stone, foundations without a building on top aren't very functional. Placing new bricks, perhaps of some different colors and textures, makes the whole building stronger, more useful, and beautiful, but there is no replacement for the foundation. To move ahead in life and grow in and into each phase is never a negation of the past but rather an affirmation of how solid that past has been—solid enough to support a lifetime of building an ever-growing edifice on it.

Remind everyone this is the time a mentor can be helpful. Since reentry is actually the entering stage of the larger transition experience they are going through at this point, don't forget this is when TCKs most need a good mentor, as discussed in chapter 13. Reentry is the key period when TCKs are most vulnerable to being swept up in a group of friends they would never have chosen under normal circumstances, and they can get into drugs, alcohol, or other behavior they previously would have spurned. A good mentor can be a positive role model and lead them in the other direction too. If possible, it's wonderful to have that mentor be a TCK/CCK who has some expertise in the field of study and work that is of interest to the reentering TCK.

Parents must remember it's okay when their children don't share the same sense of national identity as they do. Sometimes this can be a source of great stress in a family if the TCKs are rejecting, at least for a while, identifying with the home country. Hopefully, parents can understand this is an expansion rather than an exclusion of the TCK's worlds and embrace the mosaic that their children have become, even if the differences hurt a bit.

Parents have the ultimate responsibility for helping the children through reentry. Sometimes TCKs arrive at universities with no clear idea of where they will go for long weekends, during school breaks, or even during summer vacations. It's not enough to presume that relatives at home will automatically pitch in to take care of a "homeless" TCK. Any time parents send their children back home (or to a different country altogether for university) while they themselves remain overseas, parents are still responsible for making sure their children are protected and cared for. It's their absolute responsibility to make sure their children have a designated "home away from home."

TCKs going to university don't always have appropriate footwear or clothing for the weather they will experience, nor access to the resources for basic needs. Perhaps this happens most frequently when the "reentry" is to attend a university not in their parents' passport country or in a very different area geographically from where the parents had lived, so the parents are simply unaware of some basics needs. The world of the university student has changed drastically since the parents went to university, so it would be a good idea for the parents and prospective TCK student to talk with current students at the university or other universities in that area.

It's okay for families to customize their approach to reentry depending on their circumstances. One family's story shows how creative some parents can be to fulfill their parental roles, keep their children ready throughout their expatriate journey to repatriate at some point, and still accomplish their career assignment well. Ria attempted to help her children stay conversant in their mother tongue of Flemish. Read what else she did:

> All through their years living abroad, Ria continued to help her children learn Flemish. When it came time for university, the two older kids chose to return to Belgium and enter university with others who had been raised in Belgium. But the Verrijssens soon realized they had to make some radical decisions to help their children adjust as they made a major transition to the passport country.
>
> The Verrijssens bought an apartment near the university in Belgium so the siblings could stay there together, and they decided that Ria would travel back to see them every six weeks. This frequent traveling, along with Erik taking side trips to them whenever his business travel took him into the region, meant the kids got the right support in addition to all the other support they enjoyed from Ria's and Erik's families and friends in Belgium.
>
> While this obviously cost the family much in terms of both money and time, it made this transition back easier for their children. After one year, both of the Verrijssens who were in university felt settled in their "new" world. The parents had made some radical decisions and found creative ways to address the reentry issues their kids faced. Now, because they can relate to their passport culture in this deep way, it can be their choice whether they stay in Belgium or venture into some international career.

Of course, not everyone can do this, but it is important for families to talk together frequently and make adjustments when needed. Some families have solved the issue by taking a leave of absence from an overseas post or a sabbatical, or asking for a reassignment to be closer to college-age children, especially in the first year. Also, a strong extended family can help the process greatly, especially if both the relatives and the TCKs already feel comfortable with each other.

If no extended family is available, close friends can help. But if there is no safe harbor available for their TCK, parents should think seriously about staying home themselves until their child is secure in his or her new life. This may cost the parents of such TCKs a few years of their careers, but failure to do so may cause their children lifelong harm because of mistakes these TCKs make or the abandonment they feel as they try to adjust to a world they have never known.

A "journey of clarification" later on can be helpful. Ultimately, one of the best things to help TCKs resettle in their home country on a long-term basis is to provide an opportunity for them to revisit the host country where they feel most deeply rooted. It's easy for that past experience to become so idealized or romanticized in the transition to their home culture that it grows to larger-than-life proportions. Going back can help put it into perspective. Going back does something else as well. It connects the past and present worlds of TCKs and reminds them that their past is neither a myth of their imagination nor totally inaccessible. In addition, such a journey reminds them that things never stay the same, and allows them to see in ever-clearer light that ultimately the past is now their foundation for the future.

How Reentry Becomes a Plus

While the preceding discussion of what happens in reentry and what TCKs and their parents can do about it are hopefully helpful, it has focused on prevention of potential problems. Reentry can also be an exciting time—a time of new discovery and joy and of affirming the amazing gifts of this globally nomadic life. And from it, TCKs bring many gifts with them to each situation they are in—including reentry.

Think about it. Of the countless TCKs we've asked, "What is the greatest gift of your experience?" most will list "Having the opportunity to meet people of many cultures and getting to know them" in their top five. While the world is trying to figure out what to do with "diversity" based on traditional models that primarily define it by many of the externals of the cultural iceberg, most TCKs have lived a life where, indeed, they saw the person first and the details of race, culture, or economics second or third or not particularly at all. They have lived the reality of knowing the likeness of being human with others as well as the uniqueness of being themselves—over and over. When a TCK sits by the fire in the village and asks his friend questions about his life, the two are connecting as people. In sharing their stories, both are meeting the fundamental needs of relationship—being known and knowing others. The details of the stories are different, but they understand the shared emotions of gladness when stories of success are told or sadness when stories of a child's death emerge. This is why the same person who sat around a village fire in Papua one day with a tribal friend can fly to a resort in Bali the next day to meet another friend who works for the World Bank.

So how does this relate to reentry? Simply this. TCKs who have related to people quite different from themselves so comfortably need to remember a couple lessons they have learned from their cross-cultural life experiences when they return home.

1. *People from the home culture are persons too.* They want relationships: they feel and they can create and think like others around the world as we discussed in chapter 6 for TCKs. Again, their circumstances may be different, but their shared humanity is not.

2. *People from the home culture also have a story.* Once TCKs and ATCKs understand this, instead of waiting around to be asked their own fascinating story, they can take the initiative to ask those in the home culture about their lives. Just as it was in any other culture, through the stories of those who live in a community, we learn about the history and culture of that place as well as about that person.

3. *People from the home culture can understand the emotions of your story even when they don't share in the details.* TCKs must remember that when we tell each other our stories, we may not have the experience hooks to take in and retain all the exotic (or ordinary) details, but we can both connect over the emotions we experienced and relay to one another.

4. *People all around you have lived far more similar stories than they may have yet recognized.* Part of the beauty of expanding the scope of this work to look at the world of CCKs is in seeing how many, many people are, in fact, living similar lives of cross-cultural interactions, moving around the world for a wide variety of reasons, and interacting in worlds their parents never knew. Some families have been doing it for generations without the recognition of a label. Again, the details may differ, but in these stories of relocations, adaptations, losses and gains, and identity and belonging searched for, there are intense places of specific shared connection where deep friendships can be formed. When we draw in local friends and other TCKS, we become relational bridges, crossing divides that others might not, with the ability to connect people who might otherwise not meet—and one never knows the good that might come from that.

When TCKs (and all others) see this most fundamental truth of shared humanity, they don't need to fear losing their sense of identity, no matter where they are, reentry or not. And then, in the mystery of life, they can look without fear at where they also differ from others, for we also have a need to be unique!

Many TCKs look back on their reentry period as one of the more stressful parts of their TCK experience, yet they wouldn't choose to miss what they learned from the process. Often they emerge from reentry with a sharp awareness of how their own culture works in ways those who have never left don't, and can't, see. This awareness can help them decide, perhaps more proactively than they might have otherwise, which values of their own culture they want to keep or let go. Most also come to appreciate the special gifts they have received from each culture that has been part of their lives, including this one called "home."

Expanding Our Vision

One of the first "Aha" moments for Ruth regarding the expansion of the TCK concept to the larger area of CCKs came while listening to members from an immigrant community trying to understand what was "wrong" with their first- and second-generation U.S.-born children. For the first time she saw clearly the reality of how much more mobile immigrant communities are in today's world and how much the concept of "reentry" applies to them each time they visit their parents' former homeland. Educational CCKs who attend school in a different language or cultural base than their home culture have a certain type of reentry every night when they go home. Certainly these realities also apply to many of the other groups, including international adoptees who may visit their birth country where they will look alike but not be alike. Recently Michael has developed relationships with NGOs working with "returning citizens" from prison and human trafficking and has found that the principles absolutely apply to these subcultures who are also experiencing reentry. This is the gift CCKs can share: helping all of us move beyond stereotypes and boundaries to meet the real people behind our assumptions so we can find common ground and shared vision

Questions for Chapter 14

1. Many TCKs look back on their reentry period as one of the more stressful parts of their TCK experience. If you, as a TCK, or others you know including your children, experienced a difficult reentry, what do you think could have helped make it smoother?
2. The Transition Challenge Matrix (figure 14-2) has several indicators of particular dimensions and factors that can impact reentry. Think about your own reentry, or that of a TCK you know, and tell that story through this grid (as was done with Ted and Trisha). How did the story you are thinking about

work out if you look at it through this grid and consider what factors were or were not special stressors? Explain, please.

3. Can you relate to any of the "reentry stresses" the authors talk about, such as expectations of sameness or reverse culture shock? What rings true for you or others you know?

4. What are some lessons you or others can, or have, taken away from a reentry experience?

5. Sometimes what was hard in the past has now become a great story (especially if we can laugh at our mistakes or tell what we learned)! Share some fun stories about what you or others have experienced during reentry.

6. Is there any advice you might give TCKs or their families who are about to experience reentry?

CHAPTER 15

Enjoying the Journey

I am from Belgium, where the clouds are usually soaked in
   rain,
I am from Italy, where the clouds are always cleared by
   sunlight,
I am from Poland, where the sky is as dark as coal,
I am from Mozart, whose music charmed peoples' hearts
   and woke their souls,
I am from my dreams and nightmares, where my imagina-
   tion takes over,
I am from Egypt, whose mysteries haunt peoples' minds,
I am from the ocean, where the waves calm my thoughts,
I am from the mountains, where the echo calls my name,
Most of all, I am from my family, where my heart truly
   belongs.

—"I am from . . ." by Hendrik Verrijssen

Belgian citizen Hendrik Verrijssen wrote this poem at the age of twelve. In these few lines, he captures the incredible wealth of his experience, the challenge of defining his roots geographically, and the comfort of defining them relationally. He gives evidence that while mobility may interrupt the traditional patterns of developmental flow and relationship building, globally mobile families can reach the same goals of helping their TCKs develop to their fullest potential and maintain relationships through less traditional, but equally positive, patterns of family living. Where do we start?

HAVE FUN!

Never forget that one of the best aspects of a TCK lifestyle is the fun it can be. In his book *Living Overseas*, Ted Ward emphasizes the importance of enjoying the adventure—of *living*.[1] Having fun in the journey is another great way to tie the many elements of a TCK's life together into a cohesive whole that is essential for building a strong sense of identity.

Unpack Your Bags and Plant Your Trees

Without knowing he had a name for his TCK experience, Ruth's dad, Charles Frame, gave her solid, lifelong advice.

> "Ruth, wherever you go in life, unpack your bags—physically and mentally—and plant your trees. Too many people never live in the now because they assume the time is too short to settle in. They don't plant trees because they expect to be gone before the trees bear fruit. But if you keep thinking about the next move, you'll never live fully where you are. When it's time to go, then it's time to go, but you won't have missed what this experience was about. If you never eat from the trees, someone else will."
>
> And he followed his advice by planting trees all around their home in Kano, Nigeria. Twelve years after going back to the United States, Ruth made her first trip back to Kano. As she picked and ate an orange off one of his trees, she knew he had been right.

For any member of a globally nomadic family, following this simple piece of advice can make all the difference in whether it is a positive experience or not. It means you have made a choice to embrace all the possibilities and live with an openness to all the opportunities this life affords rather than to live in a self-protective mode. As parents model this, TCKs get the picture and will do it themselves.

Tour When Traveling between Countries

Stopping off in various countries while traveling between home and host countries is another experience that adds fun to the third culture lifestyle. Such stops expand the world of TCKs and create lifelong memories. Courtney had this to say about her travels:

> My memory is much bigger than most of my friends' memories because of all the exciting places my parents took me on our trips between Saudi Arabia and America. When we went to England or Germany, for example, knowing I loved art, my mom would take me to the museums while my sister

and dad went off on other excursions. I learned so much by
absorbing the cultures we encountered; we would take tours
and soak up the information the guides told us.

My parents may not realize that the most profound
thing they did for me was to take me to Dachau. I must have
been about eleven or twelve. We walked the grounds; we
looked at everything; I cried. My parents did not protect me;
they exposed me to everything—including the crematoriums,
gas chambers, photos. When you read about World War II
and the concentration camps, I can't imagine how you can
truly understand it without seeing it. I just stood there, overwhelmed, and thought, How is this possible? It was so big.

I am filled up when I think of all that I've seen and
touched, and how much I want to return and touch them all
again.

One note: Parents can be creative here to make such side trips happen inex-
pensively. Ruth's family did not have the money for fancy hotels or restaurants,
but her parents made reservations at rooming houses; bought bread, cheese, and
meat for Mom to make sandwiches; and took local transportation to get around
town. They figured it didn't cost any more for the airplane tickets to get off (way
back then anyway!) in the cities where the planes refueled. They built wonderful
memories for the family, and made "going local" part of the adventure.

Explore and Become Involved in the Surroundings

When families arrive at their overseas assignment, parents shouldn't forget the
plans they made beforehand to get to know their host country. Ironically, the
richness of their lives can become so routine that TCKs and their families forget
to notice it. Learn about the country's history, geography, and culture. Families
should pretend they're tourists once or twice a year and plan trips just to see the
sights. Courtney's parents also helped her to explore their host country—Saudi
Arabia. "My parents often took us out into the desert to look at various natural
treasures such as sharks' teeth, sand roses, and arrowheads. It was exciting to
imagine this place underwater millions of years ago." These may seem like simple
memories, but they've left Courtney with a deep sense of connection to her past.

As a corollary, a common regret we hear from ATCKs is they never really
got involved with the surrounding culture when they were children. Whether
it happened because they lived on a military base, went off to boarding school,
or played only with expatriate friends, many consider this a loss. As adults they
realize they could have learned so much more and wish they had studied the language or taken time to learn how to cook the wonderful local dishes they enjoyed
when they went out, or simply found a way to make friends among those from
the local culture.

KEEP RELATIONSHIPS SOLID

Over and over TCKs echo what Hendrik says—that the ultimate place of belonging and home comes in relationships, not place. Relational anchors and relational bridges must be pursued and maintained. These are the pieces of life that cannot be taken away when they are built well, for they are the places of the heart.

Develop Family Traditions

Traditions bind people and groups together. They are visible markers of shared history and celebrate a unity of thought, purpose, or relationship. Every nation has them, every ethnic group has them, and, hopefully, every family has them. Often a family's traditions evolve without special planning. Uncle Fred pulls out his mandolin at every reunion and family members old and young sing along. No one has consciously decided this will be a tradition, but the family gathering wouldn't be the same if Uncle Fred and his mandolin weren't there. These are the moments that build a family's unique sense of identity and belonging.

   Third culture families have at least as much need for traditions as other families do—maybe more. But, because they aren't always at the family reunions to hear Uncle Fred, they may have to do a little more conscious planning. It's important to develop at least some traditions that are transportable and replicable in whatever culture and surroundings the family might be. These traditions may be as simple as letting each family member choose the menu for his or her birthday supper every year or as complicated as making a piñata stuffed with candy for a particular holiday once a year.

   Developing traditions in cross-cultural settings isn't just important—it's fun! As new ideas gleaned from different places are incorporated, traditions also become a way of marking family history. In Liberia, a hot dog roast on the beach defined Christmas Eve for some expatriates—not a traditional custom in most snow-covered lands, but a nice one to carry back home (even if the hot dogs must be roasted in a fireplace!) as a distinctive reminder of the family's history.

Build Strong Ties with Community

TCKs usually grow up far from blood relatives, so finding substitute aunts, uncles, and grandparents wherever TCKs live can be very important in creating "extended family." Sometimes these people will be host country citizens; sometimes they will be within the third culture community itself. Parents can foster such relationships by inviting these special people to join in celebrating the TCK's birthday, allowing their child to go shopping with them, or in other ways appropriate for the situation. This created extended family gives TCKs the experience of growing up in a close community, even without blood relatives. As ATCKs remember their childhood, some of these relationships rank among their fondest memories. And don't lose touch with this *family* when you move. As much as possible, continue this thread of connection to help TCKs feel that their life is a continuous process, not one broken into many pieces.

Build Strong Ties with Extended Family

Relatives in the home country (or wherever they live) are another important part of a TCK's life, and relationships with them need to be fostered. A great way to cultivate these relationships is by bringing a grandmother, grandfather, aunt, uncle, or cousin to visit. A visit not only helps TCKs get to know their relatives better, but also lets relatives see TCKs in their own environment—the place where these children do, in fact, shine. It also builds a place of shared history with extended family that TCKs may otherwise miss. In addition, TCKs love to return "home" and be able to talk to family members who know what they're talking about. Even if relatives cannot make a trip to see them overseas, it's important for TCKs to maintain contact with their relatives as much as possible through Skype, Facetime, Instagram, Facebook, instant messaging, email, faxes, telephone, and pictures. This type of relationship building goes a long way to creating a sense of continuity throughout life.

Developing closeness with relatives at home becomes especially important if and when the time comes for TCKs to repatriate while parents continue living overseas. These relatives' homes can be the places where TCKs go for school breaks, vacations, and weekends when parents are away.

One reminder here: the time to plan for this interaction with extended family starts at the beginning. This contact also helps keep children fluent in the mother tongue of their parent(s). Here is what happened to one family who didn't maintain this contact.

> My parents-in-law, who are German and do not speak English, feel they have missed fun years with their "two English-speaking grandsons." Both boys now speak reasonable German, but that is a fairly recent change. They are now both teenagers, so Oma and Opa have had ten years of little or no real communication with their "foreign" grandsons.[2]

When this happens, everyone loses—so don't forget learning/teaching the language spoken by grandparents and extended family as part of your plan if this is needed.

Build Strong Ties with Friends

Friends are an enormous blessing for many TCKs. Indeed, many TCKs thrive in international schools and communities where there is no given norm for race or nationality. In many places, public transportation systems make it easy to form social gatherings at a favorite cybercafe on weekends. As they move from country to country, TCKs can keep up with friends in ways never before possible. Yet this here-and-now communication system can affect new connections as we have already discussed in chapter 11. Finding the balance between staying connected to the past and moving on to the new will always be a bit of a challenge, but it is one of the new normals in today's world. However, if this pattern persists for a long period and their children refuse to engage in the local scene, parents should find ways to encourage face-to-face contact in the new surroundings. They might invite another family over who have children of similar age, or find an area of particular interest, such as a sports team or choir, that the child could join.

In the end, however, as TCKs move on through life and become ATCKs, it is often reconnecting with friends from the past that validates the TCK experience and proves that the third culture world and experience wasn't a dream. Attending school reunions and returning to visit the home or homes of their childhood are all ways TCKs and ATCKs can maintain connections with the various threads of their lives. Such friendships are a gift that tops the list for many ATCKs when they look back at their past.

Return to the Same "Home" during Each Trip Back to Passport Country

Whenever practical, third culture families who are living outside their passport country should return to the same basic place in that country each time they go back. Children who change countries every two or three years, as well as those who stay in one host country their entire lives, need the sense that there is at least one physical place in their passport country to identify as "home." How much better if it is near the grandparents or other family members they do not otherwise often see. When staying in the same physical house isn't possible, families should try to relocate in the same basic vicinity so that TCKs can keep the same school, church, and friends. It's also helpful when visiting friends or relatives in other places to stay long enough to establish a basis for the relationship that can be built upon for the next time you come.

While it's good to foster these relationships in the passport country, families shouldn't spend all their time at "home" visiting people. When every evening is spent with the adults chatting happily in one room and the TCKs and children from the host family eyeing each other warily in another, and when every night is spent in a different bed, this overload of travel can be stressful. But these trips can also be enjoyable when parents include fun, kid-friendly activities. Wise parents make time for nights in motels, camping trips, or other private times during their travel to reinforce their sense of being a family in this land as well as in the host country.

Acquire "Sacred Objects"

Artifacts from countries where they have lived or visited eventually become the TCK's portable history to cart around the world in future years. It's important to take back meaningful, portable objects from each place TCKs have lived, or even visited. These help to connect all the places and experiences of their lives. During her childhood, ATCK Jennifer acquired a set of carved ebony elephant bookends, a lamp (whose base included more elephants), feather paintings, and other ebony carvings to hang on the wall. At university and in the sixteen locations where she has lived since her wedding, when the bookends are in place, the paintings and carvings hung on the wall, and the lamp turned on, she's home.

One German TCK, Dirk, summed up best what we are trying to say. When we asked him what he thought of his experience as a TCK, he said, "The thing I like best about my life is living it!"

That's what it's all about—living and enjoying the world of TCKs. As parents help their children do that, they are building into their TCKs' lives a solid sense of who they are as individuals and as TCKs. They are giving them a deep sense of relational belonging, a connection to many geographical sites, and the freedom and courage to fully participate in life no matter where their feet land. It's a good place to be.

Expanding Our Vision

Perhaps the application is simple: Whatever our life circumstances, wherever we live, whatever opportunities we have, no matter our cultural interactions or not, "unpack your bags and plant your trees." The specifics of how we do that may be different, but the principle is universal for those who want to live life out fully and with as much joy as possible.

More specifically, however, for other types of CCKs, the rich opportunities for families from several cultural backgrounds to build traditions from each historical root and create a new sense of "us" through these unique blends of traditions are great. The need to maintain the original language or languages of the family for immigrants is also important for their children also to be able to interact with the families they visit back in the land from which they came, or for when family members come to visit them. Borderlanders can plant trees in both lands. Again, many principles here apply much more universally than only for TCKs and their families.

Questions for Chapter 15

1. What would your "I'm From" poem include? Why not spend some time and journal this?
2. Describe one experience in your life—TCK or not—that you look back on as particularly fun—an experience that brings memories of joy and laughter.
3. TCK or not, how have you literally and figuratively "unpacked your bags and planted trees"?
4. What are some family traditions you celebrated as a child and now that have created stability for you even when the world is changing?
5. Describe your "sacred objects." Why are they sacred? What do they represent of your life no matter what your story is—TCK or not?

CHAPTER 16

Adult TCKs: There's Always Time

I was in my late thirties when I first heard of the term TCK. I was a firefly lighting up for the first time, suddenly noticing others who had the same little light flickering at their hearts, unbeknownst to them. I buzzed the revelation to those around me, joyous when they too lit up, disappointed when [they were] nonchalant.

It was liberating to have an identity connecting me to a group beyond nationalities and race. Years later, at my first FIGT [Families in Global Transition] conference, an evening flew into wee hours of a morning sharing, laughing, and sobbing with a soul mate I had just met; who had nothing in common except the lasting emotions imprinted from growing up in different worlds.[1]

—Isabelle Min
Founder, TCK Network in Korea
CEO, Transition Catalyst Korea Institute

In spite of the growing efforts to help current TCKs better understand and use their cross-cultural experiences, many ATCKs, like Isabelle, have grown up with little assistance in sorting out the full effect of their third culture upbringing. No one understood that help might be needed, let alone what to do if it were.

Even so, as Isabelle expresses, once these ATCKs and other ACCKs discover they have a name, that there are others who understand them in the places they have long felt shame and wondered, "What's wrong with me?" a huge load lifts. Stories abound of those who move from wondering, "What's wrong with me?" to seeing, "What's right with me," as they come to terms with the inherent losses and develop a positive sense of identity. They have learned to use their heritage in personally and/or professionally productive ways. Isabelle is an amazing example of such a person. Not only did she start the TCK Network in Korea, she is an intercultural trainer, a cofounder of Families in Global Transition, Korean Affiliate, and mentor to countless other ATCKs—and a wonderful person.

Unfortunately, other ATCKs still continue to be caught by the challenges of their childhood. They haven't yet felt fully free to use or celebrate the benefits. Depression, isolation, loneliness, anger, rebellion, and despair have felt more like at least the undercurrent story of their lives even if they are living outwardly successful lives. And for some these realities are more than an undercurrent, as these emotions have ruled their lives despite their best intentions or desires.

Other ATCKs believe they're just fine, but spouses, children, friends, and coworkers know better. There is a shell around them that no one can penetrate— even in the closest of relationships. Some of them grew up in organizational systems where extended periods of separation from their family seemed so normal at the time that they never considered how these separations might have affected their lives. Others went through periods of war or conflicts in their host country with or without their parents being present. TCKs have experienced emotional, mental, physical, and spiritual abuse, or at least trauma, as they have traversed their worlds, but because these worlds vanished with one plane ride, they have never been able to sort things out—the experiences and their contexts simply disappeared. Often ATCKs are stuck in one of the stages of unresolved grief without realizing it. All they know is that they are trapped in some place or behavior from which they can't break free.

So what can they do now? Is it too late for these ATCKs to put the pieces together? When they have been stuck for a long time in a self-destructive lifestyle, is it possible for them to learn to use their past constructively rather than be bound by it? The answer is, simply, yes. It's never too late to deal with unresolved grief, identity issues, or other challenges related to the TCK lifestyle. Ruth never began to understand the undercurrents of depression in her life that ran deeper than others could see until she began to journal about it at age thirty-nine.

But how does healing occur? Obviously, ATCKs and their parents can't go back and relive their transitional experiences or undo the separations. The years of family life lost are irretrievable. In fact, most ATCKs can't recover any of their hidden losses. They can't reclaim the sights, sounds, or smells that made home "home" as a child. They can't stop the war that displaced them or the abuser who stole their innocence. What they *can* do, however, is learn to put words to their past, name their experiences, validate the benefits as well as the losses, and ask for help from their families and others. They can learn to name the gifts they have been given and are often unconsciously using productively in one way or another. One ATCK wondered why she had always felt drawn to work with the homeless when her family had often lived in beautiful homes around the world. As she understood her own story better, she could continue her work in ways she hadn't considered before.

What ATCKS Can Do

NAME THEMSELVES AND THEIR EXPERIENCE

For many ATCKs, simply putting a name to their past—"I grew up as a third culture kid"—opens a new perspective on life. Discovering there are legitimate reasons for their life experiences and the resulting feelings not only helps them understand themselves better, it also normalizes the experience. Some who have spent a lifetime thinking they're alone in their differentness or wondering, "What's *wrong* with me?" discover they have lived a normal life after all—at least normal for a TCK.

Somehow the concept of normalcy is very liberating. It doesn't solve every problem, but it gives permission for a lot of self-discovery and frees ATCKs to make some changes they may not have thought possible. For example, rather than remaining eternal chameleons and continuing to try fitting in everywhere, they can focus on examining who they are, where they do fit, and where they can best use their gifts. If ATCKs can understand such questions as why they chronically withdraw before saying good-bye to others, they can purposefully choose to stay engaged in relationships until the end.

> Since one ATCK discovered withdrawal was her consistent pattern before moving, she now tells her friends a month before the departure date, "I want to let you know what a great friend you've been, because I might not be able to tell you at the end. I also need to tell you that I've hurt a lot of people by acting like I don't care when it comes time to say good-bye. I'm going to try not to do that, but if I start to withdraw, you let me know." And her friends do.

This simple acknowledgment both helps others understand this ATCK's potential behavior and helps her remain emotionally present in relationships both before and after she leaves.

For other ATCKs, discovering they have a name—that they are adult third culture kids—and are members of a group whose membership extends around the world finally gives them a feeling of belonging. Instead of feeling their history is a piece of life's puzzle that will never fit, they now see it as the key piece around which so many others fall into place.

NAME THEIR BEHAVIORAL PATTERNS

I LEARNED TO LOVE THE BOMB
fire is when the knots that are you or anything, get undone.

I like the smokestack, it feels like home
I like the pipe protruding from the wall
keeping me company
in the shower stall
the mad sparrows
I do like them
I do like them all / this place my home / I like it some
why do I want it all to feel like home so much
knick knacks are not enough love? mildly suggests
why do I want it all to feel like home so much
because you can get drunk on desperation
and turn the house
into the crater of a bomb
and you can keep the chimney
for a crutch. And walking cheerily
into the sun. You can see all that
smoke rising
and feel you like it some

This poem by a young adult TCK hints at some of the destructive potential in a highly mobile life. One way to see the poem is to recognize that the home TCKs are trying desperately to create often comes undone and they move on. What happens when "blowing the house up" and starting over becomes a pattern in life? What if "liking it some" becomes not knowing how to live life another way? Another way to see the poem is if the "you" is another, who destroys the house. What happens when ATCKs expect that a significant other in their life will always wreak havoc on the "home" they are creating? What do you see in the poem?

Once ATCKs realize their past has undoubtedly influenced their present life and their choices, it's time for them to make an honest assessment. Are there certain lifelong, repetitive behaviors (such as chronic moving or failure to allow intimacy in one relationship after another) that they have always excused as "That's just the way I am"?

After looking at such repetitive cycles, ATCKs need to ask themselves some questions: Is my anger, depression, or other behavior often out of proportion to its context? Is this behavior related to a confusion of identities? Is it related to one of the expressions of unresolved grief? Is it totally unrelated to anything except a personal or family matter? If it seems to be a personal matter, how might the influences of cross-culturalism and high mobility have added to that stress?

NAME THEIR FEARS

Often a major barrier to healing is fear—fear of facing the pain, fear of taking a risk again, fear of rejection. This fear is hidden behind such statements as, "I don't see any reason to look back. Life is to be lived in a forward direction." Or, "That TCK stuff is bunk. I'm just me, and my life experiences have nothing to do with the way I am. I'd have been the same no matter where or when I grew up."

It is scary to go back, but it can be helpful to realize that no matter how badly a certain situation hurt, you have already survived it and that situation is now past. Facing the pain will hurt for a bit, but it can be grieved and dealt with in the end. Not facing it may well continue to drive the ATCKs into far more pain-producing behaviors than they can currently imagine.

NAME THEIR LOSSES

After deciding that healing is worth the risk of pain, it's important for ATCKs to look back and try to identify some of the losses they haven't been fully aware of before. Journaling is one effective way to do this. Hopefully, you've been able to use some of the questions at the end of each chapter to think through your life story. You might go through the list of hidden losses in chapter 5 and see if any of them resonates with your story. Or you can also try answering such questions as these:

- Think of one of the countries you lived in. What was something you loved about that time that you lost when you had to make your next move?
- When you think of roles you had in another place, what was something you could be or do there that you may have not found repeatable since that time?
- What happened to your pets?
- Where is your *amah* (local caregiver) now?

Some use means other than journaling to look at these questions, such as combining the many pieces of their life into magnificent artwork, decorating their homes with symbols of past places and people, or writing stories or poems. All of these can help to put into tangible form things they so deeply loved that have simply disappeared with seemingly no way to retrieve them.

Having named the losses, it's not too late to go back and do the work of mourning that should have happened as the losses occurred. It's astonishing the severity of losses some ATCKs have experienced in their childhood: death in the family while the TCKs were away at boarding school; sexual abuse they never told anyone about; and wars that uprooted them in the middle of the night. So many of these have been covered over with no proper period of mourning or comfort to deal with the losses. Many ATCKs have simply disassociated themselves from the pain, but the grief merely surfaces in the other forms mentioned earlier. If ATCKs dare to face the losses in their lives, to acknowledge and grieve for them, they will discover that proper mourning takes away the power for those losses to drive their behavior in ever more destructive ways. We talk about mourning in more detail in chapter 13, but the bottom line is that we need to face our losses consciously (as in a funeral) and find ways and rituals to honor that loss and process it so we can move on to a life without what it is we have lost.

For those who weren't able to mourn properly as children, what are some ways to do that grief work as adults?

The methods are as many as the ATCKs who create them. Some have literally gone back to the sites where they grew up and planted a tree as a lasting connection, found their past *amahs* and friends, or carried back a rock from the sea. Others continue the journaling or artwork in which they first named the losses. Some go on Facebook and begin to reconnect with friends from these days. (Some blogs, Facebook pages, and artistic endeavors can be found in the Resources.)

In any type of community, whether online like Facebook.com/TCKid or TCKIDnow.com, or through school reunions or conferences such as Families in Global Transition, where many fellow ATCKs often attend, ATCKs can offer great support to one another. One class reunion from an international school concluded their weekend together by bringing a large fishnet into the middle of the room. They brought many types of cloth, string, pieces of wood, paper, buttons, and other random articles. Each ATCK had to create a montage of some sort representing his or her life story. From where they sat around the edges of the net, they then wove that montage into the fishnet toward the center. After it was completed, the ATCKs took turns explaining the meaning behind his or her creation. Not only was it wonderful to tell and hear the stories within a community who cared, but visually seeing where they were together in the center of the fishnet at the end was an incredibly powerful experience for the participants. Other groups have invited attendees to bring their sacred objects and tell their life story that way. What this does, of course, is not only validate the past journey, but give a way to normalize the experience by relating it in the context of others who understand.

When the pain has been severe, good friends who listen and support well are essential, but there are times when professional help may also be needed. (See *www.internationaltherapistdirectory.com* for a list of therapists around the world who are ATCKs themselves or who have a specialty of working with ATCKs and TCKs.) Some ATCKs have had severe trauma, perhaps in an unplanned evacuation or from sexual, physical, or emotional abuse. These things can happen in any background and require extra help. In the past, it was often difficult to find someone who understood the underlying theme of the TCK experience. Sometimes ATCKs felt more misunderstood when their counselors weren't familiar with the nontraditional places grief might be coming from. Hopefully, this is changing, but many ATCKs proactively give their therapists information on this part so they can know what might be "normal" and what issues might be tied to other events in the ATCK's life. *Belonging Everywhere and Nowhere: Insights into*

Counseling the Globally Mobile, by Lois Bushong, is a great resource for therapists working with ATCKs.

One word of warning: Sometimes when ATCKs first acknowledge some of their hidden losses, part of the grief process is a newfound or at least newly expressed anger at various people whom they feel are responsible for those losses. Lots of ATCKs (to say nothing of the people they're angry at) are so upset by this phase that they back off from going further. Don't give up on the process if this begins to happen! The angry phase *can* be a very difficult period of the healing process for everyone involved, but remember it is a normal stage of grief, and it can be worked through to a stage of resolution as the ATCKs (and those around them) persist and give the healing process time.

NAME THEIR WOUNDS

Even retrospectively, it's important for ATCKs to name not only their losses, but also the ways in which they have been hurt and how they have hurt others. Why is this important? Everyone has been hurt by other people, and each of us has hurt others. Some of the wounds, whether intentional or not, have been significant, and they must be acknowledged to be dealt with properly.

Once we have identified a wound, we have to make a critical decision. Will we hold on to our anger forever or will we forgive the ones who have hurt us? Some ATCKs are living lives bound by bitterness. They have turned their pain into a weapon with which they beat not only the offender but themselves and everyone in their world as well. It seems that the hurt becomes part of their identity. To let it go would be to leave them hollow, empty. The problem with that is that the anger and bitterness destroy as much as, or more than, the original wound. Many are unwilling to forgive because they feel the offender will "go free." They believe that saying, "I forgive you," means, "It doesn't really matter what happened."

Forgiveness is not something lightly given without looking at what the situation cost the person who was wounded. Without forgiveness, however, the offended person's life continues to be ruled by the offender. It's important to acknowledge the offense, but forgiveness is making a decision to let go of the need and desire for vengeance—even if the offender never has to pay. Forgiveness is the only thing that ultimately frees the wounded one to move on to true healing.

None of us is perfect. Healing also involves looking at how we ourselves have knowingly or unknowingly hurt others and asking for their forgiveness. It's amazing to listen to stories of rage against parents, siblings, relatives, friends, and administrators in the sponsoring organizations from ATCKs who seem to have no perception that they are doing similar damage to their own children. Some who complain of emotional abuse or separation from parents one moment are yelling at their own children the next. Some who complain of abandonment in their childhood are workaholics who may not send their children away to boarding school but still never seem to have time for them. It becomes a repeating cycle. Until and unless we are willing to acknowledge our own sins and failures against others, true healing is stymied, for we will have to continue living in our self-protective modes, shutting out anyone who would dare approach us and mention our offenses against them. We need to identify specific places where we have wounded others, and when we recognize the offense, we need to be the first ones to go and ask for forgiveness, not waiting for them to approach us. Doing this both heals important relationships in our lives and also frees us from having to defend and protect ourselves. Instead, we can begin to live more openly and with greater joy.

NAME THEIR CHOICES

Dealing with the past in a healthy way frees us to make choices about the future. We are no longer victims. Each of us must ultimately accept responsibility for our own behavior, regardless of the past. That doesn't mean that we're responsible for all that happened to us. A sexually abused child isn't responsible for the abuse; a child who felt abandoned is not responsible for the parents' choices. But as adults, we *are* responsible for how we deal with our past, how we relate to those around us in the present, and what we choose for the future. ATCKs must ask themselves several questions as they sort through their past in order to get on with their future: *Will I forgive? Will I retaliate? Will I succumb to the message that I am worthless? Will I look at what it means to be a person and realize that it's okay to think, to create, to have emotion? Will I dare to find ways to express these parts of myself?*

LEARN TO TELL YOUR STORY

Stories are one of the important ways we express ourselves to the world of other people. This is how we come to know and be known; we are made to need other human beings. Since TCKs tend to share stories quickly with one another as a way of establishing friendship, many ATCKs are marvelous storytellers! Christopher O'Shaughnessy,[2] Mary Bassey,[3] and Marilyn Gardner[4] are just three of the fabulous current storytellers. Yet, many ATCKs who find themselves in families and communities without those of similar background believe they can't tell their stories because they are "so different." Never forget that as you tell your story, "emotions are the universal language." The point of storytelling isn't to share facts to impress, but to share where and why these facts impacted our lives. Others will relate to the human places and emotions in your story, even if the details are different.

Having said that, it is true that each of us can learn to tell stories in ways that can help achieve the goal of being known and, in return, knowing others, as your story on this level invites them to respond with theirs. Being fully known and fully loved is a divine goal, so it's worth aiming for! Here are a few tips.

1. *Seek to know the stories of others and cultivate deep listening skills.* Listen for their hearts, not the facts.
2. *Learn the cultural way stories are told in the context you are in;* at what point in the relationship are they told, in which settings do people choose to share, and what is avoided as controversial or offensive? Revise accordingly.
3. *Timing is not everything, but nearly.* The longer you live, the less you will be able to tell your full story at one sitting! When and what to say takes discernment. Summarizing your story briefly and listening to the other person's story might lead to setting up more coffee or lunch dates to mutually hear and share more.
4. *Clarify your point of reference;* it can be confusing to others. When you are a hidden immigrant and tell a story as a person growing up as a foreigner, it raises many questions. Beginning with a "point of view" reference such as, "Being a kid in Kiev gave me a different perspective," helps the listener orient.
5. *Check your motives.* Ask yourself why you are telling the story: is it to connect or to impress? Is it to emphasize your similarities or is it to show how special your experience has been? Make sure you share themes you have learned that are universally applicable, no matter the details of your story compared to theirs.
6. *When your story has a "wow" factor, understate it.* Especially in egalitarian cultures, stories in a faraway setting can seem exotic and create distance. Again, emphasizing the human quality, poking fun at yourself, or emphasizing what can be commonly understood (such as the human emotion involved) can lessen distance and increase the connection.
7. *Don't assume your audience will or will not connect with your story.* Asking questions may also reveal that your listeners can relate more easily than you think, because they have had experiences that you don't know about.
8. *You have to know your story before you can fully share it.* Take time to dig into your own story, put the pieces together (physically this can help) by mapping it, outlining it, charting it, or drawing it out. Identify the losses and gains, the major events and transitions, the characters both virtuous and villainous, and work to fill in the holes. Holes come because we don't have the collective memory of folks who live in one place and are reminded or corrected by others or we've blocked something out, or we didn't realize something until later, like that a beloved caregiver had a full name. Sometimes we stumble on the vocabulary for our stories unexpectedly and we have to look at the whole narrative again with a new lens, as Mary Bassey did.

> As the professor was lecturing about the concept of culture clashes, I noticed that it was through a monocultural lens; one script per person to adhere to in order to feel more at home or deviate from in order to feel alien. But in my hand

were three scripts: one from Nigeria, my birthplace; one from
Canada, the height of my childhood; one from the United
States, the country that has held most of my life. The Canadian and American scripts are very similar on the surface
but can be surprisingly disparate. For example, in Canada,
I am usually primarily seen as a Nigerian immigrant; my
blackness is visible but it is rooted in the Canadian history
of immigration. In America, I am primarily perceived to be
black before I am an immigrant (if people see I am an immigrant at all). With the history of transatlantic slavery in
the United States and other periods of oppression against
people of color, racial identity is a much larger part of the U.S.
cultural script. And when they are both compared to the Nigerian script, the chasm widens. In Nigeria, I am part of the
majority because of my nationality. But I am also a minority
because of my American-sounding accent and Westernized
values.

 After thinking about this clash of cultures, I raised my
hand and asked my professor, "What if someone is juggling
multiple cultural scripts? Is it at all possible for them to feel
at home in different countries and cultures?"

 "No, it's not possible," he responded with a slight smile
that his face often carried, his eyes speaking directly to my
personal dilemma. "People who balance multiple cultures
at once because they have grown up in different places are
called Third Culture Kids." At this point in my life, I was
nineteen years old and yet this was the first time I had ever
heard the term "Third Culture Kid" (TCK). The rest of the
lecture was a blur to me. I was so fixated on this new term
that the anticipation of researching more about it consumed
me for the rest of the class.[5]

9. *Telling your story may open up doors with and for others with similar stories
   and those who simply never thought about life from your perspective.* Mary
   in the story above began writing and sharing her story at conferences and
   online, including at The Black Expat blog, founded by Cameroonian ATCK
   Amanda Bate. She found that there were myriads of others who had experiences in common with her who were ready to support, connect, and build
   friendships.

 The choices ATCKs make in response to these questions can make all the
difference for those who feel bound by the past but are longing to move on to
freedom in the future.

We wrote this chapter focusing on what ATCKs can do for themselves because how they deal with their history and how they can best use it is ultimately their responsibility. They can heal and find fulfillment in life even if others never understand their background. However, those close to the ATCKs can be immensely helpful if they try to understand the struggle and freely give their support during the time of healing.

How Can Parents Help Their ATCKs?

Without doubt, family relationships are key to a TCK's well-being while they are growing up. This is also true for ATCKs who are still struggling with the challenges from their TCK experience. Parents can often be partners with their ATCKs during this healing process. If parents can be supportive and understanding rather than defensive of or threatened for themselves or their organizations when ATCKs are sorting through the past, they can help open the way to much faster healing for their adult children. Support throughout an ATCK's healing process is the greatest gift a parent can give. The following sections discuss some specific ways that parents can help.

LISTEN AND TRY TO UNDERSTAND

This may seem simple, but it's not. ATCKs sometimes turn against their parents when they begin verbalizing their feelings about the past. When the accusations rage, parents often try to defend themselves with the facts: "We *didn't* send you away for six months. It was only three." "We never *made* you wear those hand-me-down clothes. You *wanted* to."

However, the facts aren't the main issue here; the issue is how ATCKs *perceived* the event. For them, the separation *felt* like six months. In other words, they really missed their parents. When they were laughed at for their attire, they *felt* they'd had no choice in what to wear. Like everyone else in the world, the ATCKs' perceptions of reality have been shaped by the emotional impact of their experiences. That emotional reaction is real, and it's far more important at this point for parents to deal with those perceptions of certain events and the feelings behind them than to argue about the facts. Arguing the facts only proves to the ATCK that the parents never understood anyway—and still don't.

Sometimes parents not only argue with the facts ATCKs bring up during this time but also with the feelings ATCKs express. For example, the ATCK tries to express how lonely he or she felt when leaving for boarding school, and the parent replies, "You never minded going off to school. Why, you smiled and waved and always said you had a great time there." Or the ATCK talks of how hard it was to leave the host country and the parent interjects, "How can you say you were heartbroken to leave Port-au-Prince? You always told us it was too hot and you couldn't wait to get back to France."

Perhaps nothing will shut down communication faster between parents and their ATCK than such a response, because no one can tell others what they did or did not feel. Outer behavior often masks inner feelings. That's why it is critical that when ATCKs try to tell their parents, even years later, what they were feeling as they grew up, parents need to listen and simply acknowledge and accept it. Parents might say, "That must have been so difficult for you. I'm sorry that we did not understand your feelings at the time. Can you forgive us for not recognizing or adding to your hurt?" This kind of acceptance opens doors for far more fruitful discussion between the parents and their ATCKs than trying to prove this isn't what the ATCKs felt.

Parents may be stunned when suddenly confronted with feelings their ATCKs have never expressed before—especially when the ATCKs are in their thirties and forties. These feelings may not be easy for parents to hear, but it's important for parents to keep in mind that life has stages, and that often children can't fully deal with or understand what is happening at a certain time in their lives. Many TCKs, like people from any background, in all sorts of situations, do experience the cycle of "grief, despair, and detachment" John Bowlby talks about. When children face any trauma, they can first feel grief, which then turns to despair when it seems the situation can't be changed, and then detachment— moving to a place virtually outside the feeling.[6] Hopefully, they will look at it later when it is safer to examine the full impact of a situation. For many ATCKs, this is likely the first time they have allowed themselves not only to name it, but to feel it and grieve whatever these losses might have been.

Children basically have to deal with life's traumas in a survival mode— whether it be someone calling them a bad name, their own physical handicap, parental divorce, major separation from either or both parents, abuse, or death. Some kids escape into fantasy. Others block out the feelings of pain with denial or rationalization. Compulsions may be another child's attempt to control the pain. It's not the *how* that's significant; it's the fact that children have to survive, and they must use everything at their disposal to do so.

As life proceeds, however, the pain remains until finally the day comes when adults decide to face their inner wounds.

> Many people have asked Ruth how she remembered so many details of her childhood to include in *Letters Never Sent*. She always explains, "I didn't remember; I reexperienced those moments. But as an adult, I had words to describe the feelings I felt but couldn't explain as a child." After one such discussion, Faye, another ATCK who had been through a similar process of retracing her own childhood, challenged Ruth. Faye said, "I don't think we reexperience those feelings. I think we allow them to be felt for the first time."

On further reflection, Ruth agreed. She realized that when she was six and the lights went off at bedtime her first night in boarding school, she felt an immense sense of isolation, aloneness, and homesickness that threatened to squeeze her to death. To give in to that much pain would surely have meant annihilation. So, like most kids, she tried everything she knew to dull the pain, to control it somehow. Ruth's solution involved "trying harder." She prayed with great attention to style—carefully kneeling, giving thanks in alphabetical order for everyone and everything she could think of—so God would stay happy with her and grant the requests to see her family again that she would sneak onto the end of the prayer. She tried to meticulously obey all the rules at school so she wouldn't get in trouble. Keeping track of the details of life took a lot of focus and attention away from the pain.

When she picked up her pen at age thirty-nine and wrote, "I want my mommy and daddy" as part of the letter her six-year-old self would have written if she'd had the words, Ruth felt that same horrible squeezing in her chest that she'd known as that six-year-old child. This time, however, she didn't need to put it away or work against it. She had already survived it and could allow herself to feel the anguish all the way to the bottom of her soul in a way she couldn't have when it actually happened.

But perhaps one of her greatest gifts is that when she became brave enough one day to show her mother what she had written, her mom wrote back, "Thank you for sharing. I read it and of course, I cried. I wish I could give you a big hug right now. If we had known, we might have made other decisions but we didn't. May your story be used any way it can be." Her mother acknowledged what she had written, acknowledged her pain in receiving it, but didn't go through defensiveness or wallowing in her own self-blame. Instead, she blessed her, which opened the door for many other moments of discussing the past, present, and future together. In time, her mom helped Ruth proofread those early journals turned into a manuscript for publication as well as the manuscripts for earlier editions of this book. Such is the power of a parent who will hear the story of the ATCKs.

This pattern of midlife clarification of the past seems to be *common* for many ATCKs, but it's a process that brings great consternation to some parents. It's helpful for parents not only to accept that ATCKs may need to deal with their emotions many years after the events themselves, but also to see that their ATCKs' attempts to share feelings with them—though initially some may be expressed in anger—are because the ATCKs still want and need their parents to understand what they felt during their moments of separation or other experiences of childhood. Consciously or unconsciously, the ATCKs desire to be in a closer relationship with their parents or they wouldn't bother trying to communicate these feelings. After all, these are the only parents the ATCK will ever have.

COMFORT AND BE GENTLE

Offering comfort is a key factor in any grieving process—even when that process is delayed by decades. Remember, comfort is not encouragement. It is being there with understanding and love, not trying to change or fix things.

> One ATCK in college in the U.S. visited her Korean parents in Zambia. She had been hurt and angry with them even though she still loved them. On the advice of a care-specialist she shared with them a letter she had written explaining how wonderful it was growing up in Zambia, how hard it was going away to boarding school, how much she was struggling with not being Korean enough to feel comfortable in her "home" country, and that it was hard for her to express her feelings to them because they were more Korean and she felt more Western. Her mother and her father cried, which she had never seen him do. They hugged her, apologized, and asked if there were some things they could read or people they could talk to so they could learn how to help her now. She forgave her parents with her whole heart and they began the work of healing and rebuilding.

The first comfort came with the acknowledgment that her parents understood and accepted the feelings she expressed. The fact that they hugged her, not a common form of parental expression in Korea, showed they would meet her where she was. Then they took some next steps together to address the situation now. Her parents never refuted or denied her feelings, nor did they wallow in self-blame or defensiveness. Instead, they blessed their daughter. Parental listening, understanding, comfort, and blessing are huge, wonderful steps in the healing process that parents can provide for their children—even when those children are now adults.

DON'T PREACH

Almost all parents find it difficult not to preach, but for parents who have often spent their lives serving in causes they see as greater than themselves, this may be especially hard. Take, for example, parents of adult missionary kids who have spent their lives dedicated to a religious cause, or military parents who have given their all to defend a particular country. There is probably no greater anguish a parent can feel than when their ATCKs reject the system for which the parents have stood—particularly when it is the faith or freedom they have gone halfway around the world to share or defend. Often, the sense of urgency to convince their children to believe in what they themselves believe grows as parents watch their ATCKs fall into increasingly self-destructive behavior: "If they'd just get their lives right with God, they'd be fine." Or, "If Suzy would just enlist, the Marines would shape her up."

To that we would respond with a "yes, but" answer. Yes, what the parents desire for their children is valuable, but ATCKs who suffered within a religious system must first sort out their pain in terms of who God actually is compared to the rules and culture of the religious system that seeks to represent God. Until then, preaching—or worse, words of spiritual reprimand—will only fuel the anger. A lecture on what a great country this is and why they should be grateful to be part of it may all be true, but is not helpful for a military ATCK trying to understand the many nuances of his or her story. All ATCKs need, at some point, to differentiate between what parts of their experience are basically "normal" for being a TCK and what parts are particular to their family structure or the organization under which the parents worked.

Is there never a time for third culture parents to talk forthrightly with their ATCKs both in response to the accusations that are being made as well as the destructive behavior parents see? Of course there is. When parents have listened and understood what their adult child is feeling, there *is* an appropriate time to express their own feelings and beliefs. But it must come as a sharing of who they are and their perspectives rather than as a denial of what the ATCK has shared or is feeling.

FORGIVE

Sometimes parents need to ask their ATCKs for forgiveness. They have made mistakes too and shouldn't run from acknowledging them. If their ATCK has been extremely hurtful and rebellious toward them, parents will also have much to forgive. This can be very difficult, particularly if their adult child is not yet acknowledging how badly he or she has hurt them. But if parents are able to forgive and ask for forgiveness, it can be a major factor in their adult child's healing process.

ASSUME YOU ARE NEEDED

Parents should assume their adult children still need and want them as part of their lives.

They may tell parents not to bother coming for a birth, graduation, or wedding, saying, "It isn't that big a deal," and these ATCKs probably believe that's how they really feel. They are used to the Ocean in between for birthdays and holidays and that is OK. But it makes a big difference—even to those who don't think they need their parents any longer—when parents make the effort to remain involved in a caring (not suffocating!) way in their children and grandchildren's lives as adults. Sometimes those years together as adults finally make opportunities for new relationships after the separations of the past.

Of course, we also recognize there are some situations where, for whatever reason, the adult TCK is so angry at the parents, perhaps blaming them for abandonment or whatever, that they have specifically told the parents not to make contact. If that is the case, then parents should not force themselves on their children but be patient and try to understand their anger without becoming defensive. Sometimes parents may need professional help in such situations as well.

What Friends and Other Relatives Can Do

Sometimes friends and other relatives can help ATCKs take the first major step in the healing process because they stand outside the emotionally reactive space occupied by the ATCKs and their parents. What can they do for the ATCKs they love to help in the healing process?

LISTEN TO THE STORY AND ASK GOOD QUESTIONS

Many ATCKs feel their childhood story is so far removed from their present lives that they have nearly forgotten it themselves. Few people cared to know more than the cursory details when they first returned from their third culture experience, and they quit talking about it long ago. To have someone invite them for lunch, ask to hear about their experiences, and then actually listen may be such a shock to some that they seem to at least temporarily forget everything that has happened to them. But persist. When friends or relatives initiate the conversation and clearly express their interest, the ATCK knows it's bona fide. It may even give them the first chance they've ever had to put words to their experiences.

Questions such as these can also help the process: "How did you feel when you said good-bye to your grandma?" "What was the hardest thing about returning to your home country?" "What did you like best about growing up that way?"

These kinds of questions prove the friend is listening closely enough to hear the behind-the-scenes story and may even challenge ATCKs to consider issues they never stopped to think about before.

DON'T COMPARE STORIES

Friends and relatives shouldn't point out how many other people have had it worse. Generally, ATCKs already know they've had a wonderful life compared to many others. That has often been part of their problem in trying to understand their struggles.

Most ATCKs will first relate the positive parts of their story. They won't tell the difficult aspects until they feel safe and comfortable with the listener. Once they do begin to share the darker times, don't try to cheer them up by reminding them of the positives. Both sides of the story are valid.

COMFORT IF POSSIBLE

Sometimes friends are the first ever to comfort an ATCK. There are ATCKs with amazing stories of pain that came through an uncontrollable situation such as a political evacuation under heavy gunfire, or simply an insensitive remark that has cut them deeply all their lives. For ATCKs who went through political stress and resulting physical danger in days gone by, few had any debriefing teams. People celebrated their survival but never addressed the trauma. When a situation like that comes out, it's helpful for the listener to take a moment and say, "That must have been incredibly scary," or, "I am so sorry that happened to you. If you were ten years old, that would have felt terrible." The ATCKs may reveal terrible things that have been locked up as their secrets throughout life, once someone begins to truly listen. If you feel overwhelmed by the story they tell, you can still find ways to acknowledge their loss or grief even as you realize they might need to discuss the events and feelings with a professional counselor at some point.

One point to bear in mind is that, initially, comfort can sometimes be hard for the ATCK to accept. Many feel as if admitting to any pain is the same as disowning their parents, their faith, or the organizational system in which they grew up. Sometimes ATCKs become angry when others try to comfort them, because they refuse to admit they might need it. So offer comfort, but don't push if they aren't ready to receive it.

AFFIRM GIFTS FROM THE EXPERIENCE AND LOOK FOR APPLICATIONS

Sometimes ATCKs wish they knew what they could do with some of the many experiences of gifts they have received from their lives. Depending on where they live and what they are doing, at times it feels as if there is a disconnect from who they were and who they now are. A significant portion of their lives doesn't seem to relate to their present environment.

Others, of course, like Isabelle Min, are using their story every day in the workplace and life. They are in situations where language and cultural experience are valued, where adaptability and empathy for others are given worth, where a global perspective is shared and considered. That's terrific, and their experience of growing up among many worlds is affirmed.

But for those whose everyday lives seem a bit more disconnected, friends can help them consider what their experiences have been and point out ways they may already be using their story (like the woman mentioned who taught writing to the homeless without realizing the connection to her story of rootlessness). And friends may also encourage them to more proactively seek places where they can connect. Maybe an ATCK doesn't think she knows a language well enough to use it in an official way, yet she can easily chat with a visiting businessman or help interpret for a refugee family if the friend encourages her to try.

When friends and relatives understand the ATCKs' strengths as a whole person and point them in the direction of a need or opportunity, a very positive integration may take place.

> Swedish-born ATCK Lucas grew up in Paraguay and spoke both Spanish and Guarani. As an adult he found work at a magazine in California as a photojournalist. One of his first stories that garnered attention was about homeless shelters that turned away Spanish-only speakers. Blonde and blue-eyed Lucas felt out of place and didn't want to pick up the story because he felt he didn't know enough to jump in. His friends pushed him, citing all his background credentials. Lucas didn't just write the story; he began volunteering as an interpreter at the shelter.

Being known and supported can mean, for anyone, the difference between the courage to try something new or not. For ATCKs, recognition and encouragement to develop and use diverse gifts can be transformative.

How Therapists Can Help

We don't presume to tell therapists how to counsel ATCKs, since professional therapy is outside our domain. As mentioned earlier, Lois Bushong has written a great book for therapists precisely on how to work with TCKs and ATCKs called *Belonging Everywhere and Nowhere: Insights into Counseling the Globally Mobile*. We hope, however, that we can help therapists understand the problems specific to the TCK experience, such as where TCK grief often comes from, where the early attachments between parents and children might have been broken, and how TCKs' concepts of identity and worldview have been affected by cultural and mobility issues. Our goal is to help therapists understand the basic life patterns of the third culture experience so they will be better prepared to assist their TCK clients. Hopefully, a careful reading of this book by therapists will have done that. An interesting occurrence when we have given seminars for therapists is that after our presentations, our audience begins to redefine the topic by explaining it back to us and one another from therapeutic models such as attachment theory, triangulation, or posttraumatic stress syndrome, with which they are already familiar.

> After attending a conference on TCK issues, one therapist said, "We used to think that if a child was adopted at birth, that child would have no different issues to deal with than a child born to the adoptive couple. Now we know anytime a client comes in who was adopted, there are certain questions to ask.
> "It seems to me the TCK issue falls in that category. Being aware of this experience can help us ask better questions when we realize our clients are TCKs or ATCKs."

RECOGNIZE HIDDEN LOSSES

Therapists who understand the nature of the third culture experience may be the first to help ATCKs identify the hidden losses that are part of the TCK experience but which TCKs themselves are often not aware of. The Cycles of Mobility Chart (see figure 16-1)[7] can be a useful tool in this process. Many ATCKs do not recognize the degree to which separation has been an integral part of their lives and how it has contributed to feelings of loss and grief. (A copy can be found at www.crossculturalkid.org in the resources section. You have permission to download and use from there as well.)

Instructions: Make a time chart of the separation patterns for the first eighteen years of the ATCK's life, using different colors to fill in the spaces for when and where he or she lived.

For example:

Blue = time living with parents in the home country

Green = time living with parents in the host country #1

Purple = time living with parents in the host country #2

Yellow = time living with parents in the host country #3

Brown = time spent away from parents in boarding school in the host country

Pink = time spent away from parents in boarding school in the home country

Orange = time living with anyone other than parents or boarding school

Age in Years	1	2	3	4	5	6	7	8	9	10	11	12	13	14	15	16	17	18
January																		
February																		
March																		
April																		
May																		
June																		
July																		
August																		
September																		
October																		
November																		
December																		

Figure 16–1: Cycles of Mobility Chart
©1999 David C. Pollock/Ruth E. Van Reken

This chart can be modified to fit the specific situation of each ATCK. What's important is for the therapist—and the ATCK—to see the overall patterns of mobility: where the transitions between various cultures happened, what ages they occurred, and so forth. As the times of transition, separation, and loss become obvious, therapists may discover the roots of some of the issues they see in their ATCK clients. This insight can help them aid their ATCK clients in recognizing the areas that need healing. Therapists should also help their ATCK clients carefully think through the issues regarding the impact of culture on a TCK's developmental process. Some of the feelings ATCKs struggle with may, in fact, be largely a result of cultural imbalance.

RECOGNIZE THE IMPACT OF THE SYSTEM

One major factor that many therapists of ATCKs overlook or fail to understand is the powerful influence of the military, mission, business, or other organizational system under which these ATCKs grew up. Often the ATCKs' anger or hurt stems directly from policies that either controlled their lives on a daily basis or took away choice when it came to schooling, moving, and so on. On the flip side, ATCKs who were used to being protected or nurtured in that system (for example, the perks like free medical care or inexpensive housing) may not know how to cope comfortably in a larger, less structured world where they are expected to depend more on themselves. Therapy is sometimes stymied if issues are dealt with only in the context of family relationships rather than understanding the operative system that often superseded family decisions. The appendix in Lois' book has a detailed chapter on the system's impact on TCKs, which is also available online.[8]

RECOGNIZE THE PARADOX

Often ATCKs are defensive in therapy when asked about the painful parts of their past. They don't want to negate the way of life that is the only one they have known and is a core element in their identity. Corporate kids may feel they are discrediting the many privileges they have known if they say there was anything hard about the experience. Missionary kids may have trouble acknowledging the pain because they feel that to do so will negate their faith. It is hard for many to know how much of that system they can examine, and potentially give up, without renouncing what they value in the process.

Acknowledging the paradoxical nature of their experience may be particularly important in relationship to a client who attended a boarding school. These ATCKs may have many great memories of the camaraderie experienced there and friendships made and maintained through the years. How could there be any negatives? In addition, for some TCKs who were boarding students for as long as twelve years, their identity is deeply tied in to the boarding school experience. To acknowledge anything but the good would threaten their entire sense of self. But young boarding students feel unprotected; a six-year-old child going to boarding school may actually experience something akin to becoming an orphan. How can ATCKs acknowledge the loneliness they felt without seeing it as a denial of the good they have also known at school? For these, or any ATCKs who grew up in strong systems and feel closely identified to that system, questioning system policies can be such a threat to their core identity that they may refuse to continue with the therapy they need.

That is why those working with ATCKs must never forget to recognize—and help the ATCKs recognize—what we have tried to stress time and again. Looking at the TCK experience from the perspective of the adult TCK will reveal many paradoxical realities. Therapists must affirm the positive elements as well as identify the stress points to give their ATCK clients the permission they need to look at all sides of their past experiences. It's also helpful to remind them once more that if there hadn't been so much good to lose, there often wouldn't have been so much grief at its passing.

Expanding Our Vision

Looking at the impact of our childhood experiences on our adult lives is an important part of each person's journey in moving to a fuller understanding of who we are, ATCK or not. But CCKs from the other types of cross-cultural experiences mentioned in chapter 3 seem to face the same types of specific issues mentioned here. Often their own hidden diversity—that place that has been shaped by their various cultural worlds—remains unseen to others who judge them based on old models of culture and ethnicity. Without language and understanding, other CCKs also have no way to process what they have been experiencing. For all parents and therapists of ACCKs, there must be a realization of the changes between their perhaps more traditional upbringing and that of their children/clients. The lessons above apply to ACCKs just as much as to their ATCK counterparts. We are indeed facing a new normal in this world, and the more we all understand the changes, the better we can move ourselves and each other forward with confidence and hope, not with fear or rejection, no matter our story.

Questions for Chapter 16

1. For ATCKs and other ACCKs, how/when did you discover you were a TCK/CCK? Did it change your perspective on yourself, your childhood, or on life in general?

2. Reflecting on life from an adult perspective is different from simply living life as a child. As you consider your story or that of others you know, what

are some ways you are using some of the skills or outlook on life that you received from your background?

3. If you are the parent of an adult TCK/CCK, what are some of your reflections after reading this chapter? What did you like best about raising your child(ren) in another country? What was hardest?

4. Make a copy of the Cycles of Mobility Chart from www.crossculturalkid.org and fill it in. You can be from any background, as it is just as valid if your story is all one color as it is if your story is full of colors! After you do this, reflect on the patterns you see there. Share your story by using this chart with another in the group or perhaps over coffee.

5. Share any other thoughts or reflections you have from looking more closely at all your stories.

Maximizing the Benefits; Overcoming the Challenges

Part IV takes a major bend in the road from the way—not the reason—the book has been written to this point. Parts I, II, and III have been for all to read—those who are or have grown up cross-culturally; those who parent, teach, educate, or counsel them; or those who are simply curious about them. The next two chapters are written specifically for two groups who are heavily invested in this experience—parents of today's TCKs and the HR/personnel/member care departments for corporations or other sponsoring organizations who send their people overseas. To take full advantage of Michael's many years of experience working directly with both of these groups, he wrote these two chapters from his perspective and particular expertise while continuing to build on the solid principles his father laid out for the good "flow of care" needed to help globally mobile families be successful.

Overview: Bridging Transitions through Care. Michael explains the rationale and importance of establishing a caring community for families as they move around the globe. The overview lays out the principles underlying the specifics of the strategies in chapters 17 and 18. Be sure to read it.

Chapter 17: Bridging Transitions: How Parents Can Help. While there are many general strategies parents have, hopefully, picked up in earlier chapters, this chapter focuses totally on strategies parents can use with their families to help their children grow in all ways to their maximum potential.

Chapter 18: Bridging Transitions: How Organizations Can Help. Using material he has presented at workshops for corporations and organizations, Michael gives practical ways organizations of all types can support and care for their members/employees and their families effectively through the process of global relocation.

And then, the grand finale!

Chapter 19: Where Do We Go From Here? As promised from the beginning, a major reason for looking deeply into the traditional TCK experience is to *also* learn lessons that might be applied in many other places, to many other groups, in our fast-changing world. In this chapter, Ruth and Michael each share their personal dreams of all the places and ways to continue exploring, using, and building on and with what we have already learned. Add your dreams to theirs and together we will see where this topic takes us!

Overview: Bridging Transitions through Care

Love seeks one thing only: the good of the one loved. It leaves all the other secondary effects to take care of themselves. Love, therefore, is its own reward.

—Thomas Merton[1]

By substituting "care" for "love," we realize that caring for people in the vulnerable spaces of transition and adjustment is its own reward for parents and schools and for sponsoring businesses, organizations, and agencies. It is simply the right thing to do.

THE EMPHASIS IS ON CARE

Caring for TCKs in the context of their families and schools requires coordination and communication so that the ball is not dropped between entities as we walk with TCKs in our capacities as parents, educators, administrators, member care and human resource staff.

We are also concerned with what Merton called the "secondary effects," as research continues to underscore what we have intuitively known all along: Caring for the people in our families and organizations is essential to reaching our fundamental goals.

Thirty to 85 percent of expatriate assignments end in failure, defined as early return or less-than-satisfactory performance.[2] An oft-cited study in 1999 revealed that of the placements that fail, 86 percent fail due to stresses on the family.[3] Although the numbers seem to be trending lower, family stress is still often given as the number one reason for failure. Given that the cost of preparing and sending a family overseas is estimated to be around $100,000 today, premature ending of assignments affects the sponsoring organization's bottom line. The parents at the center of the transition cannot be expected to perform at optimum level in the capacity to which they have been assigned if the family is not functioning well. Unhappy, struggling spouses and children in high-profile communities will not represent the sponsoring organization to its benefit. And families that do not make the transition well will cost the sponsoring company or organization dearly, not just in the financial cost of the overseas placement investment, estimated at two to three times the cost of the annual salary in the passport country per year, but in time, productivity, replacement costs, and often damage to the reputation of the sponsor.[4] A poor record of member care can undermine trust in the home department and hinder further recruitment and fund-raising efforts for cross-cultural assignments.

Keeping employees with strong cross-cultural skills also helps an agency's performance in relationship to the host culture. New people trying to learn those skills are bound to make more professional and social gaffes that hinder their effectiveness than someone who has already gone through the process of cross-cultural adaptation. After all, there are lessons about crossing cultures that only time and experience can teach. Agencies benefit financially if they can keep their seasoned, internationally experienced employees from departing prematurely.

Also, it does not take long for word to get around the expat community when an agency or corporation fails to consider the well-being of its staff and employees with compassion and competence. The reverse is also true: a company or organization that looks after its people quickly makes a positive impression—increasing loyalty, productivity, and retention—and makes the prospect of relocating across cultures an attractive enterprise.[5]

There are two other costs revealed by current research. We think of these as the hidden cost of mobility on learning and healthy development through midlife. In *Safe Passage* Ota cites research from John Hattie's 2009 meta-study of education that concludes "moving harms learning." Ota contends that it doesn't have to be that way if needs are addressed.[6] In September 2016 the *American Journal of Preventive Medicine* published a study led by Dr. Roger Webb of Manchester University on the long-range impact of mobility.[7] The study, which included all 1.45 million Danes born between 1971 and 1997, focused on the impact of moving before the age of fifteen. The negative outcomes screened for were suicide (attempted), violent crime, psychiatric disorders, drug abuse, and unnatural/early mortality. Moving, especially during the adolescent years of eleven to fourteen, showed significant increases in all four of these negative outcomes later in life. Even acknowledging potential reverse causality (that the problems children were having caused the moves) and cultural difference (if one is not Danish), this broad study is significant and compels us to seek the best ways to address the needs of highly mobile and cross-cultural people.

The bottom line is that moving, especially in adolescence, can increase and even double the likelihood of negative impacts throughout life. Our recommendation is not to avoid moving or moving with children, but to consider moves thoughtfully at the family and organizational level. When moving is appropriate, it is essential to work toward optimal care and support.

The final cost of neglecting to care for the children and families of cross-cultural workers may be the hardest to assess and the most hidden, but is relevant nonetheless as the cost of lost potential. In the TCK and CCK milieu it is common to hear talk about young and middle-aged adults being *lost, sidetracked,* or *derailed.* The numbers are difficult to ascertain and more concrete research is needed, but the challenges that TCKs face can prevent them from becoming fully the persons they were meant to be—thriving in life and contributing to the good of others. While the general need for TCK care is no different from the needs of their monocultural peers, there is reason to cultivate citizens and leaders with transcultural skills and mind-sets. While some might argue for nationalism versus globalism, there is a growing need in society, at all levels from local to global, for empathy, cross-cultural understanding, and an ability to see and understand multiple perspectives without losing one's own value base. Third culture kids have grown up in an interstitial culture that generally requires those traits and skills and, as David Livermore states in *The Cultural Intelligence Difference,* "the ability to function effectively across a variety of cultural contexts is an increasingly necessary and useful skill set in business, education, development, government, and faith-based enterprise."[8]

Picture the transition experience as building a bridge from "here" to "there" and back again. Constructing the bridge are the parties involved in the move: the senders, the goers, and the receivers. The sending organization acts in an oversight capacity so that no planks are missing and no family falls through. Member care and human resource departments bring experience and analysis to policy and procedure, guiding families through a process and building trust. Parents take the care and help given to them to help their children.

In the following chapters our goals are twofold: first to reiterate some of the common challenges and opportunities in the transition process, and second to share insights and strategies for bridging the distance from Involved to Reengaged, as we looked at in chapter 13. When we speak of care we include several layers, including self-care, family care, peer care, and institutional or organizational care.

David Pollock began working with Kelly and Michele O'Donnell on a model in the 1990s to visually incorporate the levels of care and where resources intersect. After Dave's death, the O'Donnells have continued to shape the model, which they presented and explained fully in the book *Doing Member Care Well: Perspectives and Practices from around the World* and updated in *Global Member Care, Volumes I and II.* The model derives from a Judeo-Christian perspective and begins with a heart of care called "Master Care," expressing the love of God for people. It is similar to what psychologist Carl Rogers referred to as the ethos of care or "unconditional positive regard." Caring for oneself and one's teammates and community members is enfolded into the care of the sending agency for all members from recruitment to retirement. Specialist Care is a resource to all of the aforementioned groups addressing a variety of needs from health to legal support. Network Care is the basis for sharing resources, research, and best practices and connects the four major sectors of international work.

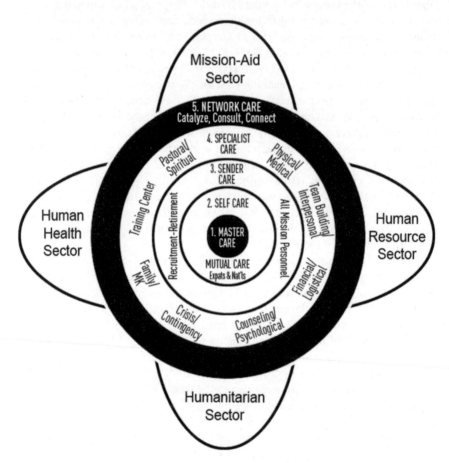

Figure IV–1: O'Donnell Pollock Member Care Model (Adapted)
©2017 O'Donnell/Pollock. Used by permission

Michael developed an approach to identifying the needs of transition based on his own transitions and those of the myriad families who passed through his care. The Transition Needs Table is a matrix of Abraham Maslow's hierarchy of needs and David Pollock's (his father's) Transition Model. As a holistic educator, Michael approaches transition the way he approaches teaching and learning: by addressing the totality of the person and that person's context. It will be necessary to give an overview of the hierarchy of needs that Maslow developed before walking through the application to transition care. With the matrix as a scaffold we can then address needs and strategies from three relevant perspectives:

- The parent perspective
- The organizational/sponsoring perspective
- The international school's perspective

MASLOW'S HIERARCHY OF NEEDS: A REFRESHER

Maslow's hierarchy might be summed up as a framework of human needs from the most essential to the limits of potential.[9] He believed that in order to fully flourish, all individuals must become fully what they are and what they have the potential to be, making us better people and the world a better place. Keep in mind that fulfilling this purpose requires that our more basic needs are met, *even if that is not 100 percent.* The hungry sculptor may still create beautiful art or the war zone journalist may report with excellence under threat of harm, but those lower-order needs of food and safety are going to cause stress and strain on the system.

If one pictures the hierarchy of needs as "nestled into each other" and not "stacked" it helps to perceive the organic nature of meeting the basic needs before moving on to the next tier, as follows:

1. **Tier one: Physiological needs** are the basics such as air, drink, food, sleep, and shelter. Maslow's worldview included human beings as spiritual beings intertwined with biology. He contended that the highest potentials were reached when we see and experience life as fully sacred. In the model I represent this as "integration."
2. **Tier two: Safety** needs encompass physical health and social and emotional safety. Sufficient resources are needed that provide safety nets and margins to absorb life's unexpected shocks.
3. **Tier three: Belonging and love** include being known, cared for, affiliated, accepted, and connected to others. Ranging from emotionally and physically intimate to casually social or functional, these relationships are critical. We also note the interrelatedness of this tier, as being known and cared for will usually increase our safety and our resources for physiological needs.
4. **Tier four: Esteem** derives from our ability to contribute and be noted for our areas of excellence and giftedness. Esteem needs are based on respect or positive regard, which often has a performance aspect; it must be earned. Even in cultures where respect is granted automatically, respect and regard can be lost due to performance or behavior.

Maslow considered the first needs "deficiency needs" in which people are motivated by the lack of the thing. Practically, we expect to have those needs met. The following needs are "growth needs," and motivation comes not from a lack but from a desire for more.

5. **Tier five: Cognitive needs** include increasing our knowledge and understanding, expressing our curiosity, seeking meaning and predictability, and exploring ideas as well as geography.
6. **Tier six: Aesthetic needs** include the pursuit of beauty, order, balance, and form as well as appreciating serenity and refreshment.
7. **Tier seven: Self-actualizing needs** are the desire to grow, create, and share generously. We are drawn toward a "consciousness of the universe"—to something greater than ourselves. The result can be described as happiness and includes a stable sense of well-being, joy, wonder, gratitude, and other-centeredness; it is a satisfaction with life. Interestingly Maslow notes that moving toward self-actualization includes life-affirming humor, a lessening influence of general or "pop" culture, and a kinship with the human race.[10] What a fantastic picture of healthy adult TCKs!

Maslow pointed out that the first four levels of human need are "deficit" needs, indicating that they are most keenly noted when they are not present. When feeling a need, people respond in three ways. Either they push through to higher-tier needs with gritted teeth (the starving artist who eats paint to keep creating art); move "sideways," finding alternative ways to meet needs (the spouse who feels unloved and enters an affair); or regress to a lower-tier need that can be met (the lonely expat who submerges in video games and cupcakes).

On the other hand, growth happens when our lower-tier needs are *sufficiently* met and we find even a bit of boredom in our current state. Good critique of Maslow's work includes consideration of developmental stages that "reorder need priorities" (adolescents may value belonging over safety) and also cultural differences (some cultures will prioritize group needs before personal needs).[11] The more recent and global work of Luis Tay and Ed Diener reinforces the universality of needs and subjective well-being (SWB) while emphasizing that SWB seems to depend more on a "some of each" approach to needs rather than a strictly hierarchical one.[12] This research should inform our practice through understanding that well-being does not depend only on "covering the basics" but on looking to the spectrum of human need.

We must also keep in mind some key dimensions of what it means to be human, lest we fall into the trap of cookie-cutter solutions. The complexity of our many facets as human beings makes caring for each other interesting and challenging as we attempt not to use a mechanistic formula of "input to output," but to ask questions more integratively to understand how human survival becomes human thriving in the context of cross-cultural mobility and transition. In social media contexts Michael simply shortens this to the concept of "thrival," which encompasses well-being across the spectrum of being a person. What it means to be a human being is explored in chapter 6. The elements as presented in Michael and Ruth's 2014 seminar at a Families in Global Transition conference included the following:

- Four dimensions of human existence—Physical, Spiritual, Emotional, and Intellectual (body, soul, heart, and mind);
- Three actionable aspects—people are Relational, Creative, and Volitional (interconnecting, productive, and needing to have choices);
- Two inherent truths—people are Valuable and Integral (their worth exists aside from what they can produce, and people cannot be dissected to be understood but must be taken as a whole entity).

The implications are deep and wide for how we care for TCKs and their families. A framework for strategic planning needs to incorporate the flow of transition with the understanding of human needs, keeping in mind the full spectrum of human flourishing. The Transition Needs Table is one practical way to accomplish the integration and simultaneously create a communication tool between globally mobile personnel and their sending organizations. Over time, use of the tool may lead to observable patterns of strengths and weaknesses, suggesting improvements.

What is Needed?	Leaving Pre-departure	Transit "In Motion"	Entering/ Settling	Re-Engaging/ Staying	Responsible Entities & Choices
Physiology food clothing shelter integration					
Safety protection resources health safety net					
Belonging affiliation acceptance friendship intimacy					
Esteem respect recognition contribution status					
Cognitive understanding exploration discovery					
Aesthetic serenity refreshment creativity order					
Self-Actualization mastery autonomy service					

Figure IV–2: Transition Needs Table
©2014 Michael V. Pollock

CHAPTER 17

Bridging Transitions: How Parents Can Help

I t is never too early to begin preparing your children for a cross-cultural experience. More than likely if children do not move out into the world with their parents, they will find that the world is coming to them.

Involvement Stage

Addressing this stage as a foundational springboard for healthy transition is helpful, but it is not always accurate to state that healthy and satisfying involvement is a determinant for healthy and satisfying reengagement; nor is the reverse true. We are all aware of stories in which people in unsatisfying circumstances made a cross-cultural jump and discovered a renewed sense of home. Pico Iyer's discovery of peace and belonging in Japan is a strong example, and there are many others. The question of whether certain cultures and indeed geography are more suitable to certain personalities and dispositions is a fascinating study beyond the scope of this book. Let's consider, then, practices, attitudes, and foundations in the involved stage that lend themselves to a strong cross-cultural transition.

CULTURAL PREPARATION BEGINS AT HOME

Critical observation and thinking skills while withholding judgments can be practiced while one is still comfortably embedded. Asking questions and digging deeper into one's own culture while remaining curious about other cultures is a core skill. Anthropologist Charles Kraft used sets of questions to help understand culture from the visible objects and behaviors to the deeper and unseen values and worldview.[1]

- **What is valuable?** What symbols are acquired with discretionary funds, prized, and displayed?
- **What is acceptable?** What behaviors are normal versus embarrassing or illegal? How do people dress and eat?
- **What is important?** How do people spend discretionary time? What value is placed on human dignity and life?
- **What is true?** What is considered to be "right" or "wrong"? What is considered the basis for moral and ethical decisions?
- **What is real?** What is the ultimate view and value of humankind? What is the meaning of life? How is truth determined? Who or what is "God"/god?

We can increase our readiness by practicing multiple perspectives in our current context, reading broadly, listening to a variety of narratives, and considering the merits of accepted positions and opinions. Establishing an honest current baseline of health and well-being for yourself, in your family and within community relationships, allows for both adjustment and improvement now and a comparative standard later. Finally, practicing gratitude is a strong component of well-being, and acknowledgment of the good that we are currently experiencing strengthens us both to acknowledge the good that is lost in change as well as the good that is gained. Individuals, families, and organizations can all practice and promote these strategies in various ways as a type of *cultural* or *contextual mindfulness* that will support, when it comes, a healthy transition through change.

MEDIATING THE MOVE

Wise cross-cultural parenting doesn't just happen. Moving to a new culture far from familiar support systems causes new stress for everyone, and we know there is no magic formula for making everything work out as we wish. Parents need to ask some important questions before committing their family to such a major move as part of that baseline assessment.

1. *What are the family's needs that require attention regardless of location?* For example, does any child have a learning challenge, physical disability, or chronic medical condition that requires special care? If so, parents must make sure that those needs can be met in the new location. Will homeschooling or tutoring be sufficient if special education programs aren't available in the regular school? Will medical facilities be adequate? In addition, a child's age and level in school are important factors to consider. For instance, the last two years of secondary school aren't usually a good time to uproot teenagers. Not only will they miss graduating with their friends but it makes planning for the future more difficult logistically. College visits may require

a plane ride, residency required for tuition breaks may be an issue, and/or summer employment before and during college becomes more complicated to set up. Internet and smartphones can help but are not consistent in every location.

2. *What are the policies of the sending agency or corporation?* Does it look carefully at family and educational needs when moving personnel? Is it clear what kinds of safety nets are in place and who is responsible for such things as health or evacuation insurance? In addition to reading the stated policies, parents should also talk with peers in the organization who have already made such a move.

3. *How will existing family patterns and relationships be affected by the move?* Are there aging relatives in the picture who might not be there when the family returns? Are there dear pets who will not travel with the family? In the home culture, parents generally have a support system of extended family, friends, and people from school and church to help raise their kids. A cross-cultural move radically disrupts that support system.

> A Nigerian man told of the surprise he'd felt when he and his wife first moved to the United States so he could pursue a graduate program. In Nigeria their family had lived in close proximity to grandparents, aunts, and uncles who often functioned as surrogate parents for their children. Finding a babysitter in Nigeria was never a problem. In the U.S., however, they were on their own. No one offered to take their children when they needed to go to class or the store. The special nurturing that comes from living in an extended family had disappeared, and the couple had to develop completely new patterns of parenting.

4. *Do both parents favor the move?* This is a key question. If both parents aren't fully committed to a cross-cultural move, the experience often ends in disaster. Any reluctance easily turns to resentment and hostility under the pressure of adjusting to the assignment. An unwilling parent may use extremely damaging passive-aggressive methods (e.g., emotional withdrawal, drug or alcohol addiction, generalized hostility, or destructive levels of personal criticism) to sabotage the experience for the entire family.

5. *How does the family—and the individuals in it—handle stress?* Parents must realize that not only they but also their children will experience stress in a cross-cultural move. Obviously, stress is part of everyone's life, but sometimes specific individuals or families have a particularly hard time dealing with it. If someone in the family, or the family as a whole, becomes seriously depressed or reacts in an extreme way to stress in general, parents would be wise to seek outside counsel before planning a cross-cultural move. One family whose son had a learning disability decided not to move again until their son finished high school because they realized he could not adjust to

new classroom situations and new language environments without going into major withdrawal and depression.

6. *If the family does decide to move, how will it take advantage of the cross-cultural opportunities ahead?* It's a sad waste for families to live in another country and culture and not be enriched by the experience. Without some planning, it's easy for life in the new place overseas to become as routine as it was in the village, suburbs, or city back home. Is the move only for the purpose of work, or will the family take hold of the learning and growth opportunities? One ATCK lamented that while living in the rich history, politics, and geography of Kazakhstan, she had no idea what was really around her until she returned to her passport country and took a university course on her former country of residence.

7. *What educational options are available in the new setting?* This is a crucial matter to consider before accepting any particular assignment. In the early years of global mobility, schooling options were limited and most TCKs attended boarding school. This has largely changed, but it means parents need to think through even more options.

8. *How will the family prepare to leave?* Once parents decide to make the move, they must consider how to help their children through the transition process (see Transition in chapter 13 for a detailed discussion). Closure is as important to a child as it is to an adult. Leaving well has as profound an impact on the ability of children to enter well and adjust successfully as it does on adults.

Cross-cultural living can be a wonderful experience in countless ways, but it is far better when it begins with clear thinking and good planning rather than with naïve visions of a romantic adventure. Of course, there can be much that is unforeseen, but those storms are better weathered when there has been thoughtful preparation.

STRONG PARENT FOUNDATIONS FOR HEALTHY TCKS

Over our years of study, practice, and observation we have identified four core areas of family life that have a direct impact on the stability and sense of safety for TCKs as they develop. Recognizing that life rarely operates on optimum levels is no excuse for not aiming for those targets. We know that an engine runs best if it is clean, well lubricated, and firing on all pistons. If one spark plug is not firing efficiently, the car still runs, but you will see the effect in lost efficiency and you will hear a difference. Moving children cross-culturally means they will become TCKs, and that has great benefits along with the challenges. As with any child, having a consistent, stable, and loving family matters; when life is shaken up by a major move or series of moves, it is even more critical. Let's consider the four following foundations, like four pistons in the "family engine."

Parent-to-Parent Relationship

We realize not all TCKs live with two biological parents. Some families are blended through marriage or adoption; other TCKs are raised in single-parent families. Regardless, the relationship between parents is of vital importance. There are three critical areas parents must examine.

1. *Commitment to each other.* Commitment may be an unfashionable word to some, but it remains an important one. Commitment draws a couple closer in the face of life adjustments because they are "leaning in" and interdependent. Commitment requires parents who may no longer live together to work out their differences in a way that considers the good of their child. Commitment keeps us working for solutions in new and challenging circumstances rather than throwing in the towel. It's how we grow. Parents considering a change as major as a cross-cultural move need to make sure they are sufficiently committed to one another, their relationship, and their family to make the necessary personal sacrifices to achieve their common goals.
2. *Respect and support for one another go hand in glove with commitment.* When kids know their parents' relationship is solid, they feel secure, particularly in the midst of the chaos of a move. They also need to see that their parents like each other. Small signs of affection—hugs, a quick kiss on the cheek while passing, or holding hands while watching TV—may not seem very important, but for children, these types of actions assure them that all is well with Mom and Dad. That's one area they don't have to worry about. If parents are no longer together, showing respect and not demeaning the other parent to any child is also important.
3. *Relationship nurturing by choice and intention.* A new cultural environment can change a couple's traditional ways of investing in each other. Elegant restaurants may not be available for a lovely anniversary meal. Visitors may pop in unannounced any time of the day or night, restricting the opportunities for private conversations. It takes time to develop trustworthy childcare so parents can enjoy a stress-free date. Couples in cross-cultural settings often have to find creative ways to keep their relationship vibrant; realizing this is vital to their family as well as themselves.

Parent-to-Child Relationship

Parents are the most important caregivers in any child's life. Indeed, researchers say that this relationship is the single most significant factor in determining how TCKs (or any kids) ultimately fare. This is where children form their first inklings of personal identity. They begin to discover where they belong, that they have value, and that someone believes in them. This profoundly important relationship must be nurtured intentionally and various needs must be addressed, especially in the midst of cross-cultural stress and the chaos of moving.

Children need to be provided for. This might seem like the most obvious point, yet a child who is being moved from a place of comfort and provision may first wonder about the mundane aspects of life—"What will we eat? Wear? Will we have a house? Will there be . . . Can I bring my . . . ?"—and all of those questions are important and valid. When parents address those basic needs and give children space for their own questions and concerns, children can assure themselves that their needs are being considered and they will be taken care of. Because reassurance may need to come regularly for some time until the child feels settled again, patience is required of the parents.

Children need to be protected. A special challenge for parents of TCKs is that their children are often growing up in a different world from the one they knew as children, and there will be new threats, both perceived and real. Because the parents are seeing this new world through adult eyes, they may not realize how stressful some cross-cultural situations can be, at least initially, to their children. Some ATCKs have told us of the extreme fear they felt when they first did such a normal thing as going to a local market—they were targets of constant attention and rude remarks simply because they were foreigners. When their parents said, "Don't be silly; no one is going to hurt you" as they continued walking through the crowd, the fear—and shame for being afraid—only increased. Others have known tremendous stress because of the political climate in the new country.

New cultural values and new cultural rules may mean new risks for children, and parents need to learn both what is acceptable and what is safe. Consider that in many places a young woman walking without a male "chaperone" and not dressed according to local standards attracts unfavorable and even threatening attention. Walking alone to the store might be safe in one environment and risky in another. Parents used to the safety of public transportation in Japan never thought twice about putting their children in a taxi in another country during their vacation. Unfortunately, the taxi driver robbed the children and left them off in a totally different place from where the parents expected them to go. Sometimes a child's interpretation of events leads to anxious thoughts and feelings.

> International businessman Byron and his family experienced a coup close up, seemingly unscathed in spite of machine gun fire in their front yard one night. Shortly after the coup, however, one daughter became panicked when the family car developed a flat tire and they stopped by the side of the road to fix it. After a second flat tire the very next day, this daughter refused to take any more car trips with the family.
>
> Why did a simple flat tire cause her so much panic? When questioned, she said something about the "soldiers"; when questioned further, however, the cause of her panic finally became apparent: the first tire went flat near an army

barracks, where soldiers walked around with guns promi-
nently displayed. Their daughter had panicked, afraid that
if the soldiers came after them or started to shoot, there
would be no way for the family to escape because of the flat
tire. With soldiers present throughout the city, she didn't
want to risk being caught in such a situation again.

TCKs who are hidden immigrants in a new country may feel a special sense
of confusion and pain socially. Sharon, a Chinese Canadian whose parents moved
to Beijing, was often shamed by locals for her poor Mandarin, which was decent
even though spoken with an accent. Her blonde English friends, however, were
praised for their few, halting words. Because Sharon looked Chinese, she was
scolded, even when she protested that she was Canadian. Her parents wondered
why she preferred to read inside rather than venture out; socially, Sharon did not
feel safe. When children feel uncomfortable, parents need to listen carefully to
understand their child's concern and the reason for the behavior, and not brush
it off as silly.

We stress the importance of protection because of the deep expressions of
pain TCKs who have felt unprotected by parents or other caregivers express.
Sometimes they felt pushed out on their own too soon into a new school or community, especially when they didn't know the new language yet. They felt it during leave when it seemed, to the TCKs, that they were put on display against their
will for church congregations, functions of state, or for relatives. Children who
will attend a school in a new language need to learn at least some words before
they begin. TCKs who express resistance at being "little missionaries" or "little
ambassadors" shouldn't be forced into that role. Children are persons in their
own right, not merely extensions of their parents. They need to be respected as
such.

The most heart-rending stories, however, are from those who were left with
a caregiver—whether a dorm parent in a boarding school, a domestic worker, a
fellow expat in the host country, or a friend or relative in the home country—and
were emotionally, physically, or sexually abused by the person parents trusted to
take care of them. The trauma is intensified, of course, if the parents refuse to
believe what has happened, sometimes sending their child back to that same situation. Although no parent would knowingly send a child to an abuser, the fact
that often TCKs have been abused by the very people parents trusted can make it
seem at some deep level that the parents themselves sanctioned the abuse. This is
one reason it often takes years before the child (now an adult) will tell the parents
what really happened.

With fewer young children away at boarding schools, and with email, instant messaging, Skype, and cell phones, it's much easier to make sure there is a
way for children to have direct contact with parents when they are away. Contact
must be a priority when children are at school in more remote areas where some
of this technology may not be as available. As for all children, it is important to

teach TCKs concepts of personal safety and private body zones. Children need to be reminded that their parents will always believe them and protect them—no matter what anyone else might say. And then, if the child does report some potential or actual infringement, parents must be prepared to intervene on that child's behalf—even if doing so may put their career at risk. One of the dangers that we perceive in the international community with the issue of abuse is that there is often so much riding on the investment of sponsoring organization and family that it can be difficult to acknowledge actions that are so damaging and life-changing. That needs to change. Since the first edition of this book, the number of documented stories about child abuse has increased. We believe one reason may be that parents trust others in their expatriate or local communities they know and forget to take precautions they might in other situations. Another reason for an increase in reporting is the courageous revelations of people like Wes Stafford, director of Compassion International and author of *Too Small to Ignore: Why the Least of These Matters Most*, who revealed his own story of abuse at the hands of mission school staff, and Wm. Paul Young, author of *The Shack*, who shares his story of abuse at the hands of indigenous tribespeople. Groups like MK Safety Net now provide essential supports to protect children and offer healing and hope to survivors of abuse.

Children need to know that they belong. It's likely the more questions that parents can answer, the more their kids feel valued. Children need to be special. A parent's greatest gift to the children is letting them know beyond any doubt that there is somewhere in this world where they are unconditionally loved and accepted and that no one else could ever replace them. That place is in the family.

For many TCKs, however, the need to feel special is an area of particular vulnerability. Many have parents who are involved in important, high-energy, people-oriented jobs. Sometimes TCKs feel their needs are less important than those with whom their parents work, but this may not be expressed until years after the fact, and parents are surprised. Expressions of "I felt abandoned" or "I felt like an orphan" shock parents who never knew their kids wanted them to be more emotionally or physically present. Parents of TCKs need to make sure that as they are out dealing with the world, there are spaces reserved for family time—no matter what other apparently urgent matters arise.

Children need to be comforted. We talked about the importance of comfort in chapter 5. Being comforted communicates that parents care and understand, even if the situation can't be changed. Parents should remember, particularly in any transition experience, that the quietest, most compliant children may be grieving and need to have their losses acknowledged and to be comforted.

Children need to feel valued. Being known (what we think, feel, enjoy, dislike, etc.), pursued, and prioritized lets us know that we are significant to others.

Children are no different. Parents of TCKs communicate that they value their children in all the usual ways parents normally do: by listening when children talk, by asking good questions, by seeking clarification when a child speaks or acts in a way parents don't quite understand, by giving a quiet hug. On top of that, encouraging and valuing our children's unique contribution to the world builds esteem whether it is for humor, writing, athletics, creativity, or any combination of skills, abilities, or characteristics.

The following list of questions from cross-cultural educator Shirley Torstrick[2] helps parents assess how well they have been listening to their child.

- What makes your child really angry?
- Who is your child's best friend?
- What color would your child like his or her room to be?
- Who is your child's hero?
- What embarrasses your child most?
- What is your child's biggest fear?
- What is your child's favorite subject in school?
- What is the subject your child dislikes most?
- What is your child's favorite book?
- What gift from you does your child cherish most?
- What person outside your family has most influenced your child?
- What is your child's favorite music?
- What is your child's biggest complaint about the family?
- Of what accomplishment is your child proudest?
- Does your child feel too big or too small for his or her age?
- If you could buy your child anything in the world, what would be his or her first choice?
- What has been the biggest disappointment in your child's life?
- What does your child most like to do as a family?
- When does your child prefer to do her or his homework?
- What makes your child sad?
- What does your child want to be as an adult?

Children need to be heard and to have input in decisions. Another way to let children know they are valued is to include them in the discussion of decisions that will affect them, such as the possibility of a global move. Sometimes parents try to protect their children and keep them from worrying by not telling them about an impending move until just before it happens. Despite the good intentions, such a delay prevents children from having the time to process the changes that are ahead. Of course, kids don't have the final say in their parents' career choices, but when included early in discussions and preparations, they hear the all-important message that their needs are respected. They'll know they are valued members of the family.

Children need to be provided with means for appreciating beauty, pursuing mastery and autonomy, and service to others. In following the ideas expressed in Maslow's hierarchy and the current work in well-being, we can't forget that our children are also in need of beauty in the natural created aesthetic world. In some overseas posts, trees, grass, running water, and the like have to be sought; in others works of art and music are challenging to come by, and we need to seek opportunities for our children to play, appreciate, and create. Moving can also disrupt the practice and mastery of pursuits.

> Alegra was a girl growing up between Kentucky, U.S.; the Egyptian delta; and Lebanon. She loved everything equestrian. She was learning to ride, care for, and train horses, and saw herself one day being a therapist using the relationship between humans and horses to heal. She struggled each time her family moved to find or reproduce the means to pursue her dream: to work with and ride horses. For three years in Egypt, she didn't have a single opportunity. In Kentucky there were multiple options. When her parents announced the family was moving to Lebanon, she was angry and frustrated until her parents discovered the reason, did research together, and located a stable and riding school in their new city. They even let the locations of the stable and international high school help them choose where they would live.

Not every solution can be as neatly worked out as Alegra's, but even the act of trying to do so and working together communicates value and care.

TCK Perception of Parents' Work

"He who has a why to live for can bear almost any how" is attributed to Nietzsche. TCKs who understand and value what their parents do are more willing to work through the challenges than those who don't.

Many TCKs feel pride to have parents involved in careers that can make a difference in the world. They feel part-owners (and thus significant) in the process because their family traveled together so Mom or Dad could do the job. Any challenges are small compared to what is being accomplished.

Other TCKs, however, express great bitterness toward parents involved in international careers. What makes the difference? Certainly the parents' attitude toward the job, the host country and culture, and the sincerity of the political or religious beliefs that motivated them to go abroad in the first place are critical factors. Parents who feel and act positively toward their situation and the host country people with whom they are working communicate that attitude to their children. On the other hand, the parent who shows disrespect for the people or culture of the host country can make the young TCK observer wonder why the family is there at all. When the going gets tough, the question can quickly change from, "Why are we here?" to, "Why don't we go home?" Once that question is raised, the TCKs often begin acting out in ways that may be disruptive to the parent's career: international business kids end up breaking local laws; foreign service kids start covering the embassy walls with graffiti; missionary kids blatantly smoke, drink, use drugs, or get pregnant; and military kids may join an antiwar demonstration.

A particular irony can happen, however, when parents feel it's time to repatriate. Some TCKs who have valued what their parents are doing question how these parents could be "giving up." For them, leaving may cast a retrospective doubt on their whole experience. Once more, communication is important: parents must let children know of the upcoming move and the true reasons for it—even if the children have difficulty listening.

Positive Spiritual Core

This foundation block is the child's awareness that there is a stable spiritual core in their parents' lives and in the life of the family as a whole. Sojourning across cultures not only brings us face to face with different beliefs and practices but often does so after we are torn out of our routines, lifted from our communities of faith, and removed from our places of worship. David Pollock spoke often of having a persistent and practical faith. By this he meant pursuing matters of belief and faith with rigor and honesty and applying those beliefs in practical ways at home and throughout all of our interactions and decisions. He believed this did not exclude people who profess "no faith at all," as he saw that as a belief system requiring faith. Knowing what one believes and what is at the core of your sense of what is real, true, and good is a compass for all of life, and that is no less true for families than for individuals. Barbara Schaetti talks about this as a final step in a TCK's identity development.

> Certainly it is valuable to be able to understand different truths as represented in different cultures, to withhold judgment and interpretation. This is part of the global nomad birthright. At the same time, however, it is important for the adult global nomad to plant his or her feet in personal truth, one not dependent on circumstance. "This is what I believe, regardless of the cultural context in which I find myself. I may alter my behavior according to changing circumstances, but my truth remains my truth."[3]

In a world where moral values and practices can be radically different from one place to another, this block of maintaining a constancy of identifiable core beliefs and values is the key to true stability throughout life. When it is strongly in place, TCKs are equipped to remain on a steady course, no matter which culture or cultures they live in.

Obviously not all of the items mentioned will be possible to do before one decides to make the leap into another culture and maybe across the world.

However, the more solid the platform in the involvement stage, the more successful the next stages are likely to be.

Leaving

BUILD A RAFT

As decisions are made and the leaving process begins, remember that now the orientation is to the future, and events seem to move faster and faster. Intentionally planning spaces to think together as a family, make checklists, check on progress, and ask questions is like creating airholes on a frozen Arctic ocean for mammals to breathe. Anticipating the "tunnel vision" of being in motion helps to take a wide look around and make sure everyone is preparing. Parents need to address their children's issues developmentally, giving both responsibility and support where appropriate. It is now high time to build the RAFT we discussed in chapter 13. If you have internalized the RAFT process already, feel free to jump ahead!

Let's look at the RAFT from the parent's perspective. The following steps in the RAFT and the ensuing points are not an exhaustive list, nor are they a talisman to ensure a stress-free transition, but they are an effective way to prepare adults and children for the next destination on an international journey. When I talk with younger children, I encourage them to craft an actual raft for their trip, labeling the planks as we work on them and taking their raft for a test run in the tub or on a local pond. Some teens enjoy this too, especially if it involves a competition!

- **Reconciliation:** Ensure that relationships are healthy and repaired before leaving. Address and try to resolve conflicts. Ask for and give forgiveness; settling accounts well will prepare you for your new environment. Carrying unresolved emotional and interpersonal baggage with you into the new situation will only increase the difficulty of adjustment.
- **Affirmation:** Take time to thank people and be thanked and recognized for your part in the community. Make time for a "send-off" party with friends. If they don't initiate one for you, give one for them! Spend time sharing stories and reviewing accomplishments and growth experienced in your current setting. Demonstrate gratitude for those who shared your life.
- **Farewells:** Make time to say good-bye to people, places, even pets that were important to you while you were in this place. Help children make a list and follow through with visiting important people and places. Be prepared to give them some privacy with people and places as they desire. Children who move often may develop small rituals that help them with leaving, and we parents can encourage those or even help to create some for our children if it is the first time they are moving.

- **<u>Think Destination</u>:** Look ahead to who and what is coming up, what to expect, and when to expect it. Talk with your children about what they think will happen and help them keep expectations reasonable. Who will they see? Where will they stay? Tell them what the plans are so far and what is still unknown. Give them time to ask questions and to share concerns. Parents can help their children by looking up facts together on the destination city, finding out about activities, climate, places of interest and vacation opportunities. Looking forward to particular aspects of a new home can help relieve anxiety.

For the youngest children or those whose language needs to be more simplified, one of Michael's teaching staff in China, Dani Beth Barsalou, created the SHIP version to convey the main concepts as follows:

S —Saying sorry and I forgive you—Reconciliation
H —Heartfelt thanks for each other—Affirmation
I —It's time to say good-bye—Farewells
P —Plan for the new place—Think destination

Take a Treasure Box

It is common for children to have special items that mean a great deal to them as part of current life. Encourage your child to make a small "treasure chest" to take on his or her "raft." (It might include photos, a stuffed animal, trinkets, jewelry, or even natural objects like a stick or stones.) Older children may later be encouraged to bring an item or two that reminds them of the place they are leaving. Packing has limits, but your child will appreciate your support even if the item does not make sense to you. Thinking ahead and planning a little may save some last-minute desperation as a child can't find a special object in the final whirl of leaving.

Build Relational Bridges

Since belonging is so critical to wellness, people leaving and people being left can help each other by being intentional about whether and how a relationship will continue over distance. Helping our kids create a plan, such as Skyping with grandparents every week, or keeping up with a friend daily on Instagram, may need to be adjusted, but it creates a helpful framework. With family and close friends it can be helpful to have a conversation about the long-term plans and hopes of the family. Is repatriation expected? Will the family return to the same area? Are you planning to keep a residence in the area? Is there a geographically stable friend or family member who would be willing to host you on visits back to the area? Deployments for the military, appointments for the State Department, or assignments for some NGOs and businesses might be unpredictable, while other contracts and assignments are more stable or up to the family. While there may be few solid answers, it helps to chart the territory as far as you know it. Keep in mind that the bridge you are building is two-way, and one day you, or your children, may desire to traverse that bridge back into your passport country. What you, or they, will find in the way of relationships may depend on how well you construct and maintain that bridge.

On the far side of the move are the people with whom you are going to live, work, play, and perhaps worship. If the sponsoring organization will allow it or has already set it up, try to reach out to the folks on the other side as you are in the preparation stage. Their experience and knowledge are invaluable to you, and you may make a friend in the process.

> While heading to China for the first time, Michael and his wife, Kristen, read a touching testimonial from one of their future team members. They wrote back expressing their thanks for the insights and transparency and a friendship was born. Three months later, they moved into their "randomly assigned" apartment above their new friend, and the relationship continues to this day.

One sure-fire strategy for making new friendships in an overseas post is to ask the other expats what they would love from "home" that they can't find in their present location. You have to be careful, since sometimes the coveted items are difficult to transport. A Sierra Leonean friend working in Asia asked her newly arriving compatriots to bring "bonga," a pungent dried fish in the sardine family, which brought them some unexpected attention in Beijing customs.

Another source of connection is the expat and repat community online. Folks who used to live in the place you are headed are once again an excellent source of connection and information. You might, indeed, find a neighbor with an unexpected history by doing a simple Internet search.

Key areas for information gathering and preparation in the leaving stage include: educational opportunities, health (including dietary needs) and recreation, housing and transportation, communications (not only telephone and Internet but language and cultural styles), and basic knowledge of the legal and social system into which the family is moving. There are many available resources online, and they cycle and renew so quickly that taking time to list them here would be wasted space.

Plan for Educational Concerns

Taking extra time to think through and plan out the course of educating your children is time that will reward you well. Keep in mind also that education and development are much broader than "schooling" alone, and it is the role of parents to best advocate for and pursue what each of their children needs. The following are time-tested principles that will serve you well:

1. *Consider the end goal.* What are your expectations for learning? Are your goals for your children developmental, social, linguistic, cultural, academic, or all of the above? How do you prioritize those goals? Where will your

children pursue tertiary or higher education? What are the requirements of language and prerequisite study in those institutions? *Please go back and read the final two questions again.*

Time and again as an educator, Michael has witnessed students near or at graduation at loose ends. Sometimes the problem is figuring out their educational plan in conjunction with required military service. Sometimes the challenge is language related.

> Uwe is a German TCK who related his story that upon graduation from an American-based school in Taiwan (Chinese Taipei), his German wasn't strong enough for German university. His parents struggled with the reality that if he studied in the American school for high school, he would not be German. When he graduated, neither his Mandarin nor his Cantonese levels were compatible with university study in Taiwan or China. He didn't have any connections in the U.S. besides some of his school peers, but decided to apply and was accepted by a small liberal arts school that was impressed with his ToEFL score and decided to give him a chance. Uwe married an American woman and they returned to China to work, where he helped start two international schools. He is currently in Taiwan, having founded an organization for children with special needs. He says although his parents struggled with the decision about his education, they have never regretted it.

Considering the end goal of your child's primary and secondary education prepares you to "work backward," keeping the primary objectives in view so that planning and decisions remain in alignment.

2. *Understand your alternatives.* Are you seeking public education, private education, homeschool, correspondence school, online school in a group setting, or online school with an individual task orientation? All these options and more exist and some parents choose a combination of strategies. When it comes to developing your child, there are no wrong answers.

3. *Understand your child's learning styles and needs.* If your child has had or you suspect he or she needs educational testing, it is usually better to get that done before leaving your home area. If a new system affords what you feel is superior educational opportunities, it might be helpful to do a second round of assessments to compare. It is important not to do any educational or psychological assessments until adjustment has taken place (three to twelve months), as transition stress and language issues could skew results. (See the Resources at the end of the book for helpful organizations.)

4. *There is no perfect scenario that is right for every child.* Children are complex beings and may respond well to different types of schooling at different developmental stages and in varying circumstances. The best policy is frequent

interaction with them, good counsel from friends and educational consultants, and making judgment calls based on the best information one has.

5. *Know your sponsoring agency's and the host country's educational policies and laws.* For instance, homeschooling is illegal in Guatemala, Germany, and Albania, but while some countries allow private education or exceptions for expats, some do not and laws can change quickly. Some sponsors have strict rules about attending a particular school or may simply give or withhold incentives to encourage members. For instance, some Korean companies will offer more tuition assistance to their employees for particular schools based on the status of the school and tuition fees.

6. *Understand the educational philosophy of the country, culture, or system that your child will enter, particularly if you intend to use local schooling.* This might sound like common sense but many families have been surprised to find that grading, behavioral expectations, workload, behavior management, corporal punishment, conflict resolution, parent-teacher relationships, homework, work ethic, and progress reporting all have cultural overtones and values. Those differences can be stated or implied or be invisible. As principal of an American international school in China, Michael was not surprised that "American" had a very international flavor—this was true of many international schools. He found the atmosphere charged with an Asian sense of rigor even at an elementary level. However, he was surprised at first to find how strongly the Korean culture influenced the school's social structure and how a Confucian view of family and relationships impacted all aspects of school life. Only after a crash course with "old hands" staff and reading Jonathan Borden's classic Confucius Meets Piaget did he begin to understand and work more successfully with the implications.

Rebecca Grappo, founder and president of RNG International Educational Consultants, LLC, has some wise words for parents as they consider different educational options for their children:

> There are many important factors for parents to consider when selecting the right school for their child overseas. These factors might include the language of instruction, training of teachers, accreditation, safety concerns, curriculum, administrative supervision, proximity to home, transportation, disciplinary methods, classroom size, etc. But perhaps the most important factor is the focus on the fit and match for the student's individual learning, social, and emotional needs. Does this school have the kind of culture and atmosphere that will serve your child best? Is this a school that can meet your child's learning and social needs? Will he/she fit in? If so, then you are probably on the right path.

> If you feel any of your internal alarm bells going off, then it
> might be a signal that the school really isn't the best fit.[4]

When the considerations and planning are done, or the departure date arrives (the latter sometimes coming before the former), it is time to "batten down the hatches" and do the final checking to make sure the family "ship" is airtight. Before embarking, do a final check-through with family members for all the important details and communicate as thoroughly as possible how the process will go. Give children a chance to ask questions even when your answer is an honest, "I'm not sure; we'll have to see." There are many good resources online, including government websites addressing specific expat needs and specialized blogs tuned into the area where you are headed.

Transit

Remember now that the time orientation is future but the experience is present, as internal systems go on high alert: "What's next?" is the common question from children with variants like, "When will we . . ." When parents provide their children with a mental or physical map or list of events, it reduces the sense of being lost and reduces anxiety. Just because we told them something does not mean they are going to remember it through the journey. Children will take many of their cues from their parents, and if attitudes are positive, open, flexible, and good humored, the kids will often follow.

Children's needs are going to vary, but there are some basic things to remember. Using Maslow's hierarchy to plan could result in reminders like these:

- Normal food and sleep patterns are going to change and that can throw children off. Carrying a child's favorite snack can be a plus. Keep everyone hydrated and nap when you can.
- Weather along the journey may vary and clothes should be planned accordingly.
- Safety issues include preparing your kids to know what to do if they find themselves separated from Mom and Dad. Some parents assign each child to one adult or an older sibling.
- Providing copies of travel documents to each family member creates a backup.
- Giving each person an appropriate role in the trip nurtures a sense of belonging. And noting a "job well done" builds esteem.
- Having something engaging to do during the waiting periods can create a respite for everyone, from a small child's activity book to music, books, or cards.
- Planning for learning some geography, history, and culture of places along the way encourages growth.

- Appreciating art and architecture along the way can increase a sense of wonder.
- Cultivating an awareness for opportunities to be kind and helpful to others on the way can lift your own spirits too.

Whatever the specific applications, the point is that the process of thinking through the needs of children in a hierarchy puts an emphasis on what has to be prioritized and what can also be an aim that is enriching to all. Caring for basic needs can reduce the sense of chaos and anxiety that is normal in the transit stage.

Remember that this liminal, or in-between, space can include lots of varying emotions for all members of the family. Children may be processing grief during transit, especially in the quieter moments: sitting at the gate, after the plane takes off, or arriving at a hotel and settling in. Asking questions, acknowledging losses, being present or focusing on the child, and providing comfort all address the need of connection, safety, and belonging.

Entering

We like to think of the parent's role as a strong fence around the children, providing safety from without, boundaries from within, and space to explore. When a family arrives at the destination, one task of the parent is to increase the boundary of the fence in a way that is appropriate for the child and to do it incrementally as each child is ready for it.

> When Michael was eight years old his parents moved from Vermont, U.S., to Kijabe, Kenya. Even though his father was an adventurous outdoorsman, he was extremely cautious when they first arrived in their new home. He did not allow his four children to play in the field of long grass below the house because of concern about snakes. After setting up their rooms, Michael and his brothers got permission to flatten the grass using cardboard boxes as sleds in the sloping field under their father's watchful gaze. All went well, and before many days the three boys were roaming in the forest and over several square miles of the mission station. After some months in Kenya, with no snakes discovered, the story became something of a family joke until a neighbor moved into a nearby house and the young daughter discovered a pair of venomous mambas in her toy box.

Both parents and children benefit from mentors in the new setting! Knowing from old hands where and how to buy necessities, what is safe and what is not, and the basic knowledge that comes only from experience can even help build new friendships. Modeling dependence on mentors can be more difficult for some people, depending on personality and culture. For one Malaysian family, leaning into the community for help was natural.

> Our first encounter with a mentoring community was very helpful. One family provided our first meals, took us shopping, and gave us their number in case we needed any help, especially with language. Once we settled into Ulaanbaatar, a Canadian family in their second year in Mongolia helped us very much. I think they remembered what it was like! By Christmastime, our families were friends and we traveled to Harbin, China, together to visit the ice festival.

If there is not a mentoring-type program for children in the new setting, it is appropriate to ask human resources, the school counseling office, or member care providers for some help. We encourage parents to remind the children that this person does not need to be their best friend but a person who can answer their questions and instruct them on what is expected of them, what is happening in the culture, and how to avoid dangers or unnecessary risks, especially in the first year.

There is usually a period of marginality, and different children will cope in different ways. Some children will charge in and announce, to anyone who will listen, how great they are and the things they can do, and at the other extreme some children will not want to leave the house and will bury themselves in books, video games, social media, and small projects. Parents can act as wise guides to help kids find a middle ground. Once again this is a time when the family feels vulnerable and it is normal to proceed with caution.

Getting to know the geography, people, and culture of the new place is a major task for children, and parents can help by giving them tools, resources, and an appropriate amount of support. If parents enter in with a learner's posture, the children have a head start. A common acronym for entering into the new culture that David Pollock taught and Michael has revised is ROMEEEE (think "when in Rome, do as the Romans do"):

Research: Be a learner; use the Internet and local sources.
Observe: Watch what's going on and reserve judgment.
Mentor: Find someone to be a support and teacher.
Expect surprises: Treat the unexpected as adventures.
Explore: Don't hide or look for a way to escape; get out and try things.
Explanations: Look for the reasons behind what people do.
Enjoy: Make it play; have fun; laugh at yourself and with others.

There are many wonderful aspects to exploring a new environment and getting to know new perspectives and new people. There is nothing like firsts: eating your first delicious street food, seeing your first snowfall, getting caught in a tropical deluge in a tuk-tuk, or standing in awe at your first sight of an ocean or a high mountain range. At the same time, if the new things are startling or unpleasant, and come too quickly, high stress can result. Parents are the only ones who know the baseline for their children's behavior and hold the vital role of observer and initiator of intervention.

Some of the signs of high stress seen in infants are delayed development in language or other skills and milestones, increased fussiness, and regression to earlier stages. School-age children may show stress with attention deficit, "quick trigger" tempers, moodiness, secretive behavior, hostility toward peers, hyperactivity, insomnia, physical ailments like head and stomach aches, and underachieving in school. Adolescents may exhibit similar signs and additionally may have trouble studying and organizing themselves mentally, be unable to keep friends longer-term, regress into childhood conflicts with parents, or express feeling incompetent and inadequate in sweeping ways. Keeping track of your children's progression through the entering stage and balancing their growing autonomy with their need for support may mean creating spaces where the pressure is reduced and/or getting professional help for your children.

Reengagement

Time orientation in this stage is once again focused on the present. Modeling is probably the strongest teaching tool parents possess. When parents approach the new context with openness, trust, and acceptance rather than suspicion, fear, and prejudice, they create a strong climate to meet cultural differences, frustration, and tension with grace. If parents then choose to observe more rather than judge, to inquire and listen, rapport and understanding are the likely outcomes.

As parents it is important for us to ask our children how things are going, to listen to them with compassion, and even wait with our good advice until they are ready to listen to it. It will be normal for them to feel out of place, to wonder why they had to leave home, and to feel critical of the new culture. Patience with children's concerns and affirmation of held values that are supracultural go a long way toward helping them through the ups and downs of the adjustment cycle. *Expect this process to take a full year!*

Help your children to remember that you and they both are in a *process* of adjustment that is normal, if difficult at times; it will not last forever. Help them also to remember that they have much to learn as well as contribute, that adjusting takes time, and that they will benefit by deciding to be fully present and to get reinvolved in a new place, to take some positive risks, to make some new friends, to keep developing their unique gifts and talents, and to invest in the community around them. We as parents can walk alongside of our children as they seek the security of understanding and fitting in to the new culture and, in time, often quite short, new families find that they are the "stayers" and are able to help arriving families make a strong adjustment.

A powerful technique in making the adjustment into the new community is teaching children to tell their story. We all want to be known, and children have experienced a cutting off of their life-story line! Becoming storytellers takes practice. What are the most important points? How long should the story be in a particular setting? What parts of my story (and our family story) are public and what parts are private? Parents can work with their children as they learn to narrate the story of where they came from for a new audience. Dr. Rachel Cason is an ATCK using storytelling as a therapeutic tool as well as a community-building resource.[5] When children become tellers of their own story, they can also develop the empathy to listen to the stories of others. Both telling and listening are crucial to creating a continuation of a child's life story in a new setting.

Continuing and blending the new story with the old is just the right encouragement to value, celebrate, and cultivate both the home culture and the host culture—language, relationships, holidays, historical setting, etc. By doing this parents create a bridge that helps their child absorb the benefits from both "worlds." Modifying and adapting the excellent work of John W. Berry[6] in acculturation theory and Y. Y. Kim[7] in integrative communication, positive integration happens when both cultures are highly valued. Practically that means maintaining the first culture and pursuing relationships in the second that result in adopting new skills and cultural practices and values. If the host culture is

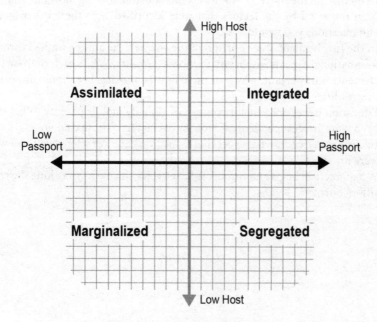

Figure 17–1: Host Passport Scale
©2017 John W. Berry. Adapted with permission

valued and pursued over, and at the expense of, the passport culture, the child will often be assimilated and may lose important aspects of identity and belonging. If the passport culture is valued and pursued over the host culture, the child will be segregated and lose out on many of the gifts of cross-cultural life. And if neither the passport culture nor the home culture is valued and pursued, the child will be marginalized, often feeling at home in neither culture.

Positive integration or adapting is the result of pursuing and cultivating the richness of both cultures in language, customs, and understanding. A well-supported and nurturing transition process creates the basis for internal well-being and positive interaction with others in the host and cross-cultural community.

Questions for Chapter 17

1. How might the "care model" proposed in the introduction make a positive impact on you or your family's transition? What aspects of care would you add?
2. What examples have you or your family experienced in the "flow of care"? What aspects were missing?
3. In mediating the move, or questions to ask before leaving, how has your life been impacted by the factors that were identified? Are there other factors and questions you would add?
4. In the Involvement Stage portion of the chapter, the author walked through foundational aspects important to mobile families. While each of these four elements is important, which of these four factors has been most important in your life?
5. Education issues are a major concern of globally mobile parents. What have been your greatest challenges? How have you faced those challenges?
6. In your experience, what aspects of transition care were done well and what were missing?
7. What practical helps and resources have been valuable to you along the transition journey?

CHAPTER 18

Bridging Transitions: How Organizations Can Help

In the thirty years of sending employees abroad, I have always known the financial loss, but I considered it part of the price of doing international business. Now, however, as I retire I am asking myself, "What was the cost in terms of broken families and destroyed lives of those for whom we have not sufficiently cared?"

—Business executive quoted by David Pollock[1]

The policies and the programs (or lack thereof) of sponsoring organizations weigh heavily in the equation. Even if parents and TCKs do everything we've suggested to maximize the TCK experience, CEOs and human resource managers of international organizations need to realize that their personnel policies have a profound effect on the employee's family—for example, a company that asks its employees with children to move in the middle of a school year or an organization that only pays for one type of schooling may be causing one or more of the children great anxiety and grief or loss of support for learning disabilities. At home, employers rarely have any influence on the schooling and living choices of their employees, but in cross-cultural situations the ramifications of corporate and organizational decisions filter down through the family.

Administrative decisions based solely on the interests of the international organization or the short-term bottom line of the international company are shortsighted. Of expatriate assignments, 30 to 85 percent will end in failure.

Failure is defined as early return or less-than-satisfactory performance.[2] Agencies should consider family needs as part of the corporate needs when planning to send an employee overseas for the reasons we outlined in the Overview for Part IV prior to chapter 17:

1. It's for the long-term benefit of the company.
2. Sound family-aware corporate policies are not only good for the family, but also good for the corporation or agency.
3. Appropriate care demonstrated through well-developed policy and procedures enhances the image of the organization. Lack of care tarnishes the image and decreases recruitment.
4. In some instances, competent and compassionate care is the embodiment of the organization message.

If you have not read the Overview for Part IV, please read it now so that this chapter makes sense as you read it.

In 2008, Robin Pascoe, a true pioneer in spousal and family issues for expatriates, did a "Family Matters!" survey of 656 expatriates living in sixty-two countries and representing forty-four countries. She wrote, "In serving family needs, it's not only a company's bottom line which is at stake in areas such as attracting and retaining good employees who are productive and loyal and will not walk out the door to the competition upon repatriation. The family system—the relationships between partners and their relationships with their children—is also put at risk when a deployment is handled badly or with indifference."[3]

When corporate or organizational decisions are made with families in mind, the family feels protected and cared for, a relationship that any organization should wish to cultivate as part of the organizational or corporate culture. With each family member having space to grow and develop, parents can make decisions only they are qualified to make—decisions that will help their children effectively use their cross-cultural heritage—and, in turn, the organization or corporation is able to retain these highly qualified parents as now well-contented and highly qualified cross-cultural employees.

When considering the needs of the mobile family, it is not necessary for the sending organization to take care of every detail at every level of need. The trick is discerning and communicating that the needs are understood, the circumstances of the overseas assignment can be predicted to some degree by research and experience, and that policies and procedures are in place to be supportive. Using the Transition Needs Table (figure IV-2) in the part IV overview of needs and care, organized around Maslow's hierarchy of needs and David Pollock's stages of transition, is one way to identify the needs of the family, who is responsible to meet those needs, where gaps exist, and who is responsible to fill those gaps. The Transition Needs Table becomes a tangible checklist as well as a communication tool between the bridge-building parties.

How Agencies Can Help Prior to the Overseas Assignment

In the "Family Matters!" survey, Pascoe compared the responses from the employees of international organizations and their families related to preassignment preparation. Two-thirds of the employees said they had no predeparture help offered. Only about 20 percent of the accompanying partners received help, 12 percent of the employed partners had predeparture training, and 6 percent had assistance for the entire family. Since nearly 70 percent of the respondents listed family reasons, including marital breakdown and children's education, as the top reasons for failed assignments, it is important for corporations and sponsoring organizations to work hard in this area of support for families.[4]

Schaetti notes:

> In all my travels, conversations, and research, I've discovered that the only people who had relatively easy identity encounter experiences related to growing up globally were those who had been introduced to the terms "global nomad" and "third culture kid" while still living overseas, or those who were offered repatriation services upon coming "home" and heard the terms that way (or at least subset terms like "missionary kid," "oil brat," "military brat," and so on).[5]

If an organizational culture cannot own the fact that by sending families overseas they are creating TCKs, they will be even less likely to have appropriate programs in place to reduce the impact of the challenges and to enhance the benefits of the experience. So the process begins by naming, recognizing, and appreciating the TCKs in an organization, not as a surprising by-product but as an expected and welcome benefit of the endeavor.

One of the most important steps an organization can take for its overseas employees is to *make sure the employees know the schooling options they will have well before the date of departure.* Corporations and organizations must make clear their policies and practices regarding educational costs and choices. Of those surveyed, 50 percent said they were *offered a trip during that period to go to the new location, see the schools, and consider their housing,* and they felt this preparation was extremely helpful.[6]

A second valuable step is to *implement a careful screening process for potential overseas employees.* The best people should be sought and vetted for excellent character, competence in their work, and experience in cross-cultural environment when possible, but at least trained in intercultural intelligence and understanding. "Screening in" is the second step, which requires understanding of best fit in the organization, including personality cohesion and maturity along with matching skills. Anyone working with children, of course, should be fully vetted, especially if they will be working in the realm of international education, refugee services, or development work where frequent moves may conceal harmful behavior.

A third step is to *plan a preassignment orientation*. This training should include tips for living in a new culture as well as for transition itself. Some international agencies are doing an excellent job of this, offering workshops for both the employee and the employee's spouse and children. Other agencies, however, still think only of the employee and make no preparation for the intercultural adjustments the employee's family will inevitably face. Such agencies should seek outside help from cross-cultural training consultants and organizations. A Shell Oil program of three days of predeparture training for expatriates to Saudi Arabia reduced the failure rate to 5 percent, and a six-day program reduced it to 1.5 percent.[7]

Finally, organizational managers need to gather information on how often and why personnel are transferred to new locations and to look for ways to reduce mobility, especially when families include early adolescents. Since many challenges of the TCK experience are so closely tied to high mobility, administrators must look for ways to minimize the frequency and severity of the transition cycles. For example, do embassy personnel change posts every two years because of staffing needs or security reasons, or is it simply tradition? Similarly, when a business decides to send a person overseas, or a mission agency decides to offer incentives for early retirement, is it essential that the employee relocate in the middle of the school year? Sometimes moves can't be avoided, but other times, with creative thinking, perhaps they can either be avoided or their consequences can be mitigated. Simple matters like examining the options for moving a family during a school vacation or after a child graduates can make all the difference as to whether a family thrives or barely survives in a cross-cultural lifestyle.

How Agencies Can Help during the Third Culture Experience

> Why have international schools worldwide been slow to establish the kinds of programs necessary for dealing with the issues described? Why are there so few comprehensive transition programs when the issues at stake are so clear and pervasive?
>
> Grief. The word makes us uncomfortable. We are biologically designed to deal with grief over the course of a lifetime. Mobility puts the normal cycle of life into warp drive.
>
> —Dr. Doug Ota[8]

Both the organizations that do the sending and the international schools that do the receiving must do a better job of tackling mobility care issues. An agency's responsibility to the family's well-being doesn't end after the final plans for departure are made or good-byes are said. To increase a family's chances of success abroad, the agency should have a plan in place that includes the following components.

1. *Have an entry team or a designated employee to welcome new employees on-site.* This was at the top of the list when Pascoe asked her respondents what the sending company or organization could do to help the families.[9] Each agency should have a formal plan for introducing new people to both the host and expatriate community as quickly as possible. Newcomers need to be introduced to local contacts for business as well as for the practical issues of life that long-time residents take for granted. We know of one young couple who went overseas and, after their initial welcome at the airport, were left on their own to figure out how to get their driver's licenses, find someone to install a phone, and even locate a doctor when a family member became sick. The problem was that the home office assumed that families in the overseas branch would take care of orienting new arrivals, but nobody had a formal (or informal) plan in place. Sometimes people are assigned to a post where they are the only employees from their home country. Those from the local culture may work hard to make the newcomers feel welcome and introduce them to local customs and stores, but other expats know about things like which of the local products can substitute for what they used at home. They might think to explain that a siren going off in bad weather means a tornado approaching. Local residents are so accustomed to these things that they don't think to explain.

2. *Help employees evaluate schooling options using the compiled list put together before departure.* Agencies should never insist on one particular method of schooling for their families; parents must have the freedom to consider each child's personality and needs. Agencies must also take into account the additional costs of education for expatriate children. Part of the employee's salary and benefits should include helping with those costs. In the home country, educational expenses for children are rarely discussed when negotiating a job contract, but schooling is often a complex and costly issue for expatriates.

3. *Establish a flexible leave policy.* Policies for leave vary from agency to agency. Some insist their employees remain onsite for four years, followed by a one-year home leave. Others have a cycle of sending people overseas for eleven months, then home for a month. Between those two ends of the spectrum lie other alternatives. There are pros and cons to each—both for the sponsoring organizations and the families. Wise administrators are willing to negotiate mutually beneficial leave packages if the standard policy for that organization doesn't work for a particular person or family.

4. *Make provision for children who are attending school in the home country to visit parents during vacations.* Traditionally, many sponsoring organizations have

paid for TCKs to return home for vacations if they were away for schooling through secondary school, but once those children returned to their home culture for university, those benefits ended. It's during those post-secondary years, however, that many major life decisions are made, years when parental support and guidance are crucial. Many organizations lose valuable employees whose children are at this critical life crossroads; many employees would rather resign than be separated from their children for long periods of time—particularly if the parents are in a situation where they can't afford to pay personally for frequent trips.

There is a fairly simple answer. Paying for children who are attending school in the home country to visit their parents for vacations should be a normal benefit for those working with international organizations. That policy change alone would likely prolong the careers of many employees and go a long way toward reducing many of the most challenging aspects of this globally mobile lifestyle.

5. *Create policies that reflect an understanding of TCK experience and needs.* Support re-entry seminars, transition coaching, mentoring programs, and gap year programs. If your organization has not done so, expand the resources available to families whose children have left home to attend college. The difference between retaining and losing valued employees may be simple support at critical junctions like starting college.
   a. Give leave time to settle young adults in the passport/university country.
   b. Pay or help with travel expenses for the student and the parents.
   c. Consider sabbatical time for long-term employees.

6. *Support international community efforts to provide ongoing expatriate family services.* Factors contributing to the relative success or failure of an overseas assignment include the degree to which a sponsoring organization provides ongoing assistance abroad. Barbara Schaetti, a consultant to the international expatriate community whom we quoted earlier, suggests that the challenge for a company lies in how to provide such assistance in every one of its international locations. She notes that, historically, most have relied upon their network of expatriate spouses. Support has been limited to paying membership dues to international women's clubs and contributing funds to international school parent/teacher association programs. Some companies are taking a more proactive approach and contracting with International Employee Assistance Programs (IEAPs) to provide expatriates with access to confidential mental-health services on demand and provide Internet-based resources. Still others sponsor events such as Families in Global Transition, where global nomads and those who work with them meet for continuing exploration of how best to support globally mobile families.

7. *Create or support programs for TCK development and adjustment.* Sometimes the school or expat community has to multitask in countries where sports teams, youth groups, clubs, libraries in the primary language, and programs like driver's training are limited or nonexistent. Innovative companies and

organizations that address resource gaps for children and teens will benefit on multiple levels.

8. *Help families prepare for repatriation and organizational reentry.* Not only do companies lose valuable employees during the posting abroad, but disappointing statistics indicate that 10 to 60 percent of the overseas workforce will quit the company within a year of returning.[10] Repatriating, or returning home, is frequently more difficult than moving abroad in the first place. Many, especially corporate employers, have been out of the loop while they were overseas. Someone else has filled the old job, their career is off track, and the company doesn't know what to do with them or how to use the international and cross-cultural skills they've acquired. Also, while overseas these employees may have had a good bit of autonomy as decision-makers or leaders, but at home their position is subordinate and one study of 750 companies found that 61 percent of returning managers felt they could not use the knowledge they had gained. No wonder the repatriate turnover is 25 percent, or double what it is in the passport country![11]

Unfortunately, agencies and employees who prepared well for the original cross-cultural transition may forget to prepare equally carefully for the transition home. Ideally, before the family leaves the host country, a formal or informal briefing should be provided by people who have experienced this type of transition before. Families should be reminded it is as important to build the RAFT (discussed in chapter 13) during this transition home as it was for any prior transition. The military has a great model for preparing both the deployed spouse and the family at home before they are reunited. Before the reunion, all members of the family—the service person at the place of deployment and the family members at home—go through training on the common challenges reuniting families often face to try to help them prepare better for the inevitable readjustment they will face as a family, despite the joys of being reunited.

9. *Offer reentry seminars for both parents and TCKs soon after repatriation.* Several organizations sponsor week-long seminars every summer for TCKs who are returning to their home country, and some agencies hold debriefing seminars for the adults. Recently, some groups have begun offering programs for the entire family. Some agencies include support for their TCKs to go to reentry camps offered in different places around the globe.

How Agencies Can Help Their TCKs in the Long Term

> The Jack Welch of the future cannot be like me. I've spent my entire career in the United States. The next head of GE will be somebody who has spent time in Bombay, in Hong Kong, in Buenos Aires.[12]
>
> —GE CEO Jack Welch

Think of how advantageous it would be for a company or organization if these children brought their cross-cultural skills back to it when they are ready for their own careers. Facilitating connections between TCKs and ATCKs and their past is one way to pave that road. A majority of TCKs grow up with a strong sense that friends from the sponsoring agency or their international school are a part of their extended family. This group and way of life become part of their very identity. It may be the one place outside their family where they have a deep sense of belonging. They want and need to stay connected to this support system in some way even when life takes them in a different direction.

Here are some ways administrators can play a vital role in helping TCKs who have grown up in their communities continue to thrive—ways that can also help in the healing process for those ATCKs who still need help adjusting.

1. *Support an alumni newsletter, blog, or Facebook site.* A growing number of agencies and international schools already help their TCKs and ATCKs maintain a sense of connectedness by giving them an alumni page on their websites. These forums not only distribute information, they also give opportunities to discuss relevant issues from their past, to offer suggestions for the present, and to stay a part of the "family."
2. *Utilize the experience of TCKs and ATCKs.* It's ironic to see an organization bring in "experts" about a particular subject or country while ignoring the wealth of knowledge and experience of their own ATCKs.

> One ATCK sat through a meeting where a medical facility to be established in Brazil—modeled after one in the United States—was being described and discussed. She knew from the beginning that it wouldn't work because the philosophical concepts on which the project was based were very different from those that shaped Brazilian thinking. When she attempted to raise a few questions, she was disdainfully put down. Three years later, after vast sums of money had been spent on the project, it folded—a complete failure.
>
> In New Zealand, an organization asked Ruth to speak about using the resources of the ATCKs in their organization. She asked how many ATCKs there were in the audience and invited them to come forward and form a panel. As they fielded the questions from fellow employees, Ruth never had to answer another question. The fact was they had this resource right among themselves and never thought to tap into it. The ATCKs themselves seemed surprised at what they had to offer.

Agencies that honor and leverage the knowledge and experiences of their ATCKs will tap into a vital source of insight and potential growth.

3. *Own and apologize for past organizational mistakes.* When poor administrative decisions from the company or sponsoring agency have caused suffering, acknowledging the fact and making appropriate changes can initiate healing. Some policies on relocating families, for example, have caused needless separations. Some trusted and vetted caregivers in boarding schools have done harm. The damage may not have been the result of willful actions, but they did happen. Even when those who made the decision have since left the organization, it helps the employees—and the TCKs who were hurt by those policies—to know that the system itself is taking responsibility and that someone representing that system or organization is willing to apologize for past mistakes, take preventative steps against future harm, and, where needed, offer restitution or help with counseling.

4. *Support a TCK's "journey of clarification."* Some agencies already offer a trip back to the host culture during or immediately after university for all of their TCKs who grew up overseas, even if the parents are no longer abroad. As mentioned before, going back to their roots and validating past experiences helps TCKs move on more smoothly to the next stages of life. But when the agency itself is willing to pay for such a trip, the journey becomes even more healing. TCKs receive the important message that they do, indeed, belong to a community that cares for them—not one that discards them at a certain age with no concern for the impact that growing up as a member of that overseas community had on them. It's another way of validating the value of their heritage and inviting them to build on it rather than disown it.

5. *Consider the long-term affiliation of ATCKs to the company, organization, or school.* Much can be gained on both sides of the equation when a "system identification" is a positive and affirming relationship. When an army brat, MK, DipKid, oil rig monkey, NGO kid, or international school grad can say they "loved the experience and wouldn't trade it for anything," the statement is a win-win for former dependents and their overseas agency. Invite ATCKs to reunions, conferences, think tanks, and panels. Consider incentives to bring them back for internships and potential job opportunities. Give them the opportunity to belong and to contribute. Even if they decline, the offer is a gift.

6. *Seek qualified TCKs and CCKs for positions in global mobility, member care, and human resource departments.* One far-reaching study reported that in 450 companies, only 11 percent of HR managers had worked abroad, and most had minimal understanding of the unique challenges or benefits involved. The result is lost opportunity and strategic development. Direct recruitment of experienced transnationals can reverse the flow to positive growth.[12] The fact that the study from *Harvard Business Review* is eighteen years old and still being cited suggests that an update in the research is warranted.

In conclusion, international organizations must face the fact that they bear responsibility not only to their individual employees, but also to their families once they begin to give employees international assignments. Too often administrators have blamed failures totally on the person who didn't succeed rather than looking at the part their agency or corporate policies and decisions may have played in the matter. We're grateful for the growing awareness among companies and sponsoring organizations of their role in helping cross-cultural families be successful.

Expanding Our Vision

There may be sweeping changes coming to the realm of TCK care. Safe Passage kicked off an introductory conference at The Hague in the spring of 2017; the Global Member Care network continues to grow and create networks for resource hubs, with close to 2,000 members on their Facebook page; and the international mental health and the relocation and transition service sectors are growing rapidly. Human resource personnel from different corporations and various human resource agencies have attended and participated in the Families in Global Transition conferences. The World Bank has a highly active department for family care. Certainly the military, in certain countries at least, has long promoted family care. In some countries, the foreign service also has support systems in place for their families.

A simple reality: While family has the greatest impact on every child's life, the community and the various organizational systems in the community also impact the child directly and indirectly. Real people decide on laws, policies, and procedures that affect the lives of colleagues and employees. It's important that in all arenas they consider the human factors along with efficiency and profitability, which is good not only for the individuals, but also for the community, the organization, and all those under the influence of their decisions. Consider the following story and how organizational policy, including school policy, might have impacted Marnini (not her real name).

> Marnini's parents (black African dad and white American mom) met working for the same organization in Kenya. Their marriage resulted in both of them being let go as a matter of policy. The family moved to Tanzania for work and Mom worked at an international school. Dad's work took him to the U.S., while Mom stayed in Tanzania to honor her contract. Marnini stayed with her. When Marnini's mother joined her father, the school allowed Marnini to finish high school, living with a school staff/faculty family who became her legal guardians, and becoming a big sister to a newly adopted girl. Repatriating to the U.S. for college far from home, Marnini was "adopted" by a local family who provided transition information, practical assistance, and

a welcoming home. All along the way official decisions and support or lack thereof impacted Marnini's life. In her own words:

"As of now I am torn between two cultures, two races, three nationalities, and three families. A part of me fits perfectly into each of these groups, but there always remains the rest of me as a reminder of what doesn't. My mother is white and my father is black, and I am a half-caste (it's the first word that I learned to describe someone of mixed race and since then has become a fixed point in my identity; if I am nothing else, I am for sure a half-caste). As I got older, when I would talk to my Tanzanian friends about their home lives, I would immediately know what they were talking about. I knew what it was like to grow up with African parents, but at the same time I would talk with Americans and be able to relate to their home lives as well. I've always been caught in the middle.

When my parents were cut off from the organization, we were African. My mom didn't really talk to her side of the family much, and there were no partners to visit because, despite the projects my parents had done, we weren't [officially part of the organization]. Why not, though? I mean my parents definitely felt called to [the work], they had a passion for that kind of work, so why not turn that into a paid position instead of struggling to fund projects as well as a family?

When I started to live with [the school staff family], I started to go to the [organizational] monthly meetings. And, boy, was that a tough crowd. I finally began to understand how my parents felt. They all looked at me like I didn't belong there. I mean, I was only supposed to be living there for a year, so they didn't really take the time to get to know me."

Before college, Marnini's birth parents divorced, creating more chaos as she was leaving for college:

"A friend's parents started parenting me shortly after my family splintered apart. They have become two of the most influential people in my life. I love them with all my heart. They were the ones to move me into my dorm room, they are who I call when I have questions about insurance, and they are who I have spent most of my holidays and breaks with since I have been in college. In a very deep way I feel a part of and connected to their family, even though I'm not really.

"So, there you have it, three families, two cultures, two races, and three nationalities, but one God. He is the only one with whom I completely belong. And that's a tough pill to swallow. I have spent my entire life (all eighteen years of it) searching for a people to belong to, a place to call home, and all I have ultimately come up with has been disappointing, painful, sometimes including betrayal—empty and lacking. Nothing has been able to fill that hole in my heart, to satisfy my desire to feel safe and known."

Noting the organization roles in Marnini's complicated story both garners praise and raises concern over how individuals are impacted in the short and long term by policies and practices. Did Dad's company consider the children in the international move to the U.S.? Did Mom's school counsel the couple and provide options? Do organizations have practices to welcome nontraditional dependents? Do Marnini and others like her fall through the cracks because the categories of their experience haven't existed before? Do college personnel have training and preparation to meet the needs of students like Marnini? Certainly parents own the most responsibility for care and grounding, yet how might supportive and flexible organization structures have helped stabilize and root development? We hope these kinds of questions will lead to more research and stronger family-friendly practices.

Questions for Chapter 18

1. In what ways do you wish "member care" or "family support" or whatever name your group calls it had been involved in your life, and/or in what ways was it involved in a helpful way? What kind of help from your sponsoring agency would have been beneficial to you and your family during or before an overseas assignment?

2. If you grew up overseas, were you aware of organizational support for you or your family? If not, do you think your current "self" might be different if you had received it then? Explain.

3. What more can be done by corporations and organizations who send employees overseas to ensure the physical, emotional, social, and spiritual well-being of their children growing up in international contexts?

4. Can anything be done for corporate employees and organizational members who don't want help/oversight but whose children might need it?

5. Some corporations and organizations now offer debriefing and if necessary counseling on reentry for the children. But what about the next years? When should their care stop?

6. If you went to an international school or boarding school overseas, explain how the administration and teachers helped you with your transition to school and getting ready to leave. Is there anything else you wish they had done?
7. If you are in charge of member care or an HR director, what ideas did this overview and chapter give you for better supporting your families stationed globally?

CHAPTER 19

Where Do We Go from Here? (Part I)

by Ruth E. Van Reken

The Little Ones

Lord, who are these little ones?
The faces of panic staring out
From an overturned train.
Faces pressed against a window,
Pressured by the unseen faces behind.
All wanting to be free
But no way to free themselves.

While they wait
We do our things,
Keeping our own safe and dry
Preparing rescue paths—
But in the fixing and the preparations
We forget that there are real people trapped in there.

We cannot hear their screams
For the windows are closed
And we are busy.

But when we remember to look—
The faces stare back.
Gaunt cheeks, hopeless eyes

Fingers trying to get the window down
That can only be released from outside.

Who are they?
Now lifted out one by one by one—
Will the flow never cease?
But look around—
How do they get to safety?

We need a human chain
But we're still so busy getting ready—
Putting our emergency plans in place

We forget the people.

Whoever these little ones are
They need help.
Forgive me for my preoccupations
With protecting me and my own.
Send me forth with urgency and clarity
To lift them from this potential prison of death.

But send the rest of the laborers
To pick them up and carry them off to
True Safety.
I cannot do it all—but let me see
What I can—and should.

Ruth E. Van Reken, January 1990

In 1990, I (Ruth) woke up one morning with a clear vision of a train wreck and grabbed a pencil to write these words before I lost the picture. What did it mean? What did my life have to do with train wrecks? And then I knew.

In 1984 I had done some journaling trying to understand my TCK story, and when it became published as *Letters I Never Wrote* (now *Letters Never Sent*), I began to hear from people all over the world. Many thought they were the only ones who had cried when the lights went out at boarding school. They didn't know others had struggled through reentry, or felt the loss of their host worlds as a death experience. Phone calls came ostensibly to order the book, but two hours later the person was still telling me his or her story. What was going on? My heart was filling up both with sorrow for so much grief flowing in, but also with a burning sense that "somebody needs to do something." But who? What?

I knew it couldn't be me. In 1990 I was (and still am!) a suburban housewife in Indianapolis, Indiana, U.S. Besides, my education was in nursing rather than any of the social sciences like psychology or anthropology or sociology. Surely, surely there were far more capable folks who could offer much more effective help than I ever could.

Of course, there were the academics who were studying TCKs—Ruth Hill Useem, Ann Baker Cottrell, Richard Downie, Kathleen Jordan, and others. Their work was vital or we wouldn't even have known there was a topic or name for our group. But Ruth Useem told me herself that her job was not to apply it, but to study it.

I knew Dave Pollock was trying to reach as many as he could by spending countless weeks and months each year circling the globe, speaking to TCKs, their parents, educators, and organizational administrators. Many ATCKs had their "Aha!" moment at one of his seminars. But the response from organizations and even, at times, parents was slow. Some wondered if he was, in fact, creating the TCK Profile simply by talking about it! Norma McCaig spent her retirement money to bring together the first Global Nomads conference in Washington, D.C., in 1988 because few believed this topic really mattered enough to help sponsor her.

But again—what to do? I had no idea. Any ideas to reach out felt like drops in a bucket compared to the need. It seemed too big.

And then I woke up one morning and saw the train. How? I can't explain. But however the picture came, I saw it lying on its side, tipped off the tracks. People were panicked inside and trying desperately to get out. For some reason, however, the windows could only be opened from the outside. As those further back in the crowd of folks in each car pushed those who were at the windows, those in the front had their faces flattened against the glass and panic was setting in.

I looked at the faces in front of me and then I looked behind me. Who was coming to help? Surely someone saw this mess. Behind me on a small hill, all the emergency crews were getting organized—but no one was coming to open the windows. I felt a bit of panic myself, but then realized, *Well, I don't know how to do the rest, but I can open the windows.* And so I went to the first window and opened it. As people streamed out, I went to the next one, and the next one until the end. They all ran past me looking for safety. I don't think they even saw me, but I watched and my heart was glad. They were safe!

Then I knew the meaning of the vision. For sure I couldn't figure out how to do all the "big stuff" needed for those who were contacting me almost daily, but maybe I could open some windows.

And so we started, believing each phone call, each email, each personal encounter somehow mattered. Dave Pollock continued his speaking tours, Norma organized as many Global Nomads groups on campuses as she could and wrote her articles, Barbara Schaetti did the first Ph.D. on TCK/global nomad identity and began her seminars, and the momentum began to grow. Each person opened another window for someone, and look what has happened. A topic that began over fifty years ago by two researchers who were initially studying something else has grown into a worldwide phenomenon. Why? Because each person did what he or she could.

So where *do* we go from here? None of us really knows, but we do know that for all that has already been done, there is an amazing sense that, in truth, we have only just begun. There are still people waiting to be released from wherever they feel imprisoned by feelings or responses they don't understand from their own cross-cultural experience.

Back to the question: Where do we go from here? What is left to be done? What new insights, ideas, or research might we need or desire?

As a beginning, I see three areas where we can move ahead.

- Continuing the research going on for globally mobile youth.
- Connecting with other communities of fellow CCKs.
- Raising awareness that "hidden diversity" needs to be recognized along with more-traditional forms of diversity.

Expanding Our Vision for TCK Research

There are many new academic researchers in place now to carry on where past academicians have left off. Momo Podolsky researched Japanese TCKs early on and compared the studies in Japan to what we were learning about TCKs in the West. Anastasia Lijadi, Ph.D, is a current researcher interviewing and studying TCKs during the years this experience is forming them, not retroactively as we are perhaps more prone to do. Rachel Cason, Ph.D., emphasizes the importance of hearing the story in her studies. Katia Mace has done brilliant research on globally mobile youth as a Ph.D student in England, and there are countless more. Danau Tanu is a Japanese Indonesian ATCK who finished her Ph.D. work on the Asian TCK experience and is becoming a major voice for examining the nontraditional ways children are growing up internationally. See Appendix C for some of her growing thoughts, but here are a few for starters . . . .

> My mobile upbringing is typical among young people who attend international schools and who are popularly referred to as "Third Culture Kids (TCKs)." Much has been said of their experiences of the many childhood hellos and goodbyes as well as the cultural displacement that comes with an intensely mobile lifestyle, and the impact that these experiences have on a child's sense of identity and belonging.
>
> But there are many aspects of my experiences of mobility and English-medium international schools that are missing from the literature on privileged international mobility and schooling. My own experiences of mobility and the gap that I felt between my home culture and that of the

international schools I attended raise questions about the
cultural hierarchies embedded within the social worlds of
so-called cosmopolitan elites and the way these hierarchies
shape the way children interact with one another across
difference.[1]

Myra Dumapias, current CEO of TCKidnow.com and daughter of a Filipino diplomat, concurs that the past writings on TCKs have not included enough
perspectives on different economic and class differentials within the traditional
TCK community. We quoted from her thoughts in chapter 2, and here are a few
more thoughts.

In actuality, it all depends on the context of everything and
class experience really is in relation to one's contexts. I say
contexts as plural because there is the context of the passport or sending country's wealth, the context of the host
country's wealth and the context of the family's wealth.
How all these contexts interact together, and the individual's
response or attitude towards privileges, luxuries or conve-
niences or lack thereof, is the individual's class experience.
. . . On a more macro level, when you consider the varying
cost of living standards around the world and the salaries
that career diplomats have per their passport countries,
there is a wide range of class experiences for career fields
that are global. I have heard similar stories for the engi-
neering and other fields.[2]

Distinctiveness

John Barclay[3] did his Ph.D. work focusing on Korean and Indian missionary kids
(MKs). Here is a quote from a symposium where eleven Asian MKs gathered to
make a statement to their parents' organizations explaining how they also had
"extra stuff" to deal with from the traditional TCK literature.

We are ethnically Asian, often influenced by at least three
cultures—our home culture, multiple fields, the Western
culture, and a plethora of religious backgrounds. While we
recognize and value our strong family and socio-cultural
heritage, we struggle with the expectation to uphold the innate obligation to show respect to elders, and adhere to the
"save-face" culture so as not to disrupt the status quo or
bring shame to the family. Asian MKs also face the challenge of maintaining their mother tongue, returning to
monocultural contexts for some, and fitting into predeter-
mined roles.[4]

Isabelle Min leads the way in developing a network for TCKs in Korea and at Families in Global Transition (FIGT) conferences. She explained how Korean TCKs are judged based on what language they learned while overseas as TCKs and how this complicates their reentry process.

> While I had spent fifteen of my early eighteen years of life living on five continents, my Korean was fluent when I repatriated in the early 1980s in high school. I had no idea how different I had become as the result of Italian, American, British, and international schooling. Little did I know I would soon be the subject of envy among my classmates as English fluency was, and still is to this day, a key competency in Korean society.
>
> Korean TCKs' visibility combined with self and social pressure and bewildering, mixed messages around English leads some to simply bury their past and numb their senses by focusing on their privileges. As for those ATCKs who repatriate without English, such as the case of a missionary kid who grew up in Mongolia with Mongol and Chinese, repatriation is met with social dismissal. This young man wrote me sharing his fear of never making it into the mainstream of Korean society despite his multiple efforts.
>
> ATCKs' initial yearning to conform to their perceived parental expectations eventually conflicts with those values instilled during Western academic upbringing, frequently disconnecting them from their parents and society at large.[5]

So these thoughts are just the tip of the iceberg. We haven't looked here at what might be specific for African TCKs, or South or Central American, or from other Asian countries than those listed above—let alone all the other groups of CCKs around the world. As so many countries urbanize or major cultural shifts occur, the domestic TCK is surely one group that deserves much study as well. As you can see, there are many windows still to open. Ruth Useem was right when she said that concepts will grow and change with time.

And yet, despite all of these specific differences among the groups of TCKs, there is something in the human story of those mentioned above and all whom they study that transcends those differences. It seems the basic issues of finding a sense of identity and issues related to loss still resonate with the hearts of TCKs of every nationality, class, and economic status. If anything, the previously unrecognized factors these researchers talk about appear to intensify some of the core issues we have discussed in this book of the longing many TCKs express to find a place of belonging and deal with previously unrecognized losses and grief. We look forward to all that is discovered by these and many others who are now officially and unofficially researching this topic of children who grow up globally mobile. Our TCK tent is large and expanding as the story grows and grows.

As before, the hope then is to not keep this new wisdom for ourselves alone, but to share with others what we learn about commonality of the human experience that goes beyond our traditional ways of dividing ourselves into "us/them" groups. It would be wonderful to move beyond being the individual prototype citizens Dr. Ward predicted to being a "prototype group"—a place where we and others can see that it is possible to connect in meaningful ways with one another in this way.

Expanding Our Vision for Other CCKs

I am excited for the many new findings researchers are discovering for internationally mobile youth. But I keep wondering if other groups of CCKs (in addition to the domestic TCKs just mentioned) know they belong to this larger group of others who have also grown up cross-culturally in some way. There is no question by now that those who grew up in any one or any number of CCK communities (chapter 3) have connecting points with TCKs and other CCKs. How can they discover that they belong to this growing new normal of individuals raised cross-culturally? Might they also have an "Aha!" moment that *I am not alone; I'm not crazy; I do fit*? And then to see the gifts of their experience that they can use to the good of themselves and many others instead of being caught in the challenges?

That is my dream as I watch the world tumble and change around us—that those growing up without the traditional anchors and mirrors in their lives can find their place and sense of belonging in the bigger story of those also growing up in this new normal of growing up cross-culturally. How can they too celebrate being "all of the above" instead of being forced to choose identity based on old standards?

Again, the job seems too big as the mass of this group grows, but if we go back to one step, one window at a time, there is joy to see that some are not waiting for a rescue but taking their own steps to get to where they need to and can go. And many are doing so from the "other" circle of CCKs, not even ones we traditionally named.

LESSON FROM THE DEAF WORLD

Oya Ataman is my first star for that. She is an example of someone who figured out for herself how the TCK principles related to her mostly invisible (to the rest of the world) community and culture. Be as inspired by her story and what she has done as I am.

I first met Oya in 2014. She is a hearing child of Deaf Turkish immigrants to Germany. Somehow Oya found out I would be in Berlin, and emailed me to ask if we could meet for an hour or so. Oya explained that when she picked up a copy of the original TCK book, she put it down after the first chapter believing it didn't apply to her. But when she saw the CCK model in the revised edition, things clicked, even though we had not listed any disabilities in our CCK examples. I was intrigued and happily agreed to meet. On the appointed day and hour, I took the elevator from my room to the lobby. As I got off, I saw a beautiful young lady looking around for someone. We sat and she told me her story.

> I grew up among many cultures because my parents were Deaf immigrants. There are distinct Deaf cultures—ones that have their own language, ways of doing things, and worldview that are very different from the hearing world. I am part of both. My parents, who were Turkish, immigrated to Germany before I was born. Because they were poor, however, my mother went back to Turkey to give birth, and then she went back to Germany, leaving me with my grandmother until I was five. It was not uncommon for Turkish immigrants to have children brought up by grandparents in the old country, but in the case of my parents it was also taken for granted by everyone that they, being Deaf, would not do a good job of raising children because they couldn't teach them to speak. Nevertheless, I picked up sign language from my parents and other relatives.
>
> At any rate, I lived there until I was five with my parents frequently visiting but then disappearing again. I had no way to contact them while they were away. When I moved to Germany, I was the only hearing person in the family. I learned German within a year and became the family interpreter and manager. When I talked on the phone with officials they would think they were talking to a grown-up. Back then, discrimination against Turks and Deaf people was open and abundant and I heard and understood all of it.[6]

I felt blown away as I spent the afternoon learning about a world and its people of whom I had previously known nothing, so had not thought about as another cultural entity (nor mentioned in the book!). But Oya had!!! So many pieces of the TCK story seemed to fit her situation. At the same time, I felt growing excitement that what we had learned from the TCK story *per se* really could be helpful in giving language and understanding to others with various types of cross-cultural childhoods . . . even groups I had never considered or known anything about! In the time since our meeting, Oya has started an amazing blog where she also explores not only the circle related to her CCK circle concerning those who have grown up like her—hearing children of Deaf parents—but also the growing cultural complexities many in her community face. In our ongoing interactions, Oya explained to me that, "We say Deaf world and mean Deaf culture world and when we use the adjective "Deaf" we capitalize it in order to make the point that this world is as real as a German, French, Nigerian, Brazilian, Mexican, or Kazakstanian cultural world is for those who are part of them."

APPLYING CCK LESSONS FROM THE PAST TO THE PRESENT

Eva László-Herbert is my second star for someone who opened my mind to previously hidden types of CCKs/ACCKs. She is a professional conference interpreter, translator, and writer who has lived in four countries and speaks six languages. When Eva gave the closing keynote at the 2012 Families in Global Transition conference, a whole world of new and lasting thinking happened for me—and likely all who were there.

The title of Eva's talk was "The Building Blocks of Me, Myself and I When Life Takes You Places—Identity vs. Nationality vs. Citizenship in the Global Village." She shared her story of how she grew up behind the Iron Curtain in Romania and is the daughter of an ethnic Hungarian and an ethnic German. Eva pointed out how, from a formal point of view, they are all citizens of Romania. However, they are not Romanians—neither in their identity nor in their culture. Eva believes that, based on her experience, living in a country in which nineteen officially recognized minorities have lived together for centuries is much easier than being the only "other" in a monolingual, monoethnic state.

During her speech, Eva took her rapt audience through the history of her family, indirectly covering relevant parts of twentieth-century history in Central and Eastern Europe, eloquently showing how, in the course of a lifetime, the same person could have had four citizenships and lived under three or four political regimes without ever moving an inch. It was amazing and gave flesh and blood life to vague stories I had studied long ago in history classes. To me, these statements were key:

> Following WWI and WWII Europe was cut up and put together again several times; borders were moved and some new states emerged . . . . and whilst the citizenship of their inhabitants changed with every geopolitical patch-up, their nationality remained unchanged. Especially within the cultural and political landscape of what had formerly been the Austrian-Hungarian Empire, nationality and citizenship were and still are, to this day, two fundamentally different concepts. *Whilst citizenship is seen more or less as a formal rapport defining the duties and rights of an individual living on a particular territory related to the power in place, nationality is very much a matter of emotion, tradition, custom, heritage, and—ultimately—identity. It is only within the mental and geographical boundaries of monolingual and monoethnic states that one can afford the negligence*

> *to believe that citizenship and nationality can be used as
> synonyms.* [italics added] Many of present-day conflicts, big
> and small, stem from this key moment: when an individual
> is applied a label that does not match his or her identity.⁷

After hearing Eva give these historical thoughts, I met a high school student
born and raised in the United States who told me she was surprised when others
thought she was an "American." To me, that was a surprising statement in itself!
I asked, "Why is that?" "Because I'm Mexican." For her, her national identity had
nothing to do with citizenship. This young woman's parents were from Mexico,
and she speaks only Spanish at home. Like TCKs before her and the many CCKs
Eva describes, passport is no longer the defining word for a person's sense of nationality and emotional belonging.

Wow! I didn't realize people in my neighboring town in Indiana would be
essentially saying and feeling the same differentiation as what Eva had spoken
about in Europe. This young woman definitely distinguished between her sense
of nationality and citizenship.

Eva goes on to mention one more important reason we need to sort out this
cultural conundrum:

> To give but one example: Belgium has the highest number
> of youth fighting along ISIS in the EU—although most of
> these are Belgian citizens, they are the sons and daughters
> of (inter alia) Moroccan immigrants, who still define them-
> selves as Moroccans albeit being born and raised in Belgium.
> To explain it in overly simplifying terms: they feel excluded
> from their "Belgian" life, as many of the "native" Belgians
> still see them as the "others" and therefore [they] seek sol-
> ace in what is the "felt/perceived" home country they often
> know from family holiday visits, at best. Although both
> "old" and "new" Belgians are citizens of the same country,
> the great rip between old and new communities and eth-
> nicities sadly persists. Possibly also because no one ever
> thinks about WHY some Belgian citizens feel threatened and
> other Belgian citizens feel invisible in the country of their
> citizenship.

Seen through this lens, the question of citizenship vs. nationality becomes
not only interesting but also sobering. Sadly, the example Eva gives could be applied to many other situations where local people are surprised fellow citizens
would be carrying out terrorist acts against their shared country. Is it possible
bringing to the table some of the lessons TCKs have learned about embracing
a positive but more fluid identity through their experience covering multiple
country and cultural borders might be useful in addressing some of these important global issues?

If so, where do we go from here with other groups of CCKs? I envision joining all types of CCK communities (including "other"!) in some type of forum where the commonalities as well as the distinctives of each type of experience can be explored. In doing so, we could at least start and, hopefully, help CCKs of all backgrounds, all economic groups, all classes, with parents of any vocation, see and use with joy the gifts this life is offering them in our changing world, rather than being entangled and caught in a world of confused (multiple) identities. For these and more reasons I dare say: the time is ripe for a paradigm shift.

Expanding Our Vision for "Hidden Diversity"

One last place that needs more exploration. How do lessons from the TCK experience apply locally as well as globally? I confess I will be writing here from a totally U.S. American perspective as that is where I live and it's what I know, but I believe this relates to the stories from Oya and Eva. It's the issue of "How can we help people in every local community recognize the hidden diversity present among them as well as more traditional forms of diversity?"

Some years ago I realized I had no clue what the term *diversity* meant in the U.S. I thought *diversity* meant *difference*, including any kind of difference. In 2001 when an international company with local headquarters asked me to talk about TCKs through their diversity department, I tried to figure out the segue from my topic of TCKs to their theme of diversity and had an "Aha!" moment. If I changed the "hidden immigrant" label we used for TCKs to "hidden diversity," I could give them a title for my talk that matched their stated goals of diversity and inclusion! Since the date for the presentation was two days after 9/11, most of my intended audience was stranded in airports around the world, so my vision of a lively discussion of "diversity" did not take place, but the groundwork was laid.

Later, Paulette Bethel and I wanted to talk about TCKs in the local classrooms. For our session, we decided to try the term again and defined it as: "a diversity of experience that shapes a person's life and worldview but is not readily apparent on the outside, unlike the usual diversity markers such as race, ethnicity, nationality, gender, and so forth."[8] Again, the audience was small and the spark didn't seem to ignite many flames.

Only years later did I realize that the term *diversity* had a different meaning than I had been assuming (which is likely why my "hidden diversity" career wasn't flying!). Through conversation with a diversity expert, I learned that the word was not what I thought at all, but in the U.S. was (and is) more about race and equity than cultural diversity. I could understand that since prejudice first comes in terms of the visible aspects of a person, racial heritage, gender, and such were and are important topics and need to be addressed, but how about the "hidden diversity" within any racial group?

The question puzzled me and then I met with Shelly Habecker, an ATCK who grew up in Liberia and did her Ph.D. in anthropology at Oxford and her field research for her thesis in Eritrea. She gave an observation she had made. "Ruth, it seems like when people talk about 'blacks' in the U.S., there is no separation by experience or background. Everyone is in the same pile. However, I am meeting many children of African parentage who are very different culturally than African Americans, but it seems there is no space to recognize them on the forms."

Shelly began some significant research on this topic and met with African teens and parents in different settings as well. She asked the teens what they did when they wanted to be seen as Africans and what they did when they wanted to be seen as African Americans. There were a lot of laughs as they told their stories, but it was very clear they knew which behavior or dress was which and they knew how to code switch well! At school, of course, they simply maintained their African American sense.[9]

Definitely Shelly was on to something but I only saw it firsthand a few months later. I was asked to do something for a local school district because they were beginning to have a lot of immigrants and children of refugees moving to the area. They wanted to help their teachers understand more about these kids. I was delighted. I went to the district's website to see what I could learn about them and their level of awareness on cross-cultural matters so far.

When I opened the admission form, it asked the standard U.S. government–required questions of ethnicity and race. "What is your ethnicity? Are you Hispanic? Yes or no? Are you black or white (if Hispanic)?" And the person can check the box. The next section was "What race are you? American Indian, Black, Asian, Hispanic, White, Multiracial, Native Hawaiian or other Pacific Islander, or Other." Well, that seemed like quite a list to choose from and my mind was left to wonder about a host of folks I wouldn't easily know how to categorize except as "other." And I admit on such forms I have often checked "other" out of pure annoyance with the questions!

Next I went to look at their enrollment demographics. The title across the top said "Enrollment by Ethnicity." And then it listed the groups in the bar graph as American Indian, Black, Asian, Hispanic, White, Multiracial, Native Hawaiian or other Pacific Islander, or Other. What???!!! They only had one ethnicity question on their form but the title was "Enrollment by Ethnicity"? How could that be? Everything else they listed on this chart as "ethnicity" had been asked on the questionnaire in relationship to race, not ethnicity! I was astounded. How many different ethnicities are there among white people? Or black people? Or Asians? Or ??? How could a group of presumably university and above administrators name the chart so differently from the questions they had asked? My mental puzzle nearly fell into pieces at that point!

The day for the seminar came, and we began with a panel of various types of CCKs going to the public schools. They had amazing stories to tell of how they were perceived and how it felt. Many listeners were moved to tears. Between the "Enrollment by Ethnicity" chart and listening once more to these CCK stories, I became more passionate than before that somehow, someone needs to raise the wake-up alarm that our conversations on diversity, particularly for those working with children, must include the types of hidden diversities we have looked at in story after story in this book. And Eva's story, and so many others, let us all know this is important not just for the children themselves, but for our world. Yes, we need equity for sure. No question there. But a big part of making that happen is recognizing the unseen places of diversity so many young people now bring to our schools and workplaces. Sadly, when these things are not recognized, not only do we lose the gifts they bring, but also many students become alienated and seek other ways and places to fit.

REASONS TO HOPE

Meanwhile, I have hope. Again, all around are people living out their amazing stories with strength and joy. They are also doing something to spread the word of this growing new normal of so many who grow up as CCKs in one way or another. Doni is one of them. She is an amazing woman, founder and publisher of *Culturs*, a multicultural magazine. Doni also is a faculty member in the Department of Journalism and Media Communications at Colorado State University (CSU) and director of marketing at the Lory Student Center at Colorado State. In recent years, she has successfully advocated for topics related to hidden diversity to be in their annual diversity conferences and developed a strategic partnership with the university to create a home for globally mobile students. Speaking of cultural complexity, few stories can beat hers. But read what happens to that complexity when she is assigned a role that is given by her appearance and not her story. We told more of her story in chapters 6 and 12,

> As an ATCK who identified with seven cultures and lived in five countries before adulthood, my life was THAT full of mobility from place, to people, to family, and more. What you see is not what you get when you look at my outward appearances (accent, skin color, dress, etc.).
>
> By the time I entered university, Colorado had been my home through my three years in high school. Little did I know, however, that the population of people who "looked like me" would cause my first experience of culture shock. Being a United States citizen, with a decent foundation of the country's cultural norms, of Afro-Latina Caribbean heritage and global mobility, along with the potential to carry three passports, can create a potentially confusing cultural milieu. Yet, I was used to living in countries full of tan-, brown-, black-, or white-skinned individuals without skipping a beat. Who would have known that a couple hundred black faces—faces that arguably looked like my own—would cause

more cultural consternation than the tens of thousands of white faces around me?

African American. It's used as a racial identifier in the U.S.—the most recent one—as icon Oprah Winfrey recounted the descriptors that had been used to identify her during her lifetime: "colored, then black, then African-American, now 'person-of-color'." But for me, based on my background and upbringing, this is more a *cultural descriptor* than a racial one. It took longer for me to identify, learn, and mimic cultural expectations of America's Black population than it ever did to fit into the majority population in America. The definitions and expectations of music, dress, hair, manner of speech and more were infinite and mind-blowing to someone for whom being "Black" was just the color of her skin—and everything "she was" fit into that realm—it was just another piece of me. Every other "Black" person I knew spoke, dressed, cooked, etc., in a manner not out of the norm, as we each were individuals, and the overall culture was that of a nation, not necessarily a subset of one.

Just when I was figuring it all out, as a teenager, I suspended U.S. studies to attend university in recently opened East Berlin, immediately after the fall of the Berlin Wall. Coming back to the U.S. meant marathon weekends watching *In Living Color*, finding out the latest dance moves and slang in my African American community. Coming back to the white community at my university, however, didn't cause me one bit of strife: "*Macht nichts*," as the Germans would say. I fit in easily and effortlessly. But finding a place to call home while bringing my hidden diversity and global multiculturalism to my Black community in Colorado? That was entirely another story.[10]

I am grateful for all Doni and others like her are doing to expand our vision on diversity. I know more windows are being opened every day for people of all backgrounds and various racial heritages through her work at culturs.guru online magazine and its print counterpart.

And so, while a great deal of good has already happened for globally mobile and other cross-cultural families, much more is yet to come. How do we include the wave of refugees in our hearts and discussions? How do we embrace children and families of those who move seasonally from one country to another to harvest crops? How do we continue to discover the subcultures related to those with disabilities and how that affects families? Our world is culturally mixing and matching in ways that have never happened since the beginning of time until now. Maybe if we can see some of our connecting points just a little bit more clearly, we can share with others some of what we have learned that has been helpful to us. And if we can make that little bit of difference for another person or family, if we can open one more window, let's see how big those little things can grow to give hope and help for the generations now and to come.

~~~~~~

Where Do We Go from Here? (Part II)

by Michael V. Pollock

> Your calling is to the place where your deep gladness and
> the world's deep hunger meet.
>
> —Frederick Buechner[11]

Growing up as Dave Pollock's son meant sharing his genius, and gigantic pastoral (shepherd, caregiver) heart with the world, at significant personal cost. I chose to hone my craft as an educator and put down roots in a community in the U.S.—rejecting the role of "global champion of cross-cultural care" or anything that would seemingly impoverish family and community at the expense of a bigger vision. Yet I still desired a deeper understanding of my own story and that of other TCKs.

Although I never met Dr. Ruth Useem, I read her work and sat at the table with Dr. Anne Cottrell through Families in Global Transition (FIGT). I had the pleasure of meeting Norma McCaig in Washington, D.C., in the 1980s and was charmed by her warmth and impressed by her insight and commitment to caring for global nomads. I met Ruth Van Reken first through her book *Letters I Never Wrote* (now *Letters Never Sent*) and was moved by her discoveries. When we finally met in 2013, she became a mentor and sounding board and a dear friend. I am truly standing on the shoulders of many educators, coaches, counselors, and trainers who have pioneered, sacrificed, and made deep and lasting impacts on my life.

What I realized somewhere in the midst of teaching and administrating in the U.S. and China was that the seeds my father had planted in me were simply taking root in different soil: I was working to see young people flourish through overcoming challenges, to develop competence and character, and to cultivate leadership formation in them. Applying that vision to international school students and families simply brought the two realms of education and cross-cultural work together; children can't optimally learn and grow if they are not safe, cared for, included, and valued regardless of the setting.

True understanding becomes wisdom when applied to our fellow sojourners. If we apply understanding of the Third Culture and of the people who grew up in it to improve care—body, spirit, and soul—we will cultivate human thriving. Broadening the lessons to apply to the increasing number of people in cultural and geographic mobility seems a natural progression. We have something important to share with the refugee, the immigrant, the migrant worker, the hearing children of Deaf parents, the formerly incarcerated, the trafficking survivor, the LGBTQ community, and other minority populations. We also have receptors tuned to hear their stories.

Our two key purposes in rewriting this book were to clarify where we have been (the history and evolving understandings of the TCKs) and to build on that understanding so that further energy might not be wasted identifying "what and who we are talking about" but will instead be focused on:

1. To whom do these understandings and principles apply?
2. What needs to be done next to help overcome the challenges involved and to capitalize on the benefits?

So what do I see from this unique vantage point? What indeed needs to be done?

Building Relationships

I see the changing formation of relationships moving from traditionally small, trusted, yet exclusive communities to large open networks of people with weaker affiliation due—in part—to the connective yet isolating power of current transportation and communication technology (the airplane, the Internet, and the smartphone). We may soon long for the days when friendships and loyalties were rooted in "place." If our inability to gather our close friends into one location is frustrating now, how will TCKs/CCKs find relational anchorage when the landscape is increasingly flexible? We need a new vision for community, for connecting in "real time" and in the flesh. We need tools for creating healthy attachments to others, both mono- and multicultural.

Additionally, existential and postmodern philosophies may further alienate people from shared relationships and shared truths. These powerful currents challenge old loyalties as they also challenge old prejudices. Will the move toward globalization and global monoculture continue unabated, or will there be a backlash of nationalism and a new kind of tribalism? Are the metaphors of "melting pot" and "mosaic" that are seasoned with mutual respect and affirmation possible? Where does that vision put the TCK/CCK, careening between worlds and looking for "tribe and home"? Rather than deny the need, we must continue to visualize the kind of society we want to live in, and be willing to invest in the processes that will bring it about even when it would be far too easy to play the tourist and complain about the scenery.

Is there a leading role for the TCK/CCK in empathy, in hope, in peaceful coexistence? And what is the role of religion and spiritual commitment? Is there a core difference between the two? Can TCKs/CCKs model a new kind of social alliance not based on externals of race, gender, ethnicity, socioeconomics, or culture but on the principles of shared humanity and values? The potential is certainly there! We need to cultivate leaders who will boldly articulate a vision and empower those around them to live out a society that recognizes our shared likeness as humans even while recognizing the differences among us.

Using Abilities and Experiences

Conflict seems to be rising over ideologies and resources on the planet, and there is a pervading sense of "Me/Us First" in the global air; indeed, an American President just declared it a focus of his administration. I believe that we can offer a better vision of the future—one where an individual can be free to be just that, and still find acceptance and belonging, growth, and opportunity to serve others in the local and worldwide community. In the case of nations, strengthening one's own platform, if not at the expense of antagonizing and impoverishing others, is an excellent goal that creates opportunities for individuals and organizations to serve across national boundaries. TCKs' abilities to bridge differences and engage "the other" constructively must be affirmed and fostered so that they can take advantage of these opportunities.

How do we get to a place where the virtues of love, joy, peace, patience, kindness, goodness, gentleness, and self-control are valued amid a myriad of cultural and religious expressions? Ruth and I have written all through this work on the application of care, which I believe derives its mandate from the Spirit of Love, and whose end is to act on behalf of another for their good, demonstrating what that spirit is truly like. My worldview includes that this Love was embodied in the person of Jesus Christ. I do not know anything more real. I also believe that the underpinning values can be a common goal for people of all cultures and faiths, or no declared faith at all. When those values are pursued and lived out, questions of identity, belonging, and life purpose find their answers.

The pathway to "the virtuous home"—as I think of it—lies along the dual tracks of care for people: (1) helping them to overcome challenges through mutual comfort, healing, and (2)understanding and encouraging them by helping them find the courage to take hold of their gifts and experiences.

When people feel understood and comforted, they can learn to weave their gifts and experiences into competencies that build strong character and result in a joyful, thriving life for the benefit of themselves and those around them.

Caring for People

Significant obstacles remain. Ignorance of the needs of people living between cultures, and a lack of will to act on those needs, requires action; research that leads to understanding and "best practice" application is essential. It matters that we understand shifting trends and nuances and help those "in the trenches" of global mobility and cross-cultural transition to have tools and resources that are practical and timely. Five trends noted in a 2015 survey of 2,700 expats working in 156 countries:

1. U.S. expats remain the largest group but have shrunk 24 percent since 2001.
2. Asian expat numbers increased while European numbers decreased.
3. More expats are deploying for shorter periods (under a year) and are leaving families behind than in previous studies.
4. Global mobility is becoming a career in itself as numbers of assignments and years overseas increase significantly.
5. The two overwhelming requests of expats surveyed were for better **mentoring** in the new culture and stronger **repatriation** services upon their return.[12]

Changing trends have changing impact on families, and that requires a determined will to keep up with changing needs.

If we are going to improve the lives of TCKs/CCKs, then our organizations, schools, business enterprises, and government agencies must put their money where their mouths are and develop concrete programs and practical applications for paving the "flow of care" highway. The research that already exists insists that investing time and funding in member care and human resource departments will pay long-term dividends.

One application of the flow of care is the work of Doug Ota and the Safe Passage Across Networks (SPAN) movement. Having paddled in the river of international education, I am enthusiastic about this work and the best practices approach for creating welcoming and safe places to learn—harbors, if you will, on the global mobility ocean. What other harbors are needed? What would happen if universities and colleges, city councils and workplaces, churches, temples, synagogues, and mosques had training and understanding to receive, cultivate, and steward their globally and culturally mobile populations?

There is much hope for and much work to be done on the concept and practice of the "flow of care." I am encouraged by the nexus organizations like Families in Global Transition (FIGT), Society for Intercultural Education, Training and Research (SIETAR), and Global Member Care (GMC), which are linking strategies and resources across the globe. However, caring for people who move geographically and cross-culturally is not the job of "someone else, out there" but is an organic need in each school, workplace, house of faith, and hall of government.

Creating Transition Resources

Transition itself is such a major part of the TCK/CCK experience that many care providers see a need for a multilayered resource accessible to families and practitioners all over the world. The concept for the Transition Resource Cube (or TR3[13]) was born out of work with MK caregivers and is in the development phase. How many other resource projects are out there that may be unknown and untapped by individuals and families?

Hand in glove with the need for ongoing CCK research and networks that aggregate and disseminate findings is the need for more administrators, teachers, counselors, mentors, and coaches who are experienced and trained to understand and respond to TCK/CCK challenges and benefits, and to actively design and implement curricula and programs. We may, indeed, need a "TCK/CCK Institute" for research and training that is both global in scope and broad in application.

Addressing Needs

And what of the TCKs/CCKs themselves? What difference does it make to our peace of mind to know we are not alone and we are not crazy; our experience is normal? Although no one wants to be labeled and stuck in a box, how does normalizing the experience impart freedom as individuals choose to move, or stay put, fitting into local culture and yet remaining essentially who you are, yourself? It is this freedom we are after—to understand our experiences and ourselves and then to choose our next avenue of growth.

If we can address those concerns, there might be a great collective sigh of relief, already begun, but gathering in scope . . . and I imagine that as TCKs relax into who we are, there will be a greater outpouring of gifts, insights, and perspectives. How many TCKs and other kinds of CCKs remain hidden, experiencing hopelessness and alienation? Any at all is too many. There must be a concerted effort to name the third culture, acknowledge its participants, and disseminate what we know about life patterns. I believe we need to find new platforms and high-profile spokespersons to put our knowledge and experience to work.

We, as TCKs /CCKs, need not depend on others to advocate for us but must learn to advocate for ourselves, for each other, and for the millions of others who share aspects of our experience. Here I am thinking about cross cultural adoption, human trafficking victims, refugees and other displaced persons, and the numbers are staggering. If we have learned how to overcome the challenges of the globally mobile life, we need to reach a hand to those behind us. If we have been gifted with a 3-D view of the world, it is incumbent on us to work to affirm what is good: to see past race, gender, and class; to bridge the gaps of culture, economics, privilege, and creeds.

Mahatma Gandhi, a beautiful, flawed, cross-cultural human being, said,

> We but mirror the world. If we could change ourselves, the tendencies in the world would also change. As a man changes his own nature,[14] so does the attitude of the world change towards him.

By taking hold of the gifts of our experience and serving our fellow human beings, each of us has the possibility to become fully who we were intended to be. I believe this joyful selflessness could change the world.

Epilogue

By Ruth E. Van Reken

When I heard the sad news of David Pollock's impending death in April 2004, I felt as though I was about to lose half of my brain. For so many, the size of Dave's heart is what they remember most. Time and again at his memorial service, individuals spoke of how, when they met him, Dave's undivided attention made them feel as if they were the most important person in the world. At that moment, they were.

I too have no question of the size of Dave's heart. When I sent him the journaling I did at age thirty-nine trying to figure out my own journey, Dave not only responded but worked out a way for me to attend the first conference on these topics in Manila and encouraged me to publish my writings in what ultimately became *Letters Never Sent*. But what I also came to value beyond measure was the size of David's mind. Rarely have I known someone with his capacity to listen patiently to someone explain an idea, bounce it back and forth, synthesize it into a form that had shape, and then guide it into a crystallized, usable form as the Big Idea (e.g., the Pol/Van Cultural Identity Box). It was through countless conversations such as this with TCKs and their families around the world, with people like Ruth Hill Useem, originator of the TCK term; her co-researcher, Ann Baker Cottrell; Norma McCaig, founder of Global Nomads; and others in the field that he formed his TCK Profile and The Transition Experience models. Now, with Dr. Useem having died a few months before and Norma battling her own illness, I wondered: *With these leaders gone, what will happen to this topic they pioneered with such passion? Who could I think with?*

And then I had a mental image of Dave at the top of a long, vertically ascending, single-file line of people rising toward the sky—almost as if those in this line were climbing some invisibly suspended stairway to the stars, each person tucked in behind the one ahead. The line wiggled and wove its way up until, suddenly, it completely collapsed because the leader who held us together—Dave—was gone. For a moment, it seemed all was lost. But suddenly I saw something else. In that collapse, everyone in the line was flung far and wide. And then this verse came to my mind: "Except a seed of wheat fall into the ground and die, it abides alone. But if it dies, it springs forth and brings forth much fruit." In that moment, I realized that the seeds Dave had gathered from others and replanted in so many lives had and would continue to take root in countless places around the globe. Instead of dying, new life and growth would spring up everywhere. Updating *Third Culture Kids* for the first time in 2009, with the hope of sharing more of Dave's growing vision as well as my own, was my way of distributing those seeds.

With incredible awe, I see the fruit trees growing all over the world. There are books, seminars, webinars, conferences, chat rooms, and blogs hanging from those in beautiful, life-giving fruit. The seeds Dave planted in so many of us have, indeed, grown and been watered, I trust, by his work that remains in written form.

As we write this new edition, we need fresh seeds falling from those trees to be planted even further. Dave's son, Michael, has been out in the world gathering these fresh seeds from all those trees, which are growing faster than I can count. He has brought them and together we have planted the seeds in this book so they can begin growing as seedlings for the current and next generations. While the generation before me, and many of my own generation, never got to see the trees they planted grow to the size they are now, I rejoice that I did.

I feel as if I have come full circle. To know that what Michael has planted in this book will continue to water the trees his father only knew as seeds, gives me joy. His seedlings will start new trees in other regions. It has been my great honor to be a holding link between father and son for such an important and great topic as this one.

Remembering David C. Pollock

by Betty Lou Pollock

O ur daughter, Michelle Pollock Bower, likened her father to a great spreading oak tree, having deep roots and spreading branches. How apt a picture. His roots rested deeply in the soil of faith and hope.

David endured massive storms while providing rest, shade, and enabling for many; his networking resembled not only a root system to sustain him but to connect others who became more effective for their interrelatedness to him and others. David was a catalyst and connector; he was always pleased to foster growth and development in others. Branches do not thrive and grow expansive without strong roots.

Many have asked how David became interested in *third culture kids (TCKs)*. It was largely due to his exposure to internationals, international students, and missionary kids, some of whom were also TCKs. Dave realized that "someone should do something for these people"—that is, to help them ameliorate the challenges and enhance the benefits of their mobile childhoods. Words of a Dutch diplomat years later underlined this. He said that the benefits (of being a TCK) are social; the challenges are personal. Yes, and if the personal challenges are addressed, people grow freer to use their talents and knowledge.

David was equally at home behind a lectern in a Singaporean suit or running his chain saw in jeans frayed at the cuffs. He was comfortable in so many places in the world striving for cultural balance and assisting others in achieving that as well. Dave was a lifelong learner and was always proud of our family learning new things, even when we were separated due to his travels and life work. He loved teaching to make a positive difference.

David never believed it was a bad thing for parents to live and work and raise children cross-culturally. He did believe that preparation, intervention, and care could promote fewer shocks or trauma and greater health on all levels for entire families. He used to say that when TCKs were in charge of the world leadership, different decisions would be made, because he understood the hearts and minds of those who know that humanness is universal.

In April, 2004, David collapsed in the middle of presenting his TCK Profile to a group of teachers at the American International School in Vienna. He died nine days later, on April 11. Over many years and since his death, I have heard from countless TCKs who tell me how much David's work changed their lives. We still feel the expanse, the spreading branches of that oak tree.

History and Evolution of Third Culture and Third Culture Kids Concepts: Then and Now

In our first two editions, we basically gave a "fast-forward" synopsis on the history of the *third culture* term itself in order to focus more on what this idea has become in relationship to the TCK topic, per se. With increased interest (and sometimes confusion) about what the third culture concept is, however, it is important that we give a more expanded review of the historical development of this *as well* as what it has become in regard to third culture kids (TCKs). (Some segments of this have been used in chapter 2, but for continuity's sake, we leave them here as well.)

For the sake of reference, we reiterate David Pollock's definition of TCKs in chapter 2:

> A Third Culture Kid (TCK) is a person who has spent a significant part of his or her developmental years outside the parents' culture. The TCK frequently builds relationships to all of the cultures, while not having full ownership in any. Although elements from each culture may be assimilated into the TCK's life experience, the sense of belonging is in relationship to others of similar background.[1]

The Third Culture as Originally Defined by the Useems

A common misconception about third culture kids is that they have been raised in what is often called the "Third World." While this might be true for some TCKs, the Third World has no specific relationship to the concept of the third culture. TCKs have been born and grown up everywhere, including such places as Abu Dhabi, Accra, Amsterdam, Bangkok, Caracas, Kunming, London, New York, Singapore, Sydney, Timbuktu, and Vienna. Where, then, did this term develop?

In 1958, two sociologists from Michigan State University, Dr. Ruth Hill Useem and her husband, Dr. John Useem, coined the phrase *third culture* when they went to India for a year. They wanted to study how, in the changing world of post–World War II and postcolonialism, U.S. Americans who lived and worked there as foreign service officers, missionaries, technical aid workers, business-people, educators, and media representatives would interact with their Indian colleagues (and vice versa) as the traditional power bases were also shifting. Ann Baker Cottrell and Richard Downie, former graduate students of the Useems, tell us more of those days:

> "Third culture" was initially [the Useems'] own shorthand term to describe what they observed in the interaction of Americans in India and their Indian colleagues. In addition to the two national cultures they saw [a] different culture in the interaction which reflected both [national cultures] but was definitely not a blended culture. They intended to create a more sociologically meaningful term but before that hap-pened, the State Department got hold of "Third Culture" and the rest is history.
>
> The Useems defined Third Culture as: The behavior pat-terns created, shared, and learned by men (sic) of different societies who are in the process of relating their societies, or sections thereof, to each other.[2]

Initially, for this particular research project, the Useems identified India (or a local non-Western culture) as the *first culture* and America as the *second culture*, and the interactions between the people from the first and second cultures as the *third culture*. It is true, however, that when researchers set out to explore one topic, they often make unexpected discoveries in other areas, as what they thought they were studying grows and changes in unforeseen ways. So it was for Ruth Useem in particular.

> Ruth and John were equal partners in this research, but Ruth, as an expat wife and feminist, associated with and took interest in the wives of the men they were study-ing. Many of the wives were involved in establishing an

American School for their children, thus Ruth took a special interest in their children. She dubbed these children, who were growing up in the third cultures established by their parents and Indian counterparts, Third Culture Kids. It is important to note that as originally defined, TCK is a child of parents working outside their passport countries in representative roles, i.e., they [the parents] are sponsored.[3]

As Ruth began to focus more on the spouses and children of the Americans of all sectors, she recognized that they were part of a larger whole of Westerners who were living as expatriates in non-Western countries during this post–World War II era. In writing about them, Ruth noted that "each of these subcultures [communities of expatriates] generated by colonial administrators, missionaries, businessmen, and military personnel—had its own peculiarities, slightly different origins, distinctive styles and stratification systems, but all were closely interlocked."[4] In other words, there was something they shared that transcended their subcultures or *sectors*. In this article, however, Ruth does not *specifically* define either the first or second culture, per se.

Ruth's early studies of TCKs included children from all the expatriate sectors but she had two constants in her continuing studies. The children's families were from the U.S. (she did not include the Indian children whose parents were interacting in this third culture with the U.S. Americans) and all of their parents were overseas because of a parent's *sponsored* career (meaning they had gone under the aegis of a specific international agency of one sort or another).

This model represents some of the groups Ruth Useem included in her initial studies and what their sponsoring organizations might be.

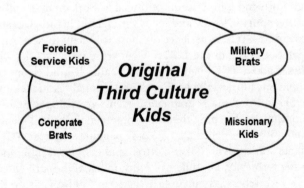

Figure A–1: Original Third Culture Kids
©1996 Ruth E. Van Reken

Because those children she studied had parents who were clearly identified with the agenda of their organization, much of Dr. Useem's groundbreaking article on TCKs in 1973 focused on how she believed this reality impacted the children because she saw them growing up in what she called *representational roles*. In other words, people around them (including parents) expected the children's behavior to be consistent with the goals and values of the organizational system for which the parents worked. These TCKs were seen as "little ambassadors," "little missionaries," or "little soldiers." If their behavior fell short of these expectations, the children could jeopardize a parent's career in a different way than that same behavior might have done in the parent's passport country. Instead of being merely an individual or family matter, misbehaving TCKs could reflect poorly on the very reasons the parents and/or their organization were there in the first place.[5] Useem saw this factor as a key part of the TCKs' identity formation and one of the main reason for some of the different characteristics she saw between TCKs and non-TCKs.

Ruth Useem also believed this strong sense of identity with the parents' sponsoring organization is what made the TCK experience distinctive from other ways children might grow up cross-culturally, such as children of immigrants or bicultural parents. Interestingly, however, Ruth did not include this fact regarding the parent's occupation in her actual definition of a TCK. Instead, she simply said that TCKs were "children who accompany their parents into another culture."[6] Perhaps in those early days of increased global migration she did not foresee the countless other ways future children might also grow up accompanying their parents into another culture but not under some organization's sponsorship. This has sometimes created confusion for later researchers as they tried to identify exactly who was or wasn't a TCK based on her definition alone. Even Dave Pollock's definition does not specifically state *why* the parents are in another culture. Neither definition clarifies that this other culture is also in another country, although that seems to have been the underlying assumption at the time these definitions were written.

Although Ruth and John Useem continued to work on many other research projects, Ruth's enduring legacy and focus throughout her life was studying the lifelong impact of the TCK experience on those who have lived it. Almost ironically, while later criticism of the TCK concept arose from skeptics who said the ideas and theses about TCKs had no good research behind them, the truth is this entire topic was born in the heart of a professional researcher and research community. She enlisted many graduate students at Michigan State University to help her continue researching the TCK phenomenon she had identified. Even after retirement, Ruth launched a large study of adult American TCKs with her former graduate student Ann Baker Cottrell and help from John and Kathleen Jordan (another former Ph.D. student).[7] Sadly, much of the early research seems lost to today's researchers, as apparently the term "Third Culture Kid" wasn't specifically included in the title of the earliest dissertations and thus does not come up during Internet searches. Richard D. Downie was among the first of her graduate students to make "third culture experienced youth" a part of his dissertation title in 1976, a new beginning in making the research more accessible for researchers who were to follow.[8] Truly, Ruth Hill Useem deserves the title of "Mother of TCKs," as she has affectionately been called by many.

Other Pioneers in the Field

As is normal with any major sociological change, the awareness of these changes—and the implications for what these changes could mean for a society and those within it—often begins to sprout up in many divergent and seemingly unconnected places at approximately the same time. Eventually, these initially separated pieces begin to coalesce and become visible as a more unified whole.

So it was in the days when families began to move internationally on a scale not seen before. Others besides the Useems also began to notice that something was different for the internationally mobile children compared to those who grew up in the more traditional monocultural environments of the past. Here are others who helped add key beginning pieces to the emerging TCK puzzle.

In 1936, more than twenty years before the Useems' initial research, Dr. Allen Parker, head of Woodstock School in India, wrote his master's dissertation on characteristics he saw among students in his international school whom we now call TCKs. At that time, his students were virtually all missionary children, so his studies focused on that particular sector.[9] Many of those characteristics—such as a wide perspective of the world but ignorance of home [passport] culture—reflect what later researchers also described as common for TCKs of all sectors. But his observations were an important beginning, even though Dr. Parker wrote before he had common language to connect his students to the greater whole of other globally mobile youth.

But for many years after Ruth Useem first coined the TCK term, those living it still had little awareness that there was universal language for their experience. Ruth primarily looked at the educational implications for her findings and worked with educators to seek changes, but she did not work as directly with the families and TCKs themselves as others did later.[10] In fact, when Ruth Van Reken talked with Ruth Hill Useem at a Global Nomads conference in December 1988 and asked Dr. Useem how she saw her findings being useful to TCKs or ATCKs, Dr. Useem answered, "It's my job to study this, not to apply it. That's for others to do."[11]

And she was right. While various Western researchers had begun to look more closely at their particular populations, such as military, missionary, or foreign service kids, during the eighties, and researchers such as Momo K. Podolsky were doing research in Japan on children of international businesspeople, two people stand out as those who took the research and growing awareness that this was more than sector- or culture-specific to the folks who were living it. Those two pioneers were Norma M. McCaig and David C. Pollock.

Norma McCaig became a key player in translating theory into practical wisdom. Her father had worked overseas for a drug company, but she attended a missionary kid boarding school in India. Perhaps that is where Norma developed her keen sense of the cross-sector nature of this topic and worked diligently to promote that groundbreaking awareness. Until then, while the foreign service, military, and missionary communities had begun to notice the long-term effect of a global childhood and had made beginning steps to try to help their families, each community operated within its own parameters, with little collaboration between them.

Although Norma had the highest respect for Ruth Hill Useem and her work, she didn't like being called a "kid" when she was an adult. The Adult TCK, or ATCK, terminology had not yet been introduced to distinguish those who were still in the "kid" phase and those who grew up as TCKs but were now adults. Norma changed all of that when she began Global Nomads International, a group for Adult TCKs (ATCKs) from all sectors, nationalities, and backgrounds. Norma had a great skill in putting catchy phrases together to name some of the realities such as *cultural chameleon* or *hidden immigrant*, but *global nomad* is the one that is most frequently associated with her.

Norma also rightly feared that because neither Ruth Useem's nor Dave's definitions for TCKs specifically included that TCKs were children whose parents had gone to other countries due to their career choices, it would one day be difficult for researchers to study them specifically. She (and others) believed if all internationally mobile children were included under the TCK umbrella no matter why their parents had made such moves, the variables would be too many for meaningful research. So in 1984 she coined the term *global nomad* and defined it: "A global nomad is a person of any age or nationality who has lived a significant part of his or her developmental years in one or more countries outside his or her passport country because of a parent's occupation."[12] For the most part, the terms *TCK* and *Global Nomad* are used interchangeably.

In December 1988, Norma organized the first International Conference for Global Nomads in Washington, D.C., and until her untimely death in 2008 was a true visionary and leader in the field of raising awareness that this is a legitimate topic profoundly affecting the lives of those who live it, both for great good and with identifiable challenges along the way. Sadly, since her death, the term *global nomad* has become popularized. For most in the general public or press, it has lost its meaning as referring to a person's childhood experience. Instead, it seems anyone who has lived globally or traveled widely refers to themselves as global nomads, but that doesn't change that Norma's definition was clear and precise.

David C. Pollock is the other person who took this topic from theory to practical application. In 1977, almost twenty years after Ruth Useem created the TCK acronym, Dave and Betty Lou Pollock went to Kenya with their four children. There the Pollocks served as dorm parents at a large international school. As they interacted with their students, Dave also noticed common characteristics among them that differed from the young people he had worked with in the U.S. Over and over Dave heard the same story that the land the parents called "home" was a strange one to these students. He soon realized how traumatic reentry to that "homeland" was for many and wanted to help organizations become more aware of the needs of the families they sent overseas. With that in mind, the Pollocks returned to the U.S., where Dave set up Interaction, Inc., and in time began his endless trips to international schools in countless countries, sharing what became his signature seminars, *The TCK Profile* and *The Transition*

Experience. His passion became helping parents, teachers, and the TCKs themselves find language and understanding for their experiences. Repeatedly we hear stories from adult TCKs who had their "Aha!" moment at one of his seminars—that moment they found out there was language and context for their life stories. They were not alone!

The Third Culture as Currently Defined

Because Dave died in 2004, we can't ask him where or how he first heard the TCK term, but obviously whenever he discovered it, he recognized that the terminology described the students at his school, and the characteristics Ruth Useem described confirmed many of the behaviors he had noted. The main difference was that those he initially studied were not just U.S. Americans, but included children from other primarily Western countries who had grown up in different African nations, not India. Because of that, in order to simplify the concept and make it applicable to his increasingly international audiences, in time he began to talk of the *first culture* as the *home culture*, meaning the country issuing the parents' passports; the *second culture* as the *host culture*; and, ultimately, the *third culture* as "the way of life shared by those who live or have lived an internationally mobile lifestyle." At this point, we would add "the third culture is the way of life shared by those who live or have lived an internationally mobile lifestyle due to a person's or parent's career choice" to differentiate it from other ways individuals or families may be internationally mobile, such as refugees or immigrants.

This diagram gives a picture of our understanding of the third culture in that emerging picture of it and how we use the term in this book.

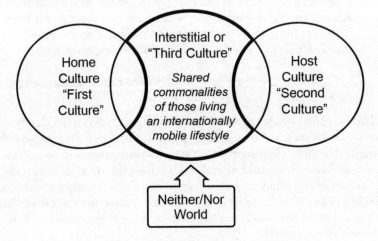

Figure A–2: Original Third Culture Kids

©1996 Ruth E. Van Reken

When Dave and Ruth asked Dr. Useem about this way of describing the different cultures as it emerged for us, she replied, "Because I am a sociologist/anthropologist I think no concept is ever locked up permanently. . . . Concepts change as we get to know more; other times concepts change because what happens in the world is changing."[13] That, in itself, is an important lesson to remember as the world continues to change. Rather than living protectively about her research, Dr. Useem wasn't afraid to let others build on the foundations she had laid or let the practitioners apply it and take it to the people she had studied who needed language for their experiences.

So these were some of the people beginning to come together on this topic. But those were not easy days for them because, as is the case with many pioneers, they were ahead of the curve in seeing how the world was changing. As this topic became more popularized, some observers—including academicians—were skeptical and said it was all some sort of pop-psychology without any real basis in academic research. Somehow the truth that Ruth Useem birthed the TCK concept in solid academic research became lost along the way. There is no question that through her lifelong personal work and via her graduate students, including the groundbreaking ATCK survey she did with Ann Baker Cottrell in 1993,[14] she created a strong academic foundation upon which others have built. In this transition of research to application, however, that research piece became more invisible and is one reason we have expanded this section on the history of this term and its evolution to the present.

Please read chapter 2 for more about the distinctives of this third culture as we see it now. As we say there, for our purposes in writing this book, we are trying to go back to the original intent and define TCKs as

> *A traditional third culture kid (TCK) is a person who spends a significant part of his or her first eighteen years of life accompanying parent(s) into a country or countries that are different from at least one parent's passport country(ies) due to a parent's choice of work or advanced training.*
>
> *An adult third culture kid (ATCK) is someone who grew up as a TCK.*

This is not to exclude anyone, but to set the parameters more clearly so the conversation can grow rather than being stuck on who is or isn't included if TCKs are simply those going into another culture with their parents. In 2002 Ruth Van Reken coined the term cross-cultural kid (CCK—see chapter 3) to include this larger cohort of children who grow up cross-culturally for many reasons, again with the hope of enlarging our conversations and understanding of how what we have learned in the past from the TCK model can apply more universally to others in our changing world.

Of course, many others are trying to find the right term as well. We hear of terms such as transnational kid, transnational person, transcultural kid, global citizen, and more. There are problems with each, just as there are strengths with each. Researcher Danau Tanu states (2015) that "it is important to treat the 'third culture' as dynamic and changing in relation to specific socio-historical contexts . . . only then can we begin to situate the existing study of Third Culture Kids within the broader study of migration and identity."[15]

So there is plenty for researchers now and in the future to study. But this is where the topic started and where it is at this point. We look forward to seeing all that is ahead!

Our Tribal Elders and the Global Nomad Medicine Wheel (Excerpts)

by Paul Asbury Seaman

Paul Seaman attended Murree Christian School in Pakistan (1963–1973). He is the author of Paper Airplanes in the Himalayas *(1997) and* Far Above the Plain *(1996) and is currently seeking a publisher for his novel about the Great Bhola Cyclone in 1970 and the Bangladesh Liberation War a few months later. He lives in the San Francisco Bay area with his wife, Catherine Lockhart-Seaman.*

> This is a much-shortened version of an article about four of the founding pioneers of the TCK community. The full text can be found online at: www.djiboutijones.com/2015/03/our-tribal-elders-part-1

Isaac Newton once wrote, "If I have seen a little further it is by standing on the shoulders of Giants." American Indians would call this honoring the Grandmothers and Grandfathers. Four people who have had the most impact on identifying the TCK subculture, and who dedicated their lives to developing a global nomad community, are Ruth Van Reken, Ruth Hill Useem, David Pollock, and Norma McCaig. Placing each of these "tribal elders" in one of the four quarters of the medicine wheel can highlight their distinct contribution. These are *heart, identity, wisdom,* and *integration.*

Heart . . . Ruth Van Reken (b. 1945) The first quadrant is East, the direction of the rising sun, of new beginnings and family. The heart is where we feel the ache of displacement and it is through the heart that we redeem our sense of belonging. Ruth Van Reken's grandfather was a U.S. American doctor who set up a Presbyterian hospital in Resht, Iran [then Persia]. Her father was born there and became an educator/administrator himself for an international organization serving in Nigeria. Ruth was born in Kano, Nigeria, where she lived until she was thirteen. Van Reken's first book, *Letters Never Sent* (1988), grew out of her struggle with inexplicably persistent depression as a happily married adult. It is presented as a series of letters she might have written to her parents—if she had been able to name her feelings—beginning with her first night at a boarding school in Nigeria. With its portrait of accumulated loss over multiple transitions, her modest little book is now something of a classic in global nomad literature and has helped thousands of people get in touch with grief. It would be hard to find someone who is a more fully present listener than Ruth Van Reken, and for all her organizational involvements, that may be her greatest gift.

Identity . . . Ruth Hill Useem (1915–2003) There is power in giving something a name; it can make things less scary, easier to manage. Ruth Hill Useem was the first one to name us. The second quadrant of the medicine wheel is South, where we grow into and affirm our individuality and sense of purpose. Dr. Useem was a sociologist at Michigan State University. From 1952 to 1985 she studied expatriate communities, overseas schools, and the discrete subcultures of organizations working abroad. Her later work on the impact this had on minor dependents would take her to seventy-six countries. The first cross-cultural research conducted by Useem and her husband, John, was on the Rosebud Sioux Indian Reservation in South Dakota. Ten years later they went to India and made a second, yearlong trip in 1958 to study American expatriates. They discovered that these families, businesses, embassies, international schools, military commissaries, and mission compounds all developed patterns of interaction with their host country that incorporated elements of both the *home culture* and the *host culture* into what the Useems called a "Third Culture." Thus, Ruth coined the term "Third Culture Kids" to refer to the children who grow up in such an environment.

In the late 1960s Ruth Useem actively recruited graduate students with third culture experience. The effort resulted in nine Ph.D. dissertations on TCK issues. In thinking about Ruth Useem, I am reminded of another diminutive Ruth: Supreme Court Justice Ruth Bader Ginsburg. Both were early feminists and pioneers in their male-dominated professions.

Wisdom . . . David Pollock (1939–2004) The western quadrant holds the Magician archetype; it is a place where we confront the unknown and learn to work with it. If wisdom is the combination of knowledge, experience, and insight, David Pollock was the embodiment of those qualities. Prematurely gray, with a neatly trimmed beard, he resembled both Sigmund Freud and

Ernest Hemingway. Pollock combined heart and intellect and packaged them into his "TCK Profile" traveling medicine show. He was almost always on the road speaking to sponsoring agencies, teachers, parents, and adult TCKs around the world, and it's what he was doing when he died unexpectedly in Vienna on Easter Sunday 2004.

Pollock understood the power of myth—in the truest sense of that word: to impart guidance about life through universal stories that resonate with the individual. Pollock was an alchemist, a master at using anecdotes to illustrate a principle or make the research personal. And the result was gold. After graduating from Moody Bible Institute, Pollock attended Houghton College in western New York. He pastored a church in New Jersey for seven years. Then, from 1977 to 1980, Pollock worked at a Bible college in Kijabe, Kenya. With a daughter and three sons of their own, Dave and Betty Lou also served as home boarding parents for high school boys attending Rift Valley Academy, a school for missionaries' children. Pollock had become, in the language of anthropologists, a "participant-observer"—in effect doing the same kind of field research the Useems had done in India twenty-five years earlier.

When they returned to the States, Pollock founded Interaction to help bring more focus on the needs of internationally mobile families. He developed the "TCK Profile" and a flow-of-care model, which together would form the basis of *Third Culture Kids*, written with Ruth Van Reken. In 1983 Houghton College asked David Pollock to come back and help internationalize their curriculum. In 1984 Interaction cosponsored the first International Conference on Missionary Kids (ICMK) in Manila, Philippines. This was followed by two more—in Quito, Ecuador (1987), and Nairobi, Kenya (1989). Dave was codirector of all three and on the board of many of the growing number of organizations related to TCK issues, including Association of Christian Schools International, Mu-Kappa (aimed at college-age MKs), Families in Global Transition (cofounded by Ruth Van Reken in 1998), and Global Nomads International (created by Norma McCaig in 1984). The TCK workshops he presented took him all over the world. Van Reken recalls that when she first visited Pollock at Houghton College, "I was shocked to see that all this worldwide operation happened in a little office with a copy machine and one volunteer secretary." If Van Reken's early focus was on healing, Pollock's was about prevention. He spent more time working with sponsoring agencies than he did with adult TCKs themselves. Dave had the passion of a political activist but also the easy good humor of someone who has learned not to take life too seriously. One of Pollock's memorable gems, poking fun at stereotypes, was the comment, "All Indians walk single file; at least the one I saw did."

I first learned I was a TCK in 1990—at one of David Pollock's seminars. It was spooky to have someone I'd never met describe my emotional history in exact detail. I discovered there is a reason I was who I am—the different perspective, the trouble fitting in. But more than an explanation, my "TCKness" gave me a sense of belonging for the first time in my life. By focusing on the lifelong impact of a globally mobile childhood, the stereotypes we had about each other quickly became irrelevant, regardless of what kind of organization had employed our parents.

Integration . . . Norma McCaig (1945–2008) On the medicine wheel North represents the Elder stage of life, coming fully into our own in both responsibility and self-expression. It is the embodiment of mindful stewardship: having the ability to effectively apply our knowledge and resources for the greater good. Norma was born in Teaneck, New Jersey. Her father was an executive with an international pharmaceutical company, and when she was two years old the family moved to the Philippines, where Norma attended the American School in Manila. When she was fourteen her parents moved to Sri Lanka and Norma spent a year and a half at Kodaikanal International School, a missionary boarding school in South India.

At the Meridian House in Washington, D.C., McCaig worked as home hospitality coordinator, providing orientation for foreign students and government employees coming to live in the United States. This experience became the foundation for her life's work. In 1984 Norma went to a reunion of Kodaikanal International School and was struck by an incredible sense of homecoming, far beyond what nostalgia might warrant. Not satisfied with the colloquial connotations of "third culture kids," she wanted something more inclusive, something that would describe how wide this experience truly was—a phrase that alluded to our continuing journey as well as our upbringing. Thus was born "global nomads."

In 1987 McCaig attended the Second ICMK in Quito, Ecuador, where she met Ruth Van Reken. Norma stayed up all night reading *Letters Never Sent* and wept throughout (as I had). The next night she and Ruth discussed the commonalities between MKs and business-kids, along with those from volunteer agencies and foreign service and military backgrounds. Where these experiences overlap—and what we carry into adulthood—is what offers the most insight. Norma McCaig was the first to see this so clearly.

McCaig borrowed heavily from her own retirement accounts, and in December 1988 representatives from all these communities came together in Washington for the first conference of Global Nomads International (GNI). Norma never married or had children of her own; while this was not necessarily her preference, it did give her the freedom to pursue her vision. Norma's life was about making connections—between individuals, groups, and ideas. She could muster an impressive turnout for a meeting, a project, or a social event—better than anyone I've known. GNI never became the institution McCaig hoped for, with chapters across the country and around the world; but her vision of a vibrant, interactive global nomad community has become a reality—in no small part because of her efforts. Norma worked harder than anyone to make us a culture, not just an identity or a researchable "population." Then, in a few short years, our tribe lost three of its guiding lights. Ruth Useem died in 2003 and David Pollock in 2004, and when Norma McCaig died in November 2008 after an unexpected relapse of bone cancer, it felt like the end of an era.

The beauty of the medicine wheel is the way it represents the seasons of our lives but also the *cycles* of growth—in a spiral that moves us toward grace and contentment. Our founders gave us tools and opportunities to integrate and expand upon our special legacy, with a stronger sense of identity rooted in elder wisdom and connecting from the heart. Ruth Useem's research led to David Pollock's TCK Profile; his articles on that topic led Ruth Van Reken to write *Letters Never Sent*. Van Reken's book helped clarify to Norma McCaig our striking commonalities across widely different contexts. It is the interconnected nature and cumulative impact of these four lives that make them significant. Ruth Useem allowed us to see for the first time what was distinct about our heritage; Norma McCaig enabled us to celebrate it. Dr. Useem gave us a name; Norma gave us an address. Just two months after Norma died, Barack Obama—a global nomad—moved into the White House. She would have enjoyed talking about that.

Hidden Diversity of TCKs

by Danau Tanu

Danau Tanu was born in Canada to a Japanese mother and Chinese Indonesian father. She grew up in Indonesia, Japan, Canada, and Singapore. Danau received her Ph.D. in anthropology and Asian studies from the University of Western Australia (UWA) in 2015, and her book Growing Up in Transit: The Politics of Belonging at International School *is forthcoming. She has since been an Australian Endeavour Research Fellow with the University of Indonesia while researching young refugees who move multiple times as they are growing up, and is now an Honorary Research Fellow at UWA.*

When I first read about Third Culture Kids, I found that I could relate to much of what had been written. Yet, there was an element of my experience as an Asian kid at an international school that was missing from what had already been written. The pursuit to fill this gap then became one of the main focuses of my doctoral research, which I summarize briefly in this appendix.[1]

As an anthropologist, I went back to high school in 2009 to immerse myself as a participant observer for one year in the lives of teenaged students at an international school in Jakarta, which I dub "The International School (TIS)." When I began the field research, I thought it would be easy to decide who to include as "Third Culture Kids." It soon became clear, however, that it is often difficult to categorize who is or is not a "Third Culture Kid" because children are experiencing international mobility in increasingly diverse and complicated ways.

Within the first few weeks, I became aware that the teachers and other school staff felt that many of the Asian students—namely the Koreans, Japanese, and local Indonesians—were "not really Third Culture Kids."[2] These students were seen to have somehow failed in becoming Third Culture Kids because they were perceived to be ethnocentric and not "international" enough. However, when I spoke to these students, I found that many had grown up in several countries or were of mixed heritage. In fact, some groups that were accused of "self-segregating" were quite diverse and not at all ethnocentric.

Why then were they seen as not international and not TCK? To answer this question, we need to understand the diversity of ways in which children experience mobility and the international school setting.

Being "International" or "Western"?

Almost two decades ago, Barbara Schaetti pointed out that research on TCKs have yet to address "issues of power and cultural dominance in international microcultures" and its impact on "the global nomad experience."[3] This neglect remains broadly true today and it influences the way we define being "international." At TIS, being international was epitomized by the flag procession or multicultural food festival carried out during United Nations Day, the biggest celebration of the school year, as well as the many drawings of flags that decorate classroom walls, among other things. The assumption is that anyone can participate in this form of internationalism and diversity on an equal footing, but this is not entirely true.

The student groups that the school teachers and administrators perceived as "international" appeared physically (or "racially") diverse in terms of skin tones but were also highly Westernized. The way students themselves described these groups best illustrate this point as I have published elsewhere.[4]

> "So, who are the popular kids?" I asked a couple of seniors.
>
> "Well, popularity isn't such a big deal here, but I suppose the white kids that like to sit over there are considered popular," Melinda answered as she pointed at the benches near the high school office.
>
> "The white kids?" I repeated suspiciously, as I was sure they were not all "white."
>
> "Yeah, the white kids."
>
> I leaned over to do a double take on the group she was referring to. Many of them were Caucasian, but there were also two blacks, one South Asian, and at least three were of mixed Caucasian and Asian descent. Melinda did not notice the irony in her choice of words.
>
> On another occasion, a couple of students from the group referred to as the "white kids" helped the Korean students set up a tent during a senior sleepover at school. All were male. One of their friends came over and said, "Hey, the

white kids are helping the Korean kids!" There was a pause as we all tried to digest that statement. One of the "white kids" broke the silence, "Dude, I'm Pakistani." The other "white kid" added, as he held on to the tent he was working on, "Yeah and I'm Asian. My mom is Chinese . . . and you're half Japanese." It was only then that the student realised the inaccuracy of his statement.

The "white kids" are at other times referred to as "Western." These labels alluded to the fact that these groups of students used English as their main mode of communication and were the most Westernized among the students. They shared a sense of "cultural sameness."[5] But because they *looked* diverse, these groups were also often referred to as "international" by both staff and students at TIS. However, the label "international" may be misleading. Not all students— regardless of how internationally mobile their upbringing had been—were able to comfortably join these English-speaking groups if they did not speak English well or were not Westernized enough.[6]

Western by Day, Asian by Night

Korean, Japanese and Indonesian students alike said that the reason many of them did not hang out with the English-speaking groups is not due to a lack of trying. They did try, especially when they were new to the school. But they gave up after the first few weeks because they felt discouraged that their efforts did not pay off. Take for example, the story of a Korean student.

Yoo Mi had spent most of her elementary school years at an international school in Indonesia and learnt English. She used to have friends of other nationalities, or "blond friends" as she called them. Then in Grade 5 she repatriated to Korea. By the time Yoo Mi returned to Indonesia and enrolled in Grade 10 at TIS, she had lost most of her fluency in English. She also found it difficult to befriend her new classmates who were more westernized than her. Try as she may, Yoo Mi's attempts at striking up a conversation with those from the English-speaking groups never developed beyond on-the-surface talk. If she asked about homework, they would only respond about homework. Yoo Mi found that her classmates boxed her up as "Korean" and showed little interest in getting to know her. In contrast, when she asked Korean classmates the same question, the conversation would quickly evolve and soon they would be talking about other things.[7]

When I interviewed Yoo Mi, she was already in Grade 12 and hung out mostly with her Korean friends while on campus. Sometimes she also hung out with her Japanese friends. Those from the Japanese and Indonesian-speaking groups described similar experiences of trying to join the English-speaking groups and then giving up because it was too hard.

For some, being thrown into an English-speaking environment was a difficult experience. For example, a Korean student said that he had nightmares during his first few weeks at TIS due to the stress of having to engage in English—a language that he could not speak. Others recalled similar experiences in childhood of when they first attended English-medium international schools. A male Japanese student remembers punching a classmate when he was in elementary school after feeling frustrated that he could not make himself understood in English. A female Japanese alumnus said that she once yelled at her international school teacher in Vietnam for similar reasons.

> Ayumi was new to the elementary school and could not understand how to purchase food at the canteen using the ticket system. When she approached a teacher for help, she felt that the teacher spoke impatiently while rattling something off in English to her. Ayumi's English was not very good, so she could not understand. This made her feel stressed. So Ayumi loudly blurted out one of the few phrases she knew in English: "Shut up!" The teacher, offended, walked off. Left on her own, six-year-old Ayumi then hid herself because she was scared and did not know what to do.[8]

Yoo Mi, Ayumi and others like them fit into the TCK profile described by Dave and Ruth in this book. They grew up outside their passport countries and faced similar issues to other TCKs of having to cope with the many hellos and goodbyes. At the same time, their experience of the international school was like that of CCKs as Ruth has outlined. Not only were they temporarily living in host countries (Indonesia and Vietnam) whose language and culture were foreign to them, they were also spending the most significant part of their days in an international school environment that used yet another set of foreign language and culture that they had to learn.

For many of the Asian students, the experience of being at an international school was like that of a second-generation immigrant child living in a Western country. At school they had to learn English and become Westernized. After school, they had to enter another world, which for example, centered around their Korean- or Japanese-speaking families. They were "Western by day and Asian by night."[9] Unlike American TCKs who may feel comfortable in the international school setting but become like migrants when they repatriate, many other TCKs become like migrants when they enter the international school environment and then again when they repatriate.

Setting an Example

It was common for Asian students at TIS to comment that they felt their teachers preferred students who spoke English or were Westernized. For example, the Korean students who spoke English fluently said that they felt uncomfortable when their teachers showed them preference over their fellow Korean students who were not able to speak English as well as they could. Precisely because they were aware of this, the Koreans who were confident in their English would often try to help those who were not by sitting next to them in class. In one of these classes, one of the two Korean students in the class always placed an electronic dictionary on her desk, while the other would sit next to her and occasionally lean over to translate some English words into Korean for her. Even then, the teacher would assume that the two Korean students in class were self-segregating because they had failed to become international or TCK (the two labels were sometimes used interchangeably at TIS).

Ironically, the English-speaking expatriate teachers and school staff who criticized the Korean, Indonesian, and Japanese students for self-segregating were unaware that they behaved similarly. Some of the teachers would refuse to have lunch in the comfortable staff lunchroom because, they explained, they felt out of place among the Indonesian staff who ate there. Instead, these teachers would sit outside in the student canteen. Even when they occasionally did sit in the staff lunchroom, they would sit with other expatriate teachers—most of whom were white and from English-speaking countries—at a different table from the Indonesian staff who could also speak English.

It was also not uncommon for the teachers and students from the English-speaking groups to live in countries like Indonesia for many years—sometimes more than a decade—without gaining a functional knowledge of the local language. Yet, they seem to place higher expectations on their students and classmates in terms of learning to speak a new language (English) and operate in a new cultural environment.

Changing Friendship Patterns

Many of the Asian students who had been at TIS for a long time said that their friendship patterns changed as they grew up.[10] They were friends with "everybody" when they were in elementary school. At that age, nationalities, languages, and cultural background did not matter much. But as they grew older, especially as they entered high school, their friendships became increasingly influenced by their linguistic and cultural backgrounds.

> Seung Gi had been at TIS since elementary school. Back then, he had friends of many different nationalities. But as his friends left and new students came, Seung Gi found

it more and more difficult to become friends with his new Westernized classmates. He did not feel as though he could "connect" with them. So by high school, Seung Gi hung out mostly with his Indonesian friends because he could speak Indonesian even though he was not fluent. He also shuttled back and forth among other groups of friends, including his Korean friends.[11]

Seung Gi was a "stayer" as he had stayed at TIS since elementary school. But his life was affected by the high mobility that characterizes the TCK experience as he watched his friends leave and was forced to find new ones. Other Asian students at TIS who had moved around noticed the same changes as Seung Gi in their own friendship patterns. New Korean students who had only joined TIS in high school and spoke English fluently also found it easier to befriend other Koreans or Asians for similar reasons. There were also other reasons. For example, they had more opportunities to meet fellow Koreans through their parents and afterschool life, such as at cram school, where they prepare for university entrance examinations back in their passport countries.

It is easy to accuse these students of simply failing to be "international." But it is important to understand that many factors other than ethnocentrism are at work in the formation of linguistic and cultural groups that are often seen in international schools.

But were the students who did not join the English-speaking groups really self-segregating? For example, was Seung Gi the only non-Indonesian who joined the Indonesian groups?

Hidden Diversity

At TIS, there were student groups that were accused of self-segregating based on ethnicity or nationality. In reality, these groups were not always as homogenous as they were made out to be. Here is my description of one of the groups:

> Among the 12th graders, there was a large group of 30 or so students that was labeled "Indonesian." I suspected that this was not an accurate label and decided to check by hanging out with the group one day. To my surprise, the group turned out to be more diverse than I had thought. Certainly, most were Indonesian nationals of different ethnic backgrounds, such as Chinese (the majority), Indian and Javanese. But the group also included Kenji who was a Japanese national of mixed heritage. His father was Japanese and his mother was Javanese Indonesian. There were others who were like Kenji, such as Shane who was a British national because his father was (white) British though his mother

was Indonesian, and others who were Indonesian-Thai, or Indonesian-(white) American, and so on. More importantly, there were also two Koreans, two Taiwanese and two Filipinos who were permanently part of the group, as well as students from Japan and Hong Kong, among others, who regularly visited the group.[12]

The so-called "Indonesian" group was not so Indonesian after all. What they had in common was the fact that most spoke Indonesian well—though not all were fluent—and they often mixed Indonesian and English in their speech. Their choice of language made them appear to be Indonesian even though they were not. Furthermore, most also looked physically "Asian" even though some were of mixed European/white descent. Their racially similar physical appearance hid their diverse nationality and cultural backgrounds.

If we put all of the above examples together, we begin to see a pattern: there is a tendency to think of cultural similarities and differences in racial terms. Being Westernized or English-speaking is seen as being "white." Looking "Asian" and speaking, for example, Indonesian is seen as being "Indonesian." Even though the concept of "race" has been scientifically debunked as a marker of difference, we still have a tendency to subconsciously use "race" to categorize others. Consequently, groups that are racially diverse are perceived to be "international" as they are assumed to be color-blind. The fact that they are Westernized and English-speaking—a characteristic that makes it difficult for others to join the group—becomes invisible. It is a form of hidden homogeneity. Meanwhile Indonesian-speaking groups that are not as racially diverse are perceived to be homogenous. Their diversity, in terms of nationality, culture, and language, becomes invisible. It is a form of hidden diversity.[13]

Internalized Racism

The appearance of being color-blind is often taken as evidence of caring less about race or cultural difference, when this is not true. Given that many still think of diversity in racial terms, being color-blind is an illusion. It is important to understand this because glossing over the continued influence of "race" on our perceptions can make us oblivious to their negative consequences. At TIS, many students experienced a sense of internalized racism, which is common among children of culturally marginalized minority groups.

Neil was a white American who was married to an Indonesian woman. He felt that there was "institutionalized racism" at the international school where he was teaching and his daughters were studying. By this he meant that nobody was consciously trying to be racist, but "the very make up" of the school unintentionally taught the wrong message.

Most teachers were expatriate, white and English-speaking. Neil explained, "the vast majority of our students . . . see Indonesians in subservient positions—primarily drivers, nannies, maids, gardeners, secretaries, electricians and what have you."

In his view, students subconsciously learnt that being white or identifying as white made them superior to Indonesians and others. Neil could see the effect of these unintentional messages in his daughter's behavior. He felt that his seven-year-old daughter wanted to identify with him, her white father, rather than her Indonesian mother.[14]

Neil expects his daughter to grow out of these perceptions as she matures. Having also interviewed adult TCKs, I have found that many of those who have similar experiences of feeling inferior for not being white do learn to dismantle these perceptions as they grow older. In some cases, it is an emotionally involving process.[15]

Researching TCK Diversity

What then are the implications of these findings on the way we carry out research on Third Culture Kids and international schools? We need to remember that concepts such as "Third Culture Kids" are research tools that we use to categorize and understand phenomena, such as the impact of mobility during childhood. Sometimes these research tools can have a profound influence on the community that it describes, like in the case of TCKs, because it gives voice to experiences that were previously not discussed. But this does not mean that the concept cannot change (see Chapter 3) or that it needs to be used all the time. As researchers of TCKs—many of whom also identify as one—or practitioners who work with TCKs, we often lose sight of this fact due to our personal attachment to the concept, which may limit our understanding and interpretations of what we have observed.[16]

It would be unfortunate to use the "TCK" label to create a new identity box that includes and excludes people based on the language they speak, the color of their friends, and so on. The TCK concept has been influential because it provided a sense of belonging to those who did not fit into the boxes created by traditional notions of belonging, such as nationality and culture. But we need to remember that there are many different ways of being a TCK. There are also many different layers to our life experiences, identity, and sense of belonging. Being a TCK is just one of them.

Notes

INTRODUCTION

1. *Esther 4:14. The Bible.* King James Version, Public Domain.

CHAPTER 1

1. Smith, Carolyn D. (1994). *The Absentee American.* New York: Aletheia Publications.
2. www.aaro.org/about-aaro/6m-americans-abroad
3. https://advance.org/australians-abroad-preliminary-findings-on-the-australian-diaspora
4. www.stat.go.jp/english/data/nenkan/1431-02.htm
5. www.iscresearch.com/information/isc-news.aspx
6. Ward, Ted. Personal conversation with David C. Pollock, ICMK conference, Manila, Philippines, October 1984.

CHAPTER 2

1. Pollock, David C. Definition in *The TCK Profile* seminar material, Interaction, Inc., 1989. p. 1.
2. Cottrell, Ann Baker, & Downie, Richard D. "TCK—The History of a Concept." http://tckresearcher.net/TCK%20Hist%20'12%20FIGT%20res.%20Newsltr%20copy.pdf
3. Ibid.
4. Useem, Dr. Ruth Hill. Personal letter to Dave C. Pollock, February 1994.
5. Vidal, Ximena. "Third Culture Kids: A Binding Term for a Boundless Identity" (Senior Essay, April 10, 2000).
6. Dumapias, Myra. Personal email to Ruth E. Van Reken, January 7, 2017
7. Global Nomads International is an organization formed by Norma McCaig in 1986 for TCKs of every background and nationality.
8. Families in Global Transition is an organization that sponsors an annual conference for those living and working with globally mobile families of all sectors. See www.figt.org.
9. Wu, Alice Shu-Hsien. (2011). "Global Nomads: Cultural Bridges for the Future" in *Writing Out of Limbo: International Childhoods, Global Nomads*

and Third Culture Kids, edited by Gene H. Bell-Villada and Nina Sichel with Faith Eidse and Elaine Neil Orr. UK: Newcastle-upon-Tyne Cambridge Scholars Publishing. pp. 332–353.

CHAPTER 3

1. Brice Royer, founder of TCKID.com, in a personal email to Ruth E. Van Reken, September 28, 2008. Used with permission.
2. We understand that "race" is a social construct as scientists have shown there is only one human "race" but we also recognize in our world, the factor of how "race" has traditionally identified groups is a significant reality for many. Using the term "mixed-racial heritage" is our attempt to acknowledge both realities until, perhaps, a better term emerges.
3. Anonymous personal conversation with Ruth E. Van Reken, December 22, 2008. Used by permission.
4. Personal conversation with Joyce Mann, circa March 2011.
5. Personal conversation with Ruth E. Van Reken, circa March, 2011.
6. Mann, Joyce. "At home in the world, and just as much a Hongkonger," June 13, 2013. Retrieved from www.scmp.com/comment/insight-opinion/article/1259275/home-world-and-just-much-hongkonger
7. Ataman, Oya. "Third Culture Kids." Retrieved from https://signsandwords.com/new-page/identity/tck-english-i

CHAPTER 4

1. James, Alex Graham. (1993). "Uniquely Me," in *Scamps, Scholars, and Saints*, edited by Jill Dyer and Roger Dyer. Kingswood, SA, Australia: MK Merimna. p. 234.
2. Andersen, Hans Christian. (1999). *The Ugly Duckling*, adapted and illustrated by Jerry Pinkney. New York: Morrow Junior Books, William Morrow Publishing Co.
3. Hiebert, Paul G. (1983). *Cultural Anthropology*, 2nd ed. Grand Rapids, MI: Baker Book House. pp. 28–29.
4. Ibid., p. 25.
5. Weaver, Gary. "The American Cultural Tapestry," *eJournal USA*, June 2006. http://usinfo.state.gov/journals/itsv/0606/ijse/weaver.htm.
6. Ibid.
7. From the musical *Fiddler on the Roof*. Book by Joseph Stein, music by Jerry Bock, lyrics by Sheldon Harnick, based on Sholom Aleichem's stories, *Fiddler on the Roof*, 4th Limelight Edition (New York: Crown Publishers, 1964). p. 29.
8. Figure 4–2 is adapted from a figure by Norma McCaig.

9. Denver, John. "Leaving on a Jet Plane." ©1967. J. W. Pepper Sheet Music, Exton, PA.

10. McDonald, Joseph. Personal email communication to David C. Pollock, October 1995. Used by permission.

11. Tanu, Danau. Personal email to Ruth E. Van Reken, January 19, 2017.

12. Nicolás, Eleanor. Personal email to Ruth E. Van Reken, January 30, 2017.

13. Wertsch, Mary Edwards. (1996, reprint from 1991). *Military Brats.* Putnam Valley, NY: Aletheia Publications. p. 6.

14. Bushong, Lois, & Van Reken, Ruth E. (2013). "The Powerful Impact of Systems on the Globally Mobile." Appendix A in *Belonging Everywhere & Nowhere: A Guide to Counseling the Globally Mobile.* Retrieved from http://quietstreamscounseling.com/wp-content/uploads/2016/05/The-Powerful-Impact-of-Systems.pdf

15. Tanaka, Ken. "What Kind of Asian Are You?" www.youtube.com/watch?v=DWynJkN5HbQ

16. Bethel, Paulette M., & Van Reken, Ruth E. "Third culture kids and curriculum issues in the international school system: recognizing (and dealing effectively with) the hidden diversity of third culture kids (TCKs) in the classroom." Paper presented at "A conversation on educational achievements globally," Comparative and International Education Society Annual Conference, March 12–16, 2003, New Orleans, Louisiana.

CHAPTER 5

1. Tabor, Sara Mansfield. (1997). *Of Many Lands: Journal of a Traveling Childhood.* Washington, DC: Foreign Service Youth Foundation. p. 1.

2. Willmer, Sharon. "Personhood, Forgiveness, and Comfort," in *Compendium of the ICMK: New Directions in Mission: Implications for MKs,* edited by Beth Tetzel and Patricia Mortenson. West Brattleboro, VT: ICMK. pp. 103–18.

3. Seaman, Paul. *Paper Airplanes in the Himalayas: The Unfinished Path Home.* Notre Dame, IN: Cross Cultural Publications, 1997. pp. 7–8.

4. White, Frances J. (Fall 1983). "Some Reflections on the Separation Phenomenon Idiosyncratic to the Experience of Missionaries and Their Children," *Journal of Psychology and Theology,* 11:3, 181–88.

5. *Merriam-Webster's Collegiate Dictionary,* 11th ed. (2003). Springfield, MA: Merriam-Webster, Inc.

6. Kübler-Ross, Elisabeth. (1997). *On Death and Dying.* New York: Touchstone Books.

7. James, Alex Graham. "Mock Funeral." Used by permission.

8. Boss, Pauline. (2000). *Ambiguous Loss: Learning to Live with Unresolved Grief.* Boston: Harvard University Press.

9. Dumapias, *Myra.* "Refusing to be Erased." *http://news.tckid.com/refusing-to-be-erased/4/*

10. Wertsch, Mary Edwards. (1996, reprint from 1991). *Military Brats*. Putnam Valley, NY: Aletheia Publications.
11. Bowlby, John. (1982). *Attachment and Loss: Attachment*, Vol. 1. New York: Basic Books.
12. *Merriam-Webster's Collegiate Dictionary*.
13. Simens, Julia. (2011). *Emotional Resilience and the Expat Child*. Great Britain: Summertime Publishers. p. 40.

CHAPTER 6

1. Sophia Morton. "Let Us Possess One World," Third Culture Kids: The Experience of Growing Up Among Worlds, 1st ed. by David C. Pollock and Ruth E. Van Reken (Boston/London: Nicholas Brealey Publishing/ Intercultural Press, 1999, 2001), 307-312.
2. Willmer, Sharon. "Personhood, Forgiveness, and Comfort," in *Compendium of the ICMK: New Directions in Mission: Implications for MKs*, edited by Beth Tetzel and Patricia Mortenson. West Brattleboro, VT: ICMK. pp. 103–18.
3. Schaetti, Barbara. "Phoenix Rising." www.worldweave.com/BSidentity.html
4. Lijadi, A. A., & Van Schalkwyk, G. J. (2017). "Place Identity Construction of Third Culture Kids: Eliciting Voices of Children with High Mobility Lifestyle." *Geoforum*, 81. pp. 120–128. *doi: 10.1016/j.geoforum.2017*
5. Nelson, Monica. "Mango Rains," in *The Worlds Within*, edited by Eva László-Herbert and Jo Parfitt. (2014). Great Britain: Summertime Publishing.
6. Lijadi, Anastasia. Personal email to Ruth E. Van Reken, April 1, 2017. Contact at anastasia.lijadi@gmail.com.
7. Ambrosine, Donnyale. Personal correspondence to Ruth E. Van Reken, February 5, 2017.
8. Schaetti, Barbara. "Phoenix Rising." http://www.worldweave.com/BSidentity .html
9. Ibid.

CHAPTER 7

1. Schaetti, Rachel Miller. (1994). "Great Advantages," in *Notes from a Traveling Childhood*, edited by Karen Curnow McCluskey. Washington, DC: Foreign Youth Service Publication. p. 9.
2. Luce, Henry. http://en.wikipedia.org/wiki/Henry_Luce
3. Zakaria, Fareed. "The Power of Personality," *Newsweek*, December 24, 2007.
4. Ibid.
5. Butovskaya, Maya. Personal email to Ruth E. Van Reken, January 22, 2017.
6. Ibid.
7. Fritz, Jean. Homesick: *My Own Story* (New York: Bantam Doubleday Dell Publishing Group, 1984). pp. 148–50.

8. Callow, Paisley. Facebook posting on Third Culture Kids Everywhere, January 18, 2017, www.facebook.com/groups/2204737296/permalink/101543 63348447297

9. Eisinger, Steve. (1994). "The Validity of the 'Third Culture Kid' Definition for Returned Turkish Migrant Children," research report submitted to The Ministry of Culture in the country of Turkey, August 31, 1994. p. 16.

10. Podolsky, Momo. (2009). *Third Culture Kids: Growing Up Among Worlds*, rev ed. Boston: Nicholas Brealey Publishers. Appendix B.

11. Iyer, Pico. "The Empire Writes Back," *Time*, February 8, 1992.

12. Ibid.

13. Nicolás, Eleanor. Personal email to Ruth E. Van Reken, January 30, 2017.

CHAPTER 8

1. McCaig, Norma M. (1996). "Understanding Global Nomads," *Strangers at Home*. New York: Aletheia Press. p. 101.

CHAPTER 9

1. Atkins, Andrew. (July 1989). "Behavioral Strings to which MKs Dance," *Evangelical Missions Quarterly*. pp. 239–43.

2. Ruth, Nancy Ackley. "What the World Needs Now . . . Global Skills," seminar presented at Families in Global Transition, Houston, Texas, March 6–8, 2008.

3. Venezia, Nilly. "Ethics of Intercultural Education and Training," paper presented at SIETAR Europa Congress 2007, April 24–29, 2007, Sofia, Bulgaria.

4. Heny, Jeannine. (1994). "Learning and Using a Second Language," in *Language: Introductory Readings*, 5th ed., edited by Virginia Clark, Paul A. Eschholz, and Alfred F. Rosa. New York: St. Martin's Press. p. 186.

5. Filippi, Roberto. "Bilingual children show an advantage in controlling verbal interference during spoken language comprehension." www.bbk.ac.uk /psychology/dnl/personalpages/Filippi_etal_14.pdf

6. Limacher-Riebold, Dr. Ute, private email to Ruth E. Van Reken, December 22, 2016.

7. Ibid.

8. Rosenback, Rita, personal email to Ruth E. Van Reken, February 2, 2017.

9. Rosenback, Rita. (2014). *Bringing Up a Bilingual Child*. United Kingdom: Filament Publishing.

CHAPTER 10

1. Agnoli, Benedetta. "Third Culture: Soon to Be Our Culture," Retrieved from www.fractuslearning.com/2016/11/07/humanist-lesson
2. Wu, Alice. "Global Nomads: Finding Home in the Age of Technology." *Global Living Magazine*, Issue 20, Sept/Oct 2015.
3. Ibid.
4. Ibid.
5. Ibid.
6. Ibid.
7. Derragui, Amel. "Lost and Found Between Homeless and Homefull," http://jessicatalbot.net/identity/lost-and-found-between-homeless-and-homefull-amIel-derragui
8. Ibid.

CHAPTER 11

1. Van Reken, Ruth E. (2009). 1986 original research survey on ATCKs, 1986. Published in *Third Culture Kids: Growing Up Among Worlds*, rev ed, Appendix A. Boston: Nicholas Brealey Publishers.
2. Wu, Alice. http://globallivingmagazine.com/global-nomads-finding-home-in-the-age-of-technology
3. Gatlin, Melissa. Personal Facebook reply, January 17, 2017.
4. Ibid.
5. Ibid.
6. Quick, Tina. *Survive and Thrive: The International Student's Guide to Succeeding in the U.S.* Boston: International Family Transitions. From the manuscript to be published in 2017. Used by permission.
7. Ibid.
8. Louis, Ard A. An email on MK issues, August 1996. Used by permission.
9. Ibid.
10. From an email on MK issues, August 1996. Used with permission.
11. Wertsch, Mary Edwards. (1996, reprint from 1991). *Military Brats*. Putnam Valley, NY: Aletheia Publications. pp. 263-65.
12. Van Reken, Ruth E. *Third Culture Kids: Growing Up Among Worlds*, rev ed, Appendix A.
13. Missildine, Hugh. (1963). *Your Inner Child of the Past*. New York: Simon and Schuster. pp. 245–46.

CHAPTER 12

1. Ambrosine, Donnyale. Personal letter to Ruth E. Van Reken, February 4, 2017.

2. Useem, Ruth Hill, & Cottrell, Ann Baker. "TCKs Experience Prolonged Adolescence," *Newslinks*, 13, no. 1 (September 1993). p. 1.
3. Ibid.
4. "When Is a Child an Adolescent?" from www.4troubledteens.com/adolescence .html.
5. Woollaston, Victoria. www.dailymail.co.uk/health/article-2430573/An-adult -18-Not-Adolescence-ends-25-prevent-young-people-getting-inferiority -complex.html, September 24, 2013
6. Ward, Ted. Private conversation with David C. Pollock, Oct. 1984.
7. Gjoen, Judith. Personal letter to David C. Pollock, November 1995.

CHAPTER 13

1. Gardner, Marilyn. (2014). *Between Worlds: Essays on Culture and Belonging*, South Hadley, MA: Doorlight Publications. p. 202.
2. Ibid., p. 162.
3. Iyer, Pico. "Where Is Home?" TED talk: www.ted.com/talks/pico_iyer _where_is_home. Brilliant presentation by master storyteller Pico Iyer of his incredible journey as a TCK and its lifelong impact.
4. Ota, D, W. (2014). *Safe Passage: How Mobility Affects People & What International Schools Should Do About It*. London: Summertime Press. p. 4.
5. Ibid., pp. 11–15.
6. Solsona, Laia Colomer. https://lnu.se/personal/laia.colomer—Facebook Group "Archeology of a Mobile Life."
7. Gardner, p. 91.
8. La Shure, Charles. "What is Liminality?" October, 2005. Retrieved from *www.liminality.org/about/whatisliminality*
9. Gould, Jim. Personal conversation with Ruth E. Van Reken, circa 2000.
10. Kramer, Jade. http://griefandmourning.com/grief-and-mourning-distinguishe
11. Fireman, David. www.griefcounselor.org/articles/grief-article-mourning -grief.html
12. Iyer, Pico. "Where is Home?" TED talk: www.ted.com/talks/pico_iyer _where_is_home
13. Jones, Jerry. Pre-Departure seminar, Tianjin, China, 2012.

CHAPTER 14

1. Eidse, F., & Sichel, N. (editors). (2004). *Unrooted Childhoods: Memoirs of Growing Up Global*. Boston: Intercultural Press, a division of Nicholas Brealey Publishing.
2. University of Rochester Medical Center Encyclopedia, 2017 www.urmc .rochester.edu/encyclopedia/content.aspx?ContentTypeID=1&Content ID=3051

3. Gardner, Marilyn. (2014). *Between Worlds: Essays on Culture and Belonging*, South Hadley, MA: Doorlight Publications. p. 152.

4. Harris, Eric. www.biography.com/people/eric-harris-235982#synopsis

5. Schubert, Esther. "Keeping Third-Culture Kids Emotionally Healthy: Depression and Suicide Among Missionary Kids" in *ICMK Compendium: New Directions for Missions: Implications for MK*, edited by Beth A. Tetzel and Patricia Mortenson (Brattleboro, VT, 1986).

6. Schaetti, Barbara F. (2006). "A Most Excellent Journey," from *Raising Global Nomads: Parenting Abroad in an On-Demand World* by Robin Pascoe. Vancouver, BC: Expatriate Press Limited, 2006. p. 214.

7. Cameron, Rosalea. (2006). *Missionary Kids: Who They Are, Why They Are Who They Are, What Now?* Queensland, AU: Cypress Trust

CHAPTER 15

1. Ward, Ted. (1984). *Living Overseas: A Book of Preparations*. New York: Free Press.

2. Gosling, Peter, & Huscroft, Anne. (2009). *How to Be a Global Grandparent: Living with the Separation*. Oakham, Rutland, UK: Zodiac Publishing.

CHAPTER 16

1. O'Shaugnessy, Christopher. (2014). *Arrivals, Departures, and the Adventures in Between*. Great Britain, Summertime Publishers.

2. Bassey, Mary. https://thedisplacednation.com/2016/03/31/tck-talent-mary-bassey-writer-storyteller-activist-and-scientist

3. Gardner, Marilyn. (2014). *Between Worlds: Essays on Culture and Belonging*, South Hadley, MA: Doorlight Publications. p. 152.

4. Bowlby, John. *Attachment and Loss: Attachment*, Vol. 1. New York: Basic Books, 1969, 1982.

5. Cycles of Mobility Chart. For printable version, go to *www.crossculturalkid.org* and check on resources. May be printed for personal or group use.

6. Bushong, Lois, & Van Reken, Ruth E., "Powerful Impact of the System," available at http://quietstreamscounseling.com/wp-content/uploads/2016/05/The-Powerful-Impact-of-Systems.pdf

PART IV OVERVIEW

1. Merton, Thomas. *No Man is an Island*. NY: Mariner Books. 2002. p. 3.

2. Human Resources Going Global: How Institutions Can Support Those Living and Working Abroad, CUPA, April 2012, www.cupahr.org/knowledge center/files/HR_Abroad.pdf

3. Storti, C. (2003). *The Art of Coming Home.* Boston: Intercultural Press.

4. Ibid., pp. 80–82.

5. Seppala, Emma, & Cameron, Kim. "Proof That Positive Work Cultures Are More Productive." *Harvard Business Review,* December 01, 2015

6. Webb, Roger T. PhD, Pedersen, Carsten B., & Mok, Pearl L.H., PhD. (2016). *American Journal of Preventive Medicine.* 51(3):291–300.

7. Livermore, David. (2011). *The Cultural Intelligence Difference.* New York: American Management Association. pp. 4, 5.

8. Maslow, A.H. (1987). *Motivation and Personality. (3rd ed.).* New York: Harper & Row. pp. 15–21.

9. Puttick, Elizabeth. "A New Typology and Sociological Model of Religion Based on the Needs and Values Model of Abraham Maslow," *Journal of Beliefs and Values,* November 1997.

10. Maslow, Abraham. (2016). "The Pursuit of Happiness," www.pursuit-of -happiness.org/history-of-happiness/abraham-maslow

11. Tay, Louis & Diener, Ed. (2011). "Needs and Subjective Well-Being Around the World." Journal of Personality and Social Psychology. Vol 101, No. 2. pp. 354-365. https://pdfs.semanticscholar.org/1b75/37995d06bae06bb739b86b 9416ed39b480f8.pdf *DOI: 10.1037/a0023779*

CHAPTER 17

1. Kraft, Charles. Creative Commons

2. Torstrick, Shirley. Seminar handout. Used with permission.

3. Schaetti, Barbara. "Phoenix Rising."

4. Grappo, Rebecca. www.rnginternational.com

5. www.explorelifestory.com

6. Berry, John. (2015). "Theories and Models of Acculturation." *The Oxford Handbook of Acculturation and Health (www.oxfordhandbooks.com).* England: Oxford University Press.

7. Kim, Y. Y. (2005). "Adapting a new culture: An integrative communication theory." In W. B. Gudykunst (Ed.), *Theorizing about intercultural communication.* Thousand Oaks, CA: Sage. pp. 375–400.

CHAPTER 18

1. Pollock, David C. (2002). *Doing Member Care Well: Perspectives and Practices from Around the World.* Pasadena CA: William Carey Library. p. 25.

2. *CUPA HR,* "How Institutions can Support Those Living and Working Abroad," http://conservancy.umn.edu/bitstream/107757/1/Cooper_umn_ 0130E_11882.pdf

3. Pascoe, Robin. ExpatExpert.com/AMJ Campbell International Relocation Survey

4. Ibid.

5. Schaetti, Barbara. Intercultural Detective at https://www.culturaldetective.com

6. Pascoe.

7. Schumpeter, "Not-so-happy-returns," *The Economist*, November 17, 2015.

8. Ota. pp. 2, 3.

9. Pascoe.

10. Schumpeter.

11. Richards, Nathaniel, & Averett, Todd. Radius World Wide blog, January 2017. www.radiusworldwide.com/blog/2017/1/how-make-most-your-returning-expat-workers

12. Black, Stewart, & Gregersen, Hal. *Harvard Business Review*, March 1999. Quoted in Nathaniel Richards and Todd Averette, Radius World Wide blog, January 2017.

CHAPTER 19

1. Tanu, Danau. "Toward an Interdisciplinary Analysis of the Diversity of Third Culture Kids." In *Migration, Diversity, and Education: Beyond Third Culture Kids*. Sarah Benjamin and Fred Dervin, eds. New York: St. Martin's Press LLC., 2015. Prologue.

2. Dumapias, Myra. Personal email to Ruth E. Van Reken, January 7, 2017.

3. Barclay, John. *Families in cross-cultural ministry—a comprehensive guide and manual for families, administrators and supporters.* http://library.mst.edu.au/liberty/libraryHome.do

4. *Adult Asian MK Statement*, Adult MK Seminar, Chiang Mai, Thailand, April, 2012.

5. Min, Isabelle. Founder, TCK network in Korea; CEO, Transition Catalyst Korea Institute. Personal letter to Ruth E. Van Reken, February 7, 2017.

6. Ataman, Oya. https://signsandwords.com/new-page/identity/tck-english-i

7. Laszlo-Herbert, Eva at FIGT Conference, 2012: http://jsimens.com/tag/eva-laszlo-herbert/

8. Bethel, Paulette M., & Van Reken, Ruth. "Third culture kids and curriculum issues in the international school system: recognizing (and deal ing effectively with) the hidden diversity of third culture kids (TCKs) in the classroom." Paper presented at "A conversation on educational achievements globally," Comparative and International Education Society Annual Conference, March 12–16, 2003, New Orleans, Louisiana.

9. Habecker, Shelly, DPhil. "Seen But Not Heard: Assessing Youth Perspectives of African Immigrant Parenting in the Diaspora," *Africology: The Journal of Pan African Studies*, vol. 9, no. 4, July 2016. pp. 253–267.

10. Ambrosine, Donnyale. Personal correspondence to Ruth E. Van Reken, February 5, 2017.

11. www.calledthejourney.com/blog/2014/12/17/frederick-buechner-on-calling

12. Cigna Health and Life Insurance Company, 2015 Global Mobility Survey October, 2015. www.cigna.com/newsroom/new-survey-results-expat-expec tations

13. www.Daraja.us

14. www.shmoop.com/quotes/be-the-change-you-want-to-see-in-the-world .html

APPENDIX A

1. Useem, Ruth Hill. (January 1993). "Third Culture Kids: Focus of Major Study." *Newslinks*, Newspaper of the International School Services 12: 3 (p. 1).

2. Cottrell, Ann Baker, & Downie, Richard D. "TCK—The History of a Concept" http://tckresearcher.net/TCK%20Hist%20'12%20FIGT%20res.% 20Newsltr%20copy.pdf

3. Ibid.

4. Useem, Ruth Hill. (1973). "Third Cultural Factors in Educational Change." In *Cultural Factors in School Learning*, edited by Cole Brembeck and Walker Hill. Lexington, MA: Lexington Books. p. 122.

5. Ibid. p. 129

6. Useem, Ruth Hill. (January 1993). "Third Culture Kids: Focus of Major Study." *Newslinks*, Newspaper of the International School Services 12: 3 (p. 1).

7. Ibid.

8. Downie, Richard D. (1976). "Re-entry Experiences and Identity Formation of Third Culture Experienced Dependent American Youth: An Exploratory Study."

9. Parker, Allen. (1936). *An Analysis of the Factors in the Personality Development of Children of Missionaires*. Master's thesis, University of Chicago.

10. Useem, Ruth Hill, 1973. pp. 136–138.

11. Van Reken, Ruth. Personal conversation with Ruth Hill Useem, Global Nomads International Conference, December 1988, Washington, DC.

12. Schaetti, Barbara. "Global Nomad, Third Culture Kid, Adult Third Culture Kid, Third Culture Adult: What Do They All Mean?" http://www.figt.org /global_nomads

13. Useem, Dr. Ruth Hill. Personal letter to Dave C. Pollock, February 1994.

14. Useem and Cottrell study, 1993.

15. Tanu, Danau. (2015). "Toward an Interdisciplinary Analysis of the Diversity of Third Culture Kids." In *Migration, Diversity, and Education: Beyond Third*

Culture Kids. Sarah Benjamin and Fred Dervin, eds. New York: St. Martin's Press LLC. p. 27

APPENDIX C

1. Tanu, Danau. (2017 in press). *Growing up in Transit: The Politics of Belonging at an International School*. New York: Berghahn Books.
2. Ibid.
3. Schaetti, Barbara F. "Global Nomad Identity: Hypothesizing a Developmental Model" (dissertation, The Union Institute, 2000). p. 74.
4. Tanu, Danau. (2010). "Educating Global Citizens?" *Inside Indonesia* 102, Oct–Dec.
5. Tanu, Danau. (2015). "Towards an Interdisciplinary Analysis of the Diversity of 'Third Culture Kids'." In *Migration, Diversity, and Education: Beyond Third Culture Kids*. Saija Benjamin and Fred Dervin, eds. 13–34. Basingstoke: Palgrave Macmillan. p. 29.
6. Tanu, 2017 in press.
7. Ibid.
8. Ibid.
9. Ibid.
10. Tanu, 2015.
11. Ibid.
12. Ibid.
13. Ibid.
14. Tanu, Danau. (2016). "Going to School in 'Disneyland': Imagining an International School Community in Indonesia," *Asian and Pacific Migration Journal*, 25 (pp. 429–50).
15. Tanu, 2017 in press.
16. Tanu, 2015.

Resources

Organizations

Anchor Education—*http://anchoreducation.org*—Multi-agency group
  providing educational counselling, workshops, and testing for families
  across Africa.
Around the World in a Lifetime (AWAL)/Foreign Service Youth Foundation—
  www.fsyf.org—Organization for United States foreign service teens.
Asia Education Resource Consortium (AERC)—*www.asiaerc.org*—Meets the
  educational needs of Christian worker families in Asia through
  consultation, training, resources, testing, and more.
Asian MK Network—*https://asianmknetwork.wordpress.com*—A network of
  Asian MKs who seek to support fellow Asian MKs.
Barnabas International—*www.barnabas.org*—Barnabas staff are passionate
  about caring for global workers through ongoing speaking, listening, and
  giving so each can thrive where planted. Offers reentry seminars.
Daraja—*www.daraja.us*—Founded in 2012 by Michael Pollock, daraja means
  'bridge' in Swahili, so it offers TCK seminars, retreats, coaching, and
  consulting to TCKs/CCKs and those who care for them, with a focus on
  young adult TCK transitions.
Families in Global Transition—*www.figt.org*—Hosts a yearly international
  conference on topics related to global family living. Has a researchers'
  network: *www.figt.org/research_network*
Interaction International—*www.interactionintl.org*—Organization founded by
  David C. Pollock. "The voice for third culture kids and internationally
  mobile families." Contains lists of books for adults and children and an
  index of articles.
Interchange Institute—*www.interchangeinstitute.org*—Offers training for
  educators, human resources personnel, and others in matters related to
  cross-cultural living.
InterNations—*www.internations.org*—Largest online expat community.
Member Care Associates—*http://membercareassociates.org*—Resources for
  those people charged with member care within their organization,
  especially when the members are or have been out of their passport
  country, started by Kelly and Michelle O'Donnell.

Military Child Education Coalition—*www.militarychild.org*—Focused on ensuring quality educational opportunities for all military-connected children affected by mobility, family separation, and transition.

Missions Training International (MTI)—*https://www.mti.org*—Develops and equips cross-cultural messengers of the Gospel through training and debriefing.

MK Safety Net—*http://mksafetynet.org*—Offers hope, help, healing, support, and advocacy for former missionary kids and all TCKs who have suffered abuse. Also MK Safety Net Canada.

Mu Kappa—*www.mukappa.org*—A fraternal organization for missionary kids on college campuses across North America.

Society for Intercultural Education, Training and Research (SIETAR)—*www.sietarusa.org*—Offers conferences, webinars, blogs, and many other resources for intercultural work.

Summer Institute of Intercultural Communications—*http://intercultural.org/siic.html*—Led by co-founder, Janet Bennet, offers workshops in intercultural communications and can be for credit.

Websites

A.H. Dance Company—*www.ahdancecompany.com*—A multidisciplinary dance production company of Alaine Handa (a TCK) that tours the world either in an educational setting or professional production. See the Chameleon Project on the website.

AramcoBrats—*www.aramco-brats.com*—For Aramco TCKs who grew up in Saudi Arabia.

Bate Consulting—*www.bateconsult.com*—Consulting with Amanda Bate, a global nomad of color.

British Expat—*www.britishexpat.com*—Full-featured site for expatriate Brits.

Buck, Leila—*www.leilabuck.com*—Writer, actor, and educator who has worked with the UN and performed dramas on stories of refugees and her own many-cultured life in over 22 countries.

CanuckAbroad—*www.canuckabroad.com*—Caters to the Canadian expatriate, but provides information and resources—including a forum—that are equally useful for U.S. and other expatriates.

Campus Sherpa—*www.campussherpa.com*—Arrange one-to-one personalized college tours from real college students.

College with Confidence—*www.collegewithconfidence.com*—a comprehensive psychotherapy service by Maureen Tillman that supports young adults and parents through the college experience into adulthood.

Cross-Cultural Kids—*www.crossculturalkid.org*—Ruth Van Reken's website with many resources and articles on and for TCKs and CCKs. Read articles by Ruth or see what books, TV shows and movies, and webinars she is finding important.

Cultural Detective—*https://www.culturaldetective.com*—Founded by Dr. Barbara Schaetti, it is an intercultural tool that will enhance your intercultural competence with better culture-general and culture-specific communication skills. Site includes webinars, newsletters, and blog.

The Displaced Nation—*https://thedisplacednation.com*—'A home for international creatives' founded by Mary Bassey.

Drs. Doug Ota Safe Passage—*https://www.dougota.nl*—Consulting so you feel at home in the world and coaching so you are at home in yourself.

Expat Clic—*www.expatclic.com*—Articles and information by expat women to help expat women and their families meet new cultures and embrace new lifestyles in an open, relaxed, and positive frame of mind.

Expat Research—*http://expatresearch.com*—Website of expatriate scholar and global Human Resources expert Dr. Yvonne McNulty.

Expat Weekly Telegraph—*www.telegraph.co.uk/expat*—An online section of the *Weekly Telegraph* (U.K.) newspaper dedicated to expatriate living, with resources, news, articles, and information.

Expat Woman—*www.expatwoman.com*—A free website helping expatriate women from all nationalities in any country in the world share experiences and advice, and find resources for living in a foreign country.

Expatica—*www.expatica.com*—This Netherlands-based website provides useful resources for those living and working in the Netherlands, Germany, France, Spain, and Belgium. It also publishes an online newsletter and hosts conferences on expat-related topics.

Global Education Explorer—*www.Globaleducationexplorer.com*—A web-based tool that enables companies and families to learn about curricula in other countries, educational assessments, and customs surrounding schooling so that they are informed before making this all-important life change.

Global TCK Care & Education—*www.iched.org*—(formerly iCHED) Provides information and materials for families and teachers of students who are studying outside of their passport country.

Grosjean, François—*www.francoisgrosjean.ch*—Website about learning another language, biculturalism, and applied linguistics.

Hardy, LeAnne—*www.leannehardy.net*—Book author who has lived in 6 countries on 4 continents; her books come from her cross-cultural experiences and passion to use story to convey spiritual truths.

Hobsons—*www.hobsons.com*—Offers comprehensive college and career readiness solutions to help students define postsecondary goals and develop plans for reaching them.

IMKEC—Intermission Missionary Kids Education Consultation—Annual meeting of evangelical mission agency representatives to discuss various aspects of the education of MKs/TCKs (missionary kids, third culture kids), develop a collective voice on MK education issues, and advocate for best practices in MK education.

International Therapist Directory—*www.internationaltherapistdirectory. com*—Website for finding mental health counselors around the world experienced with issues of mobility or stemming from being a TCK/ATCK/CCK.

Jsimens: Helping Families Worldwide—*http://jsimens.com*—Julia Simens's website to help TCKs and expats through storytelling, articles, events. See her lists of books.

Liang, Elizabeth—*http://elizabethliang.com*—Great information for creative outlets and workshops to aid TCKs and ATCKs.

MBK Conseil—*https://mkbconseil.ch*—Katrina Burrus develops professionals and leaders through coaching, speaking, and writing. An area of focus is helping expatriates, repatriates, or highly mobile leaders who want to prepare and assure their success in their transition.

McBride, Beth—*www.thefinetoothedcomb.etsy.com*—Art related to the TCK and ATCK life.

Multilingual Parenting—*www.multilingualparenting.com*—Rita Rosenback offers many helpful tips for families wanting to maintain multilingual skills for their children.

Murray, Taylor—*www.taylorjoymurray.com*—A young adult TCK who writes about the humor and hardships of cultural transition, life on the mission field, and TCK issues.

O'Shaughnessy, Christopher—*www.chris-o.com*—Having lived in, worked in, or traveled to over 100 countries, Chris uses a unique blend of storytelling, humor, and provocative insight to engage a wide array of people on topics associated with globalization and cross-cultural understanding.

Overseas Brats—*www.overseasbrats.com*—Group for military kids.

RNG International Educational Consultants—*www.rnginternational.com*—Started by Becky Grappo, they coach students applying for college from test taking to filling out applications, getting financial aid, and making the transition.

The Road Home—*www.roadhomefilm.com*—Site for Oscar award short-listed film about a poignant story of an Indian TCK searching to understand his identity. Website has other resources regarding TCKs as well.

School Choice International—*www.schoolchoiceintl.com*—Helps families with a child with special needs, for whom an overseas move is particularly difficult, both emotionally and educationally.

Sea Change Mentoring—*www.seachangementoring.com*—Ellen Mahoney began Sea Change Mentoring to help young adults identify and apply the skills and insights acquired in their international backgrounds toward their career, academic, and personal goals.

SHARE Education Services—*https://www.shareeducation.org*—Offers English-speaking ex-patriate families living in Europe, Russia, and Central Asia assistance with decisions about schooling, determining learning disabilities, finding resources.

Stephens, Libby—*www.libbystephens.com*—Pre-departure training, transition and relocation guidance, transition debriefing, Third Culture Kid (TCK) issues related to organizations, families, and their children.

TCKid—*www.tckidnow.com*—Founded by Brice Royer, current CEO Myra Dumapias. Resource-rich interactive website for adult TCKs and CCKs.

Transitions Abroad—*www.transitionsabroad.com/listings/living/resources/ expatriatewebsites.shtml#global*—A list of website addresses for expats of all countries.

Use Your Difference Media by Tayo Rockson—*www.uydmedia.com*— Community includes blogs, podcasts, columns, and videos to help TCKs use their differentness.

Ute's International Lounge—*www.utesinternationallounge.com*—Cultural consulting and coaching (live and online), language training and coaching, and workshops by Dr. Ute Limacher-Riebold.

Blogs, Forums, Chats, and Facebook Pages

* Note: These are samples of the countless blogs, forums, chats, and Facebook groups and pages now available on TCKs/CCKs and related topics.

Black Expat Blog—*www.theblackexpat.com*—Many guest bloggers, interviews, adventures, experiences, and more related to being a black expat.

Communicating Across Boundaries Blog hosted by Marilyn Gardner—*https:// communicatingacrossboundariesblog.com*—A blog that covers a wide variety of TCK issues.

Cultural Transplant Blog hosted by Lizzy Wiley—*http://tckness.blogspot. com*—Many resources for Third Culture Kids and their families.

Djibouti Jones—*www.djiboutijones.com*—A blog, newsletter sign-up, and list of published work and a cookbook by expat Rachel Pieh Jones.

European Mama—*www.europeanmama.com*—A blog by Olga Mecking about the expat life.

Facebook page (public group) hosted by Laia Colomer Solsona—*The archaeology of a mobile life https://www.facebook.com/ groups/1767502343538014/*—She displays many of the pictures and stories others have sent her, sharing the stories of what they mean and why they have carried them literally around the world!

Jones, Jerry—*www.thecultureblend.com*—Cross culture and transition blogger.

Journal of Global Mobility: The Home of Expatriate Management Research— *https://www.facebook.com/groups/705191772972428/ permalink/728747830616822*—Online magazine for researchers.

Publishers

Among Worlds—*www.interactionintl.org/amongworlds.asp*—A quarterly magazine for adult TCKs.

BR Anchor Publishing—*www.branchor.com*—Publisher of books for families on the move, including books and workbooks for young and elementary aged children.

Culturs Global Multicultural Magazine—*www.culturs.guru*—An online magazine and a marketplace of cross-cultural excellence by Doni for TCKs, Global Nomads, Military Brats, Diplomatic Kids, and Expats.

Denizen Magazine—*www.denizenmag.com*—Online magazine dedicated to today's third culture kids.

Educare Newsletter—Started and edited by Steve and Gill Bryant, it is a free educational and welfare e-magazine for TCKs, their families, and any organizations and individuals that send them. Subscribe at *mk_tck@yahoo. co.uk*

Expatriate Expert—*www.expatexpert.com*—Website for Robin Pascoe, author of *A Moveable Marriage, Homeward Bound,* and *Raising Global Nomads.*

Interchange Institute—*www.interchangeinstitute.org*—Publisher of books on the U.S. educational system for expats, moving with babies, and other resources.

Nicholas Brealey/Intercultural Press—now part of Hatchette, merged into John Murray Publishing—*https://www.hodder.co.uk*—search for Third Culture Kids and for Intercultural Press.

Summertime Publishing—*www.summertimepublishing.com*—Publishes books for TCKs and expats. TCK Bookshelf: *www.expatbookshop.com/third-culture-kids* and Expat Bookshelf: *www.expatbookshop.com*

Books

Andrews, L. A. (General Editor). (2004). *The Family in Mission: Understanding and Caring for Those Who Serve.* Palmer Lake, CO: Missionary Training Institute.

Bell-Villada, G. & Sichel, N. (Editors). (2012). *Writing Out of Limbo: International Childhoods, Global Nomads and Third Culture Kids.* Newcastle Upon Tyne, UK.: Cambridge Scholars Publications.

Bowers, Joyce M. (Editor). (1998). *Raising Resilient MKs.* Colorado Springs, CO: Association of Christian Schools International.

Bradbury-Haehl, N. & McGarvey, B. (2011, Kindle 2013). *The Freshman Survival Guide: Soulful Advice for Studying, Socializing, and Everything In Between.* Boston: Center Street, a division of Hachette Book Group.

Bushong, L. (2014). *Belonging Everywhere & Nowhere: How to Counsel the Globally Mobile.* Indianapolis, Indianapolis: Mango Tree Intercultural Services. (Great list of famous TCKs as well as list of movies about TCKs at back.)

Cameron, Rosalea. (2006). *Missionary Kids: Who They Are, Why They Are Who They Are, What Now.* Queensland, AU: Cypress Trust.

Cameron, Rosalea. (2008). *The Ecology of Third Culture Kids: The Experience of Austrailasian Adults.* AU: VDM Verlag.

Copeland, A. (2004). *Global Baby.* Brookline, MA: The Interchange Institute.

Crossman, T. (2016). *Misunderstood: The Impact of Growing Up Overseas in the 21st Century.* London, UK: Summertime Publishing.

Devillers, J. (2006). *The College Dorm Survival Guide: How to Survive and Thrive in Your New Home Away from Home.* New York: Three Rivers Press.

Eidse, F., & Sichel, N. (Editors). (2004). *Unrooted Childhoods: Memoirs of Growing Up Global.* Boston: Intercultural Press, a division of Nicholas Brealey Publishing.

Franklin, K. (2008). *International Parents Guide to Undergraduate Study in the USA* [NAFSA Brochure]. Washington, DC: Association of International Educators.

Gardner, Marilyn. (2014). *Between Worlds: Essays on Culture and Belonging.* South Hadley, MA: Doorlight Publications.

Ho, Polly C. (2015). *Rice, Noodles, Bread, or Chapati? The Untold Stories of Asian MKs* (2nd ed.). Order from Polly Ho at *books@cimi.org.hk.*

Hofstede, G., Hofstede, G.J., & Minkov, M. (2010). *Cultures and Organizations: Software of the Mind. Revised and Expanded* (3rd ed.). New York: McGraw Hill.

Hulstrand, J. (2007). *What Parents Need to Know* [NAFSABrochure]. Washington, DC: Association of International Educators.

Iyer, P. (2000). *The Global Soul: Jet Lag, Shopping Malls, and the Search for Home.* New York: Vintage Books.

Kohl, R.L. (2001). *Survival Kit for Overseas Living* (4th ed.). Yarmouth, ME: Intercultural Press.

László-Herbert, Eva & Parfitt, Jo. (Editors). (2014). *The Worlds Within.* London UK: Summertime Publishing.

Lipson, C. (2008). *Succeeding as an International Student in the United States and Canada.* Chicago: The University of Chicago Press.

Livermore, D. (2011). *The Cultural Intelligence Difference: Master the One Skill You Can't Do Without in Today's Global Economy.* New York: American Management Association.

McCluskey, K. (Editor). 1994. *Notes from a Traveling Childhood: Readings for International Mobile Parents and Children.* Washington D.C: Foreign Youth Service Foundation.

Molinsky, A. (2013). *Global Dexterity: How to Adapt Your Behavior Across Cultures without Losing Yourself in the Process*. Boston: Harvard Business Review Press.

O'Donnell, Kelly. (2013). *Doing Member Care Well: Perspectives and Practices from Around the World* (Globalization of Mission Series). Pasadena, CA: William Carey Library.

O'Donnell, Kelly. (2014). *Global Member Care: Volume One: The Pearls and Perils of Good Practice*. Pasadena, CA: William Carey Library.

O'Shaughnessy, Christopher. (2014). *Arrivals, Departures, and Adventures In-Between*. London UK: Summertime Publishing.

Ota, D. W. (2014). *Safe Passage: How Mobility Affects People & What International Schools Should Do About It*. London UK.

Pascoe, R. (2003). *A Moveable Marriage: Relocate Your Relationship Without Breaking It*. Vancouver, CA: Expatriate Press Limited.

Pascoe, R. (2000). *Homeward Bound, A Spouse's Guide to Repatriation*. Vancouver, CA: Expatriate Press

Pascoe, R. (2006). *Raising Global Nomads*. Vancouver, CA: Expatriate Press Limited.

Pearson, Barbara Zurer. (2008). *Raising a Bilingual Child*. New York: Living Language.

Quick, T. (2017). *Survive and Thrive: The International Student's Guide to Succeeding in the U.S.* Boston: International Family Transitions.

Quick, T. (2010). *The Global Nomad's Guide to University Transition*. London, UK: Summertime Publishing.

Rader, D. & Sittig, L. H. (2003). *New Kid in School: Using Literature to Help Children in Transition*. New York: Teachers College Press, Columbia University.

Raguenaud, V. (2009) *Bilingual by Choice: Raising Kids in Two (or More) Languages*. Boston: Intercultural Press, a division of Nicholas Brealey Publishing.

Romano, D. (2008). *Intercultural Marriage: Promises and Pitfalls*. Boston: Intercultural Press, a division of Nicholas Brealey Publishing.

Rosenback, R. (2014). *Bringing Up a Bilingual Child*. Surrey UK: Publishing Ltd.

Simens, J. (2011). *Emotional Resilience and the Expat Child: Practical Tips and Storytelling Techniques That Will Strengthen the Global Family*. London, UK: Summertime Publishing.

Smith, C.D. (1996). *Strangers at Home: Essays on the Effects of Living Overseas and Coming "Home" to a Strange Land*. Bayside, NY: Aletheia.

Storti, C. (2003). *The Art of Coming Home*. Boston: Intercultural Press.

Storti, C. (2001). *The Art of Crossing Cultures*. Boston: Brealey.

The College Board. (2007). *Meeting College Costs: What You Need to Know Before Your Child and Money Leave Home*. New York: The College Board.

University of Texas at Arlington. (2010). *No Limits: Foundations and Strategies for College Success*. Plymouth, MI: Hayden-McNeil Publishing.

Van Reken, R. (2012). *Letters Never Sent*. London, UK: Summertime Publishing.
Wertsch, M. E. 1991. *Military Brats: Legacies of Childhood inside the Fortress*. Bayside, NY: Aletheis Publications.

Books for Children and Teens

Appropriate for adolescents and young adults.

Barratt, Anna. (2016). *A Ball, a Book, and Butterflies: A Story About International Transition*. Publisher: Threadbare Chair English.
Bescanceny, Valérie. (2014). *B at Home: Emma Moves Again*. London UK: Summertime Publishing.
Besanceney, Valérie. (2015). *My Moving Booklet*. London UK.
Biale, Rachel. (1996). *We are Moving*. Berkeley, CA: Tricycle Press.
Civardi, Anne & Cartwright, Stephen. (1985). *Moving House*. Tulsa, OK: EDC Publisher.
*Hardy, LeAnne. (2003). *Between Two Worlds: A Novel* (for ages 9–14). Grand Rapids, MI: Kregel Publications.
Maffini, Helen. (2011). *Sammy's Next Move: Sammy the Snail is a Traveling Snail who Lives in Different Countries*. Self-published. Printed by Third Culture Kids Press CreateSpace Independent Publishing Company.
*Murray, Taylor. (2013). *Hidden in My Heart: A TCK's Journey Through Cultural Transition*. Pioneer Books.
*Pittman, Lisa & Smit, Diana. (2012). *Expat Teens Talk: Peers, Parents and Professionals Offer Support, Advice and Solutions in Response to Expat Life Challenges as Shared by Expat Teens*. London, UK: Summertime Publishing.
*Quick, T. (2017). *Survive and Thrive: The International Student's Guide to Succeeding in the U.S.* Boston: International Family Transitions.
*Roman, Beverly. (1999). *Footsteps Around the World: Relocation Tips for Teens*. Wilmington, NC: BR Anchor Publishing.
Roman, Beverly. (1999). *Let's Move Overseas: The International Edition of Let's Make a Move*. Wilmington, NC: BR Anchor Publishing.
Roman, Beverly. (2004). *The League of Super-Movers: My Moving Adventure*. Wilmington, NC: BR Anchor Publishing.
Roman, Beverly. (2006). *My Family is Moving*. Wilmington, NC: BR Anchor Publishing.
Schubeck, Carol M. (1998). *Let's Move Together*. Orange, CA: Suitcase Press.
*Simens, Julia. (2011). *Emotional Resilience and the Expat Child: Practical Storytelling Techniques That Will Strengthen the Global Family*. London, UK: Summertime Publishing.
Van Swol-Ulbrich, Hilly & Kaltenhauser, Bettina. (2004). *When Abroad Do as the Local Children Do*. NL: X-Pat Media.

Zoer, Martine. (2007). *The Kids' Guide to Living Abroad*. Washington DC: Foreign Service Youth Foundation.

DVDs, Movies, and Plays

*This is only a sampling of the wonderful and varied DVDs, movies, and plays on the subject of being a TCK, ATCK, or CCK.

"Alien Citizen: An Earth Odyssey"—*http://aliencitizensoloshow.com*—This one-woman show by Elizabeth Liang is a funny and poignant show about growing up as a dual citizen of mixed heritage in Central America, North Africa, the Middle East, and New England.

"BRATS: Our Journey Home" produced by Donna Musil—*www.bratsourjourneyhome.com*—The first documentary about growing up military, featuring narration and music by Kris Kristofferson.

"Neither Here Nor There" DVD produced by Ema Yamazaki—*www.neitherherenorther-thefilm.com*—Interviews with TCKs/CCKs of very different backgrounds who tell their own stories of identity and cultural complexities.

"The Road Home" DVD produced by Rahul Gandotra—*www.roadhomefilm.com*—20 minutes—Beautifully filmed in India, it is story of a British young man returning to where his parents consider "home" and his struggle to find his place. Great discussion starter.

"Where Is Home?" TED talk by Pico Iyer—*https://www.ted.com/talks/pico_iyer_where_is_home*—Brilliant presentation by master storyteller Pico Iyer of his incredible journey as a TCK and its lifelong impact.

Index